The Civil War Years in Utah

The Civil War Years in Utah

The Kingdom of God and the Territory That Did Not Fight

John Gary Maxwell

To New Hanover County library with compliments of the author
John Gary Maxwell

UNIVERSITY OF OKLAHOMA PRESS : NORMAN

ALSO BY JOHN GARY MAXWELL
Gettysburg to Great Salt Lake: George R. Maxwell, Civil War Hero and Federal Marshal among the Mormons (Norman, Okla., 2010)
Robert Newton Baskin and the Making of Modern Utah (Norman, Okla., 2013)

Library of Congress Cataloging-in-Publication Data

Maxwell, John Gary, 1933– author.
  The Civil War Years in Utah : the Kingdom of God and the territory that did not fight / John Gary Maxwell.
    pages cm
  Includes bibliographical references and index.
  ISBN 978-0-8061-4911-0 (hardcover : alk. paper)
  1. Utah—History—Civil War, 1861-1865. I. Title.
  E532.95.M39 2016
  979.2'02—dc23
                              2015030111

Interior layout and composition: Alcorn Publication Design

highlanders would claim her;
but a lowlander chanced lucky!

born into adulthood,
from her alchemy comes laughter,
and her love erases years!

Contents

Illustrations

Preface

There once were two cats of Kilkenny,
Each thought there was one cat too many,
So they fought and they fit,
And they scratched and they bit,
Till (excepting their nails
And the tips of their tails)
Instead of two cats, there weren't any!

In the Civil War years, non-Mormons in Utah Territory were merchants, appointed federal officials, usually well-educated, skilled in language, and socially adept. The largest numbers came as officers and soldiers in Union volunteer infantry and cavalry units, from urban, mining, or farming backgrounds in California and Nevada; a substantial percentage were foreign born.

The Mormons' parallel universe had similarities. Leaders were better educated than followers, who were predominantly converts to the Church of Jesus Christ of Latter-day Saints: farmers, industrial workers, artisans, and laborers mostly coming out of the poverty of Great Britain, Scandinavia, and Europe. Because they were isolated by geography, language, illiteracy, and religious fanaticism, points of friction characterized their interaction with the non-Mormon world.

The folk poem is credited to Ireland's County Kilkenny, where it is alleged that several soldiers, time heavy on their hands, attached two cats by their tails. Their conscience perhaps blunted by liquid anodyne, the troopers awaited the inevitable. Each cat consumed the other—or so it is told on the Emerald Isle.

Brigham Young, the second Mormon prophet, and other Mormon leaders repeatedly used the phrase "Kilkenny cat" in alluding to the 1832 prophecy made by their first prophet, Joseph Smith, Jr., that a great war would begin in South Carolina. Prophecy also held that, in the combatants' mutual destruction, God's purposes would be served. Men of the Mormon priesthood could complete their formation of a literal geographical, political, theocratic entity, their Kingdom of God on the earth. Out of America's ashes, the Mormons—under God's revelations—would take up the reins of a new government and lead the nation, then the world, into righteousness, preparing all for the approaching millennium, for Christ's return to the earth.[1]

Non-Mormons might use the phrase "Kilkenny cat war" to add a touch of levity to the war's tragic reports. At a pause in the terrible Battle of the Wilderness, where "it was man to man and bayonet against bayonet," with visibility measured in yards, General Grant is said to have remarked while vigorously smoking his briar-root pipe: "Well (puff), if Lee does want to make this a Kilkenny cat fight (puff, puff,) I am sure we'll win; (puff, puff,) for we've got the longest tail."[2]

Before firing began in Charleston, Brigham Young spoke of those who had opposed and oppressed the Mormon people: "I would fight them if I had to fight them alone, until there was not as much left of them as was left of the Killkenney cats, the last that Joseph Smith saw of them was the ends of their tails. God . . . will rend them to pieces, and put them to the sword, and that by one another."[3] Shortly after Lincoln's 1864 reelection, Young proclaimed: "The North prays that their swords may strike into the heart of every rebel, and I say *Amen*; and the South prays that the North may be cut down on a thousand battlefields, and again I say, *Amen*. The congregation responded 'Amen'; and as Brigham's utterances are considered inspired, they probably believe the war will have a Killkenny cat termination."[4]

LDS Church members selling foodstuffs to the California and Nevada Volunteers at Camp Douglas were said to "gloat over the prospect of a universal inheritance of the riches of the entire nation when the Gentiles [non-Mormons] . . . shall be wiped out in true Kilkenny-cat style."[5] Speakers could make the Mormon Tabernacle's walls "ring with jibes and sneers at the Government, calling the war 'a Kilkenny cat affair' and vieing [sic] with each other in their atrocious abuse of everything loyal and patriotic," wrote the editor of the *Daily Union Vedette*. The *Vedette* was the newspaper of the California Volunteers, non-Mormon troops stationed near Great Salt Lake City.[6]

Several LDS leaders saw polygamy as ameliorating the war's Kilkenny cat tragedy. As one wrote, "[Millions] will fall upon the battle field, . . . and widows will be left to mourn the loss. What will become of these females?" They would be gathered with the Saints in Zion, there to obtain husbands for eternity, was the answer.[7] Mormon poet William W. Phelps put it to verse:

Should Johnny war do brave awhile,
And waste his men a tryin'
What host of wives, and babes will come
To seek the peace of Zion?[8]

An anonymous poet was succinct:

Fight on, till all your men be dead,
And Mormon saints your widows wed.[9]

Apostle Parley Pratt explained in 1841 that the Kingdom of God on earth would begin in conflict, one "more important in its consequences—than any which man has yet witnessed." God would "set up 'a new and universal Kingdom, under the immediate administration of the Messiah and his Saints.'"[10] In the *Millennial Star* of 1842 it was proclaimed that "the kingdoms of this world are [to] become the kingdoms of our Lord, and of his Christ."[11] In 1843 Joseph Smith, Jr., predicted 1890–91 as the time of Christ's return, and in 1844 he organized the secret Council of Fifty because, he asserted, "Church must swallow up State" before the Kingdom of God could come.[12] In 1848 Orson Pratt wrote that the Kingdom of God "is the only legal government . . . in any part of the universe."[13] In 1856 Brigham Young said, "As the Lord lives, we are bound to become a sovereign State in the Union, or an independent nation by ourselves."[14] The U.S. Army was marching to Utah in 1857 when Young said, "The time must come when there will be a separation between this kingdom [of God] and the kingdoms of this world."[15]

"Kingdom of God" carried meaning beyond allegory, far more than a special synonym for the Church of Jesus Christ of Latter-day Saints. Millennialism under Young supplanted and exceeded that of Smith. The Saints' elite held no doubt that a political kingdom of God was about to supersede that of the United States, bringing about the political transformation of the world, just as its unique religion was to bring about the world's religious transformation.

Acknowledgments

Teach me to hear mermaids singing,
or to keep off envy's stinging,
And find
What wind
Serves to advance an honest mind.

JOHN DONNE (1573–1631)

I have been fortunate to have found my way to the community of scholars and historians who do their best to follow the wind that the poet found elusive. They overlook that I do not present decades of experience in the history of the land into which my Scots-Irish ancestors came in 1854 and by handcart in 1856 from the hopelessness of Scotland's mills in Lanarkshire and its crowded Glasgow tenements.

Independent historians David L. Bigler, Will Bagley, and William P. MacKinnon, all authors of many important works, including the Kingdom of the West Series, have generously kept a river of suggested source material flowing to my electronic and paper libraries. The ever-modest historian Floyd O'Neil must be prominent on the list of those whose criticisms have been both wise and kind, and whose encouragement has been invaluable. Michael W. Homer, Chair of the Board of State History of the Utah State Historical Society, together with the J. Willard Marriott Library's Associate Dean for Special Collections,

Greg Thompson, who with Walter Jones have been unfailing with their help and friendship. For the images from the Special Collections, my thanks go to many at the J. Willard Marriott Library of the University of Utah, including Kristin M. Giacoletto, Assistant Photograph Archivist; Betsey Welland, Senior Library Specialist; Elizabeth Rogers, Archivist; Lorraine Crouse, Photograph Archivist; and Luise Poulton, Managing Curator.

Thanks are due for the warm reception of Brad Westwood, Director of the Utah Division of State History. Doug Misner and Greg Walz, Research Managers, and Heidi Stringham Orchard, all of the Utah State History Library, have each given valuable assistance.

The Fort Douglas Military Museum is situated on the Camp Douglas site laid out by Col. P. Edward Connor in 1862—a military base of central importance in Utah Territory's history through the Civil War years. Director Robert Voyles and historian Su Richards made much-appreciated contributions to the stories of the California and Nevada Volunteers at Camp Douglas. Rosemary Wetherold's sharp eye and masterful attention to detail have once again made mine a better work. For this and for her courtesy and warmth, I am indebted.

I gratefully acknowledge genealogist, researcher, and historian Connell O'Donovan, who has helped bridge the gap between North Carolina and Utah, and Gerald McDonough for his passionate explanation of Irish history in Utah. Researcher Joseph Soderborg selflessly led me to little-known facts regarding Walter Murray Gibson. Melanie Sturgeon, Director of Archives and Records Management at Arizona State Library, shared portions of her work on the life and 1862 murder of Olive Curtis Coombs Higbee. Brian Reeves, Chad Orton, and Michael Landon all deserve thanks for their aid at the LDS Church History Library.

Recognition is due several outside of Utah: to Cindy VanHorn, Lincoln Librarian, Allen County Public Library, Fort Wayne, Indiana; to Debbie Hamm and James M. Cornelius, PhD, Curator, Lincoln Collection, Abraham Lincoln Presidential Library and Museum, Springfield, Illinois; to Geoffrey Stark, Special Collections, Mullins Library, University of Arkansas, Fayetteville; and to Isabel Planton, Lilly Library, Indiana University, Bloomington. Marsha Hayes of the New Hanover

County Public Library was helpful and supportive in obtaining material from other institutions. Julie Pagel, Vice President, Winnebago County Register of Deeds, Oshkosh, Wisconsin, helped with efficient searching of the records for James Duane Doty.

My great-grandfather John Maxwell left Scotland to travel in 1854 to a difficult land and a unique religion. He repeatedly answered the call of his church leaders to give up all, move himself and his family, and start over. Sadly, neither he nor his children left any known personal record of their reaction to polygamy, their opinion of Brigham Young, their experiences during the Utah War or the Civil War years, or his membership as a piper and soldier in the Nauvoo Legion. They passed the challenge to me—and to all—to "advance an honest mind" in the complicated, divisive, conflict-laden history of the Latter-day Saints and others in Utah Territory.

The Civil War Years in Utah

Introduction

The work of making the kingdoms of the world [into] the kingdom of God and his Christ has commenced; and all the inhabitants of the earth, without exception, will yet acknowledge Jesus to be the Christ.

BRIGHAM YOUNG, 1862

By any measure—lives lost, societal disruption, racial conflict, economic impact, or persisting aftereffects—the Civil War's magnitude is judged by many historians and social scientists as beyond that of any other event in this nation's history until the attack on Pearl Harbor and World War II.[1] In the 1860s, Utah Territory was unique—very little of the Civil War's disruptions were experienced there. No other state or territory gave less in resources and lives than Utah, and none was less afflicted by the war's costs and sufferings. Notably missing from Utah's history is any self-imposed sense of guilt or accountability for not responding to the war's ultimate crisis. Rather, in the telling of Utah's Mormon history it has been said many times, with implied pride, that during this war, ninety-five men and a dozen teamsters formed—by a presidential request sent not to the territorial governor but to LDS Church president Brigham Young—a cavalry company that served as a U.S. volunteer force. For ninety days in the spring and summer of 1862, they patrolled the mail and telegraph lines and overland traffic. In so doing, they battled neither Indians nor Confederate forces. In this service, Mormon men did not risk life for the cause of union or to end the practice of one man owning the body of another. Utah saw no crude amputations, no lives lost to starvation in filthy prisons, no fields or farmhouses burned by occupying forces. No civilians were ravaged or Utah Mormons killed fighting for a cause shared with millions of Americans.[2] Nonetheless, the territory's ninety-day contribution of men and matériel has become an integral part of the larger legend of Mormon heroism in the face of persecution, of the service of Mormons to a nation they were absolutely certain did not serve them justly. Mormons focused unwaveringly on their own sovereignty, on the establishment—in their lifetime—of the Kingdom of God on earth, on the restoration of the one and only true Church of Jesus Christ, on the practices of their religion unfettered by a government they judged immoral and evil.

God was busy from 1860 to 1865. God was with the South, as church leaders overwhelmingly held unshakable belief in God's commitment to their cause and to perpetuating his sanctioned institution of domestic slavery. Even after Atlanta's September 1864 fall, clergyman Daniel R. Hundley wrote from prison, "The South will surely triumph in the end. She is fighting for the correct principles of civil and religious freedom, and panoplied thus in the armor of divine truth and justice, she can never be conquered."[3]

God was with the North. Religionists saw in their mounting victories evidence of God's favor and of divine chastisement for the South's sins of secession and slavery.

And God was with the Mormons, clearing away the sinful of both camps in millennial preparation.

In one sense the Latter-day Saints' view of the Civil War was no different from that of the majority of Americans. They shared with people in both North and South the overriding belief in a "pervasive, providential interpretation" of human events.[4] History was directed, for "God was in charge," and "all events reflected God's will."[5] However, at another level the Mormon perception of the causes of the war and its unfolding was profoundly different, unrelated to the abolition of slavery, or tariffs, or state's rights, or the preservation of union. When abolitionist John Brown, of Harpers Ferry, held that "the crimes of this guilty land will never be purged away but with blood," he was referring to the guilt arising from the evil of slavery. Mormons viewed the Civil War carnage as God's just punishment for the evil perpetrated on them. For the Mormons the "guilty land" was several counties in Missouri. There the events leading to the murder of their prophet Joseph Smith and his brother Hyrum were set in motion. Mormon stalwart George Q. Cannon wrote: "Missouri, whose soil is drenched with the blood of Saints! . . . over whose surface Prophets and Saints were hunted and driven with cruel and fiendish violence—has become the theatre of stirring events. . . . A fearful retribution is being exacted from the wicked inhabitants of that poor State for their base conduct towards an innocent and unresisting people."[6] As the Civil War expanded, the breadth of those deserving punishment also expanded, until it included the entire populations of North and South. "May the judgements Continue [sic] to be poured out upon this land of North America untill [sic] the Blood of Prophets and Saints is avenged before the Lord," prayed Mormon leader Wilford Woodruff.[7]

Understanding Utah's place in the Civil War—and the war's relevance to the Mormons' Kingdom of God on earth in preparation for Christ's return—must begin within the larger framework of Mormon history from 1830 to 1861. From a church begun in 1830 by Joseph Smith, Jr., near Palmyra, New York, there were soon branches in the cities of Colesville, Fayette, and Manchester, New York. In 1831 the Mormons moved to a "way station" in Kirtland, Ohio. Membership increased, and they moved to the spot their prophet claimed had been the site of the biblical Garden of Eden, near Independence, Jackson County, Missouri. Troubles and violence from non-Mormons forced another migration, this time to an Illinois city on the eastern bank of the Mississippi River that the church members rebuilt by industry and forbearance, renaming it Nauvoo.

When Joseph and Hyrum Smith were assassinated in 1844 in a lopsided gun battle with their assassins while under arrest, charged with treason at Carthage, Illinois, Brigham Young took up the church leadership and, after a delay, the mantle as their prophet. Mormons fled from several counties of Missouri and from Illinois, either because of unwarranted persecution and violence—as they claim—or because they were forcibly expelled for unlawful behavior and their peculiar, unacceptable "marriage" practices—as non-Mormons record. Their unlawful behavior, political manipulations, and devotion to one-man rule proved more causative than any of their singular religious practices. By whatever cause, the members of the LDS Church, some ten thousand strong, crossed the frozen surface of the Mississippi in the bitter winter of 1846, in a hegira of immeasurable personal sacrifice, forging westward to an interim refuge they called Winter Quarters, near present-day Omaha, Nebraska. Under great hardship, many Mormon emigrant groups pressed farther westward—following Brigham Young's first trip in 1847 to found Great Salt Lake City. When the United States took possession of an immense land tract west of the Rocky Mountains as a provision of the Guadalupe Hidalgo Treaty at the end of the Mexican-American War, the Saints were again ruled by a government they feared. By 1850 they once more sought sovereignty, not by further emigration, but by requesting a state of the Union, one that they would control and wished to be named Deseret. Instead, Congress granted a United States territory named Utah, after one of its several native Indian tribes, and the Saints became subject to the laws applicable to other U.S. territories and subject to the federal oversight they despised. Young blamed the denial of statehood on deceased president Zachary Taylor, exclaiming, "[He] is dead, and in Hell, and I am glad of it."[8]

Overt disloyalty and treason blossomed in Utah from sedition's seed planted by LDS leadership in 1845 in Nauvoo, Illinois.[9] William Smith, brother of slain Joseph and Hyrum, alleged that fifteen hundred followers of Brigham Young had been ordered to swear in the temple "that you will avenge the blood of Joseph Smith *upon this nation,* and so teach your children; and that you will from this day henceforth and forever begin and carry out hostility *against this nation,* and keep the same a profound secret."[10] Slight variations of this unwritten "oath of vengeance" or "oath of retribution" became an integral part of the Endowment House and Mormon temple ceremonies. Contemporary corroboration of the oath as part of ritual comes from several former Mormons, including T. B. H. and Fanny Stenhouse, Catherine Lewis,

and John Hyde, Sr. Writing of his 1855 visit to Utah, visiting French-
man Jules Rémy stated that Mormons "swear to cherish an undying
hatred for the government of the United States, because it neither
avenged the death of Joseph Smith nor repaired the outrages and
losses suffered by the Saints during their persecutions; to do all that
they can to destroy, overturn and molest this government."[11] In 1889,
Utah judge Thomas J. Anderson dealt with the issue of whether taking the Mormon oath of vengeance disqualified one for citizenship.
Lawyers Robert Newton Baskin and William Dickson called eleven witnesses who admitted to the oath as part of the endowment ceremony,
while fourteen faithful Mormons denied it.[12] The oath of vengeance
became a significant issue in the prolonged investigation at the seating
of Senator Reed Smoot at the beginning of the twentieth century.[13] It
was not until 1927 that the First Presidency of Heber J. Grant, Anthony
W. Ivins, and Charles W. Nibley directed Charles F. Richards to inform
those at the St. George Temple to "omit from the prayer in the circles
all reference to avenging the blood of the Prophets . . . [and] all reference to retribution."[14] Presumably this was part of a general instruction
to all temple officers.

In 1850 Franklin Langworthy, an Illinois emigrant to Utah, reported
a July 24 message prophesying "that the total overthrow of the United
States was near at hand, and that the whole nation would soon be at
the feet of the Mormons, suing for mercy and protection."[15] In Salt
Lake City in January 1851, Presbyterian minister Jotham W. Goodell,
bound for Oregon, reported hearing Governor Young proclaim, "No
other person shall hold that office while I am alive." The federal government might send a governor to Utah, but Young asserted, "We will
send him back or send him *duck hunting*."[16] In the fall of 1851 the
Nauvoo Legion's Daniel Wells contacted arms maker Samuel Colt on
the "availability of large quantities of Colt's most powerful, sophisti-
cated, scope-equipped weapons and 'any kind of instruments you may
be manufacturing, suited to mountain warfare.'"[17] Brigham Young
acquired a revolving, rifled, long-barreled gun in the fall of 1857, but
it proved to be inaccurate on testing.[18]

Hope for isolation and the Kingdom of God's sovereignty was
quashed by the Saints' location in the path of western growth and

migration. Shiny material reflected in the wash of California's American River in January 1848 soon made Great Salt Lake City an indispensable way station for those westering "with golden visions bright before them."[19] Few of those traveling to California or Oregon saw promise in Utah's dry lands, and unless they showed interest in Mormonism, the Saints did nothing to make life there appealing. Mormon leaders established a hierarchical society where dissent was little tolerated and disobedience to eastern federal government was fostered.[20] The Saints were convinced that any government was evil if it denied them the full expression of their religion as guaranteed by the Constitution, which they believed had been divinely inspired for their benefit.

President James Buchanan's decision in the spring of 1857 to declare Utah's people in rebellion was based in part on various reports by several non-Mormon, federally appointed officials, describing the conditions in 1855–56 under Young's governorship. Less than three months after his inauguration, Buchanan ordered one-third of the strength of the U.S. Army available for frontier duty—2,500 troops—to march from Fort Leavenworth, through the middle of the continent, toward Utah. Young countered by imposing martial law and interrupting overland travel and mail, isolating California from the east. He prepared for all-out war.

Buchanan's purpose in sending the Utah Expedition was to seat Alfred Cumming of Georgia as Young's successor as governor and to install federal supremacy over the "first rebellion which has existed in our Territories."[21] Mormons interpreted the troop's movement as a threat to their survival, suspecting that another religious pogrom was unfolding against them. Young's letter to Col. Edmund B. Alexander at Fort Bridger was explicit: "As you officially allege it, I acknowledge that you and the forces have been sent to the Territory by the President of the United States, but we shall treat you as though you were open enemies, because I have so many times seen armies in our country, under color of law, drive this people . . . from their homes, while mobs have followed and plundered at their pleasure, which is now most obviously the design of the government."[22] Young warned his Saints of a life-threatening confrontation: "We are invaded by a hostile force, who are evidently assailing us to accomplish our overthrow and destruction."[23]

Young's choice of verbs was deliberate. He wished his people to believe their State of Deseret—nonexistent officially—was being illegally menaced. The September 15 imposition of martial law in a territory large enough to encompass New England, New York, Pennsylvania, and Ohio virtually divided the nation, east and west, north and south. Young knew Utah's land remained under the ownership of the United States and could be legally traversed by the U.S. Army without permission from Utah's governor or its people.[24] The Utah Expedition "compels us to resort to the great first law of self-preservation," Young proclaimed. Thus Mormon people maintained unity and solidarity, while their leaders repeatedly sounded throughout the Civil War years that annihilation lurked as the secret, true federal purpose.

Young held lifetime tenure as LDS Church president, trustee-in-trust for all its money and property, husband to many wives, and hard-line dictator of a theocracy, buttressed by several score of trusted men of the LDS Church priesthood and a private army at his call. For practicing plural marriage, his closed society was vilified for almost two decades beyond his death. He was also—until 1857—the superintendent of Indian Affairs. He vowed that ten years in Utah, unfettered by federal interference, would enable him and the Saints to "cut the threads" that bound them to any man-made, federal government.[25] Buchanan's action in sending the Utah Expedition marked the tenth year of Young's preparations, and the Mormon leader saw an opportunity to act on this promise.

Young and Lt. Gen. Daniel H. Wells ordered militiamen to seize thousands of the Utah Expedition's livestock. The loss—in mules alone—was $2 million.[26] Millions more were lost through his orchestration of the destruction of federal property carried by Col. Albert Sidney Johnston's supply train as it inched with little protection toward Fort Bridger.[27] Spared from destruction were kegs of gunpowder and other munitions that were transferred to Nauvoo Legion troops. With a pool of seven thousand Mormon volunteers, many of them Nauvoo Legion veterans, the narrow Echo Canyon approach to the Salt Lake valley was fortified with more than three thousand men. Wells formed plans and accumulated men and arms, preparing to engage the U.S. Army in all-out war if any of the Utah Expedition advanced beyond Fort Bridger or entered the Salt Lake valley by any route in the fall of 1857. "Find safe retreats in the Mountains," ordered General Wells.[28] If all else failed, Young planned "to lay waste everything that will burn . . . so that they cannot find a particle . . . of use to them."[29] Mormons would hide in the vastness and wage guerrilla war, or they might flee to another refuge, possibly to Mexico, Vancouver Island, Malaysia, Indonesia, or Alaska.

In an early 1858 visit to New York City, Young's trusted Council of Fifty agent, Horace S. Eldredge, was fresh from secret efforts in St. Louis to purchase gunpowder for shipment to Salt Lake City. He claimed religious intolerance and prejudice by the territory's appointed federal officers for the Mormons' trouble with government.[30] Had Buchanan sent "high-minded, honorable men" among them to investigate in the 1850s, they "would have found nothing" to discredit the Mormons. Eldredge noted that Mormons were "in no way troubled at the purport of an increased Army going out to Utah in the Spring," but if "troops forced their way into the valleys," a "*bloody account would have to be rendered*," since Mormons preferred an honorable war . . . *to a dishonorable peace.*"[31] A prominent southern Utah Mormon, James Henry Martineau, reported circulating rumors: "They intend to hang about 300 of the most obnoxious Mormons; Brigham to be hung any how—no trial necessary for him . . . and a form of a trial for the rest." Martineau concluded, "I . . . greatly prefer fighting to hanging."[32] The expedition forces stopped at Fort Bridger, where Colonel Johnston, his troops, and the appointed territorial officials with them endured the 1857–58 winter, short on salt but—according to the expedition's diarist, Capt. Albert Tracy—otherwise not in significant want for food.[33] Responding to the crisis, Mormon Seth Blair, a former U.S. attorney for Utah, joined with his longtime friend Texas senator Sam Houston, and the two found a way to block Buchanan's obtaining additional troops, advising him to appoint a commission to offer Mormons a "last chance to avoid the consequences of their defiance." Commissioners Lazarus Powell and Ben McCulloch did persuade Young to accede to Buchanan's April 6 no-compromise offer, and bloody war was skirted by a whisker's length.[34] On June 14, Mormons "cheerfully" but disingenuously agreed to obey federal laws and allow civil officers to discharge their territorial duties.[35]

By mid-1858, many considered the U.S. military the losers in the Utah War. Non-Mormons were dishonored by Buchanan's pardon of the Mormons' treason. Locating Camp Floyd forty miles from Great Salt Lake City prevented a prompt response to matters in the city, and Mormons in the territory's largest city could cut the military's supply line from Fort Leavenworth at any moment.[36]

Nine months into the War of the Rebellion, Young wrote to John M. Bernhisel, the territory's representative in Washington, that "if the question arises whether we will furnish troops beyond our borders for the war, . . . tell them no."[37] Young's arrogating from Utah's official governor the decision that Utah's men would or would not serve went unchallenged by Governors Harding and Doty and by President Lincoln. Lincoln neither trusted the Mormons, who three years before had earnestly prepared for war, nor did he repeat Buchanan's mistake of openly battling the all-powerful de facto governor, Brigham Young.[38]

After the U.S. Army's march from Utah to battlefields east in July 1861, an eventful eighteen-month period followed where neither U.S. regulars nor U.S. volunteers resided in Utah. The only military presence in Utah was the private Mormon army, commanded by men who did not question their leader's orders.

The single most significant Civil War event within Utah was the October 1862 march into Salt Lake City of the unwelcome seven hundred men of the Third California Volunteer Infantry and the Second California Volunteer Cavalry. Col. P. Edward Connor, placing his camp on the foothills' bench three miles from the city's center, was the first of many actions that generated conflict. Mormons saw Connor as arrogant and impertinent; Connor judged Young as disloyal and dictatorial. These perceptions would pervade their contentious interaction even beyond Connor's period of military service, to Young's death in 1877. Connor found Mormons loyal only to the government founded by men of God—namely, the Latter-day Saints' theocracy—and its developing Kingdom of God. Open warfare threatened repeatedly, and undisguised antipathy prevailed between Mormon leaders and the federal government, together with its appointed agents, throughout the Civil War and for more than thirty years beyond its termination.

In many particulars, the years of 1860 to 1865 were a halcyon period for the territory's Mormons. When the Saints entered the Salt Lake valley in 1847, the $84 in small coin brought by Brigham Young was their only official medium of exchange. A barter system quickly emerged, and paper substitutes for coin were among the first printing enterprises.[39] When Union troops arrived in 1857–58, cash began to flow readily into the territory from military purchases of meat, vegetables, other foodstuffs, wood, coal, animal feed, and range for grazing. Upon the closure of Camp Floyd, its goods sold at fire-sale prices to local Mormons. With another influx of troops in 1862, the gold, coins, and paper money in their pockets from their military salary bought entertainment, alcohol, goods, and luxuries not found in military or sutler's stores.

Setting telegraph poles and stringing lines and insulators provided employment for Mormon laborers and income for Young. Brigham's son John W. supplied many of the wooden poles, with profit to them both. Telegraph lines from the east were completed on October 18, 1861, and from the west on October 24. No longer was Young dependent on the uncertainty of "the Pony" for Civil War news or for the extensive personal letters keeping him in frequent contact with—and in control of—Mormon missionaries and church emissaries in the states and in Europe.[40]

Indian attacks on overland travelers were ostensibly behind the call of California and Nevada Volunteers to Utah. Lincoln did not call Utah's military for this task, for he wanted no risk to overland travel and communication like that which Young caused in 1857 by his illegal declaration of martial law. Moreover, Mormons were accused of complicity in Indian attacks along the Humboldt River and on the trails eastward. Boasting by Mormons that they were safe from Indian attack while traveling on the same trails strengthened the allegations of complicity. Connor was—as he is today—alternately criticized and praised for leading the California Volunteers in their attack-massacre killing of 250 Shoshonis at Bear River in the abysmal cold of January 1863. Following the official policy of harsh punishment set by the Department of the Pacific, he earned not only his brigadier general promotion but also the appellation of the supreme Indian fighter of the West and Midwest.

Connor found Young's dictatorship, the Mormons' theocracy, and the practice of polygamy unacceptable within a nation whose citizens were expected to be obedient to law and civil rule. Connor's judgment of the disloyalty of Mormons arose from treasonous speeches in their church meetings and from repeated admissions that Utah was not merely neutral in a time of moral and political crisis. The great majority of Mormon leaders openly favored the Confederacy. Celebration of Union defeats rang from the pulpits; Connor documented acts of disloyalty to his troops in the field, of refusal to aid Union troops under Indian attack, of refusal to billet officers or provide forage for animals, and of refusal to sell food to the troops except at severely inflated prices. Connor's appraisals of Mormon disloyalty were made public and corroborated by *Daily Union Vedette* editors Charles Hempstead and Frederick Livingston. Private and public remarks, together with letters and speeches by Governor Stephen S. Harding, Rev. Norman McLeod, and Judges Charles B. Waite, Thomas J. Drake, and John Titus also validated Connor's appraisal. Had Lincoln's suspension of habeas corpus, widely applied in the Northeast, been possible in Utah, many Mormons would have been arrested and imprisoned without trial, just as thousands elsewhere were, for uttering words of disloyalty even in the absence of an overt act.

Once the war passed the blood-drenched middle years, all of the states and territories in the West had either a Union or a Confederate voice, but in Utah a peculiar blanket of quiet enveloped the Mormon press. Several vignettes in 1864 and 1865 illustrate this anomaly.

On November 11, 1864, the results of the presidential election were already evident and the pages of the *Daily Union Vedette*, the newspaper of the troops of the California and Nevada Volunteers at Camp Douglas, were filled with celebration: "GLORIOUS! GLORIOUS!!" "The election of Abraham Lincoln and Andrew Johnson is beyond a doubt." "Copperheadism is forever damned." And with Thanksgiving Day approaching, "Peals from the mouths of our thousands of cannon will rent the air with the shots of Lincoln and Johnson, and millions of throats will be made hoarse with the huzzas of loyal men."[41] In contrast, not a single instance of the name "Lincoln" appeared on any of the eight pages of the November 16 issue of the weekly *Deseret News* in

Great Salt Lake City. Through November and December, that voice of the Saints remained journalistically and editorially silent, not even stating the simple fact that Abraham Lincoln had been reelected to the presidency of the United States.

When the city of Charleston, South Carolina—"the birthplace of treason"—passed into Union hands in February 1865, celebrations erupted on the snow-packed streets of Salt Lake City, with sleighs filled with the volunteer troops and non-Mormon merchants and citizens. Teams of horses were decorated with flags and patriotic banners. When they moved on to the grounds of Camp Douglas, where "in the warm and ardent clasping of manly hands; in the impulse which made men as children, embracing like brothers met after long absence; . . . in all these things we saw evidences of that deep and abiding love of country, which has borne the Nation so triumphantly through the great struggle nearly over."[42] No evidence of Mormon celebration or instance of spontaneous, joyful demonstration has yet been found. "Brigham Young will be the next President" may have been the "cardinal doctrine" of rumors in the city, according to the March visit of Dr. S. B. Bell, but Mormon leaders were stone silent on the Charleston matter.[43]

The April defeat at Five Forks, Virginia, was deemed the waterloo of the Confederacy, with the cities of Petersburg and Richmond both falling within days. "Words come not . . . when the heart overflows with emotions too deep for utterance, we can only feel the gratitude which finds no expression," wrote the *Vedette*'s editor as he sought to metaphorically sing "Gloria in Excelsis."[44] Again the *Deseret News* was silent on this news.

On April 9, Lt. Gen. Ulysses Grant accepted the surrender of the Army of Northern Virginia from Gen. Robert E. Lee, ending, as Grant phrased it, the "hopelessness of further resistance" and the "further effusion of blood." On April 11 the *Vedette* devoted two pages of five columns each to this long-desired news. Included was the letter of Secretary of War Edwin Stanton to Grant, which said, "Thanks to the Almighty God for the great victory with which he has this day crowned you and the gallant army under your command."[45] Nothing of the war's end appeared in the *Deseret News*. The speeches given by Mormon leaders in their weekend's semiannual conference gathering were devoid of any acknowledgment or words of celebration.

Public silence at the war's end was unique. The Civil War in Utah was unique. The Saints were physically and culturally isolated, and rationally and emotionally disconnected from the conflict. But disconnection was only partially explains why Mormons had no reason to celebrate the return of peace. Logic suggests that their silence had its cause in the undeniable failure of Joseph Smith's prophecy—restated many times by other Mormon leaders—of the mutual destruction of the antagonists. Thus the progression of the Kingdom of God had been interrupted. Reason predicts that unfilled prophecy would be the subject of serious discussion among the topmost men of LDS leadership. However, no public admission of the prophecy's failure appeared in the *Deseret News*.

Not until 1959, when historian Ray C. Colton published *The Civil War in the Western Territories*, did the first academic study of the war years in the West appear. However, Colton devoted Utah Territory only ten pages. Gustive O. Larson's brief 1965 article, "Utah and the Civil War," touched briefly on the subject. It remained for respected Wyoming historian Everette Beach Long to provide the first authoritative and ambitious account devoted to the broad issues in Utah in his 1981 work, *The Saints and the Union: Utah Territory during the Civil War.* David Bigler's *Forgotten Kingdom*, published in 1998, is rich with material related to the millennialism of the Civil War years, but by purpose it is not a focused treatment of the war period. In 1991 Alvin M. Josephy, Jr., published his work on the trans-Mississippi West, *The Civil War in the American West*. Richard W. Etulain's *Lincoln and Oregon Country Politics in the Civil War Era*, published in 2013, is the most recent addition.

This present study establishes that the society of the Saints in Utah contributed almost nothing to the preservation of national unity and the abolition of slavery. Utah's Mormons were not among those whom Carl Sandburg called the "immense humanity shaken with feeling that the buying and selling of human beings, even if black-skinned and primitive, should be outlawed."[46] The Saints were equipped, ready, and willing to engage in open warfare against the territory's parent government from 1857 to at least 1865 in order to establish their

Kingdom of God on earth. Documentary evidence—beyond their oath of vengeance—is abundant. No longer can accusations of Saints' disloyalty be dismissed as irrelevant and unfounded charges made by incompetent men and women whose evil purposes worked against God's plan. The Civil War created an unmeasurable crater of death, tragedy, and sorrow across the continent, but not in Utah. Seemingly infinite is the social change the war initiated outside Utah, but similar profound societal change did not follow inside.

This work visits new sources of what is known of the mistreatment of Gov. John W. Dawson and of the little-discussed association of Harding with early New York Mormonism. Gov. James Duane Doty's seemingly moderate diplomacy, his relationship with Brigham Young, and his removal from Indian relations are afforded deeper exploration. Reported for the first time is that the highest levels of the Mormon hierarchy were duped or knowingly carried out several years of personal interaction with Walter Murray Gibson, now revealed to be not only a blatant charlatan but also a notorious Confederate spy.

Collective memory and appreciation of this consequential period of the developing American nation have been the victim of the "silent artillery of time" in Utah.[47] This reappraisal of the years of 1860–65 in Utah is no less needed than the other Civil War sesquicentennial investigations that are engaging historians and sociologists nationwide.

CHAPTER 1

Transition from a Utah War to a Civil War, 1859–1860

A peace with traitors, begun by concessions, must end in disgrace.
CHIEF JUSTICE DELANA R. ECKELS

There was no winner in the Utah War. Buchanan failed to achieve federal supremacy, and the Mormons' quest for sovereignty went unfulfilled. Neither did the 1857–58 Utah War escalate into an apocalyptic end with LDS Church priesthood men surviving to take the reins of government, but soon another potential pathway to this goal opened. As matters of tariffs, abolition of slavery, and state's rights reached ignition temperatures in South Carolina and elsewhere across the South, Brigham Young and church leaders refocused on Joseph Smith's 1832 prophecy of a war of national scope that would result in Mormon rule of the nation and the world.

The *New York Times* asserted that the Utah Expedition had been an ignominious defeat for Buchanan, that affairs in Utah seemed to be "in precisely the same condition . . . as before the troops marched at all." The "insolence" of the Mormons had not been punished, and "we have neither restored the authority of the Federal Government nor secured the administration of the laws." Still remaining was the "contempt with which the Mormons treated the United States, and the open resistance which they offered to their authority." Buchanan's actions in Utah, according to the *Times*, had "ended by making neither peace, nor war, for the Mormons would neither fight nor treat." Armies and proclamations "have effected no great change."[1] The *Times* complained that Mormons "ridicule the effeminacy and credulity of President Buchanan, and boast that Brigham Young has overreached him." Furthermore, Mormons had "accomplished by strategy what they could not effect by force of arms, and . . . made fortunes while they did it."[2] The *San Francisco Bulletin* observed that Buchanan had "offered a premium to treason," for the federal government had "expended millions of dollars" and "strewn wealth and prosperity in a region that was before isolated and poverty stricken." Whenever Young desired "another harvest at federal expense," he could "incite his people to new manifestations of disloyalty," without adverse consequences. The *Bulletin*'s incisive prediction was spot-on.[3]

Secretary of War John B. Floyd's spring 1859 letter informed Bvt. Brig. Gen. Albert Sidney Johnston, commander of the Camp Floyd troops, that peace "had been restored to the Territory." However, Floyd's instruction that Johnston would activate troops only at the "written direction" of Governor Alfred Cumming, of itself, proved that peace—even among factions of the federal government—did not exist. Citizens of Salt Lake City petitioned Cumming for a military escort for safe passage out of Utah, a request that would have been unnecessary had "peace" existed. It was argued that Cumming violated the military chain of command by placing regular troops of the U.S. Army under orders from the executive branch of a territory.[4] Nonetheless, Johnston responded to Cumming's request in a May letter offering to "furnish the force for their protection" for all who wished to leave.[5] Emigrants organized; all who wished "to avail themselves of this security" were "to convene at the California House" hotel to plan for their departure.[6] The newspaper of Camp Floyd's troops, the *Valley Tan*, reported: "Treason exists as much this day as when Echo Kanyon [*sic*] with it fortifications was bristling with arms and traitors against the Government of the United States." Buchanan's blanket pardon of the Mormons was "laughed at and . . . derided, . . . in the most indecent terms." Those pardoned "sniggered at the idea," for they had "overreached the Government," whose efforts had accomplished nothing.[7] Visiting newsmen observed that conditions in Utah were "on the very eve of open hostilities . . . brought on by the firm and manly stand of the two Judges of the U.S. District Court, [Charles E.] Sinclair and [John] Cradlebaugh, . . . in their endeavors to ferret out the numerous murders that have been committed."[8] The state of affairs in Utah brought on by efforts of "the Third District Court to enforce laws and bring criminals to justice" was threatening to spark an "immediate collision between the Saints and the United States troops," added the *St. Louis Democrat.*[9]

The Judges' "Manly Stand"

Alvira Parrish set in motion a cascade of serious events when, in the district court, she accused eight men from Springville of the 1857 murder of her husband, William R. Parrish, and a son, William Beason Parrish. Among them were Cumming's restriction on the use of U.S. troops, as well as the tense collisions of the executive, the military, and the judiciary with Cumming, Johnston, and Judges Sinclair and Cradlebaugh.[10] Cradlebaugh, with only one good eye but with clear and penetrating judicial vision, issued arrest warrants for eight men accused in the Parrish killings. However, U.S. marshal Peter Kessler Dotson swore he was not able to jail any of them unless he was provided with a military posse. When one hundred infantrymen under the command of Capt. Henry Heth arrived in support, their numbers were inflated by Provo's Mormons to "1,000 bayonets" glistening on the city's foothills. Strenuous objections to the troops' presence were raised by citizens and Mayor Benjamin K. Bullock.[11] An additional eight hundred troops under the command of Maj. Gabriel R. Paul were sent to control unrest, enforce warrants, and protect federal officers. To lessen citizens' alarm, they camped four miles from the city. Governor Cumming's reaction was two-pronged: he first appealed to Secretary of State Lewis Cass, who forwarded the matter to Secretary Floyd. Then, with the cooperation of the all-Mormon legislature, Cumming gerrymandered the judicial districts of the territory, assigning Judge Cradlebaugh to appear May 1 at the post in Genoa, the seat of Carson County and six hundred miles from Provo or Salt Lake City. Formerly called

Mormon Station, near present-day Carson City, Nevada, the settlement was then within Utah Territory.

Even as the date of Cradlebaugh's banishment to Genoa grew closer, grand jurors heard abundant testimony regarding the Parrish murders, but no indictments emerged. Frustrated, Cradlebaugh dismissed the all-Mormon jury. Neighboring news editors, well aware of the happenings, reported that Utah's news seemed "to argue the impossibility of the Federal Court administering justice" and that "Judge Cradlebaugh had dismissed the grand jury, they refusing to find any bills of indictment." Also noted was that the jurors used "every other means to screen murderers and robbers from justice."[12] Cradlebaugh sent Marshal Dotson with two hundred soldiers and arrest warrants for a dozen men, including Provo's Mayor Bullock and Springville's Bishop Aaron Johnson.[13] Bullock was released a day later, but Johnson fled into the adjacent Wasatch Mountains.

On April 17, General Johnston, with Cradlebaugh's concurrence, ordered Capt. Reuben Campbell south to the Santa Clara River to investigate the much talked-of 1857 killings of more than 120 California-bound Arkansas emigrants at Mountain Meadows. Secretary Floyd ordered officers from the Department of the Pacific also to investigate. Bvt. Maj. James Henry Carleton of the California First Dragoons met Campbell on May 8 in California, where they shared what they had seen. Both officers "opened a telling [verbal] fire on Mormon settlers for committing the atrocity."[14] Deputy Marshal William H. Rogers and Indian agent Jacob Forney also searched the massacre site, and Rogers reported: "When I first passed through the place I could walk for nearly a mile on bones, and skulls laying grinning at you, and women and children's hair in bunches as big as a bushel." Rogers and Cradlebaugh named sixty white men as perpetrators.[15] Warrants for the arrest of John D. Lee, Isaac C. Haight, and John M. Higbee were issued from Provo. However, Buchanan dismissed the Cradlebaugh-Carleton-Johnston investigation of the Mountain Meadows murders—and multiple other crimes in Utah—by his order that troops were at the singular call of the puppet governor, Alfred Cumming.

Second Lt. John Van Deusen Du Bois, who rode with Johnston's troops on the June 1858 trek down Echo Canyon into Salt Lake City, left his appraisal of Cumming's allegiance: "The Governor is becoming a Mormon rapidly. Everyone is disgusted with him. He seems to truckle to Mormondom and cultivate intimate relations with Brigham Young." Federal presence failed to influence violence, according to Du Bois, for "murderers & robbers have been pardoned and now roam around unmolested." He continued, "[Young is] stronger than ever, and we have been conquered as surely by the Washington weakness as we would have been by the sword. The army . . . feels its degradation and asks nothing more [in humiliation] now except a Mormon General to command it."[16] Humiliation may have prompted Johnston's request to be relieved, suggested the *San Francisco Bulletin*, adding that "the request will not be granted at present."[17]

Peace was further disproved by the presence of two cannons "cached and guarded by three or four men on the bench north of this city, and about half a mile west of City Creek Kanyon," as Joseph R. Logue informed Marshal Dotson in May.[18] This discovery led to an inspection of the ordinance of the Nauvoo Legion by Utah Territorial secretary John Hartnett, Marshal Dotson, and Logue. The inspection report, written by Legion Adj. Gen. James Ferguson to Cumming, listed the Legion's "12 pounder Mountain Howitzer" given to the territory "in the fall of 1851" as constituting "all the public arms in the Territory."[19] Most significant in this brief report are the words "public arms," for weaponry was held in private ownership, not as the property of the territorial or federal government. Unaddressed were the origin and purpose of the Mormons' cannons situated on the commanding peaks above the city. A *Valley Tan* article further contradicted Floyd's claim of peace: "There are armed scouting parties sent out, cannons mounted, cached, and when discovered, subsequently hid," as well as "signal arrangements prepared upon the mountain heights" to communicate with other parts of the territory."[20]

Peace with Traitors Must End in Disgrace

Utah Supreme Court chief justice Delana R. Eckels' first exposure to Utah was in the winter of 1857–58, when he and Utah Expedition troops were stopped at Fort Bridger by the Nauvoo Legion. Thus he learned who controlled the territory. By the fall of 1859 he judged matters becoming "worse and worse," elaborating to Secretary of State Cass in September that when he commenced court in August for the First District in Nephi, "there were many, very many high crimes that were not passed upon by the grand jury."[21] Two-thirds of the male population fled from the prospect of being arrested or called as witnesses. Those charged with murder and grand larceny were "turned loose by Mormon officials a few days before court," and "no steps were taken to bring the perpetrators of the massacre at Mountain Meadows before the grand jury." Eckels said that Mormons were "not openly under arms," yet were "as rebellious against our form of government to-day as they ever were," since "all power, civil and ecclesiastical, is in their priesthood" in an "inseparable union of church and state." Stating that Mormons constituted "a terror to all travellers through these mountains," Eckels added: "No road from the States to California is safe. Five trains have been robbed of their stock almost in sight of our camp with impunity. . . . The Indians are blamed for it," but "whites plan and aid in the execution of these murders."[22]

Resignations and flights from the territory as described by Eckels were reminiscent of the similar exodus of federal officials in 1850–51 and again in 1856–58: "Marshal Dotson has resigned. Judge Sinclair and Attorney Wilson have gone to the States. Mr. Secretary Hartnett has gone to St. Louis, and . . . he may not return. . . . Judge Cradlebaugh will likely go during the fall, and I expect to leave in the spring." Eckels's observations led him to conclude: "A peace with traitors, begun by concessions, must end in disgrace."[23] True to plan, Eckels resigned his judgeship in March 1860. A New York newspaper noted the conflict of Sinclair and Cradlebaugh with Cumming, concluding, "Governor [Cumming] is a Mormon and the Judges are Gentiles. . . . The policy of the Administration seems to be to appease the Mormons by removing the Gentiles."[24]

"Treason and rebellion without—privation and want within," stated the *Valley Tan* of the condition of the Saints as they migrated south from Great Salt Lake valley in spring of 1858. "Treason, which then stalked openly and publically abroad, now seeks some little disguise," penned Stephen DeWolfe, the fourth editor of Camp Floyd's weekly newspaper. He went on to say that "thanks to the presence of an army here, [citizens] can dwell with some little security more than they could two years ago." No longer were they "openly told in a court . . . that their 'necks will be wrung like that of a chicken,' if they venture to assert their rights against a Mormon." Troops stationed in Utah brought other benefits to a people who in 1857 were in "want and destitution." By 1859 they had "probably never before enjoyed as much prosperity." Now able to charge "extravagant prices for all the surplus products which they have raised," they were enjoying "comforts and luxuries before unknown." Conditions were "immeasurably superior" to those prior to the federal's arrival, added DeWolfe.[25]

Annexation of Mexico

Historian William P. MacKinnon notes Buchanan's interest, long before his presidency, in acquiring Cuba and Mexico as part of the nation's westward expansion. It was possible that 1857 found Buchanan secretly planning "to stimulate a mass Mormon exodus to Sonora, Mexico, at the point of a bayonet followed by acquisition of much of northern Mexico and Cuba through a combination of diplomatic and military gambits."[26] Within weeks of his inauguration, Buchanan quietly instructed John Forsyth, minister to Mexico, to purchase a vast region adjacent to the U.S. border for $15 million.[27] When Johnston's troops met obstruction at Fort Bridger in October 1857, Buchanan may have envisioned a larger project, for three moves immediately followed: he sent Christopher Fallon to Spain in order to buy Cuba, he met with Thomas L. Kane to discuss his planned mediation mission to Salt Lake City, and he "posted a reluctant General [Winfield] Scott to California to open a second front against the Mormons to hammer them from the Pacific." British diplomat Sir William Gore Ouseley wrote privately to Lord Clarendon in England that Buchanan's Utah Expedition "ostensibly against the Mormons" extended deeper, "involving relations with Mexico and plans for the acquisition of Cuba." Ouseley pointed out, "The latter however is the real object; the other is subsidiary to it and serves to mask the real movement. The intention as to the Mormons was to bring about their immigration to Sonora and thus to turn their rebellion to account by making them pioneers for future annexation under a quasi-military colonial system." Gen. Winfield Scott would become a party to the scheme without being aware of its full scope, claims MacKinnon.[28]

When thirty thousand people left the Salt Lake valley in spring 1858 and headed southward in anticipation of the entry of Union troops into Utah's heartland, their destination was thought to be central Utah. However, other destinations were apparently under Young's consideration. Thomas Kane, heading west, had met James W. Simonton, a reporter for the *New York Times*, at Sweetwater Bridge, Nebraska Territory, and the correspondent gave him "the impression that Young, whom he had just left, was heading for Sonora."[29]

The relationship between Mormon colonies in Mexico and the U.S. government's interests there, and whether Confederates were anticipating a possible role for Mexico in enhancing slavery or supplying war munitions, apparently remained concerns in Young's mind far later than 1857. His letter of December 1859 to delegate William H. Hooper asked a question—one that he would later also pose to others, including Thomas L. Kane—that indicated curiosity, if not inside knowledge, of something afoot with Mexico.[30] Young asked, "Do you think that South Carolina means what one of her Senators lately wrote . . . [:] 'We have not enough blacks to settle the country, to raise the cotton, rice, and tobacco that are wanted. If any of them do ship from Africa [to Mexico], tell them not to say a word about [it], nor in any way let it be known.'"[31]

Representative Bernhisel, fleeing July's heat in Pennsylvania's mountains, reminded Young that the aim of creating additional slave states for Southern takeover had been operative in both the Mexican War and with the Civil War. Mexico was distracted by the prospect of procuring slave territory, but that design was frustrated by the organization of the Territories of New Mexico and Utah and the admission of California as a free state. When Kansas did not go slave, "the South designed to take Cuba, right or wrong, out of which they designed to make three slave States." If all these failed, the South "resolved on a dismemberment of the Union."[32]

Independent of any Utah involvement was Mexico's revolutionary war in January, 1858. That was followed by the intervention of Napoleon III and France's occupation of Mexico in 1864, which prevented establishing slavery routes or colonies there. Confederate forces in Texas considered land routes through Mexico to reach California, and Union forces considered shipping supplies and troops into Mexico at Guaymas. Confederate units battled Union forces of Colorado's volunteer militia, most notably at Glorieta Pass and in portions of New Mexico Territory.

Treason Is Lucky—Traitors Prosper—Repeal the Organic Act

Preceding Vermont representative Justin Morrill's bill of February 1860, to punish and prevent the practice of polygamy, was the action of Utah's Judge John Cradlebaugh, who implored Congress to repeal the 1850 Organic Act creating Utah Territory. Cradlebaugh's August 1859 arrival in Genoa was celebrated with cannons firing and "every demonstration of joy." In early October he convened court, but in December he left for Washington, focused on the Organic Act repeal.[33] Within months, Illinois representative John Alexander Logan introduced a bill "to repeal the law establishing the territorial government of Utah."[34] The *Washington Star* published Cradlebaugh's charges of Mormons' treason, murders, castrations, and shedding of blood for remission of sins. Cradlebaugh challenged William Hooper to a face-to-face public response to the accusations.[35] Young praised Hooper's nonengagement, writing: "Your course in relation to the Cradlebaugh challenge meets my entire approval, for an opposite course would only have tended to lift him from the obscurity he now <u>feels</u> to some little notoriety which he craves." Young added a crass note: "If you can manage it without any risk of its being traced . . . have a note dropped at the P. O. [box] for Cradlebaugh as follows: 'You have —— in the flax, and laid it to the hens. Now you had better write a book.'"[36]

From Alabama came support that Cradlebaugh was on the correct path: "The true remedy for the destruction of the singular society" in Utah Territory "seems to lie in the repeal of the act creating the Territorial government . . . [and] would doubtless irritate the Mormons into rebellion." The *Mobile Register*'s editor also emphasized that the anti-polygamy Morrill Bill would not find a receptive audience in his state: "The principle . . . is dangerous, almost fatal to the South, since if Congress may legislate against polygamy in Utah, it may also legislate against slavery in New Mexico."[37]

Cradlebaugh returned briefly to his Ohio home, where he was outspoken on Buchanan's failure with the Mormons. According to Cradlebaugh, Buchanan should have procured "the absolute and unconditional repeal of the organic act—blotting the Territorial Government out of existence—upon the ground that they are alien enemies and outlaws, denying their allegiance and defying the authorities of the United States." Had Buchanan seized "Brigham Young, his counselors, the bishops and the twelve apostles" and hung them, "you would never more have heard of treason in Utah." Remarking that in 1857 "the Mormons were naked and almost starving . . . but now they are clothed, and money circulates freely among them," Cradlebaugh added: "Not only are they freely pardoned, but they are rewarded with pockets full of gold." From this, Cradlebaugh concluded: "Treason is lucky and traitors prosper."[38]

James Ferguson, the Legion's adjutant general and the editor of the Mormon-run *Mountaineer* newspaper, described the war's outcome similarly: "The Expedition to Utah has fulfilled its intended mission. . . . The [federal] treasury has been plundered; the nation has been humbugged; a few individuals have filled their pockets; and the world wags on as usual. . . . Victorious or vanquished, the gains belong to Utah. The dry goods and groceries that attached the army have found here their place of final deposit; and . . . the Territory is made wealthy by the spoils."[39] The *Times* agreed, "The camp is a good market for vegetables and forage; the profits of the Mormon farmers on the sales of these articles to the troops are said to reach half a million of dollars per annum."[40] Apostle John Taylor was more plebeian: "They came to crush this people and to wipe us out of existence . . . ; but the Lord put a hook in their nostrils, stripped them of their glory, left them shivering in the cold and fed them on mule's legs. . . . We are still here, and God is controling [*sic*] matters for our good."[41]

In April, Thomas Amos Rogers Nelson, a pro-Union Democrat from Tennessee, entered a House bill that differed significantly from

Logan's bill. Nelson aimed to strike at the financial strength of the LDS Church by repealing that portion of the Organic Act that made the church a corporation.[42] Almost three decades passed before Nelson was proved correct. Seizure of the money and property of the LDS Church finally brought federal supremacy to Utah in the Edmunds-Tucker Act of 1887.[43]

The Morrill Bill passed the lower house of Congress in April. An Ohio newspaper commented that the bill "caused much fluttering among the anti-Congressional-authority-over-territories Democracts, some twenty three of whom dodged the final vote." Utah's delegate, Hooper, made two "very moderated speeches" in opposition to the bill. Asserting that "not more than one-half of the Mormons are practical polygamists," Hooper "intimated that the passage of the bill would produce rebellion in Utah."[44] A Massachusetts article addressed this possibility: "Mormons are much excited at . . . Congress making polygamy a penal offense, and are beginning to arm and drill, determined to fight for their peculiar institution."[45]

Floyd's Revised Report of Affairs in Utah

In January 1860 the *Deseret News* published parts of War Secretary Floyd's revised opinion of peace in Utah: "The army is inactive, and stands in the attitude of a menacing force towards a conquered and sullen people. I am satisfied that the preservation of right and justice . . . is impossible in that Territory. It is governed . . . by a system which is in total disregard of the laws or constitution of the land. . . . Beyond a mere outward show of acquiescence in federal authority, they [Mormons] are as irresponsible to it as any foreign nation." Although he did not name the emigrant party, Floyd revealed his knowledge of the Fancher-Baker massacre at Mountain Meadows: "Murders and robberies, of the most atrocious character, have been perpetrated in the Territory upon emigrants from the States, journeying towards the Pacific, and in some of the most shocking instances by white men disguised as Indians. . . . [T]hese murders are the work of the Mormon people themselves, sanctioned, if not directed, by the authorities of the Mormon church."[46] Predictably, Cumming joined the "Indians did it" conspiracy: "The Indians

of this territory are numerous—well armed—and somewhat warlike."
Withdrawal of federal troops would be "injudicious and unjust" to residents as well as emigrants, and "500 soldiers should be retained here,"
he asserted.[47]

Johnston Called

Camp Floyd's cannons thundered eleven times, as the salute appropriate to Bvt. Brig. Gen. Albert Sidney Johnston's departure to California on March 1, 1860.[48] The high regard bestowed on Johnston
is recorded by Capt. Henry Heth, who—like Johnston—would later
serve the Confederacy.[49] Heth said Johnston's departure was "the most
touching scene he ever witnessed, except the surrender at Appomattox Court-House," for "as he rode along the line of soldiers, drawn up
to bid him farewell, there was not a dry eye."[50] The *New York Times* was
effusive, claiming that "no other military commander of the American
army ever left a military department carrying with him so universally
the high regards and good wishes of those under his command, as
well as their approval of his official conduct." Johnston's high com-
pliment came for maintaining equanimity despite "every insult that
priestly malignity [the Mormons] could devise," for the undeserved
"gentle usage" that the Mormon populace received from him, and for
his willingness to accept that "the President chose . . . to regard the
cowardly rebels as loyal citizens." The *Times* correspondent, identified
as "Richard," decried the pending troop removal, claiming that "the
horrible butcheries that have been perpetrated within and adjacent
to this Territory in the last five or six years . . . can be traced directly
to the Mormon Church" and that "if they were not absolutely perpetrated by its orders, they at least were by the instigation of its priests
and apostles." If troops were removed, then the government should,
for national safety, "cause all emigration over these plains to cease."[51]

The *Times* correspondent then cited a *Mountaineer* article that
named Judge Eckels as "Richard" and made a "vulgar attack" on Eckels. As further validation of Joseph Logue's observation of cannons
mounted above Salt Lake City and the other *Valley Tan* accounts of

cannon held by the Mormons, the *Times* noted that General Johnston had received reports in that fall that "twenty-three pieces of cannon had passed a certain mail-station on the way to Utah" over the summer. The correspondent continued: "It is undoubtably [*sic*] true that arms and ammunition have been brought into the Territory, in considerable quantities, during the past year, by the Mormons. It is also true that there is some unusual preparation going on in Salt Lake City now, in the way of cutting [manufacturing or repairing] arms in a serviceable condition." The implication was that war weapons were being acquired in anticipation of open conflict if pending congressional legislation "hostile to the system of polygamy" passed.[52] Representative Hooper, speaking on April 5 against the Morrill Bill, confirmed that Mormons were preparing for another war: "Are we not just emerging from a difficulty [the Utah War] . . . which at one time made the danger of civil war and its attendant horrors imminent?" His concluding words carried the unmistakable message that passage of Morrill would "unite us all in opposition . . . *to put it down by force.*"[53]

Mormon apostle Orson Pratt spoke in the Tabernacle, not of patriotism and loyalty, but of invoked evil born of Satan. Pratt preached that "seduced by the instigation of the devil," some congressmen "had attempted to overrule the divine decree by introducing a bill . . . to punish polygamy as a criminal offence, thereby seeking to debar the Mormons from the enjoyment of a religious right." Pratt stated that before submitting to such a law, "he would lay his body in the cold grave." The apostle predicted that "the American Union would soon be dissolved, and the North and South would wage against each other a war of extermination, and women and children would be seen flying from city to city." Playing on the fear of Indians, Pratt threatened that Mormons would form "an alliance with the mountain tribes, and . . . prosecute a kind of guerrilla warfare against the United States."[54]

Forney's Report on Mountain Meadows

Indian Superintendent Jacob Forney submitted the first official report on the Mountain Meadows massacre on December 4, 1858, and in May

1859 he brought the surviving children to Great Salt Lake City. He provided *Valley Tan* editor Kirk Anderson with a lengthy account of site visit: "I walked over the ground where it is supposed they were killed, the evidences of this being unmistakable from skulls, & other bones and hair laying scattered over the ground." Forney visited "the three places where the dead are buried" and estimated that they contained the graves of "106 persons, men, women, and children." He added, "I made strict and diligent inquiry of the number supposed to have been killed, and 115 is probably about the correct number." Directly addressing the question of who the perpetrators were, he declared: "I deem it to be my imperative duty to say that the Indians had material aid and assistance from whites; and in my opinion the Pi-ute Indians would not have perpetrated the terrible massacre without such aid and assistance."[55] Brigham Young, presumably relieved that Forney gave no names, wrote several cryptic letters in April and May 1860 to Hooper in Washington. Young told Hooper he was pleased to learn that "Dr. Forney had acted as your friend and the friend of Utah" and that therefore "he will in no wise loose [*sic*] his reward."[56] In another letter, Young was "much gratified" that Forney had "a sufficient share of humanity and candor not to side with the reckless vilifiers who are seeking to harm us." Young's puzzling assertion was that Forney "will be fairly estimated in Utah, so far as his sayings and doings are made known to us, and will receive the largest award of credit and mete of praise that his conduct may deserve."[57] The Mormon leader's third letter alluded to Forney's financial record keeping, noting that "investigation of Dr. Forney's official acts in Utah is still in progress, under the commissionership of Mess'rs Stambaugh and Montgomery" and that its results promised to be "quite favorable to the Doctor, at least so far as any <u>dishonest</u> malfeasance is concerned." Young also expressed appreciation to Hooper: "I am glad you adopted dignified silence, so far as any public notice, in relation to Cradlebaugh, Hurt, Dave Burr."[58] In Young's letter dated May 24, he asked Hooper's opinion of a letter from Dr. Forney to General Johnston and clearly was not pleased with its contents: "What think you of the spirit therein manifested? It certainly appears to have been written without the least regard to justice or fairness."[59]

New York Times correspondent "Richard" had a different, more openly critical opinion: "Dr. Forney is one of the few Federal officers who coalesced with the Mormons, and . . . when the troops lay at Fort Bridger in almost a starving condition, he had a special weakness for writing scandalous and scurrilous reports concerning both military and civil brother officers, and for these delectable performances he received the highest encomiums from the Mormon Press."[60] Forney's being accused of submitting false vouchers for reimbursement, and Cradlebaugh's contending that Cumming's wife was receiving the salary intended for a gubernatorial secretary, added internecine feuding to the territory's unpeaceful status.

News of the appointments of Chief Justice John Fitch Kinney and Associate Justice Alexander Wilson to replace Eckels and Cradlebaugh reached Utah in mid-July. The *Times* indicated that Mormons "looked on with satisfaction . . . that the Administration, having tried force with the Mormons and virtually failed, is now fully determined to try what can be done by purely civil means." It was not only overoptimistic but also unrealistic that the new judges would have better relations with Young, while being careful to pursue "a thorough and impartial judicial investigation of the Mountain Meadows massacre."[61] Kinney would, before long, openly align with Mormon interests, while Wilson would be cited for his "masterly inactivity."[62]

Thomas Kane correctly warned Wilford Woodruff in 1849 that the limited autonomy of territorial status would be onerous when civil officers were appointed out of patronage rather than intramurally elected.[63] It was not only their "otherness" but also allegations of their poor quality that brought the *Millennial Star*'s complaint. Washington should send "men at least of good moral character, and not the rejected scum and rubbish of their political cesspool" who "in every way rendered themselves unworthy of the confidence and esteem of all right-minded and thinking men."[64] This issue galled Mormons until elections to civic office came with statehood in 1896.

In August, Young told LDS leaders that the troops at Camp Floyd were continuing the state-sponsored persecution begun in Missouri. He singled out Masons among the troops as a special threat, asserting that they and "other Masons" were sent for the express purpose of killing him and other leaders: "[T]he people of the United States had sought our destruction, and . . . have worked through the Masonic institution to perfect it."[65]

The *Times* reported on a "most extraordinary speech" by Mormon apostle Orson Hyde, heard by "nearly all the United States officers now in the city . . . and a good many of the non-Mormon population." Hyde preached that Mormons would soon "return to take possession of their 'inheritances' in Missouri and in Eastern States." As punishment for having driven the Mormons out and taking their lands and property, the people in those states would see "vials of wrath poured out upon their unbelieving heads, and lightnings, storms, tornadoes, hail, pestilence, earthquakes, war and niggers." Hyde mentioned a plan that had been "concocted in Congress" whose purpose was "seducing [Utah] women." Young followed Hyde and "pitched in hot and heavy." Their words provoked "terrible offence" among military and federal officers.[66]

The Mormons exhibited little interest in the 1860 presidential election, and Lincoln's election and the secession of several states received short treatment from the *Deseret News*, with its obtuse reference that the Constitution made the Mormon religion's plural marriages legal: "So we deem Mr. Lincoln's election, though in accordance with Constitutional forms, a violation of the spirit of the Constitution, because the party which he leads avows purposes which are utterly subversive of that sacred document."[67] Young wrote privately to Hooper, "Democrats within our borders are very much chopfallen at Lincoln's election, and several of them begin to think that they and their property are safer here than in the States."[68]

Following Buchanan's misadventure, a creative option surfaced in Congress when Representative Isaac N. Morris of Illinois proposed a three-man commission "to negotiate with the Mormons for the sale of their entire possessions, on the express condition that they remove within a reasonable time from the limits of the United States." The proposal specified that commissioners would report to the president before the next congressional session. A desperate tone was evident that "something in a tangible shape will necessarily have to be done, especially as the reports from official sources show the 'Saints' no better now than prior to Uncle Sam's troops being sent to quell their turbulence and rebellion," continued the *San Francisco Bulletin*'s report.[69] "This buying out of the Mormons will be a capital thing," the *Times* commented approvingly.[70] To allegations of disloyalty, the Lord's prophet had a hot, disingenuous response: "Have this people committed treason or transgressed the laws of their country? If any man says they have, he is a liar, and will go to hell, for he lies like hell. Those who say they have are of the Devil, and are his servants; . . . and they shall have their part in the lake that burns with fire and brimstone."[71]

In December 1860, Young told Hooper that "dissolution of the Union is sooner or later inevitable" and that "it is rather amusing . . . to note the twaddle about 'peaceable secession.'" Within a week, Young wrote Hooper: "Please ask our <u>Friend</u> [Thomas L. Kane] what his views are in relation to the permanency of our Union. The events that have transpired in the short time since he was here are strongly confirmatory that unaided human wisdom can foresee but little and only for a short distance."[72]

Frustration over Mormons' intransigence continued in Washington, but in spring 1861 began the incomparable conflagration overshadowing the relatively inconsequential concerns in Utah.

Charlatan—Confederate Agent—Pseudo Saint

The U.S. Navy issued an unsigned, handwritten confidential report, dated only as "1862," with special notice to the naval office in Hong Kong. It concerned a known Confederate agent who had had relationships with Mormon leaders dating to 1857–58:

> <u>Capt. Walter M. [Murray] Gibson</u>
> Started life in South Carolina Has two sons now in the Confederate Army. During the past year he made two journeys between Salt Lake City and the Rebel Government—
> He is a constant & confided in correspondent of Brigham Young. He is an advocate of the Rebellion whenever the opportunity offers, & serves the business of making mormon [*sic*] converts & Rebel Adherents.

He has or had when he left San Francisco, a large mass of correspondence from the <u>South</u> & from <u>Salt Lake</u> especially from Judge Mason of Va.

He was almost appointed Commercial Agent for the State of California to report on the advantages of Commerce between the Malay Islands & San Francisco[;] the vote was close & he carries the Report of the Debate . . . as introduction.

He sailed from San Francisco on the 11th or 12th of July last on the Barque Yankee for Singapore via Honolulu & Hong Kong in Company with his daughter: a young woman of 18 yrs.

His career can at any time be stopped by delivering him to the mercies of the Dutch East India company from whom he escaped some Years since.

There is good reason for asserting that he carried out Letters of Marque, & there is no doubt but that he will injure the Gov't of the U.S. if allowed to go at Large.

He has a depot for letters in San Francisco; that is letters dropped there for him will be forwarded wherever he may happen to be. He has asserted that he will always have a <u>friend in</u> the Post Office, no matter under which administration.

He made many inquiries in San Francisco concerning vessels of light Draught & corresponded with several persons concerning a small Steamer (Iron) which he represented that he desired to buy.[73]

Gibson was intellectually gifted, a charismatic manipulator whose scope was international and whose life—real and invented—before and after his time with Brigham Young has been chronicled by several authors. None has cited evidence that he was a Confederate agent, and all have underestimated his relationship with Mormon nabobs.[74] Church of England records give Gibson's birth as January 16, 1822, in Kearsley, Northumberland, a bleak, windswept expanse near the Scottish border. Far from nobility, his family raised sheep for its prosaic livelihood. The family arrived in North America by way of Montreal, Canada, where Walter spent his childhood. Adventuring at age sixteen in New York City, then into the South, he chanced into marriage to

Rachel Margaret Lewis, age twenty, in South Carolina. Rachel's death in 1844 after the birth of their third child, daughter Talulah Lucy Gibson, set him free.[75] Leaving his children with his wife's parents in South Carolina, he embarked on a worldwide odyssey to Central and South America, Indonesia, Malaysia, France, England, and the Netherlands. Shortly after the war with Mexico ended, he toured every one of its states; in New York he purchased a 153-ton schooner, *Flirt*, and loaded it with war munitions for sale to the government of Guatemala, convincing that nation it needed a navy, simply because it had none. Escaping arrest after angering various authorities, he captained his small vessel, navigating it himself from South America to the South Pacific. January 1852 found him anchored off the city of Palemburg—called the Venice of the East—on the island of Sumatra. Guilty or innocent, he was nonetheless arrested for fomenting rebellion and incarcerated for two years in a Dutch East India Company prison at Weltevreden. Sentenced to hang, he "escaped" aboard the *N. B. Palmer*, an American schooner bound for North America. It was "arranged, probably by the Dutch themselves, for ship Captain C. P. Low to take the fugitive aboard" on April 24, 1853.[76] The *Palmer* docked in New York in July, and by August, Gibson was in Washington, pressing a claim of one hundred thousand dollars against the Netherlands for his lost property and false imprisonment.

A two-year court battle ensued in Washington and the Hague, where U.S. authorities were unable to extract reparations for Gibson's vessel and imprisonment.[77] Turning failure into success, he refurbished his pockets by giving engrossing lectures on the beauty of Indonesia and by the sale of *The Prison of Weltevreden; and a Glance at the East Indian Archipelago*, the book he wrote as a much embellished tale of his imprisonment and escape.

Gibson's first known contact with Mormons was in Washington in the spring of 1857, when he became acquainted, possibly at one of his lectures on the Malay Archipelago, with Utah's Dr. John Bernhisel. On hearing that Buchanan had ordered troops to Utah, Gibson proposed a grandiose plan to move the entire Mormon population to islands in the South Pacific, eliminating any reason for sending an army. Bernhisel's interest was piqued, and in February 1858 he submitted the

Walter Murray Gibson, a consummate charlatan and secret Confederate agent, was baptized a Mormon and made welcome in the
upper strata of Mormon leaders. Claiming Japan as a mission destination, he stopped instead in Hawaii, where he established his
own version of Latter-day Saints. Following his excommunication
from the LDS Church, he held many important political offices in
the islands. Used by permission of the Utah State Historical Society.

proposition to the Buchanan administration. The proposition was
summarily rejected when Buchanan learned that the project would
cost at least $5 million. Gibson came across as selfless, his only "reason
for taking the interest he does in Mormon migration" being the "beneficial results to the civilized world."[78]

Rebounding again, Gibson wrote Young in May 1859 before leaving Chicago, bound for Utah with his purchased wagon and mules. His stated purpose: "It has been in my heart, many years, to propose to you and your people, emigration to the islands of Oceania. . . . [A]nd while I lay in a dungeon in the island of Java, a voice said to me: 'You shall show the way to a people, who shall build up a Kingdom in these isles. . . . [A]nd now I have resolved to come into your midst and declare the burden of my spirit.'"[79] Accompanied by his daughter, Talulah, and his two adult sons retrieved from South Carolina, he arrived in Salt Lake City in October. By month's end, Young reported to George A. Smith on several interviews with Gibson.[80] The *Deseret News* reported on several Young-Gibson meetings, often citing Gibson's proposal to move the Saints to New Guinea. On December 3, 1859, "Captain Gibson called in and gave the President [Young] some account of his imprisonment in Welterbreven [*sic*]"; on January 3, 1860, "Capt. Gibson called and after a few remarks with the President [Young] about the war . . . remarked he was thinking of delivering a lecture at Provo. The President said 'would you not prefer the Tabernacle or my office?' . . . Pres. Young ordered a slay [*sic*] to take the Captain home, and treated him with much courtesy."[81] On January 9, 1860, Gibson lectured in Seventy's Hall, on the beauty of Papua, Borneo, Sumatra, and Java and "the vast resources possessed by each."[82]

On January 15, Talulah and Walter Gibson answered Young's earlier challenge and were "baptized [as] members of the LDS Church by Heber C. Kimball . . . in City Creek [Canyon stream] near President Kimball's home." Young himself laid his hands on their heads to "confirm" the blessing.[83] From January through April 1860, Gibson enthralled audiences, his lectures alternating on week nights with those of Apostle Pratt. On February 21, Young "went to the historian's office to select some subjects of History for Capt. Gibson to forward to the American Encyclopedia for publication," and on February 23, Gibson "called at the Historian's Office and related some interesting incidents about the . . . the Islands of Oceanica."[84] He delivered a lecture in the Tabernacle on March 7 that was printed—in full—on the front page of the Mormons' *Mountaineer.*[85] He spoke again in the Tabernacle on March 15, on the resources of New Guinea.[86] The hospitality, conviviality, and frequency of interaction all support author Jacob Adler's claims that "there was trust, mutual respect, and social intimacy" between Young and Gibson.[87]

In late March a man who funded Gibson's coming west in October penned a long letter to Young, warning that—like himself—Young was being deceived. Gibson's adoption of the LDS faith was not genuine, he cautioned, and the schemes for Malaysia were ill-founded.[88] Young responded courteously, "You state you have been deceived by Cap. Gibson; I have not, nor do I expect to be."[89]

Gibson was made an elder on April 9, 1860. Young seemingly tested Gibson, as he often did with others, by sending him on a mission. Gibson was "set apart" on April 25 by Wilford Woodruff and Erastus Snow as a high priest in the Mormon priesthood and sent to New York City.[90] Driving an ox team, he departed Utah on April 27, 1860, leaving Talulah Lucy Gibson in Brigham Young's Eighteenth Ward household, among sixty-seven people, including many women whose surname was Young.[91]

The pacific life of a missionary did not fit for long, and Gibson returned to Great Salt Lake City on November 3, to speak the next day in the Tabernacle. On November 8, he visited Young's office, giving an interesting account of his mission; the next evening, he shared a private dinner with Young. More visits followed: On November 10, he conversed with Young and Mormon stalwart and Dartmouth College–educated Albert Carrington regarding "the character of Fernando Wood," New York City's mayor and Confederacy supporter. On November 12, Gibson "discussed . . . the Coral Isles he had seen in his travels."[92] During 1860, Brigham Young spoke extensively of Gibson in the Tabernacle on January 18, March 3, March 6, and April 5, and on November 18, Gibson shared the Tabernacle pulpit with President Young, where Gibson spoke of his future among the people, not of Malaysia or Indonesia but of Japan, claiming that he was the "only man in America who could speak with them without an interpreter."[93] Young gave Gibson his "traveling papers to the Chinese, Japanese, East Indians, and the Malasian [sic] Islands." Gibson left a locked box of personal papers in the Church Historian's Office on November 17, with instructions that it could be delivered to Lucy T. (Talulah) Gibson or Ammiel L. Willard of New York City.[94] On November 19, Gibson was blessed by Young and Apostle Heber C. Kimball; afterward they discussed "the variety of Asiatic languages" and the "Malay character."[95] Brigham Young's older brother Phineas H. Young petitioned to accompany Gibson "to the land of the Blest."[96]

Brigham Young described Gibson as "going forth fully authorized to negotiate with all the nations of this world who would obey the gospel of Christ," and he cryptically added, "If Brother Gibson would magnify his calling he would do more good than he ever anticipated."[97] Gibson and Talulah started for Japan on November 21, going by the southern route in a church train to San Bernardino.[98] He carried two certificates—both ostentatious and baroque—with yellow ribbon and seal. Gibson was authorized "to communicate unto His Majesty the Tycoon, the plan of Government, the social order, the arts, . . . and all other information appertaining to the People of Deseret." The First Presidency prayed that "His Majesty the Tycoon . . . will give protection, and assistance unto the trusty Captain Walter M. Gibson."[99] The three First Presidency men also supplied a signed "Message of Good Will."[100]

Reaching San Bernardino, Gibson notified Young on January 9, 1861, of a "pestersome nest of apostates at this place." He elaborated: "A number of the most violent are formed in a society styled 'Rechabites;' and have pledged . . . not to permit a Mormon elder to speak in this place. . . . The violent apostates . . . are almost exclusively from Australia . . . [;] however, . . . all who bear the name of Mormons . . . go together on any public question."[101] In February, Gibson wrote: "The chief grounds for apostasy here, usually mentioned; are the Mountain Meadows; the departure from 'old Mormonism;' and cupidity and election of elders; as chiefly alleged by Australians." He added, "The spirit of secession is active in California among the young politicians who pant for a Pacific Republic, with all its prospect of increase of offices and titles."[102] From Sacramento he wrote, "The lines between Northerners and Southerners are clearly marked, not only in politics, but in society. The hate is mutual and unappeasable. The Southerners . . . make up in political activity for [their] decided numerical inferiority. They are well organized and drilled; and . . . 'rule or ruin,' . . . is the pith of the principles and purposes of the pro-slavery political force in California." According to Gibson, Southerners aimed "to fascinate the restless, fortune hunting people of California with prospects of conquest in Mexico and Oceanica; and with the immigration and subordination of millions of Chinese and other Asiatics," to develop the Pacific coast just as "'tropical labour' is developing the cotton and rice fields of the Atlantic."[103]

Gibson's and Talulah's reappearance in early March in Great Salt Lake City was puzzling. By chance or at Gibson's instigation, Jefferson Davis's inaugural address of February 16, delivered in Alabama, was published in full by the *Deseret News*. Its message that "governments rest on the consent of the governed" pleased Mormons.[104] In the same issue, *News* editor Judge Elias Smith penned: "Abraham the I [Lincoln], in all probability, has been installed . . . as the successor of James the IV [Buchanan], . . . [and we] still believe, as we have for many years, that the Union . . . will go to destruction . . . and nothing can change it."[105]

Woodruff's journal revealed the reason for the Gibson's return: "I spent the time in the Endowment house. This forenoon we gave Endowments to . . . Capt. Walter M. Gibson & his Daughter."[106] Of this ceremony, biographers Adler and Robert M. Kamins note that "at least two descendants of Gibson . . . believe that Talulah was married, at least in name, to Brigham Young, though the marriage was not [known to have been] consummated."[107]

Since Gibson was in Great Salt Lake City at the time, it is confusing that Young would write to him in care of Dwight Evelith in San Francisco, but he did so, telling Gibson: "There appears no prospect that the seceding states will ever again coalesce with their free State late copartners in the general government." Inviting speculation is Young's mention that on the day of Lincoln's inauguration, "a visitor called at my house and presented me a little <u>Talula</u>, daughter of my wife Clarissa Decker," suggesting that Young named his own daughter after Gibson's winsome, eighteen-year-old daughter, Talulah.[108]

Gibson and Talulah again traveled to Los Angeles, where they made no mention that they were Mormon emissaries or that they had experienced the sacred, secret Mormon ordinance of endowment. Once in San Francisco, he disclaimed LDS membership and continued raising money by lecturing and book sales. Adler and Kamins assert that the apparent disengagement was done at Young's instruction "'not to come out too quickly and fully with professions of Mormon faith," for "hasty disclosure might 'bar avenues and opportunities for doing good.'"[109] Young wrote to Gibson, then in San Francisco, a lengthy, engaging letter of matters in Utah: "We as yet have no indication as to the policy the present administration intends to pursue towards us. . . . [However,] like the one just out of power, they can do nothing against the truth . . . for the Lord will over-rule evil purposes and acts for the advancement of his work on earth." Regarding Japan, Young remarked, "It is quite possible, as you mention, that the operations of the Christian nations in Japan may tend to pave the way for your favorable reception." Young's letter ends with everyday news that Gibson's sons "appear to enjoy themselves," adding updates on the health status and personal activities of Daniel H. Wells of the First Presidency and Hosea Stout, a Mormon leader and former U.S. attorney general of Utah Territory.[110]

In one letter from San Francisco, Gibson revealed substantial knowledge of the Confederacy's plans: "There is a large, disturbing element in this state . . . which is Southern and of course, secessionist, [and] is closely united and particularly determined—They do not hope to strike a blow in this vicinity; but will probably concentrate their strength about Los Angeles and San Diego. They want to secure the latter place, which has a fine harbor; and is regarded as the best terminus of a Southern Confederacy Rail Road, South of San Francisco."[111]

Gibson departed from San Francisco on June 12, allegedly bound for Japan, but disembarked at the *Yankee*'s first stop in Hawaii.[112] Another informative, highly personal letter went to Gibson on July 2, wherein Young explained preparations for outbound church trains and for crop harvests, as well as updating Gibson on his sons: "Your son John is still living with Pres. Wells and . . . is doing well. . . . Henry . . . some two or three months ago went as a teamster to Pike's Peak."[113] June 8 marked another Gibson letter, which Carrington read to Young.[114] In mid-September, Young again wrote a lengthy letter to Gibson in Hawaii, filled with information about matters in Utah, his trip to check on the southern Utah settlements, and his plans for enlarging the Tabernacle and building a paper manufacturing plant.[115]

Discouragement afflicted Walter Gibson in March 1862 when he wrote in his diary, "There are other things to add to my list of griefs . . . but I will only mention now the grief at the news from America. I am with the rebellion, with the struggle for independence there, but my home is not [there] with the strugglers."[116] Unaware of Gibson's actions after his arrival in Hawaii, Young wrote to Gibson in May, reporting on forming a state constitution, election results, and a request for statehood that was carried to Washington. He told of the creation of the cavalry company under Richard Burton to guard William Hooper and that of Lot Smith to guard the Overland, and of the season's immigrant numbers; he summarized the events North and South and the progress of the war.[117] On July 18, Young wrote to Gibson: "The prospects of the North's conquering the South are much poorer than they have been at any time since the war began."[118] Young wrote a newsfilled three-page letter in care of Dwight Evelith in San Francisco again on October 31, still apparently unaware Gibson's misbehavior.[119]

Gibson found Hawaii—while officially neutral—as fractioned in loyalty as California. Adler and Kamins note, "European foreign residents supported the South, and they might well aid any privateers of the Confederacy who might venture this far from the continent." But the authors observe that Union sympathizers in Hawaii soon "became suspicious of this mysterious, energetic, glib-talking Captain Gibson of South Carolina," whom they surmised "was planning a privateering venture."[120]

The Gibsons were at a gathering called by Thomas J. Dryer, U.S. commissioner to Hawaii, who told his guests that Georgia senator Robert Toombs was "a villain and a thief." Adler and Kamins summarize what happened next: "Gibson jumped up, his fists clenched," and he cried out, "My daughter was born in Toombs' late Congressional district. I know him and he is a gentleman. And you are a liar, a mean blackguard liar."[121] A year later, while calling at the U.S. Legation, Gibson was prodded into a fiery defense of Jeff Davis. Union agents missed Gibson when he and Talulah slipped aboard a boat bound for the island of Maui.[122]

Gibson adopted the Mormon view of the war, saying: "This is the time when the gentiles of America shall be swept from the face of the earth, as has been foretold in the prophecies of . . . Joseph Smith. As for Zion, her time has come to be set free, and the Prophet, Brigham Young, is to become as the King of Kings."[123] Verification of the military's ongoing concern regarding Gibson in the Far East came from the commander of the USS *Saginaw*, James Findlay Schenck, in his November report from Hong Kong to Secretary of the Navy Gideon Welles. "I have received your communication of the 1st of August, in reference to Captain Walter M. Gibson, and shall be on the lookout for him. A Honolulu paper announces his arrival at that place on the 30th of June. He is well known here [in Hong Kong], and I am satisfied he has not yet arrived."[124]

Gibson lost interest in Sumatra, China, and Japan, but he revitalized the moribund Mormon colony in Hawaii, which had languished after the recall to Utah of missionaries in 1857. His actions ranged between the same polar extremes that characterized his life elsewhere.[125] Misusing credentials given him by Brigham Young, he sold priesthood positions for cash or goods, including appointments for women. An apostleship cost $150. He used church funds to buy land that he placed in his own ownership. When LDS leaders in Great Salt Lake City heard of Gibson's actions, a team was sent to the islands; their investigation led to his 1864 excommunication.

Even with criticism surrounding him, Gibson wrote of his work on Lanai in a warm letter of March 13, 1864, to the First Presidency's George A. Smith, warning that "some good people in Washington still think they have a . . . pickle [of punishment] for you when the secession job is finished." Gibson's use of given names in his closing line underscores the affinity he still held for the Mormons: "I and Talulah send our faithful love to Bros. Brigham, Heber, and Daniel and all the Saints."[126] With excommunication pending, Gibson remained collegial, writing to Young that Talulah "remembers tenderly your interesting family" and that although Young had "dealt precipitately and harshly with me," she would never "be hostile" to him.[127] Anticipating his departure from San Francisco for Hawaii, John L. Gibson's July 15 letter to Brigham Young revealed that he thought of—or presented— himself and his brother as Mormons: "It is my duty to write you as all other missionaries," and "Henry and myself are both well and remain as your Bro [*sic*] in the gospel."[128]

Gibson moved to other profitable careers, in political scheming, newspaper publishing, and self-promotion, resulting in his holding each of the Hawaiian cabinet positions, on occasion occupying several of them simultaneously. His titles "Hawaii's Royal Prime Minister" and "the Minister of Everything" were appropriate. His grand vision for Hawaii was as the hub and ruler of a vast empire of a Pacific Island confederation. However, in all this, Gibson earned enemies, they proliferated, and he repaired to San Francisco in 1888, where he shortly died from tuberculosis and inanition.[129]

Walter Murray Gibson's controversy-pocked life is as captivating as an *Arabian Nights'* tale. Whether he was genuine in his pursuit of Mormonism or the consummate charlatan, the evidence supports the latter. Young's usual skill at rendering a person's quiddity apparently failed in this instance. Gibson's welcome into the inner circle of the top fifteen appears to have been premature, not fully vetted. Judged by their own multiple assertions that the majority of Mormon leaders in Utah favored the South, Gibson's personal associations with Young and with an impressive lineup of Mormon luminaries such as Wilford Woodruff, George A. Smith, Daniel Wells, Amasa Lyman, Hosea Stout, Erastus Snow, and Albert Carrington raise the likelihood of their having significant relationships or contacts with other Southern secessionists. That a Confederate agent occupied an intimate and trusted position with the men who were simultaneously ranking Nauvoo Legion officers and civil and religous leaders of Utah's theocracy—even addressing these men by their given names—adds significantly to the question of the Mormon's Southern allegiance during the Civil War.

Chronology
1859–1860

1859

January	Gen. Albert Sidney Johnston's troops continue to occupy Camp Floyd.
February	President James Buchanan's Utah Expedition is declared an ignominious defeat.
April 17	Capt. Reuben Campbell is sent to investigate killings at Mountain Meadows.
April 30	Pony Express from St. Joseph, Missouri, starts service to the west coast.
May	Secretary of War John B. Floyd declares that peace has been restored in Utah.
	Johnston offers protection for all who wish to leave Utah.
	One hundred infantry under Capt. Henry Heth are ordered to keep peace in Provo.
	Gerrymandering reassigns Judge Cradlebaugh to Genoa, 600 miles from Provo.
	Captain Campbell and Maj. James H. Carleton share findings on Mountain Meadows massacre.
	Hidden cannons are discovered guarding City Creek canyon.
	Indian agent Jacob Forney brings surviving Mountain Meadows children to Great Salt Lake City.
June 12	Emigrants to California are escorted by Camp Floyd troops.
August	Judge John Cradlebaugh arrives in Genoa.
December	Utah again appeals for statehood.

1860

January   Senator Alexander Logan of Illinois submits a bill
                  to repeal the law establishing Utah Territory.

                  Floyd revises his opinion of peace in Utah and
                  harshly criticizes matters there.

February 15   Morrill Bill to repeal the Organic Act creating Utah
                  Territory is entered.

March 1   Johnston leaves Camp Floyd on assignment to the
                  Department of the Pacific.

April   Tennessee representative Thomas Amos Rogers
                  Nelson submits a bill to repeal the act incorporating
                  the LDS Church.

                  Morrill Bill passes in the House.

May   Representative Isaac N. Morris of Illinois proposes
                  creating a commission to purchase Utah from the
                  Mormons, on the promise that they will leave the
                  United States.

                  U.S. marshal Peter K. Dotson is unable to serve war-
                  rants for murders committed at Mountain Meadows
                  and elsewhere.

June   Apostle Orson Hyde preaches that Mormons will
                  pursue a guerrilla war against the United States.

                  U.S. Federal Census lists Utah's population at
                  slightly over forty-two thousand.

November 6   Abraham Lincoln is elected as U.S. president.

                  Mormons complain about quality of federal appoin-
                  tees to Utah Territory.

                  Number of troops remaining at Camp Floyd is
                  down to seven hundred.

December   William H. Hooper reports to Brigham Young that
                  dissolution of the Union is inevitable.

December 20   South Carolina secedes.

CHAPTER 2

A War for the Advancement of Truth on the Earth, 1861

In wartime, truth is so precious that she should always be attended by a bodyguard of lies.

WINSTON CHURCHILL

The Saints devoted early 1861 to another appeal for statehood drafted by the all-Mormon legislature. The appeal was again denied. In the spring, Brigham Young and ranking leaders visited the red-rock, desert-dry southern parts of the territory, land alternatively blessed or devastated by the waters of the Rio Virgin and the Santa Clara. New settlements were anticipated here and in the northern green valley of Cache County, where native tribes would give way to Mormon settlements. The largest, finest theater between the Missouri River and San Francisco was constructed in Salt Lake City, as was a papermaking plant to supply the needs of the *Deseret News*. Plans were laid for more than two hundred wagons to travel out to Florence, Nebraska, with goods for sale, then back to Utah with purchased goods and converted Saints.

Hopes for resolution between the North and the South died with the shelling at Fort Sumter, and federal troops stationed in Utah were ordered east, bound for an unknown fate. The closing of Camp Floyd—renamed Fort Crittenden—met with ambivalence.[1] Although Mormons were pleased to purchase its remaining goods at a tiny fraction of their worth and to be rid of federal supervision, they lost the lucrative trade of supplying the troops. Without U.S. military presence, non-Mormons were anxious for their own safety.

Mormons were indignant that arms and munitions were carried away or destroyed when the fort was closed. Distrust of the Mormons underlay the denial of munitions. New federal officials, all non-Mormons, continued to face ill will and violence. Forces of the Nauvoo Legion were readied for war, and Mormon loyalty was further questioned. The call went to California for volunteers to keep one eye on overland travel and telegraph, and the other on the Mormons and their army. The extremes of the continent were linked when the telegraph lines—east and west—were completed in Salt Lake City. The year ended with Governor John W. Dawson's departure, setting a record for the shortest time a Utah governor was in residence. His twenty-four days had a despicable ending: en route to Indiana, he survived a severe beating by Mormon ruffians only twelve miles from Great Salt Lake City.

Mormon leaders increasingly claimed that war was inevitable. Brigham Young spun a story of a man who had either to swim a river or to meet a lion: "If he swam the river he would drown and if he met the lion he would be devoured—so with the United States, they are bound in due time to be destroyed."[2] In his fervent letter to Saints in Great Britain, Mormon leader William Clayton declared that the entire U.S. government constituted an enemy to God. The Union would be dissolved, and "blood, death, and destruction such as has not been witnessed on this continent for the last sixteen hundred years" would follow because people had "banished the people of God from their midst, after coolly witnessing the martyrdom of two of the noblest and best men that ever lived," Joseph and Hyrum Smith.[3]

Young reminded his congregation that the federal government "ere long . . . will be as water that is spilled upon the ground . . . and another government will rise that will stand forever."[4] Across the span of the war's first year, the theme of Mormon persecution in Illinois and Missouri evolved. Less stressed was that Mormons had been driven by evil legions to destitution and death. The message morphed: God *intended* that Mormons should flee to an aerie, secure from war's

Governor John W. Dawson holds the dubious distinction of the shortest tenure in residence of all Utah's territorial governors. Intending to return temporarily to Fort Wayne, Indiana, he was brutally beaten at the first stage station out of Great Salt Lake City. Used by permission of the Utah State Historical Society.

horrors. "Search . . . every geographical position on the face of the earth, and you cannot find another situation so well adapted for the Saints as are these mountains . . . the place in which the Lord designed to hide his people," Young said.[5] He told the Saints to come to the mountains' safety, for even "the nations of Europe cannot escape."[6]

Young admitted participation in bribery to accomplish his ends with government, finding it necessary to pay $1,300 "to grease the wheels."[7] Not self-serving, his purpose was "to show how minutely corruption prevails [in government] where justice should exist."[8] Threat of Utah's secession surfaced after Fort Sumter's firings, when Young instructed William Hooper to "hint" to Lincoln that "Territories as well as States are liable to become restive in these exciting times." Young's message was that granting statehood would keep Mormons loyal.[9]

"Latest News by Telegraph and Pony"

Even before "the long tongue"—as the Indians called the telegraph—shortened the continent in October, Utah's people who read the *Deseret News* were well informed about the escalation of events in the East. The eastern news was not current, for the overland mail, unreliable because of weather and Indian acts, required weeks to arrive. For an eighteen-month, twenty-three-day span, transit time was dramatically reduced by the Central Overland California and Pikes Peak Express Company—better known as the Pony Express.[10] Twice each week, from April 3, 1860, to October 26, 1861, the day or night arrival of "the Pony"—"an institution that is highly prized by all"—was eagerly awaited.[11] From its packets, the *News* issued an extra, the *Pony Dispatch*, devoted to the latest information on politics, matters in Congress, abolition, and eastern disintegration. Some perused the extra, but ranking Mormons leaders formed the "Pony Club"—first in Young's office, then in the Eighteenth Ward—to hear William Clayton read the *Dispatch* aloud. Wilford Woodruff attended on an April evening and recorded the news in his journal: "The Pony Express arived at 8 oclok P.M. I herd it read at President Young's office. . . . Massachusetts troops were attacked by the Citizens of Baltimore. 3 soldiers killed & 11 Citizens. Civil war has Commenced."[12] Since dispatches brought by the Pony contained mostly eastern news, Young asked Dwight Evelith in San Francisco about alliances there: "What is the talk in California about a Western Empire? How does California feel about the Union's splitting—the old horse's dying and being dissected in the reign of king James [Buchanan] the defunct?"[13]

Lincoln's Perilous Inauguration Path

Weeks before the inaugural, Utah readers were reminded that Lincoln did not carry the people's mandate, having received "only about one-third of the votes of the whole country, and not a vote in ten States of the Union."[14] Bound for his Washington inauguration, Lincoln was greeted by a crowd of 250,000 in New York City, and in Philadelphia his reception was grand, as "patriotic emblems were everywhere paraded in the route of the procession." In Maryland, a different sort of reception awaited. On February 21, "Lincoln was aroused and informed that a stranger desired to see him on a matter of life and death," and hearing the stranger's name, Lincoln granted an immediate interview. During a "prolonged conversation," the visitor conveyed "that an organized body of men had determined Lincoln should not be inaugurated, and that he should never leave Baltimore alive, if indeed he ever entered it." When his train left Harrisburg, it was to be derailed, killing all on board. "So authentic was the source" that, over Lincoln's objection, arrangements were made to subvert the plot. Former Illinois state senator Norman B. Judd and the informant left at 9 P.M. on a special train, with Lincoln "wrapped up in a Scotch plaid and a very long military cloak."[15]

Ward Hill Lamon, Lincoln's friend and self-appointed bodyguard, later revealed the identities of those safeguarding the president-elect that night. They were Samuel Morse Felton, president of the Philadelphia, Wilmington and Baltimore Railroad; Allan Pinkerton of the famed Pinkerton National Detective Agency; Judd; and Lamon.[16] In an unmarked railroad car, Lincoln was carried in the middle of the night to Baltimore. Lincoln and his protectors plied the city's back streets in a horse-drawn carriage while awaiting their connection with the Baltimore and Ohio line that would complete Lincoln's transport to Washington. Pinkerton agents identified the leaders of the conspiracy as Cypriano Ferrandini, James Luckett, and Otis K. Hillard and uncovered their plans for Lincoln's destruction, information that allowed Pinkerton and his team to circumvent the plot.[17] The *News* reported on the intrigue: "An organized band of 500 men had sworn that Mr. Lincoln should never sleep in the White House." Plans were

implemented for secret agents to be dispatched along the route to
Baltimore. The conspirators planned "to occupy a position as near the
President on inauguration day as they could obtain," and after one
of them shot Lincoln with an air gun, the remainder of the group
would surround the assassin and "do their best to render his detection
or capture impossible."[18] Brigham Young's reaction on hearing of the
plans and attempts to assassinate Lincoln was subdued. He considered
the president's fate to be in the hands of Providence and believed that
Congress and others could "only do . . . as they are constrained by a
Power they do not recognize."[19]

In his inaugural address, Lincoln expressed "unshaken faith in
the Supreme Ruler of nations," while stressing that, in accepting the
presidency, he was relying on "the strength of our free government
and the ultimate loyalty of the people, to the just principles on which
it is founded." Elements of the speech were considered by those of
slaveholding states as a "declaration of war."[20] "We like Mr. Lincoln's
inaugural address," Young wrote to Hooper, but also directed Hooper
to ask Lincoln "to appoint our officers from the list in your possession,
or else appoint none." Young also wanted Lincoln "[to] continue none
now in office here, except Judge [John Fitch] Kinney, and to by no
means permit Postmaster [Hirum F.] Morrell to return here."[21]

Union Service Does Not Bring Credit

Referring to the 1854 invitation made to Thomas L. Kane of a guaranteed election as Utah's representative to Congress, Young sent a February message to Hooper: "I was much gratified that you had so interesting and instructive an interview with our highly esteemed Friend, and
wish you to remember me kindly to him, his noble hearted wife, and
all his father's house, assuring him that his numerous friends in Utah
hold him and his in fondest remembrance, and have by no means given
up hope of again warmly welcoming him in our mountain retreat."[22]
In September, Young again wrote to Kane, now a Union colonel,
recalling his "patriotic enlistment of sharpshooters in the mountains
of Pennsylvania" and his "military operations since."[23] Kane had been

instrumental in forming, and briefly commanding, the Pennsylvania Bucktails, or Kane's Rifles. Wounded in December 1861 at Dranesville, Virginia, and more severely in June 1862 at Harrisonburg, Kane fought at Culp's Hill at Gettysburg in July 1863 even while still recovering.[24] Young gave his opinion of service to the Union: "Your present position and calling will bring no credit to you, nor to any other man. . . . They will find out in time that the strife they are engaged in will bring no desirable celebrity. This is for your own eye and benefit."[25]

Secessionist Indian Superintendent

Benjamin F. Davis was appointed Utah's superintendent of Indian Affairs on June 21, 1860, replacing Jacob Forney, who served during the time of the Mountain Meadows massacre.[26] Only two months into his appointment, Davis was ordered by the commissioner of Indian Affairs, William P. Dole, to examine with "rigid scrutiny of all the claims and accounts" of Brigham Young and Forney for illegal charges, particularly from the last quarter of 1856 to the first quarter of 1858.[27]

In December 1860, Davis's trip to distribute goods and food to Goshutes and Shoshonis in Ruby Valley who had been "killing, robbing and shooting at the mail and express riders all along this route from Salt Lake City to Carson Valley" received praise from versatile Mormon trail man William Adams Hickman: "By his superior knowledge of the Indian character and from his past experience, Col. Davis soon dispels their fears, and they begin to laugh and jabber as if we were all Indians together. He has literally fed the hungry and clothed the naked . . . and operates in an entirely new and different way from all other Indian officers I have seen."[28] On arrival, Davis had found Indian farms "abandoned . . . and gone to ruin" and that "the various tribes attached thereto had wandered off." All of the Indians "except those in charge of Agent Humphreys, at the Spanish Fork reserve, . . . were in a state of nakedness and starvation, destitute of shelter, and dying of want." In thirty-eight days he covered eight hundred miles, distributing "flour, bacon, coffee, sugar, material for lodges, . . . blankets, shirts, coats, pants, hats, boots, shoes, stockings, women's dresses, handkerchiefs, tobacco, ammunition, trinkets, &c., &c." On his return trip, "the poverty, misery, and wretchedness of the poor creatures, men, women, and children, who crowded the wayside . . . to shake hands and beg me to 'come again soon with presents from the great chief at Washington,' is beyond conception, much less description." Davis calculated that one hundred thousand dollars was needed for the following year.[29] However, the *News* cautioned that the Indians in Cache were "demanding a visit" from the superintendent, as were those in Sanpete County, but that his funds would not allow "his extending relief . . . as liberally as he has, to the few thus far visited."[30] Not to Superintendent Davis, but to "missionary to the Indians" Jacob Hamblin, did Young make a January appeal: "I would be much pleased to have you . . . endeavour to recover the body of George A. Smith, Jun. [Junior], for which, if it can be done, I would not begrudge paying any reasonable amount."[31] Smith's son was killed by Navajos on an Arizona excursion with Hamblin, John D. Lee, and others.[32]

By January's end, Davis was labeled a secessionist by the *Mountaineer*, a Mormon-run newspaper published as an alter ego of the *News:* "We have just been favored with the astounding intelligence that we have in this quiet and peaceful community a *great little* army of Southern secessionists who are thinking seriously of seceding from Utah! This movement, we are told, is strongly supported by the Indian Department, and the whole *imposing* array of gallantry, when properly armed and equipped, is to be commanded by *an old officer of the 7th Infantry, and hero of the Everglades.*"[33]

Since Mormon leaders repeatedly admitted they favored the South, criticism of Davis was likely tied not to his allegiance but to his unwelcome investigation of Young's finances. In February, Davis met with Brigham Young's emissary and Indian interpreter, Dimick Huntington, and with Indian agent Levi Stewart to review the Mountain Meadow accounts. Stewart and John D. Lee claimed "to have distributed more than $3,500 worth of clothing, gun powder, lead, and goods to 'sundry bands of Indians near Mountain Meadows' . . . nineteen days after the massacre." Davis was amazed that "in all his years at the bar he could not recall a single instance in which so many witnesses 'concurred with such precision and exactitude.'"[34]

By May's end, the *New York Times* reported that Davis was considering leaving, as rumors surfaced that Indian Affairs monies had been
used to purchase "feminine accoutrements" for the "copper-colored
daughters of the forest."[35] In June, George A. Smith wrote that "Col.
Davis . . . is a Secessionist and is trying to enlist some men to fight for
the South. . . . The troops [of Johnston] have had orders to move at
a moment's warning—many of the officers have seceded [*sic*] and
removed themselves." Acting Governor Francis H. Wootton resigned
and headed to Maryland.[36]

Though replaced by Henry Martin, Benjamin Davis remained in
Utah through early 1862, finishing his report on Young's financial
accounts. Young railed that the "Indian Department is very much . . .
determined to with-hold the payment of my just dues," adding that
those in Washington "are entirely too immaculate for the corrupt position they occupy." Davis decided the government owed Young $346.46
for service from July 1 to November 20, 1857. However, in 1866 Young
was paid $34,145 for alleged "Indian expenses" dating from 1852.[37]

Historian Chad Orton asserts that Davis did not command any
Utah men under the Confederate banner in the Civil War but later
served courageously in an infantry unit recruited from his native Florida.[38] Evidence is elusive as to whether a relationship between Davis
and known Confederate agent Walter Murray Gibson existed.

The Spring Trip South

With his retinue, Young made his first tour to the southern counties
from May 15 to June 8.[39] In a whirlwind trip of nearly eight hundred
miles in twenty-five days, they ventured as far south as the Santa Clara
River and visited Mountain Meadows. Among the company were Daniel Wells, Wilford Woodruff, John Taylor, George A. Smith, at least six
additional priesthood leaders, and "a goodly number of other citizens, . . . including several literary and scientific gentlemen."[40] Important facts are omitted in the LDS account of Young's first visit to the
1857 Mountain Meadows killing field, which stated: "Prest. Young and
Company visited the Mountain Meadows Monument erected at the

burial place of 120 persons *killed by Indians* in the year 1857. The pile of stone was about 12 feet high but *was beginning to tumble down.*"[41] Unmentioned in that passage were the three score or more of Mormon militiamen involved in the killings, as well as Young's instructions at the monument, given wordlessly to his assembled mounted guards, at which the pile of stones was leveled.[42] The LDS version continued: "A wooden cross is placed on the top with the words inscribed of 'Vengeance is mine, and I will repay, saith the Lord.'"[43] Not reported was Young's retort on reading the inscription: "It should be 'Vengeance is mine *and I have taken a little.*'"[44] Furthermore, the LDS account stated: "A slab at the bottom bears the following inscription: '120 men, women and children murdered in cold blood, early in September 1857, from Arkansas;' and on the south side is a slab 'Erected by Company K 1st Dragoons, May 1859."[45] Not included here were the facts that Bvt. Maj. James Henry Carleton and his Company K Dragoons, sent to investigate the massacre, had concluded that Mormon men, disguised to appear as Indians, were largely responsible for the murders.[46] According to the LDS record, Young's company "camped for the night past Gunlock Fort having traveled that day 35 miles."[47] Omitted was that while dining with John D. Lee, Brigham disingenuously told him that those killed were "the Father, Mothe[rs], Bros., Sisters & connections of those that Muerders [*sic*] the Prophets" and thus had "Merittd their fate." Lee observed, "The only thing that ever troubled him [Young] was the lives of the Women & children, but that under the circumstances [their deaths] could not be avoided."[48]

David O. Calder, Young's secretary, penned an urgent letter to Young while he was still in transit back to Salt Lake City. Primarily concerned with Hooper's misunderstanding the handling of certain monies, the letter also contained a note on territorial matters. Francis H. Wootton, previously the Utah territorial secretary, had been made the acting governor after Cumming's departure. Calder's letter gives further proof that in Utah the U.S. mail was intercepted, shared, and copied: "Secretary Wotton [*sic*] . . . wrote [attorney Stephen] DeWolfe, offering him the office of Secretary of the Territory, pro tem. The enclosed letter of DeWolfe's is his reply. . . . It is so rich I concluded to send it to you. Evidently DeWolfe's thrust wounded him, for he

[Wootton] . . . came to the conclusion that he could not conscientiously serve under the present [Lincoln] Administration, and today forwarded his resignation! Bro. Wm. Clayton was privileged with a perusal of it just before it was taken over to the pony express office."[49]

Returning to Salt Lake City, Young remarked, "The Saints South were glad to see me, and I believe my visit to them will do them much good."[50] From Wilford Woodruff's journal, the *News* published details of the trip. No further mention of Mountain Meadows was made, though the visits were to the cities through which the Arkansas train had traveled. This trip was likely instrumental in an October "call" of two hundred families to migrate and take permanent residence in the southern areas.[51] In a letter to church leaders Amasa M. Lyman and Charles C. Rich in Great Britain, Young wrote, "The settlements south . . . will rapidly . . . increase as the demand for cotton increases." He laid out plans for a cotton factory and expanded fruit production and mine output.[52]

Young called a substantial number of families to the southern reaches of the territory during the Civil War years to raise cotton and other crops that needed a warm climate and temperate winters. Sympathy with the Southern cause was prominent in these colonies. George A. Smith corroborated: "Many of them were . . . gathered from Texas, Alabama, Mississippi, and other parts of the Southern States; they were accustomed to raising cotton."[53] The 1860 census data for birthplace of men in Washington and Iron Counties confirms that all seceding states and cotton-producing states with slaves were represented, with the exception of South and North Carolina.

Utah Spared Suspension of Habeas Corpus

Six weeks after Fort Sumter's bombardment, a Maryland farmer was arrested in the dark morning hours of May 25. Union military authorities cited "vague and imprecise charges of treason against the United States."[54] The farmer, John Merryman, was alleged to command an armed group that intended to join the Confederates. Imprisoned at Fort McHenry on the shore of the Baltimore harbor, a petition was sent by U.S. Supreme Court chief justice Roger B. Taney for a writ of habeas corpus, which required that Merryman be charged with a crime or released. Taney issued the writ on May 26, but Lincoln ignored it.[55] Lincoln's decision to suspend habeas corpus in this case—and in other thousands of cases—was based on Article I, Section 9 of the Constitution, which holds, "The privilege of the writ of habeas corpus shall not be suspended, unless when in cases of rebellion or invasion the public safety may require it."[56] By June 1, Taney wrote an opinion, *Ex parte Merryman*, that was severely critical of Lincoln's treatment of Merryman and habeas corpus. Civil War historian Mark E. Neely, Jr., claims *Ex parte Merryman* as one of three documents critical to understanding Lincoln's record on civil liberties.[57] Another historian, Jonathan White, emphasizes that "*Merryman* is one of the most significant judicial decisions of the Civil War era." Lincoln's critics believed that Article I applied to actions by Congress, not those by presidential authority, and that citizens were being denied their civil rights and their right to a trial by a jury of peers.[58]

In the midyears of the Civil War, Gen. P. Edward Connor, Governor Stephen S. Harding, Judge Thomas J. Drake, and Judge Charles B. Waite frequently documented that the words of LDS leaders were evidence of disloyalty to the interests of the Union. Even Doty at times joined the criticism. Documentation of disloyalty is found in speeches in the Tabernacle, in local and regional church meetings, and on the pages of the *Deseret News* and the *Daily Union Vedette*. Had the Saints existed in the border state of Maryland, in Virginia or Washington, D.C., or in a northern state, Mormon words alone would have brought about far more serious consequences than harsh castigation by federal officers. In August in Brigham Young's office it was reported, "The feelings of the Brethren are gratified by hearing of the continued success which attends the Southern Confederacy."[59]

In September 1862, "Lincoln codified the use of military commission trials," and not civil trials, "for civilians who inhibited the draft or were 'guilty of any disloyal practice.'" In Baltimore, for example, two women were tried and convicted by military commissions for disloyal speech and conduct. One Sarah Hutchins was charged with intercourse with the enemy and violating the laws of war for having procured a ceremonial sword and attempting to send a letter to a rebel soldier. Found guilty, she was fined five thousand dollars and imprisoned for five years in Massachusetts. Washerwoman Ann Kilbaugh "was charged with 'conduct and the use of language tending to promote sedition and encourage rebellion' for verbally disparaging Union soldiers, the federal government, and loyal women who carried 'their damned old Union flag.'" Found guilty, she received a sentence of six months' hard labor, which was commuted to thirty days' imprisonment."[60] Neely estimates that suspension of habeas corpus—and the use of the military for enforcement—resulted in at least fourteen thousand civilian arrests, trials, and imprisonments. More than four thousand cases were tried in military courts.[61]

Instances of Mormons actively assisting Indians by supplying false information to California or Nevada Volunteers, thereby placing their lives in danger, would have qualified as disloyal acts. Withholding assistance and passively looking on when U.S. troops were fired upon, as reported in the after-action records of the officers out of Camp Douglas, would have qualified and would have resulted in arrests and imprisonments had Connor's military forces been able to do so without precipitating all-out war with the Mormons' numerically superior army. Secret acquisition of gunpowder, munitions, and repeated readying of the territorial militia for war against a government that the Saints were told intended their annihilation, would have qualified. Utah's population were spared punishment because of the sheer distance from Union forces and because their emboldened leader, Brigham Young, understood that the Union had neither heart nor capability to simultaneously fight another war.

The Talking Wire

In June 1860, Congress passed the Pacific Telegraph Act to facilitate communication between the nation's coasts. New York's Hiram Sibley—president of the Western Union and Telegraph Company, which was the promoter of the legislation—joined with Jeptha Wade and Benjamin Franklin Ficklin to form the Pacific Telegraph Company of

Nebraska.[62] Sibley sent Wade to California by way of the Isthmus of Panama to consolidate several smaller telegraph companies into the Overland Telegraph Company. Nebraska's Edward A. Creighton was to survey a wire line to California, with the Pacific Telegraph Company building west from Omaha. Creighton was responsible for the segment from Julesburg, Colorado, to Salt Lake City, where the Pacific wire would meet the wire built from Carson City by the Overland Telegraph Company.

Creighton left Omaha by stagecoach in November and headed for Utah, where on December 10 he met with the most influential figure in the vast expanse to be spanned. Brigham Young reported on their meeting in one of his frequent letters to Congressman Hooper:

"[Creighton] is very anxious . . . that I should become a Director in the company and take the sole management of the business in this region. It is quite likely that myself and others will take hold of the matter to a greater or less extent, say to put up the poles and stretch the wires for about 150 miles East and 150 or 250 miles West of this City, if satisfactory arrangements can be made."[63] In early February 1861, Young and Creighton met again. They discussed obtaining posts, "setting them, stretching the wire on them, etc.," but Creighton "was undetermined what course to take, waiting advices from Agent Wade in California and the Company in the East." Young claimed that Creighton was unfamiliar "with the disadvantages and extra expense attending that kind of work through the barren, unsettled region," so Young made a proposal to him: "I would furnish the wire and posts . . . and stretch the wire on them for 1000 miles from Laramie by way of this City west, at the rate of $175.00 a mile, and would take my pay in stock in the company for 250 of the 1000 miles, or . . . $43,750.00 worth of company stock." Young insisted, "I must be allowed quite a voice in the control and management of the wire and stations in Utah."[64]

In May 1861, Edward Creighton, a younger brother to John A. Creighton, met with Mormon agents in Nebraska, striking a contract for employing seventy-five Mormon men.[65] All of the crew of four hundred were well armed with navy revolvers and rifles. Supported by more than a hundred wagons and five hundred mules and oxen, they left Omaha for Fort Kearny on June 17, reaching Julesburg in time for Creighton to personally dig the first posthole of his westward segment on July 2. The *Times* reported, "Persons residing here [in Utah] have contracted for supplying the needful poles between the South Pass and Ruby Valley, at two dollars per pole, . . . the contracts to be executed by an early day. So we shall very soon have instantaneous communication with the East and West."[66] In a July 12 letter, Young recorded that Mormon men were "fast scattering poles from here toward the South Pass" and that "other companies are putting up poles and stretching the wire from Fort Karney [*sic*] west, expecting to join with the western line in this City on or before the 1st of December next."[67] A *Times* article datelined Great Salt Lake City noted that other Mormon workers were supplying telegraph poles westward to Ruby Valley, adding, "It is anticipated that the wires will meet in this city next Fall. . . . [T]hey are advancing from the west at the rate of five miles per day."[68] As the lines neared Utah, Creighton arranged to get poles from Brigham's son John W. Young. From California came this progress report: "'President' Young's teams started westward with some forty miles of poles, intending transporting them as far west as Ruby."[69] Pride and competition were injected by a provision that the first to arrive in Salt Lake City would be paid a penalty of fifty dollars per day by the slower company. Creighton completed his end on October 18, 1861. On that date, Brigham Young sent the following message to Jeptha Wade, in Cleveland, Ohio: "Permit me to congratulate you upon the completion of the overland telegraph line west to this city" and "to commend . . . the rapid and successful prosecution of a work so beneficial . . . that its use may ever tend to promote the true interests of the dwellers upon both the Atlantic and Pacific slopes of our Continent. Utah has not seceded, but is firm for the Constitution and laws of our once happy country, and is warmly interested in such useful enterprises as the one so far completed."[70] Young left it to Acting Governor Frank Fuller to send a message to President Lincoln. Fuller's language was flowery and inkhorn: "Utah, whose citizens strenuously resist all imputations of disloyalty, congratulates the President upon the completion of an enterprise which spans a continent, unites two oceans, and connects with nerve of iron, the remote extremities of the body politic with the great Governmental heart. May the whole system speedily thrill with quickened pulsations of the heart, as the parricide hand is palsied, treason is punished, and the entire sisterhood of States join hands in glad reunion around the National fireside."[71] In the privacy of his office, Young evinced a different tone, saying that he "'would be glad to hear that [Confederate] Genl. Beauregard had taken the [U.S.] President & Cabinet and confined them in the South. "That was one sentiment Young decided not to express publicly," wrote historian Michael Quinn.[72]

Anticipating the role that telegrams would serve in keeping distant Mormon leaders well informed, Young wrote to Eastern States Mission president John D. T. McAllister, instructing him to strengthen their personal contacts—for special favors: "[G]et acquainted with one or more of the telegraph operators in Philadelphia and New York, . . . that a telegram from here may reach you promptly."[73]

From San Francisco, H. W. Carpentier, of the Overland Telegraph, sent his message to Brigham Young on October 24: "That which was so long a hope is now a reality. The trans-continental telegraph is now completed. May it prove a bond of perpetual union and friendship between the people of Utah and the people of California."[74] Young answered, stressing the role played by James Street: "I am very much obliged for your kind feelings manifested through Mr. Street, in giving me the privilege of first message to California. May success ever attend the enterprise."[75] Once again, their location on the lines joining east and west brought great economic gain to Young and the Mormons.

Realizing the potential for fraud and abuse arising from the transmission of private messages through many telegraph operators, Carpentier was influential in California's legislation of April 1862 against divulging or changing contents, postponing them or sending them out of order, together with other protections against infringement on individual rights and privacy. Contracts and notices—even marriage proposals and contracts—by telegram were awarded legal status. Similar legislation was passed by Oregon's state legislature in October 1862, and notably, Utah Territory enacted such laws in January 1863.[76]

The Chief Federal Official Exits the Territory

Brigham Young noted in January that Utah's federal officials were growing restive, for "the Pony brings word from Karney [sic] of the secession of State after State, . . . and Gov't office holders are anxiously looking for still squallier times, and many of them are casting their eyes to points beyond our border, contemplating departure as soon as cold and snow abate sufficiently."[77] The news reached Utah that Col. Robert Anderson had spiked the guns at Fort Moultrie and abandoned the fort, and when the bombardment at Sumter opened outright war, Governor Alfred Cumming firmed his plans to return to his native Georgia. As Carl Sandburg phrased it, "The war of words was over and the naked test by steel weapons, so long foretold, was at last to begin."[78]

Young remarked that "the Lord controlled the Governor and he has done pretty well . . . but he had evil in his heart when he came here."[79] Cumming's wife, Elizabeth, held a different view: "Alfred has had no trouble from the Mormons. The community, en masse, seem to be thankful, that . . . they have . . . a just & honorable man who will not betray their interests." She observed that on her several visits each week to Mrs. Young, "she scarcely ever omits saying something about 'we are much obliged to Govr. Cumming.'" However, Elizabeth admitted that Alfred was overcautious, never having "entered a Mormon house, as guest, since he came here."[80] However guarded, Cumming might well have met his last day in this world when he called the Mormons' "Avenging Angel," Porter Rockwell, a Danite. After some "rough expressions," Rockwell invited the governor into the street to shoot it out at ten paces, "but the governor declined."[81]

Days before South Carolina's shelling, Young wrote to leaders in Liverpool, "Gov. Cumming intends starting for the States on the 10th of May, without waiting for Presidential action in Utah appointments." Rumors circulated that "several other incomers of the class of 1857 are expecting to leave soon."[82] Daniel Wells planned for Elder John Titcombe to drive Cumming and his wife to Florence and then return his wagon, loaded with goods, back to Salt Lake City.[83] On the day before Cumming left, Young furnished LDS elder T. B. H. Stenhouse a letter of introduction, suggesting that Stenhouse planned to accompany Cumming. Cumming, his wife, and perhaps others "quietly left Salt Lake City on May 17, 1861, bound eastward for the States."[84] The *News* considered Cumming's departure peculiar, as the governor and his wife slipped out of the city almost unnoticed.[85] The identity of those of Cumming's traveling party, or a possible need for secrecy, is uncertain, but Cumming was "somewhat eccentric," and "it seemed to be his wish to avoid any demonstration . . . concealing . . . , as far as possible, the time when it [his departure] might be expected to take place." One of his wagons was upended in the stream in Emigration Canyon, but "fortunately some men were passing at the time, who rendered efficient service in getting the wagon right side up, and the wetted freight replaced therein, for which they received a liberal compensation."[86] Cumming safely reached Washington, D.C., where he settled the details of his administration. He was not allowed to go further until mid-1864, when he was permitted to return to Augusta, where he and his family had prominence.[87]

Young explained that he had laid the threat of death on Cumming: "He understood always that if he did not do right, and step forward and defend the innocent [Mormons], all I had to do was to crook my little finger. . . . Toe the line, and mark by the law, and do it right or I shall crook my little finger, and you know what will come then."[88] Mormons knew that a crooked fifth finger directed toward them by Young was a death sentence.

As Young wrote to Hooper over Cumming's departure and the pending takeover by Francis Wootton as acting governor, Young added a unique description of the warfare beginning to unfold: "We feel secure and blest in 'our mountain home,' striving to prepare ourselves for the events that are so rapidly developing for the advancement of the cause of truth on the earth."[89] Only Mormons understood Young in this strange assertion that men dying and wounded in uncountable numbers would advance truth.

Young spoke of appointed federal officials when he told his audience that the Mormon people were served by "gamblers, cut throats, and blacklegs" but had to endure "the poor miserable curses that hold the reins [who] run away with the whole to destruction," for "there is nobody [who] can pluck the reins of Government from their hands."[90] Buchanan remained a mote in the Mormons' collective eye, for as Young said, "King James pledged . . . that . . . he would take the Island of Cuba, annex a portion of Mexico, and so obliterate the 'Mormons' that 'Mormonism' should not be known at the end of his reign." Young defiantly noted that none of the three pledges were filled.[91] Young could have told of famous Illinois politician Stephen A. Douglas, who also spoke of obtaining Cuba. In his 1858 debate with Lincoln at Jonesboro, Douglas said: "The time may come, indeed has now come, when our interests would be advanced by the acquisition of the island of Cuba."[92]

Young raised the question of taking Mexico and Cuba into the Confederacy in his letter to Col. Thomas Kane, then in Philadelphia: "The wise men of our nation have so managed that secession artillery is now trained within less than six miles of the White House. Under existing circumstances will it not be better to annex Mexico to the United States, and then go on and annex the Central States of America, Cuba—all the West India Islands—and Canada?" Assuming Kane's answer to be in the affirmative, despite his military service and devotion to the Union, Young posed a question that suggests intrigue: "What can we do to help you in this matter?"[93] It was five days before writing this to Kane, when Young and Kimball were meeting with other brethren, that Young made the remark—alluded to previously—that he would be glad to hear that "Beauregard had taken the President & Cabinet and confined them in the South."[94]

Out and Back—A Boost to Western Commerce and Migration

In 1861, as in the pell-mell days of seekers heady for the riches of California's Sierra, Salt Lake City again experienced a surge in the number of people passing through on their way west. Gold was not the principal cause; rather, uncertainty over their safety, with war threatening and spreading across the continent, now motivated them. Emigrant trains passing through the city repeatedly drew notice in the *Times:* "Emigration from the East to California continues through our city, mostly taking fine horse stock through. A few are going the other way, I suppose to fetch their relatives and friends."[95] "Emigrants from the States, for Nevada and California, well fitted out with horse and mule teams, continue to pass almost daily through our streets."[96] "Immigrants from the East to the West continue to fill our streets and stir trade."[97] Mormons constituted only part of the westbound traffic, as an excerpt from one trail journal testifies: "After we got as far as to the Platt[e] River, emigrants nearly every day from different parts of the U. States . . . brought with them some of the finest horses I have ever seen. . . . Most of these were no[t] Mormons, [but] going to California, Oregon, Montana, etc."[98]

"By the 1860s, traffic on the overland trails is more readily characterized as transportation than emigration, . . . [and] Commerce flowed on the trails in probably greater measure than emigrants," according to historian Robert M. Utley.[99] Will Bagley and Rick Grunder, investigators of westward migration, added that the various immigration strategies of the LDS Church operated as "part and parcel of the State of Deseret's singular communal society, which essentially operates as a command economy."[100] Prominent among Mormon strategies was the business-smart organization of out-and-back wagon trains. Prior to the time when entrepreneur and trader Alexander Majors proved that oxen could make two trips in a season by subsisting on forage, they were sold for meat at trail's end, with wagons that had cost $175 selling for as little as $10. Iron was salvaged from wagons that were not serviceable.[101] In 1859 the Mormons confirmed that oxen could make two trips the same season and "perform . . . better than cattle purchased [in Omaha]."[102]

In the out-and-back scheme, men of the Mormon priesthood were "called" to serve as teamsters. The use of required wagons and teams was temporarily assigned by the "call" of the bishop to faithful members, who were paid for their service not in cash but with credit at the tithing store, at ten dollars per hundred pounds for outbound freight and fifteen dollars a hundred on the return.[103] Mormon trails historian William G. Hartley estimates that more than two hundred thousand dollars in tithing credits was earned in 1861.[104] Emigrants either prepaid or were indebted to the Perpetual Emigrating Fund for food and travel costs. Emigrant numbers routinely exceeded the capacity of the loaded wagons, meaning that many individuals paid to walk to Utah.[105] Numbers of oxen and cattle, together with out-wagon freight, were sold in Omaha; profits were used to purchase goods that were loaded into the back-wagons for use or sale on reaching Utah.[106] While massive war debt was building nationally, the inventive, hardworking Saints were becoming prosperous.

Preparations began in January to field at least 150 teams for overland freight and emigrant transport. Starting in the spring from the mouth of Parley's Canyon in the Salt Lake valley, they would head to Florence—present-day Omaha—to haul freight. Between April 23 and 31, four companies under the command of experienced overland captains Joseph W. Young, Ira Eldredge, Joseph Horne, and John R. Murdock left the valley, headed "for the Missouri river to bring in the poor;" but however poor, their journey was rarely free.[107]

Young's letter to George Q. Cannon in Liverpool was detailed: "There are in the four Companies, public wagons 183, private wagons 20; public oxen 1575, private do [ditto] 124; public teamsters 194, private do. 23; and 136,000 pounds of flour to be taken beyond the South Pass for our immigration, besides an abundant flour and other outfit for teamsters, etc, 16 or 18 men as guards, 34,348 pounds of flour for sale to pay ferriages, buy wagons, groceries for return, etc. The Companies are well armed, and are strictly counseled to be very vigilant and watchful."[108]

Counsel came in four letters signed by the LDS First Presidency: Young, Heber C. Kimball, and Daniel H. Wells. Included was the need to be well armed with rifles or shotguns and, while traveling, to keep companies no more than one or two hours distant from one another, because "there is much difficulty between the whites and Comanches," and "the Sioux are disaffected about their annuities and are threatening to interrupt travel across the plains."[109] Two weeks later, another letter named a more serious threat: "The roads are infested with travelers . . . [who] will steal your flour, pick up your axes, spades, shovels, cooking utensils, blankets, pistols, guns, tin cups, whip lashes, etc. and "drive off your stock by stampede or otherwise." The brethren were advised that "the bearer of this note will aid you in forming the necessary vigilance committees and in weeding out and cleansing your camps from all such noxious vermin."[110] To those who understood the argot, this was preapproval of killing thieves or interlopers. "Let them keep clear of our camps," the letter continued, "or suffer the consequences, for in this matter we . . . have no misgivings about putting the law of right in force against them." Trail bosses should make it known "that righteous men rule and . . . that the fire of the Almighty burns so hot in your bosoms that evil doers and all workers of iniquity will surely be consumed."[111] The term "infested with travelers" is taken at face value, for Mormons would not have risked violence against U.S. troops encountered on the trail, even though some unprofessional conduct by the military was reported in trail narratives. Edward P. Thomas, of the Job Pingree Company, wrote: "That summer we met a portion of the Johnston's Army coming back from Utah. . . . They took their bayonets to our cattle and drove them into the sage brush at Devil's Gate."[112] Several members of the Homer Duncan Company remarked of uneventful encounters with the troops, while three members of the Joseph Horne Company left trail excerpts similar to that of Eliza Seamons England, describing efforts to entirely avoid contact with the troops: "One day we came close to a portion of Johnson's [sic] Army. . . . Our captain ordered us to travel around them so as not to meet them."[113] Another Horne Company pioneer wrote: "We passed Fort Laramie in the night and our Capt. . . . instructed all to go as quietly as possible, not to speak a word, not even to the oxen or to make a light. Our whole train of fifty wagons passed without the soldiers knowing it."[114] Inbound Mormons may have feared the outbound troops, but they risked being charged with treason if they were carrying gunpowder in the wagons headed to Utah. Hidden gunpowder would explain the efforts of these several Mormon trains to avoid contact with federal troops. At the least one of the 1861 trains, that of Sixtus Ellis Johnson with fifty-two wagons and some two hundred Saints, carried such a load. Seth Guernsey Johnson, the younger brother, recorded their narrow escape from disaster, explaining that when lightning struck one of the wagons, it not only killed its oxen but ignited the hay in which three hundred pounds of gunpowder in kegs lay hidden. Water from a barrel in a nearby wagon was used to extinguish the flames, and the gunpowder passed undetected into Utah.[115] Wilford Woodruff's letter to the Mormon leaders in Liverpool removed all doubt that arms were shipped: "But if the trains of waggons [*sic*] I have seen going into G. S. L. [Great Salt Lake] City, loaded with gun-barrels, ramrods, cannon balls, and cast-iron shells, mean anything, I should judge somebody was supplying the foundries and blacksmiths' shops!"[116]

Murdock and his "church" train with the paid-up-front customers of the "independent" train of Milo Andrus came in by September 12; they were joined the next day by Horne's "church" train and the "independent" emigrants of Homer Duncan, and by Ira Eldredge on September 15.[117] The eighty to ninety wagons of the train of Joseph W. Young, loaded heavily with machinery and merchandise for Salt Lake City but with few immigrants, arrived later in September.[118] Capt. Samuel A. Woolley's train of seventy wagons, composed mostly of converted Saints from Scandinavia, arrived September 22, and another train under the direction of Capt. Ansel P. Harmon arrived September 23. In July, Young estimated that "there will be some 2000 persons" in the church trains of the season, but at season's end, the *News* gave a much larger number: "Between four and five thousand persons have come across the plains this season, intending to remain permanently in the Territory." Young was pleased with the year's emigrant numbers and optimistically wrote to the Saints of Sanpete County, who had furnished much of the manpower, that "aiding that number across the plains should be a very pleasing reflection to all who assisted in fitting out and forwarding that train, and doubtless will prompt . . . more extensive operations in that direction next season."[119] However incomplete, the records from twenty-one companies of the four captains named, together with seventeen other identified companies and an unknown number of unidentified companies, show a total of approximately 882 wagons and 3,787 individuals, mostly Mormons, making the 1861 journey to Utah.[120]

Lead Became Gold

Philip St. John Cooke, respected and well known to the Mormons as the commander of the Mormon Battalion in the Mexican War, took command at Camp Floyd on March 1, 1860, as Albert Sidney Johnston headed to San Francisco.[121] By the end of 1860, many of its troops had been transferred to New Mexico and Arizona.[122] Cooke could count three hundred present in February, when the camp was renamed Camp Crittenden; he supervised the dismantling of the camp and the sale of its remaining goods to the Mormons. Colonel Cooke rode at the head of the columns leaving Utah in the last days of July.

Mormon intelligence gathering was working well in February, when the official church organ published that "Col. Cooke has received orders to have all things in readiness to march at a moment's notice." One who "had had good opportunity for obtaining correct information" regarding the events of Fort Crittenden reported that "on the 28th inst., all the employees at that post and at Fort Bridger are, by order of the war department, to be discharged."[123] Mormons were aware by February 20 that the timetable had been set for the movement of the former Utah Expedition troops. Wilford Woodruff's letter of that date said: "The U.S. Army in Utah has orders to dismiss all citizens from service. It is now reported they will leave in the Spring."[124]

According to the *Deseret News*, several of the officers "of southern extraction . . . [had] expressed their determination to resign their commissions and return home immediately on the commencement of active hostile demonstrations between the two opposing factions." Many men would be short of funds for travel, and it was suggested that LDS wagon teams headed to Florence might profit from assisting them "in their exodus from these valleys where *no laurels have been won* . . . , and from which we have no doubt, all wish to retire."[125]

Historian Thomas Alexander states that "disposal of surplus items began in July of 1859," when "the Army sold 2,000 or more mules for prices ranging from $60.00 to $140.00 each, a price considerably below the original cost."[126] On March 20, 1861, the goods and materials at Camp Crittenden were put on sale, and the *News* noted that the event was "well attended by our city merchants and speculators" and that "Mr. [William] Nixon, of this city, was the principal purchaser."[127] The Walker Brothers general store advertised its continued presence for business on East Temple Street in Salt Lake City, and on Main Street in Fairfield, near Fort Crittenden.[128] In mid-July, Young wrote to Orson Pratt in New York City, "The public buildings, . . . are advertised for sale on the 16th inst., to continue until the whole is sold."[129] In a July 18 letter, Young instructed Hiram Clawson, David Calder, and John T. Caine, then at Fort Crittenden, "to make . . . the most useful and necessary purchases at the lowest possible rates," adding, "[I] commend your policy of selling portions of what can be spared, at greatly advanced rates, to increase your funds for other purchases."[130] Young shortly informed Bishop Moffitt of Manti that "Br. Hiram [Clawson] bought a large quantity of nails, various sizes, for 6 cents a pound, horse and mule shoes for one half cent each, 200 sacks of flour for 55 cents a sack (100 pounds in each, with double sacks), new mule collars for 41 cents each, etc., etc."[131] Daniel Wells reported that "sugar sold at the lowest at twelve and half, bacon one and a quarter cents, nails six, coffee thirty cents. Tools of all kinds sold higher as a good many wanted them. Horse shoes we got about 11 tons at a half a cent apiece. Sibley Tents for $1.25 each. I suppose we have about sixty tons of stuff altogether."[132] It was estimated that "about $4 million worth of supplies sold for $100,000." Young's purchases, made through Clawson, accounted for $40,000 of that amount, yet Young claimed insufficient funds to meet the Civil War bill of almost $27,000 presented to Utah.[133] "The bullets the troops brought to shoot us turned out to be gold Eagles and landed in our pockets," said one Mormon, in reference to the sought-after U.S. gold coins, previously scarce in Utah.[134]

Young complained to Dwight Evelith: "The arms and ammunition they could not take, they were instructed by the Department to destroy—a significant index of the feeling still existing towards us."[135] In August, three Mormon men—Dr. Jeter Clinton, Bishop John Sharp, and George Goddard—approached Capt. Henry F. Clarke to purchase "two or three tons of powder for blasting purposes," as one of them "was engaged extensively in the quarrying of rock, and used considerable for that purpose." Clarke's orders "to destroy the arms, mortars and ammunition placed it entirely out of his power to accommodate us." Goddard continued, "I then tried to obtain a few hundred thousand gun caps; . . . [but] he intended to take them to the States. I then asked him what motive he had for discharging so many shells every night. He said the only motive was to destroy them."[136] To Hiram Clawson, at Fort Bridger preparing to purchase materials at Camp Scott, Young wrote: "They have burned and otherwise destroyed what they could not take, sell, or waste, and are now on their way to hell in the States where they will be wasted, burned, and destroyed."[137] Troops were "whipped in coming to Utah, are worse whipped in leaving, and thus it will ever be with all who oppose the establishment of the Kingdom of God on the earth," Young warned.[138]

The distrust of having Mormons guard the overland trails was proved when Secretary of War Simon Cameron wrote California governor John G. Downey on July 24: "The War Department accepts for three years one regiment of infantry and five companies of cavalry to guard the overland mail route from Carson Valley to Salt Lake and Fort Laramie."[139] Events were set in motion that would bring a fiery Irishman into the Utah Territory at the head of the California Volunteers. This man would vie both in verbal combat and actions with Brigham Young in an abrasive tour from 1862 to 1865, when the assignment of Gen. P. Edward Connor was transferred to the Department of the Plains. Their enmity would end only with Young's death in 1877, however Connor continued working against theocracy with the non-Mormon Liberal Party until his death in 1891.

Arms, Munitions, Loyalty

In an early January letter, Young's instructions to Hooper were that requests for arms for the Mormon's militia would go to Washington, not over his own name, but over the name of the territorial governor. Young wrote that Cumming was "anxious that Utah should have her quota of arms allowed by Government to the States and Territories." Cumming has "deemed [it] best to make Utah's requisition for her quota to be furnished in Colt's revolver pistols, navy size, delivered in Florence, Nebraska Territory, in time for transportation across the plains this season."[140]

Speculation that Mormons were accumulating gunpowder and munitions was confirmed when orders were issued by Lt. Gen. Daniel H. Wells, at the moment the U.S. army units were vacating the territory.[141] Dated August 2, Special Order No. 2 to Brig. Gen. Chauncey W. West, commander of the Weber Military District, read in part:

> It is deemed advisable [to] *quietly revive* the Military throughout the Territory. . . . [The goal is] to have our Military organizations as perfect as possible and to *have the implements of war on hand* and in good order. . . . Let the brethren provide themselves with *a good supply of powder, ball, and caps* and then not shoot nor trade it away but . . . keep it on hand and in good condition against a time of need. . . .
>
> You will also organize one company of artillery and one Battalion of mounted rifles to act as minute men.
>
> You will see that every person residing within your command . . . is enrolled . . . in readiness with Arms, Ammunition and equipments suitable to his corps for active service.
>
> . . . [I]t is considered best in the present disturbed State of our country not to exhibit too much apathy or indifference to passing events but to prepare so far as possible against any and every emergency that may arise.
>
> In fact we above all other people should ever be on the alert. It is an old saying that "Eternal vigilance is the price of liberty." Be that as it may ours consists in a union of faith and energetic effectual effort and in "keeping our powder dry." . . .
>
> As ever your Brother in Christ,
> Daniel H. Wells.[142]

Apostle Ezra T. Benson, also commander of the Cache Military District, established nine battalions totaling more than six hundred men. Wells's letter went to Maj. Gen. George D. Grant, who commanded the Great Salt Lake Military District; the district was the largest military component in the territory in 1861, consisting of brigades commanded by Brig. Gens. William H. Kimball and Franklin D. Richards. Also in this district was a regiment of cavalry under Col. Robert T. Burton, and three regiments of infantry under Cols. Almon L. Fullmer, Jonathan Pugmire, Jr., and David J. Ross. These were supported by one light artillery company, with six cannons of various sizes, commanded by Maj. Samuel G. Ladd and by Capt. Thomas Jack of Jack's sharpshooters, the Enfield Rifles.[143] Other special orders were issued: On September 2, Brig. Gen. Aaron Johnson, commanding the Utah Military District, responded to Special Order No. 5, which used some phrasing that was almost identical to that of Special Order No. 2—for example, "quietly revive" and "so far as possible [be] in readiness with arms and ammunition and equipment suitable for . . . active service."[144] One company of infantry and two platoons of "mounted minute men" were to be readied for inspection in Provo Valley by the 28th of the month.[145] On October 3, Johnson sent a similar letter to Capt. John W. Witt, specifying that a general muster of all militia in the Provo Valley was to be enrolled by the 19th of the month. Colonel Burton wrote cavalry major Lot Smith, telling him to prepare for muster and inspection of arms on October 19 at the military reserve near the Jordan River.[146]

In addition to the four military districts described, twelve others existed during the Civil War period.[147] Total troop numbers within the various Legion units available for military action in 1861 were estimated by historian Ephraim Dickson to be an impressive eight to ten thousand, substantially more than had been activated in Utah's 1857 war.[148] Just as impressive as the numbers of men and matériel available to serve on very short notice was the militia's effective organization, which facilitated the ability of Mormon leaders to simultaneously fill multiple roles as military commanders, church leaders, and civic leaders, sharing kinship and united by their society's highly effective person-to-person communication.

Speaking in Cache Valley, not in his capacity as military commander but as one of the three members of the LDS First Presidency, Daniel Wells had this message: "Learn how to clean a gun well, how to take it apart and put it together again, and how to keep it in good condition.

Learn how to load a gun properly, learn what is a proper charge, and then learn to throw the ball to the spot you wish it to be lodged. . . . We wish the military officers to lend their instructions in this way; learn the ignorant how to use and take care of their firearms, and how to keep them safely that they may be in continual readiness."[149]

Were these preparations for a strong defense that would discourage government action against them, or were Mormon leaders planning to mount another rebellion or to flee elsewhere in their quest for sovereignty? The Mormon populace was kept on high alert, with fear among the people intensified because the enemy was undefined. Warnings of an imminent but unnamed threat would be repeated from the pulpit and through military drills many times during the Civil War's duration.

No evidence of investment in the United States' future could be found in the issue of the *News* that said: "No government . . . as corrupt as has been that of the United States for the last quarter of century at least, ever continued long after it had reached and passed the culminating point of its power and greatness."[150] Young's disloyalty would be evident to any non-Mormon who heard him say, "I feel chagrined and mortified when I reflect upon the condition of my nation. . . . I have almost wished that I had been born in a foreign nation. I feel disgraced in having been born under a government that has so little power, disposition and influence for truth and right."[151] In the same meeting, Heber C. Kimball added, "The south will secede from the north, and the north will secede from us, and *God will make this people free* as fast as we are able to bear it . . . and we will be ruled by those men whom God Almighty appoints."[152] In newspapers in California, in St. Louis and elsewhere, the opinion of the *New York Times* that equated the distrust of the Mormons with that of the Indians was reprinted: "[O]rders have been issued for the immediate withdrawal of all the regular troops from New Mexico and Utah, amounting to about two thousand in the former, and five hundred in the latter. . . . [T]he worst feature of the order is the withdrawal of the troops from Utah, leaving the great overland routes to California and Oregon without protection against Indians or *hostile Mormons*."[153]

Effect of Secession in England

An article from the *London Times* held particular interest to Mormons thinking of growing cotton in the hot portions of Utah. The British had enormous interest at stake in the looming American civil war, it claimed, for "if the slaves rebel, the cotton crop perishes," in turn causing "the paralysis of our own staple manufacture." The article declared that "Lancashire depends upon South Carolina." Nearly four million people—an estimated one-sixth of the entire population of Great Britain—were "dependent on our [Britain's] cotton manufactures for their daily bread," and America had been the source of 77 percent of all the cotton used in the previous four years. Under such pressure, India might be able to supply half the amount needed. "Imagine," the *Times* suggested, "4,000,000 people in trepidation and distress. . . . Where could the relief come from?" Africa and India might rise as alternative sources of cotton production, but "if the agriculture of the slave State should be ruined, there will be a trade of £40,000,000 to be picked up by some other countries."[154]

Rockwood's Dream

A faithful Mormon from 1837 when he joined the church in Kirtland, Ohio, Albert Perry Rockwood, had been ordained one of the First Presidents of Seventies, and served in many capacities including that of the Legion "commissary general of subsistence" during the Civil War period.[155] Rockwood told of a troubling, vivid dream he had experienced in February while visiting the home of Joseph Young. Rockwood envisioned that he was in a place somewhat familiar, standing on a slight rise, looking into a small valley where he noted a number of large logs gathered together. Men appeared to be laying a log house with the foundation in place and the log walls rising about three feet in height. Rockwood reported recognizing one man as Old Priest Howe, now dead for twenty-five years, and noted a tall, elderly man with gray hair who seemed to be superintending the work party. The man reported his name as "Balteshazzar." As one log was being suspended it broke in two pieces, lengthwise; another log was too short, and yet another log was rotten at the end where it broke off. Another log had a large lump in the middle and when the men chopped it off, the log was hollow. When Balteshazzar was asked how many logs there were, he answered thirty-four. When the bark peeled off several logs, the wood was filled with many large black worms and as they fell out the men were very much annoyed. Rockwood reported that the excitement of the dream awakened him.

Apostle Wilford Woodruff volunteered his interpretation, remarkable for its insight of the Mormon's racism and subliminal perception of the events then playing out on a national scale:

> The place was Washington—the 34 logs represent the 34 States of the Union—the men were the Members of Congress—the foundation was the Constitution—Old Priest Howe represents the spiritually dead chaplains—the tall elderly man was [President] James Buchanan—the other men were the Politicians of the day—the log on the east side represents the secession of South Carolina—Balteshazzar represents the President of the United States—the log that was broken by sliding off the mountain was the sending the Army to Utah to make war on the Saints—the log that was split in two is the division of the North and South—the log on the west side that was too short was New Mexico. These logs represent the corrupt state of the Government, for there was more or less defects in all of them. The bark slipping off several logs on the south, disclosing the large black worms, represents the niggers, who have been a source of trouble to politicians for years.[156]

Over-simplification was abundant in the *News* account of the approaching conflict: "There is a decided determination in the Northern States to sustain Mr. Lincoln; and in the South, Mr. Davis has the full support of his people, even the colored population, who are reported to be preparing to fight the Northern folks, who are, at the same time, rampant to fight the Southern folks, all for and on account of those same darkies."[157]

Bark with the Dogs

In his June 12, 1857, speech at Springfield, Illinois, Stephen A. Douglas supported President James Buchanan's decision to "remove Brigham Young and all his followers from office, . . . use all the military force necessary to protect the officers in discharge of duties, and enforce the laws of the land." Not unlike the later actions of Judge Cradlebaugh and others, Douglas advocated "the absolute and unconditional repeal of the organic act—blotting the territorial government out of existence—upon the ground that they are alien enemies and outlaws, denying their allegiance and defying the authorities of the United States." He added, "It will become the duty of Congress to apply the knife and cut out this loathsome, disgusting ulcer."[158] According to the *National Era*, Douglas asserted that Mormons "do not acknowledge allegiance to our Constitution, and they violently resist the laws and government of the United States, and therefore they obtained a Territorial organization on false pretences."[159]

Chronology of Secession	
1860	
South Carolina	December 20
1861	
Mississippi	January 9
Florida	January 10
Alabama	January 11
Georgia	January 19
Louisiana	January 26
Texas	February 1
Virginia	April 17
Arkansas	May 6
North Carolina	May 20
Tennessee	June 8

The following letter, written to Douglas on May 2, 1861, from Salt Lake City, was not signed by its author but ended simply with the word "Utah."

> Sir:
> It would seem that the States are about to "apply the knife and cut out the loathsome ulcer." . . . Does not the "ulcer" prove to be located in a different part of the body-politic and to be more deeply seated that you was then aware of? Alas for human boasting, and the pride of a great Nation in its wickedness, how soon the withering touch of the Almighty can deplete an "overflowing treasury," and turn State against State in fratricidal slaughter! And do you think that your feeble influence can stay the decreed and hastening downfall of our Republic? Silly demagogue, it can no more do so than it could compass the extermination of those the Lord has chosen to bless.
> Do you not begin to realize that the prediction of the Prophet Joseph Smith, personally delivered to you, has been and is being literally fulfilled upon your head?
> Why have you barked with the dogs, except to prove that you were a dog with them?[160]

The letter's second paragraph refers to a declaration made to Douglas in May 1843 by Joseph Smith, Jr., who said, "Judge, you will aspire to the Presidency of the United States; and if you ever turn your hand against me or the Latter Day Saints, you will feel the weight of the hand of the Almighty God upon you; and you will live to see and know that I have testified the truth to you, for the conversation of this day will stick to you through life."[161]

Douglas died of "typhoid fever" in Chicago on June 3, 1861. Whether he read this letter, probably dictated by Brigham Young to a scribe, is uncertain. Hearing of his death, Young said that Douglas "should be president in the lower world, and [Missouri senator] Tom Benton should be his first counsellor."[162] However dismal was Young's opinion of Douglas, he thought even less of Abraham Lincoln, of whom he said, "Stephen A. Douglas was a far better man than

President Abel Lincoln."[163] The *Times* was well aware that Mormons "entertain certain hard recollections of the Senator, on account of his 'loathsome ulcer' recommendations," adding, "So there are no flags at half mast, no mourning appears, no tears are shed, no tokens of respect for the memory of the illustrious Illinoisan are visible, though an old neighbor in Nauvoo days."[164]

Bull Run or Manassas—A Union Wake-up by Either Name

The *Deseret News* became short of its locally manufactured paper and was not published from July 10 to September 11, eclipsing reporting on the war's first major battle on July 21 at Manassas. The Union would later favor the name "Bull Run" for the site, which was located in Prince William County, Virginia, only thirty crow-flight miles from Washington. Historian Everette B. Long credits Young with calling it "Booby Run," and with the comment that "the confusion of the people in the States was rapidly increasing, [and] they seemed as if they had lost their sense."[165] The *Millennial Star* did not specifically name either "Bull Run" or "Manassas" in referring to the battle of eighteen thousand Union troops and a similar number of Confederates, by far the most costly in deaths and casualties up to that time in the war. However, there is little doubt that the dire predictions of fulfillment of Mormon prophesy that the *Star* printed in August arose from that encounter: "The destiny of the once United States is pregnant with a dark and fearful future, as revolution and fratricidal war sweep like a simoom from north to south. Let them patch up peace, if they can,—compromise, if possible,—or cover up the canker-worm at their vitals with a hollow friendship, . . . but the word of the Lord through his servant the Prophet Joseph will have a certain fulfilment."[166] Present-day analysts of the First Bull Run suggest that it "had a curiously salutary effect for the Union side," serving as "a wake-up call for those optimists—like Seward or even Lincoln—who had hoped for, or counted on, a quick result."[167] Bull Run "struck with impelling force upon public opinion at home and abroad, upon Congress, and upon the Commander-in-chief." The failed battle "inspired a second Northern rising":

"Volunteering accelerated, 90-day men reenlisted, states rushed fresh regiments forward in plenitude. . . . As they realized victory would not come readily, a new mood fastened upon Northerners."[168] In California, Bull Run's impact was different. Brig. Gen. E. V. Sumner of the Department of the Pacific wrote to Lt. Col. E. D. Townsend, assistant adjutant general: "Up to the time of the reverse in Virginia [at Bull Run], everything was perfectly safe here. . . . Since that news . . . , I have found it necessary to take strong measures to repress any attempt . . . to thwart the Government."[169]

Among Utah's Mormons, Bull Run was a wake-up call with a very different message.

Chronology
1861

January 9	Mississippi secedes.
January 10	Florida secedes.
	Utah legislature sends another futile request to Congress for statehood.
January 11	Alabama secedes.
January 19	Georgia secedes.
January 26	Louisiana secedes.
February 1	Texas secedes.
February 6	Edward Creighton meets with Brigham Young regarding construction of telegraph line.
	Camp Floyd is renamed Camp Crittenden.
	This day's assassination attempt on Lincoln is foiled.
March 4	Lincoln is inaugurated in Washington, D.C.
March 20	Mormons benefit from the public sale of goods and materials of Camp Crittenden.
April 12–14	Fort Sumter is bombarded by Confederate artillery.
April 17	Virginia secedes.
April 23	"Church" wagons begin eastward trek to Florence, Nebraska.
May 6	Arkansas secedes.
May 15	Brigham Young makes extensive visit to southern Utah settlements, including the site of the Mountain Meadows massacre.
May 17	Governor Alfred Cumming leaves Salt Lake City, bound for Georgia.
May 20	North Carolina secedes.
June 3	No mourning takes place in Utah for Stephen A. Douglas's death.
June 8	Tennessee secedes.

	Brigham Young and entourage return from their Dixie tour.
July 10	*Deseret News* stops printing for lack of newsprint.
July 21	The Union sustains a disastrous loss at the Battle of Bull Run.
July 24	Secretary of War Simon Cameron authorizes California governor John G. Downey to form one regiment of infantry and five companies of cavalry to guard overland mail and travel between Carson Valley and Fort Laramie.
August 2	Utah's military, offically the Nauvoo Legion, is revived, reorganized, and placed on war footing.
September 20	Indian agent Henry Martin has letter published urging land in Uintah County, Utah, be made an Indian reservation, depriving it from Mormons.
October 18	Telegraph line from Salt Lake City to the East is completed. "Utah has not seceded" is the message sent by Brigham Young.
October 24	Telegraph line is completed to the west coast.
	Dr. Robert Arthur Chambers joins Dr. Washington F. Anderson in a Salt Lake City medical office.
December 7	John W. Dawson, James Duane Doty, and Amos Reed arrive in Salt Lake City to assume federal offices.
December 10	Governor Dawson makes his first speech to the Utah legislature.
December 13	Dawson chats with Mormon leaders in the LDS historian's office.
December 14	Dawson mails a copy of his speech before the Utah legislature to President Lincoln.
December 18	Bill asking for statehood is passed by both councils of the Utah legislature, and Dawson refuses to sign it.

December 21   Dawson is alleged to visit widow Albina Williams, making an offer of prostitution.

December 23   Five shots are fired at Judge Henry Crosby while walking in the street with Governor Dawson.

December 26   Dr. Chambers allegedly calls on Williams to offer money for her silence regarding Dawson's alleged proposal.

Dawson writes a nine-page professional report to U.S. secretary of the Interior Caleb Blood Smith that contains no hint of perceived danger.

December 31   Leaving Utah, Dawson is attacked at Hanks' Mountain Dell stage station, beaten, and castrated.

CHAPTER 3

Lies When Truth Is Precious, 1861–1862

Little evil would be done in the world if evil never could be done in the name of good.

MARIE VON EBNER-ESCHENBACH

Historians have not attempted a reappraisal of the life-altering tragedy that ended John W. Dawson's record-setting brief reign as Utah Territory's third governor. Dawson will always be, as historian Will Bagley notes, the front-runner in any contest for experiencing the worst New Year's Eve party of any federal official to the territories.[1] Dawson's name has been besmirched for 150 years, stemming from bizarre, one-sided allegations. The primary source material available, mainly from intramural LDS Church records, leads to a singular interpretation, but new evidence necessitates revision.

Unexamined as relevant are two widows of Thomas Stephen Williams—formerly a Mormon Battalion sergeant, an entrepreneur, a polygamist, a thief, and a lawyer—and their African American slave women, one owned by Williams and his first wife, Albina, and another owned by his fourth wife, Priscilla Mogridge Smith Lowry Williams. Not far away from the Williamses' home lived both William H. Hooper, in whose household were two male slaves, and Abraham O. Smoot, the city's mayor, who owned two male slaves.[2] Also previously unnoted is the role played by the peripatetic medical doctor Robert Arthur

Chambers, whose ambitions—well beyond his capability—led to his manipulation in participating in a shameful scheme.

Thomas Stephen Williams, born in 1827 in Maury County, Tennessee, moved with his parents and siblings to Knox County, Illinois, about 1834. The family joined the LDS Church about 1836, then shortly moved to Hawn's Mill, Missouri, where the 1838 anti-Mormon eruptions forced their relocation in 1839 to Hancock County.[3] At age fifteen, he married sixteen-year-old Albina Merrill, the first of his four marriages.

In Nauvoo, various misbehaviors made Williams a notorious figure; however, he served in the Mormon Battalion in the Mexican War, and once back in Utah, he worked to establish himself as a business figure and qualified lawyer, even serving in the legislature. In 1852 he drove a herd of cattle to California and established a freight train business running from Sacramento to nearby mining towns.[4] Returning to Salt Lake City, Williams joined with high-ranking Mormon William Hooper, freighting for his merchandising business; then, in 1854, Williams took Pricilla Mogridge as his fourth wife. Pricilla and Albina lived in the same household for a number of years after their husband's untimely death.[5] Williams's record with Utah's Mormons was checkered and complicated, with several excommunications, usually followed by Brigham Young's forgiveness and reinstatement.

In 1860 Williams and his brother-in-law Parmenio "Jehu" Jackman ventured again into freighting goods and passengers to California. On March 18, Williams and Jackman, while leading their caravan of fourteen wagons and passengers on the southern route, were attacked. Both were killed by Indians at Bitter Springs, near San Bernardino.[6]

Albina, pregnant when Thomas left for San Bernardino, likely believed, as did others, that Williams had been murdered by order of church leaders in retaliation for the negative national publicity over the burning of Williams's library, which had contributed to Buchanan's decision to send the Utah Expedition. Richard Astill, a Mormon living in Sacramento, penned his opinion to Judge Aaron Farr in Ogden, Utah, written one day after the *Sacramento Daily Union*'s publication of Williams's death. Historian Connell O'Donovan's interprets Astill's poor handwriting and spelling: "Just taking up a newspaper and seen the misfortune of Misters Williams and Jackman who were murdered on the Bitter Spring. That's what I call pretty foul play. I should not like to reason out how that was one old debt that was due from that library fuss."[7] When Albina gave testimony years later, in a hearing to obtain benefits for her husband's Mormon Battalion service, she volunteered where the responsibility for her husband's death rested: "I am sure that the Mormon leaders hired the Indians to kill my husband. . . . [F]rom what the Indians said & from the relation existing between the Mormon Church & my husband at that time I have not the shadow of a doubt but what he lost his life thrugh [*sic*] the instigation to the Mormon Church."[8]

Hooper's letter to George A. Smith in May 1860 expressed personal regret over the death of his business partner and friend.[9] The Williams widows supported themselves by laundry and seamstress work they did, aided by their two slaves. They could earn credit in the LDS tithing office, barter for goods, or earn cash from non-Mormons. The households of Hooper and the widows were in proximity in the Thirteenth Ward. If a partnership did not already exist, Hooper likely engaged the widows for laundry and seamstress services through his male slaves, encouraging the widow's silence on the matter of Mormon leaders ordering Williams's death.[10] Mayor Smoot had a family of seventeen in the city's Twentieth Ward and may likewise have engaged the widow's laundry services through his slaves. Mormons and non-Mormon federal officers, businessmen, and professionals were their clients. These mundane matters are relevant to the downfall of Governor Dawson.

Traduced by Ex Parte Evidence

Convinced that federal officials' reports had been influential in Buchanan's decision to send troops to Utah, Mormons leaders hoped Lincoln's new appointments would be more tractable men. In the fall, Lincoln appointed R. P. Flenniken and Henry R. Crosby as associate supreme court judges, and Frank Fuller as territorial secretary. Former Wisconsin Territory governor James Duane Doty, though notorious and a distrusted financial speculator, was made superintendent of Indian Affairs.[11] Newspaperman John W. Dawson of Fort Wayne, Indiana, was appointed governor.

Dawson arrived in Salt Lake City on December 7, 1861, and departed on December 31. His actions in these twenty-four days merit thorough examination, but the core issue is apparent from examining LDS congressman John M. Bernhisel's moves in mid-January in Washington, D.C. On Sunday, January 19, he read a letter mailed December 30 from Utah by Brigham Young. It contained a citizen's affidavit alleging disreputable behavior by Governor Dawson while in Utah.[12] Bernhisel hastened to present it first to Lyman Trumbull of Illinois, Senate Judiciary Committee chairman, and then to William Mitchell, the Republican Indiana representative who had nominated Dawson. Next he met with Senator James R. Doolittle from Wisconsin, chairman of the Committee on Indian Affairs, and with Ohio senator Benjamin Franklin Wade, chairman of the Committee on Territories, to whom Dawson's nomination had been referred. Wade asked Bernhisel to leave the affidavit with him, but Bernhisel planned to personally show it to President Lincoln, which he did on January 22. Both Mitchell and Lincoln were vague on how Dawson came to be selected, unable to recall details of choosing this particular politician.[13] The affidavit Bernhisel delivered to Wade, to the several senators and representatives, and to President Lincoln assured that Dawson's pending approval by Congress would be defeated.[14] Bernhisel did *not* contact the other prominent Washington federal official who had figured in Dawson's selection: fellow Hoosier and Interior secretary Caleb Blood Smith.[15]

In May 1860 a major Cleveland newspaper carried the report that "Mr. Dawson, the able editor of the *Fort Wayne Times*, . . . has placed at the head of his columns the names Lincoln and [his running mate Hannibal] Hamlin . . . [because] if elected, his administration will be wise, eminently conservative, honest and national." Historian Neely suggests C. B. Smith helped arrange Dawson's appointment, yet was concerned that Dawson's absence weakened what little Republican support for Lincoln existed in the Democratic stronghold of Fort Wayne.[16]

Born in Cambridge, Indiana, in 1820, Dawson descended from slaveholders in several states, perhaps explaining his abolitionist stance. He attended common schools in Cambridge, had two years at Crawfordsville's Wabash College, studied law by apprenticeship, and gained admission to the bar. He received additional education in law at Transylvania University in Lexington, Kentucky, and returned to Fort Wayne to purchase and edit a Whig newspaper, the *Times and Press*. His editorial partisanship vacillated, at times taking a blatantly anti-Catholic and anti-Irish position. He lost a bid for the state legislature in 1854, running under the banner of the People's Party. He turned Republican when the party formed nationally in 1854–55, but held that slavery was a state issue, not a federal one. Running for secretary of state in 1856, he was defeated. Dawson believed preservation of the Union more important than slavery's abolition.

Without substantive evidence, the charge that Dawson was "a man of loose morals" has become a recirculating denigration. "It . . . is high time to rescue the facts of his life from oblivion," wrote historian-librarian Rex M. Potterf in his study of Dawson as the Herodotus of Fort Wayne. Potterf notes, "Mr. Dawson's championship of morality and his denunciations of the scandalous conduct of young men were frequent. He kept watch on the young men . . . who patronized . . . a bordello south of Fort Wayne." Dawson threatened them with exposure unless they mended their ways. The only negative view of Dawson in Indiana is found in political diatribe appearing during Dawson's run for secretary of state. R. D. Turner—editor of the *Jeffersonian*, the opposition newspaper of Richmond, Indiana—published of his political enemy and business competitor that Dawson was "'a low blackguard bully, and a blackleg,'" adding, "'He goes armed to the teeth it is said like an arrant coward. Decent people . . . would laugh at the idea of his having any moral character. He is said to have been insane at one period. . . . [N]o man is so utterly odious and infamous as he. . . . He has waged an incessant and most unmanly and unscrupulous warfare upon the foreign-born population of Fort Wayne.'" The "warfare" mentioned was alluding to Dawson's earlier anti-Irish, anti-German editorials.[17]

Relevant to Dawson's character was an 1872 *Daily Sentinel* article describing him as "a very temperate man" who made references to "the 'Black Beast' of intemperance" and whose articles contained "frequent and somewhat lengthy quotations from the Bible."[18] Dawson's

eulogy in the *Fort Wayne Gazette,* written by a person "for years inti-
mately associated with him and had rare opportunities to observe and
learn much of his private and public life," asserted that allegations
like those of Turner were routinely dismissed as jealousies arising
from "rivalry . . . and base slanders on the part of his opponents and
political aspirants [and] never deterred him." The eulogist declared
that, in fact, "he has lived to see these calumnies fade away and his
character stand clear and unspotted." At his death, the Fort Wayne
Bar Association met in special session and gave high commendation
for "his integrity, his courtesy, his independence and his revulsion
against sham."[19]

After Mormon leaders denigrated Dawson for alleged improper
conduct, a series of authors impugned him with propaganda, incestu-
ously citing one another without citing original sources:

    ❦ Mormon Edward William Tullidge wrote in 1886 that after
       arriving in Utah, Dawson "soon fell into temptation."[20]

    ❦ Hubert Howe Bancroft's 1890 history relied on Mormon
       records that Dawson was "accused of making improper
       advances to one of the Mormon women, and . . . was glad
       to make his escape [from Utah]."[21]

    ❦ William Alexander Linn called Dawson "a man of bad
       morals" in his 1902 book, *The Story of the Mormons.*[22]

    ❦ Orson F. Whitney in 1905 made no statement as to Daw-
       son's moral character prior to his arrival in Utah, but cit-
       ing the same Mormon records, he wrote that Dawson "had
       fallen into disgrace and left the Territory[, having] . . .
       made indecent proposals to a respectable lady of Salt Lake
       City, and fearing chastisement at the hands of her relatives
       or friends, hastily departed, on the last day of 1861, for his
       home in Indiana."[23]

    ❦ Mormon apostle Matthias Cowley commented in 1909 that
       Dawson "began a course of shameful debauchery."[24]

    ❦ In Andrew Love Neff's 1940 history of Utah, charges are
       taken directly from the Mormon allegation of 1861: "A
       social and moral delinquency led to Dawson's hurried exit."

Neff cited Cowley's "shameful debauchery" and claimed that Dawson was "a known libertine and debauchee."[25]

❧ Henry J. Carman and Reinhard H. Luthin, in their 1943 *Lincoln and the Patronage*, repeated Linn's 1902 words almost verbatim.[26]

❧ Dale Morgan's bizarre 1947 comment was, "The Saints had only to take one good look at this Indiana fop to know that they wanted no part of him."[27]

❧ Citing Whitney in regard to Dawson, Ray C. Colton's 1959 work, *The Civil War in the Western Territories*, claimed that "moral standards led him to a hasty exit."[28]

❧ In his 1960 work, Norman F. Furniss labeled Dawson "a man of loose morals," by extrapolating assertions that Republicans nominated him in order to rid themselves of him as "objectionable," but the author neglected to document any moral failings. Furniss ignored reports that Dawson's selection was due to his editorial support of Lincoln.[29]

❧ Historian Mark Neely's 1975 "President Lincoln, Polygamy, and the Civil War" used the phrase "bad morals"—taken from Linn—in describing Dawson.[30]

Mary Jane Woodger's "Abraham Lincoln and the Mormons" of 2012 cites only Furniss's *Mormon Conflict*.[31] Rumors and allegations surrounding a one-hour episode undermined the personal life and ended the professional status of a federal appointee who had been vetted by the officials of his home state and whose life record after returning there was spotless.

Never raised as relevant to his character was that Dawson had been married for five years when he came to Utah. He married Amanda M. Thornton, twelve years younger than he, in Fort Wayne's Second Presbyterian Church in 1855. Dawson did not explain traveling alone to Utah; perhaps he did not wish to disrupt the life of Charles H. Johnson, the fifteen-year-old nephew living with them, or he wished his wife to continue with the domestic services of Thersa Birger Adams, age nineteen, and her eleven-year-old sister, Ida. Dawson's letters and Fort Wayne records document that he planned for only a short initial stay in

Utah and, like many a federal official, he chose not to bring his spouse until appraising the Utah situation. His marriage, though childless, survived twenty-two years despite the damning publicity focused on his life in Utah. Potterf confirms, "The marriage was permanent. In Dawson's last days, [with him] bent under infirmity, Mrs. Dawson affectionately and faithfully cared for him through the long weary years of his illness."[32] She was forty-five when he died in 1877; she did not remarry in the thirty-seven years she survived him. Her burial at his side in the Lindenwood Cemetery in Fort Wayne suggests her lifelong commitment unmarred by any moral turpitude or infidelity by her husband.

Mormon journalist T. B. H. Stenhouse, writing as "Liberal," admitted that the Mormon intelligence gathering, usually highly efficient in finding anything questionable in appointees, had found none: "Dawson, of Indiana, is expected here during the present month. We don't know the gentleman."[33] A former employee of Dawson, an editor or journalist for the *Rocky Mountain News* in Denver, Colorado, shared his appraisal of the man's capability for the office of Utah governor:

> Mr. Dawson has been for some eight years past, editor of the *Times*, Fort Wayne, Indiana, and was one of the most influential and successful editors in the State. Having been for some time an employee of his office in Fort Wayne, and by this means become familiarly acquainted with him, we speak advisably when we say that he is peculiarly adapted, both as regards mental and physical ability and energy and decision of character, to fill creditably the office to which he has been appointed, and we bespeak for him a long, happy and prosperous career in his new official position.[34]

Before leaving Indiana, Dawson was familiar with contemporary information regarding Utah's theocracy. In an October letter to Caleb Blood Smith, he wrote that Mormons "have no homogeneity in common with other citizens of the United States," that their "domestic polity is not in consonance with the Federal government, its constitution & laws," and that "though they are professedly loyal to the constitution and obedient to the laws of the United States, they . . . are inclined to independence which may approximate rebellion."[35] On the coach ride to Utah, Dawson traveled with Superintendent Doty and Amos Reed, Doty's friend and secretary. Reed, a former resident of Fond du Lac, Wisconsin, had recently worked in Washington for Representative John Fox Potter. Doty had also recently visited Washington and New York, so the long ride gave Dawson further opportunity to hear fresh eastern insight on issues of importance in Utah.[36]

If Dawson read the *Deseret News* of October 23, he would have found reason to be wary of living with the Mormons: "We sincerely hope that no other than honorable men will be appointed . . . ; and should any more miserable specimens of humanity be sent here . . . , it is hoped that *they will be induced, shortly after their arrival, to retrace their steps* or continue their journey across the continent.[37] On a list of federal officials who were recent recipients of Mormon wrath, Superintendent of Indian Affairs Henry Martin stood high. Martin wrote privately on September 3 to a friend in Indian Affairs in Washington concerning matters he considered serious that had come to his attention.[38] According to the *New York Herald*'s September 20 article, Brigham Young "intended to send about one hundred and fifty families to settle in Uinta Valley" and that it was "of the utmost importance that the Government declare that section as Indian reservation, in order to prevent Mormons settling there." Martin's letter continued: "The Mormons are declaring their design to separate from the United States, and erect their Territory into an independent province. The Mormons further declare that no more Government trains shall pass through their Territory hereafter."[39] It is uncertain whether Martin knew that Superintendent Benjamin Davis had also written to Indian commissioner William Dole on June 30, 1861, saying, "For the Utes, Pah-Utes, Pah-Vants, and others who congregate at the Spanish Fork Farm, I recommend the establishment of a reserve, including the whole of Winter [Uinta] valley." This recommendation was forwarded through Secretary of the Interior Caleb Blood Smith to Lincoln.[40] Martin's letter in the *Herald* resulted in an intimidating confrontation with Mormon leaders. Martin quickly "consented to a public acknowledgment that he told the Government a little more or less than he now considers strictly warranted by the facts in the case."[41] An additional, deeply apologetic

A Ute Indian of Utah Territory. Courtesy of Special Collections Department of the J. Willard Marriott Library, University of Utah, Salt Lake City.

letter followed in the *Deseret News*.[42] He "disclaimed," he "begged," he "most sincerely regretted," and he "assured readers" that his apology letter was "written by me of my own free will and accord without any compulsion or restraint."[43] Stenhouse commented, "Superintendent Martin's appointment was not confirmed by the Senate. I should think Martin was much relieved by his deliverance, after that unfortunate letter to the Department."[44]

Martin's exposure of Mormons' land plans remained fresh in Young's memory two years later, when he told gathered apostles, "We have it in our minds to settle Bear River Lake Valley. . . . Now if you will keep this matter to yourselves nobody will know anything about it, but otherwise it will be telegraphed to old Abe Lincoln . . . and then it will be made a reservation of immediately to prevent us getting it." Lincoln, said Young, "is a damned old scamp and villain, and I don't believe that Pharaoh of old was any worse, or any wickeder."[45]

Arrival and Preparations

Dawson, Doty, and Reed arrived in Salt Lake City in the same stage on December 7. Dawson booked quarters on East Temple Street and the next day attended Sunday's church meeting in the LDS Tabernacle. Near this time, the medical office of Drs. Anderson and Chambers was visited by vandals, smashing windows, making "a general muss of the medicine bottles," and scattering "filth on the floor." Dr. Washington Franklin Anderson, who would by 1872 become Young's personal physician and would attend him in his last days in August 1877, offered "a reward of fifty dollars for the vandals' discovery and apprehension."[46] He was recently joined in practice by Dr. Robert Arthur Chambers, a former real estate developer, financial agent, and sometime medical practitioner in the Mississippi River town of Winona, Minnesota. Leaving his wife and two-year-old daughter in Winona, he traveled to California earlier in 1861 before joining Anderson and claiming himself a specialist in eye and ear problems.[47] It was Dr. Chambers who became Dawson's physician when he became seriously ill shortly before leaving.

Dawson devoted his first two days in Salt Lake City to preparing his address to the territory's legislature. On December 10 he opened with a treatise on the causes of the Civil War, without mention of the 1844–55 treatment of Mormons in Missouri and Illinois as relevant. Listeners warmed when he said that slavery was "the creature of local law" and "the subject of local or State, not of Federal legislation," hoping Dawson would view polygamy in like manner. Instead, he added, "The people of the South have unwisely claimed a political importance and power for their domestic institution of slavery, not belonging to it." Irritating to the Mormons were his statements that "the Constitution . . . was based on compromise," that "under the name of liberty many unblushing crimes have been committed," and that all "questions of domestic or local policy" should be "*consistent with the nation's organic law.*" Of the war, he challenged, "Men of Utah, are you ready to assist? . . . what answer will you make?" He lauded Indiana's "nearly forty thousand . . . already scattered from Missouri to the Atlantic Coast, under arms for the nation's defence" and noted that "that noble State is prepared to triple, on the field of battle, the number of her sons, where when nation's need calls for them." For those who opposed with arms the policy of the federal government, "there can be no question of its final result," for "the true interest of the people of Utah is with the Federal Union . . . and let no man urge a different course, for such will be a dangerous one." Without comment on Utah's alleged cash-strapped economy, he urged the payment of the $26,982 levied on the territory to "put yourselves before the world vindicated of the charge of disloyalty, which I regret to say has obtained some credence in portions of the United States." In finishing, he urged progress on two items of public good, long-standing interests of his own, but incendiary material with Mormons: legal land ownership, by extinguishing Indian claim and completing federal land surveys; and the formation of free, public "common schools."[48]

The *News* report lacked inflammatory rhetoric but was cutting. Dawson was able to express himself "in plain English" understandable "by the unlearned." The article concluded, tongue in cheek: "There are a few things . . . the people may not . . . cordially endorse, but . . . the injunction to be true to God . . . will unquestioningly receive the unqualified approval of all."[49] Privately, Young flamed to Wilford Woodruff: "They will not collect the taxes here, neither will they get 1,000 men to join the army. . . . I do now, and always have, supported the Constitution, but I am not in league with such cursed scoundrels as Abe Lincoln and his minions who have sought our destruction from the beginning. Lincoln has ordered an army [to Utah] from California, for the order has passed over on the wires."[50]

Dawson perceived no hostile reception to his address. December 13 found him in the church historian's office "chatting with members on topography of this country, etc."[51] Pleased with his speech, he mailed a copy to Lincoln on December 14. On December 16, Dawson mailed news of Utah to his employees in Fort Wayne for publication in his own newspaper. He was conciliatory regarding polygamy, writing that "the second and additional marriages . . . make a union regarded as perfectly virtuous and honorable." Of the social and moral climate, and the tolerance of moral impropriety, he said: "If there be signs of as much sensuality as I saw every day . . . in Fort Wayne, I have not seen the first one here. . . . Indeed, purity is strictly inculcated, and any departure is severely reprobated."[52]

On December 15, Young instructed the legislature—as he had done before—to form a memorial to Congress for statehood and to draft a state constitution: "Let the Convention ask the General Government to admit us as a State," adding ominously that "if they don't do it, tell them that *we* will organize a State Government."[53] The legislators responded, "hoping that the national government," overoccupied with a devastating war, "would accept Utah statehood as a *fait accompli*," as historian John Turner phrased it.[54] Henry Martin wrote that the bill was intended to "erect their Territory into an independent province."[55] The bill sailed unanimously through both of Utah's legislative chambers. Mormon leaders were utterly outraged when Dawson refused to sign it.

Dawson's trenchant criticisms were based on four substantive reasons, each consistent with legal statutes. First, the date of January 6 for the state convention did not allow time for the bill's approval by Congress as required in the 1850 Organic Act, which stated: "All laws passed by the Legislative Assembly and Governor shall be submitted to the Congress of the United States, and if disapproved, shall be null and of no effect." Young long ignored this requirement. For eleven years lawmakers had not submitted *any* Utah territorial legislation for the required congressional approval.[56] Second, the January date did not allow time for the populace to be informed or to canvas their vote. Dawson did not recognize that Utah "elections" were simply affirmations of appointments by Young and church leaders, often by letter indicating who had been selected to represent them.[57] Dawson's third reason: the bill fixed the boundaries of the new state, a power vested exclusively in the U.S. Congress. Finally, the process to statehood began with the documentation of population, then supplying evidence of the establishment and function of a republican form of government, then petitioning Congress to pass an enabling act, which would then authorize the formation of a constitution by the petitioning body. The requirement of true republican rule was ignored, and the enabling act was circumvented.[58]

However sound his reasons, Dawson's refusal brought him a near fatal response. Mormons believed that society was rampant with apostasy from religious truth, and saw themselves uniquely responsible for establishing God's Kingdom on earth. A sovereign entity—as a distinct geographical-political-civil-religious unity, its leaders men of the LDS Church priesthood—was the requirement. As David L. Bigler and Will Bagley explain, Young saw in the 1856 violence of Kansas "portents showing that the Kingdom of God would soon take its place on earth as a free and sovereign power."[59] By December 1861 the dissolution of the Union, secession, and open warfare were stronger evidence that a new opportunity for independence was imminent. But Dawson's veto was a crushing blow, and in Mormon eyes he instantly became the enemy to God's plans. Young said, "[We] petition for admission . . . to secure to ourselves the inalienable rights of American citizens. This we do to please ourselves and our God."[60] Young had previously written, "We desire admission . . . for the independent sovereignty which the act of admission carries with it."[61]

Mormons balanced at revolution's precipice with another resolution: "Should Congress again refuse . . . our just and rightful claim to majority as a State, we [will] organize a State government *in our own way, independent of all powers,* except Him who rules above, and, that, if brought to the necessary, we maintain these rights so long as a drop of the blood of our Revolutionary Sires runs in our veins."[62] This gave irrefutable evidence that the distrust of the Mormons was based not on past issues but on contemporary ones: Mormons were taking advantage of the War of the Rebellion with threats to also secede and declare themselves an independent commonwealth.

To Thaw Out an Icy Widow

It was alleged that later on Saturday, December 21, Dawson visited the home of Thomas Williams's widows, Albina and Pricilla. If he did so, it was almost certainly to be fitted for custom-made shirts and/or to contract for laundry services, rather than, as the LDS historical account relates, to solicit sex with Albina Williams. An affidavit signed by her constituted the ex parte material that Bernhisel shared with at least four prominent Washington federal officials on January 19 and with President Lincoln on January 22. Two versions of the handwritten affidavit are found; they are not identical. The first, dated December 26, is unsigned, and the second, in different handwriting, is dated December 30 and signed by Albina M. Williams and, as notary, ranking Mormon John T. Caine. The first account, including spelling and punctuation errors, follows:

> G.S.L. City Dec 26, 1861.
> Last Saturday morning ["Dec 21–1861" is inserted above the line] there was a coulered man came to my house, he asked me if I did sewing for Gentlemen, such as making shirts. I told him I did, and asked who it was that wanted shirts made; the coulered man said it was the governor. I told him to bring the shirts himself if he wanted me to make them, for I did not wish to see the Governor. In the afternoon a couple of gentlemen drove up, hitched their horses, came to the door and rapped. I went to the door, opened it; Mr Martin the Indian Agent, and another Gentleman stood there. Mr Martin says,

"Mrs Williams, allow me to introduce to your aquaintance the Governor." The Governor walked in directly past me, set his hat on a stand, hung his can on the mantle shelf and seated himself on a chair. Mr Martin retired. I stood in the oposite corner from the Governor, he said, "Mrs Williams are you alone"? I told him no, my family were with me. He says, "Have you a father, or brothers here"? I told him I had no brother here, but my father lived in the north end of the city. (He says "You Mormons I like pretty well, but the men keep their women entirely too close) My informant tells me you are a widow, proud reserved, and cold; I thought I would come down, and see if I could not thaw you out. I want you to be my friend and confident, and to allow me to come and sleep with you." I told him to leave the house, taking the fire shovel in my hand, telling him if he did not leave the house I would use this about him, or over his head. He left saying, "You will say nothing about this, I wish to part as friends."[63]

The "coloured man" mentioned was most likely William Hooper's slave, Dan, or one of two slaves owned by Mayor Smoot. This 325-word version of the affidavit does not include any further wording.

The second version, containing 523 words and dated December 30, is more formal, with correct spelling and in different handwriting from that of the first, and is notarized by the signature of John T. Caine:

Be it remembered that on this thirtieth day of December, A.D. 1861, before me, John T. Caine, a Notary Public in and for said County duly qualified and commissioned according to law personally appeared Albina M. Williams widow, of Great Salt Lake City, County and Territory aforesaid who being first duly sworn deposeth and saith: that on Saturday morning the twenty first day of December A.D. 1861, a coloured man came to my house and asked me if I did sewing for gentlemen, such as making shirts. I told him I did and inquired who it was that wanted shirts made, he answered that it was the Governor. I then told him (the coloured man) to bring the shirts himself if he wanted me to make them, as I did not wish to see the Governor.

In the afternoon of the same day two gentlemen drove up to my house in a buggy, hitched their horses, came to the door and rapped. I opened the door. Mr. Martin Ex-Superintendent of Indian Affairs, and another gentleman stood there. Mr. Martin says "Mrs. Williams allow me to introduce to your acquaintance Governor Dawson who wishes to have some sewing done." The Governor walked in directly past me, placed his hat on a stand, hung his cane on the mantle shelf and seated himself on a chair. Mr. Martin retired. I stood in the opposite corner of the room from the Governor. He said, "Mrs. Williams, are you alone[.]" I answered him "no my family are with me." He inquired "have you a father or brother here." I replied that I had no brother here, but my father lived in the north part of the City. The Governor then said "my informant tells me you are a widow, proud, reserved, and cold, I thought I would come down, and see if I could not thaw you out. You Mormons I like pretty well but the men keep their women entirely too close, they keep all the good thing to themselves. I want you to be my friend and confidant and allow me to come and sleep with you occasionally." I told him to leave the house[,] taking the fire shovel in my hand and telling him if he did not leave my house I would use this (the fire shovel) about him or over his head. He then left saying "you will say nothing about this. I wish to part as friends."

On the Thursday following being the 26th inst. Dr. Chambers called on me at my house[,] said he was attending the Governor as a physician and asked me if I did not consider what Governor Dawson said to me, when he visited my house on Saturday last, as a jest. I told him I did not. The Doctor then said if I would contradict the statement I had made relative to that interview, that the Governor would give me a fortune, for if the story became publicly known if would injure him at Washington, and further [the] deponent saith not.[64]

That Albina immediately recognized Henry Martin implies that he had been her laundry client. The first account does not note that he was no longer the superintendent of Indian Affairs, but the version signed by Caine contains that detail, suggesting that the second version was amplified by a person better informed.[65] The question arises as to why widow Williams did not instruct Martin and Dawson to leave, after having said she did not want the governor in her home. A reader of the affidavit might question that in the city's closely monitored society any man—Mormon or non-Mormon—would be able to comment on her private behavior.

Logic dictates that a professional man, arriving in a strange city with no knowledge of the facilities available to a person living alone in temporary lodgings, would seek the services of a seamstress or laundress and would query city residents—in Dawson's case, likely Hooper or Smoot—about where such services could be obtained. Logic denies that the highest federal official in the territory, recently arrived and knowing that he was undergoing the scrutiny given all new alien appointees, having written that "purity is strictly inculcated" in LDS society, would propose a sexual contract with a Mormon woman totally unknown to him. Even the editor of Fort Wayne's rival newspaper warned Dawson that he had "an arduous and difficult task to perform—a singular and unruly people to govern—who have driven off all the officers hitherto sent among them."[66] It is unreasonable that Dawson would propose sex in a household where circumstances were ill-suited, where privacy and anonymity were impossible. The household consisted of seven children, two adult female slaves, and Williams's other plural wife, Priscilla Mogridge Smith Lowery Williams.[67] Albina's youngest child, Norma Isabella, was thirteen months old, probably still breastfeeding. Visited by customers of the women's seamstress business, this was a household with scant privacy; their hours were busy with the demands of infants, children, and teenagers, and the house was located in the Thirteenth Ward of ever-vigilant and unforgiving Bishop Edwin Woolley. It was far from being a safe or inviting site for forbidden pleasure.[68]

It is also highly improbable that Henry Martin, so recently the object of severe Mormon ire, would have knowingly driven Dawson there for an inappropriate purpose. Martin would have known of

Bishop Woolley's inflexible rules and the severe punishments handed out by his two counselors, enforcer Jeter Clinton and one of Woolley's sons, John W. Woolley. However, a character assassination was fabricated and retold many times.

On Sunday, December 22, Young spoke in the Tabernacle, telling his audience, "It is better for us to go on and organize as a State, and then go straight on, and the quicker we shall know whether we are on our own ground. . . . I wish we were a State and in 10 days these Gentiles would hustle out."[69] Two days later he added, "Most of the officers which the Government have sent here are a hiss and a by word, and a <u>stink</u> in the nostrils of all good men, and there never was a wickeder man than the President of the United States, and his associates are very wicked men."[70] In a letter to Bernhisel, Young penned, "It is our purpose to no more endure the imposition of such men as Bill Drummond, Cradlebaugh, Crosby, Eckles, Gov. Dawson and others."[71]

If John Dawson had been rebuffed and chased from the Williams house, and if Judge Henry Crosby knew of Young's preaching that their very presence was noxious to "good men," the two were foolish to be on Main Street on December 23. On that day, five pistol shots were fired at Crosby by an unknown person, with intent to kill, both men insisted. Dawson's reward offer of one hundred dollars went unanswered. The *News* belittled the event, speculating that "the Judge gave some boy fifty cents to fire a blank pistol at him to break the dullness of the times," but the editor added an ominous prediction of matters brewing: "We hear of fearful things. We hardly dare believe our own ears. Before another moon . . . we'll have something to tell."[72]

Dawson spent Christmas Day riding out the "hurricane" that swept into the city from the northwest. His letter on December 26 to Caleb Blood Smith contains no hint of perceived danger. It dealt placidly with gubernatorial business: Indian claims, Mormons, and land ownership.[73] Dawson had experienced the onset of a general illness, and under the care of Dr. Arthur Chambers missed the Christmas ball to which he had been invited. The nature of his illness is uncertain; however, LDS records describe him with a complete mental breakdown, being "insane" from the mental effort of preparing his speech and from the stress that Albina would tell of his visit.[74] Although Dawson was ill on December 26, his nine-page letter to Caleb Smith is legibly written and well organized; it provides articulate coverage of professional matters and lacks evidence of being the work of one incapacitated by anxiety, stress, or sudden-onset mental instability.

Three other surreal allegations were made: Dawson had threatened to shoot T. B. H. Stenhouse if he published the Williams incident; Dawson was "gratified by Miss Katz" before his departure; and Dawson resigned his office of governor on December 31, although Dawson's records contain no such entry or claim.[75]

A Hard Road Home

Dawson vehemently denied hiring anyone for protection as he departed Salt Lake City, insisting, "I left the city without knowing that I had an enemy therein and feeling that I had no enmity to any one there."[76] The Mormon account claims that Dawson paid several Mormon men one hundred dollars each to protect him from being killed, or "becoming qualified for the office of chamberlain in the King's palace," as the LDS record colorfully phrased it. A double entendre appeared in the *News*: "That they will *do him justice*, and see him safely out of the Territory, there can be no doubt." It was added that "he had recently done what under the common law of the country, would, if it had been enforced, caused him to have bitten the dust."[77] That death or castration was the punishment under "mountain common law" for sexual interference with Mormon women has been addressed by several historians.[78]

Accompanied by Dr. Chambers, Dawson boarded the mail stage on the afternoon of December 31.[79] Not far out, they were joined by others; first was Moroni "Rone" Clawson, sent by Ephraim Hanks as a substitute because Hanks himself was not able to accompany Dawson, even after warning him that certain disreputable men were following him. "I handed him [Clawson] five dollars for his trouble," wrote Dawson, not knowing that Clawson was soon to be his assailant.[80] Dawson and Clawson rode ahead of the stage, arriving at Hanks' Mountain Dell Station in time to eat before the coach arrived.[81] Soon the New

Year's Eve crowd "was very drunk." Dawson and Chambers noted that their blankets and a beaver skin robe belonging to Henry Martin were missing, whereupon the stage driver, Wood Reynolds, knocked Dawson down. Clawson and others joined in the beating, stripping Dawson and other passengers of s clothes, blankets and valuables.[82] Although alleged to be Dawson's agent in bribery, Dr. Chambers was unharmed. Dawson described his attackers as administering "a most serious violence" to him, "wounding my head badly in many places, kicking me in the loins and right breast until I was exhausted," but he made no mention of his doctor providing protection or medical aid. "Dr. Chambers tied up his head and wounds," according to the Historian's Office record.[83] Dawson identified his attackers as "Jason Luce, Wood Reynolds, Lot Huntington, Mat. [John] Luce, Wilford Luce, Ike Neibaur and Moroni Clawson."[84]

Dawson may never have read the affidavit, but he never gave credence to widow Williams's allegation by openly arguing it. Dawson knew that neither Frank Fuller nor Judge Kinney had made or would make any official complaint over the extralegal process to which Dawson had been subjected. Dawson would have known that, in any inquiry, Fuller, Kinney, and Dr. Chambers would testify according to the Mormons' story. His task would be to prove that an event did *not* take place, a daunting obstacle. A failed inquiry would have done Dawson even more harm.

In a January 9, 1862, letter to Lincoln, Dawson recognized that Fuller's October telegraph attesting Mormon loyalty was "not warranted by the facts." In a second letter to Lincoln, written on January 13 from Fort Bridger, Dawson reported, "Henry Martin, late Supt. of Indian Affairs . . . had desired to return with me," but "fearing violence" and desiring to make "the Mormon authorities responsible for him [Martin] asked them for protection out of the Territory and they accordingly furnished him an escort at great expense and when they overtook me I joined them [to travel] to this place. . . . Even now there is not an authority who dares to represent the truth in writing for fear of being found out and life hazarded. . . . The horrid crimes that have been committed in this Territory, which have gone unpunished, have no parallel among civilized nations."[85] By February 27,

Dawson formulated an equally strong letter regarding the affairs in Utah, addressed to Indian Affairs commissioner William P. Dole, insisting that "no Federal Governor can stay in Utah or do his duty to the Government of the U.S." Dawson specifically warned Dole that the Mormons planned a "new constitution after the State of Deseret" and that if they did so, the federal government would find—not a seceded entity—but "the anomaly of an independent government existing within the limits of Federal Territory." As others had, Dawson urged the repeal of the territory's Organic Act, along with a military rule sufficient to "expel the Mormons." He warned of temporizing, for "[Governor Cumming] tried that and failed & instead of doing any good did harm by enriching the Mormons by the expenditures not necessary to the Utah Expedition & by making them more insolent."[86]

Dawson was never afforded an opportunity to respond to the damning ex parte materials that were sent by Brigham Young and personally delivered into the hands of members of Congress and President Lincoln. He was never interviewed by Congress, the United States attorney general, or other Washington officials. According to Bernhisel, Dawson wrote to Secretary of the Interior Caleb B. Smith, who "tried to smooth the matter over" and promised to give him an appointment.[87] A crime was alleged, a verdict arranged, and severe punishment meted to a territorial governor-elect without any process of law. Dawson never showed reticence or shame regarding his Utah position, for he signed each of his many 1872 "Charcoal Sketches," articles that appeared in Fort Wayne's *Daily Sentinel,* as "Hon. John W. Dawson."

The highest-ranking presiding U.S. official between Colorado Territory and the Pacific had received the same treatment as that inflicted on many men in the deep South: an unproved allegation, followed with a midnight beating and castration by vigilantes.[88] Within a month of Dawson's violation, Mormon officials were insistent that Utah's government was "republican," superbly qualified for statehood, and possessed of unblemished fidelity to the federal government. This was claimed despite Dawson's exposure of their quixotic efforts to form a sovereign state independent of that government.

The certainty of Dawson's castration rests on the preponderance of the evidence.[89] He was in Fort Wayne, Indiana, when he wrote in

February to Superintendent of Indian Affairs Dole. In that letter, Dawson asserted that his delay in appearing in Washington to supply testimony about Indian matters as requested by Utah's James Doty was due to "my extreme illness which began in Utah & has increased up to this time—preventing me from reaching Washington."[90] Dawson's illness had its onset in the last ten days of December and was consistent with a severe viral illness.

In an 1874 letter to Brigham Young, George Q. Cannon related, "One member [of Congress] told me laughingly to-day that he was going against Utah because one of his constituents—Dawson—had been half emasculated. I told him the story in our country was that he was only whipped. He replied that the man who had attended to him as doctor informed him that an operation had been performed. He closed by relating the joke, which I believe I have heard Bro. H. B. Clawson relate, about the preacher who was unfitted for Camp Meeting duties."[91] Later recaps of the life and contributions of Dawson also suggest his castration, for "on his return from Salt Lake he was waylaid and *maltreated so that he never recovered from the outrage.*"[92] Alene Godfrey, the editor of Dawson's reprinted 1872 historical articles, repeated the assertion that he "*never completely recovered* from the effects of the unfortunate incident."[93] Potterf concludes, "They attacked him and brutally and cruelly inflicted physical punishment and *mutilation* upon him."[94] His eulogy was also consistent with a brutal castration and an accompanying permanent injury, possibly to the penis, urethra, or bladder: "From the injuries received at the hands of the Mormons, Mr. Dawson suffered long, and at times terribly, yet he bore all with patience and fortitude rarely equalled and never excelled."[95]

In most of Dawson's years after returning to Indiana, he was described as a "pitiful invalid." The diagnosis of his illness is unclear, but his chronic, recurring ill health was likely not related to injuries inflicted in Utah. "His malady was diagnosed as dyspepsia affecting both bronchial and pulmonary organs," according to an 1877 report. He "visited a number of hygienic institutions," but the state of "medical science of his day had no succor for him."[96]

The Myth of Dawson's Attempt at Dalliance

An imbroglio arose from the frustration and anger of Brigham Young and other LDS Church leaders over Dawson's block of their fifth attempt at establishing a sovereign state. Federal agents in Utah were as a "stink in the nostrils" because they impeded the Mormons' divine purposes. Others beside Dawson were aligned against them, including Indian superintendent Henry Martin, postmaster Morrell, and Judges Crosby, Flenniken, and Cradlebaugh.

Fearful of going against the LDS priesthood, distrustful of its members because of her husband's many excommunications, knowing of rumors—if not facts—about his murder, and afraid of losing laundry and seamstress work, Albina Williams reported what she was told to report, or at least she did not contradict the story.

Inconsistent with the fire shovel story was the fact that prominent Mormon Albert Perry Rockwood had been specifically commissioned by Utah's legislature to investigate the reasons for Dawson's sudden exit. Secretary and Acting Governor Frank Fuller's letter of January 4, 1862, establishes illness as the most important reason and reconfirms Dawson's prior plans for only a brief initial stay in Utah. Fuller, seemingly unaware of Albina's story, wrote: "In answer to your letter of inquiry concerning the cause of Gov. Dawson's early withdrawal from the Territory, I present the following extract from a note received by me from that gentleman on the day of his departure: '*My health is such* that my return to Indiana, *for the time being*, is imperatively demanded; hence I start this day.' Gov. Dawson *announced* to me, *on the day of his arrival, his intention to return to Indiana at the close of the Legislative session*, but I am not aware that any reason as assigned by him for his departure at an earlier day, other than the one above given."[97]

If John Dawson had propositioned widow Williams and then been publicly exposed for so doing, there would have been no need—except a cover-up—for a Mormon legislative committee headed by faithful Rockwood to officially inquire into Dawson's reasons for leaving. If Dawson felt threatened by public allegations of misconduct, he would not have written to Fuller on his last day in residence that he was going to Indiana only "for the time being" before returning to Utah. Dawson would not have proposed a contract for future sexual service in Utah when he planned—even before leaving Indiana—to return after only a brief stay in Utah. Indiana historian Neely also confirms Dawson's planned departure from Utah: he had previously made specific commitments to return to Fort Wayne by the first of February, for "his own business required his presence," and "that it was important he should return" was well known to those in Fort Wayne.[98]

Doctor Chambers's visit—if one occurred—was most likely made to pick up clothing but was transformed into a tale of his participation in a bribery attempt. Chambers's actions following his exit from Utah hold convincing evidence that he was either complicit in, or agreed to support, the allegations against Dawson. Chambers arrived at the Cold Spring mail station, twenty-five miles east of Laramie, on January 25, at least three days ahead of Dawson. There he shared dinner with a traveling companion, Mr. Eaton. The meal was provided by Joseph Silver, a Mormon agent.[99] Eaton told Silver that "the Boys" brought Dawson to the stage station and gave him "a good Whipping," but Silver's letter to Young said nothing of Chambers's caring for the injured governor, either at Hanks's stage station attack or at Fort Bridger. Chambers told Silver of his plans to return to Utah in February or March, suggesting that he either did not know of being accused of participating in the bribery of Albina Williams or saw his participation as advantageous. Chambers assured Silver he had nothing against the Mormon people.[100]

Additional evidence is found in a February 1862 letter from Chambers to Lincoln. Living in an apartment for two weeks in Washington, Chambers was frustrated by his inability to obtain an appointment to see the president, after having requested a presidential appointment before leaving Utah. He carried letters from Fuller that supported his wish to be considered for the Utah governorship or any open judicial or executive opportunity. Requests for such prestigious appointments were extremely unlikely to be made unless the supplicant had been promised support and given recommendation letters by those who knew that the governor's post would be vacant. Chambers wrote:

To His Excellency, Abraham Lincoln, President of the United States,

It is now two weeks since I arrived from California [Feb 5th] and Utah via "Overland Mail Co." & Rail Road to this city, and having been sometime in Salt Lake City, Utah. Hon. Frank Fuller Secretary of that Territory gave me a Letter to you also to Several Senators & members here, he also sent by me to you a few presents of <u>his own</u> getting up.

Chambers lamented his misfortune in losing gifts and letters he was carrying to Lincoln when his coach overturned at a night crossing of "Blacks Fork of Green River," where he was nearly drowned. Lost was a letter introducing Chambers and asking for his appointment to "one of the Judgeships in Utah." His résumé as a small businessman, a sometimes real estate agent, and a physician looking unsuccessfully across the nation for a site to practice his profession revealed weak assets for the high positions he requested:

Also please be good enough to inform me at your <u>earliest</u> convenience wether [*sic*] the office of "Resident Minister" to <u>Honduras</u> is not <u>without</u> an occupant, and wether your excellency will consider an application from myself for this position, if not, be kind enough to inform me if the office of Gov. of Utah, is not also without an incumbent, Gov Dawson having left there & came home to Indiana not expecting to go back again, and wether you will entertain an application of mine for said office at all events if there are any vacancies in the Territories, either in the Judicial or executive or elsewhere I would be pleased to <u>know</u> it, and <u>where</u> and <u>what</u> they are, as in my application I think such testimonials as will meet with your excellency's favorable consideration.[101]

Dr. Chambers made no admission of being present at Dawson's attack and no mention of Dawson's injuries or his own participation in caring for the ill and injured man with whom he had a doctor-patient relationship, yet he claimed to know that Dawson "was not expecting to go back." He closed his letter with emphasis on the letters of his recommendation to two prominent federal officers outside Utah: "Inclosed I send you a Letter from Sec. Fuller to Hon. John [Fox] Potter of Wisconsin who is absent from the city on account of sickness in his own family, also one to Mr. [Schuyler] Colfax of Indiana." After weeks of unsuccessful petitioning to see Lincoln, Dr. Chambers finally realized he had been duped, and he returned home to Minnesota to his wife and daughter, whom he had not seen in more than a year. On his arrival in Winona, he resumed activities in medicine, business, real estate, and, later, law.[102] At no time did he either repudiate or validate the Mormons' story of Dawson's downfall.

Bernhisel ironically acknowledged that Dawson's sordid treatment changed little in the course of Utah events: "The Dawson affair has created but little sensation here."[103] The several personal tragedies associated with Dawson's brief time in Utah might have been avoided entirely had Bernhisel been able to communicate more rapidly. In a letter written before he could have heard of Governor Dawson's veto of Utah's attempt at statehood, and before his injuries at the hands of Mormon men, Bernhisel reported having received unusually warm receptions in the capital city from Secretary of State William Seward, from members of Congress known from previous sessions, from "Captain, now Quartermaster General Van Vliet," and from "General [Frederick W.] Lander, late superintendent of the Pacific wagon road." Bernhisel explained, "I mention these little matters as indications of the feeling at present existing toward our Territory, indeed, we as a people were never before so popular as we are at present, and this popularity is mainly if not entirely owing to your telegraphic dispatch, saying that Utah had not seceded, but was firm for the Constitution and the Union."[104] The *New York Times* corroborated this, noting that the telegram "certainly created a more kindly feeling than was formerly cherished toward this polygamic community."[105] Bernhisel also reported that Pennsylvania's representative had said, "If you are loyal to the Union, we will let you alone, and you may have fifty wives apiece if you wish." He added further good news that addressed Young's complaint about appointments from outside the territory, with a note that "the President has promised to nominate Hosea Stout, to the Senate for District Attorney of the United States for the District of Utah."[106]

Bernhisel reported to Young that when Indiana's William Mitchell was shown the Albina Williams affidavit, he ironically mused, "In all his [Dawson's] letters from Utah to his . . . paper, he spoke in favorable terms of our people [Mormons], saying that they had been abused."[107]

The Conspirators

The portrayal of Dawson's actions is inconsistent with his personality, his past behavior, and his awareness that he was unwelcome and closely watched in Utah. Two comments regarding Dawson, made by T. B. H. Stenhouse after he left the ranks of the trusted Mormons, suggest complicity by at least two individuals in order to benefit or to save themselves: "Governor Dawson had been betrayed into an offence, and his punishment was heavy" and "He was almost immediately a victim of misplaced confidence, and fell into a snare laid for his feet by some of his own brother-officials."[108] The three men most likely to have laid the snare were Frank Fuller, who benefited immensely in the years following the Dawson incident; John Fitch Finney, who shortly—at Brigham Young's selection—became the first non-Mormon to represent Mormon Utah in Congress; and hapless Dr. Robert Arthur Chambers, to whom empty assurances of a presidential appointment were made.

It was Fuller who telegraphed his personal acquaintance President Lincoln at the eastern completion of the telegraph lines. He associated with Governor James W. Nye of Nevada, Governor William Gilpin of Colorado, Nevada's Senator William Stewart, Representative Thomas Fitch, and Samuel Clemens, whose career he boosted by sponsoring a lecture appearance in New York City.[109] In her 1868 history of this period, Catherine V. Waite, the wife of Judge Charles Waite, wrote of Fuller: "He was one of the few federal officers in Salt Lake at that time who was so fortunate as never seriously to offend Brigham Young. . . . If he saw any difficulties approaching by a little shrewd management he carefully avoided them"; and "He enjoyed for a long time the confidence and apparent respect of Brigham to a greater degree perhaps than Kinney."[110] On August 14, 1863, Fuller was made a California commissioner of deeds, and in 1865 he was one of the founders of a posh watering hole in New York City, the Travelers' Club. In the 1870s he was a journalist for the Mormon newspaper in Salt Lake City, the *Herald*; he was elected in February 1872 as a delegate to that year's constitutional convention and a month later was awarded a certificate of nomination as the Utah (State of Deseret) representative to Congress.[111] At the end of 1871 and in the spring of 1872 he was a lobbyist in Washington, working with William Hooper, George Q. Cannon, and several others attempting to achieve statehood for Utah and to blunt or defeat legislation restricting the Mormons.[112]

Kinney was warmly welcomed to Utah from his post as supreme court judge in Iowa. In January 1854 his entrepreneurial efforts led to his establishing the Union Hotel, where one of his guests was the French naturalist and traveler Jules Rémy, present in Salt Lake City to interview Brigham Young.[113] Rémy's 1856 account asserted that Kinney's reputation with Brigham Young "was so black that he [Young] is afraid of soiling his own fame by entering" Kinney's hotel.[114] One of Kinney's first official acts was his conduct of the charade—mislabeled as a trial—of several Indians accused of the killing of Capt. John Gunnison. Bigler writes that Kinney explored "new worlds of farce" in this trial.[115] Kinney returned to Iowa in the spring of 1856 "to afford his children a better opportunity for attending school" and for a run at political office, but unlike his contemporary federal officials, he did not offer any of the scathing criticism on matters in Utah that helped precipitate Buchanan's launch of the Utah Expedition. Finney was practicing law in Nebraska when reappointed to his Utah post in June 1860.[116]

By early 1861 he was the only federal official in Utah deemed acceptable to Young. According to Young's office journal for February 22, 1861, "The President remarked Kinney has done well, but just as the wind blows so is Judge Kinney."[117] Historian Catherine Waite wrote of Finney: "He is an open apologist and advocate of polygamy," adding that "the impartial truth . . . requires us to say that the uniform course of Judge Kinney has been to aid and abet Brigham Young in his ambitious schemes with but little regard to the advancement of the interests of the whole country or the requirements of indiscriminate justice."[118] Finney overtly cooperated with the Mormons in the Morrisite affair of 1862 and their subsequent trial in 1863. Young gave no public explanation when he arranged Finney's "unanimous election" in 1863 as Utah's delegate to the Thirty-eighth Congress, replacing the faithful John Bernhisel.

The evidence leads to Fuller, Finney, and befuddled Dr. Arthur Chambers as those who joined Mormon leaders to hatch the myth of Dawson's improprieties. In 1868, Waite wrote of Dawson: "Not yielding, like his predecessor, to all the views of Brigham Young, he soon became involved in difficulties from which he was unable to extricate himself. He had not the nerve and ability to sustain himself in his position. The Mormons saw this, and at once resolved upon, planned, and accomplished a brilliant *coup d'état*, similar to that [entrapment] practised upon [Lt. Col. Edward J.] Steptoe."[119] An additional entrapment would shortly be attempted on Stephen S. Harding, another Indiana man next appointed as Utah's governor.

Dawson's mistreatment in Utah came from frustrating Mormons on two pillars of the theocratic kingdom of God. Of primary importance was his obstructing the plan of Utah's Mormons for unilaterally declaring sovereignty and independence—even statehood—thereby avoiding the changes required in the prescribed pathway. Dawson recognized this, for his January 13, 1862, letter to President Lincoln laid out that "the real cause" was his veto of a bill calling for a convention for the illegal "forming of a constitution and State government."[120] The second pillar was the principle that leaders in God's Kingdom were to be appointed from loyal Mormons, not men imported from Babylon, who were ineligible for God's direction. A January 1862 letter from Bernhisel to Young also suggests the possibility that Dawson's downfall might bring Young a reappointment to the governorship. Bernhisel told Young, "I called the next morning on the President and urged your appointment," and he told Lincoln "that the people of Utah would prefer Ex-Governor Young to any other man living." Lincoln replied, "I will consider your application with others, for I shall no doubt have plenty of them."[121]

From 1851 to Young's death in 1877, the Saints claimed loyalty and love for the Constitution—as they interpreted it—and utter contempt for officials appointed to oversee its application in Utah, whom they considered incompetent and immoral. By January 1862, Judges R. P. Flenniken and Henry R. Crosby were added to the list of officials who had fled Utah in fear for their safety. Unfortunately, the next round of federal officials, Governor Stephen S. Harding, Judge Thomas J. Drake of Michigan, and Charles B. Waite of Illinois, also had traumatic experiences in Utah.

CHAPTER 4

Disloyalty amid Peace
and Prosperity, 1862

Another "rebellion" in the breeze on the far-off plains of Utah.
Here is the beginning of a new trouble. Here is a conflict at our
doors.

New York Post, April 30, 1862

The Saints devoted January to the pursuit of statehood, the Mormon legislature proceeding as though John W. Dawson had not
entered the territory and his refusal to sign the legislation for the State
of Deseret had not happened. Brigham Young did express slight concern to Representative John Bernhisel about how Dawson would "represent" his mistreatment in Washington. Young disingenuously assigned
blame for the lawless acts inflicted on Dawson to the criminal element
that came to Utah as camp followers of the U.S. troops, alleging that
"the Federal Government alone is responsible for this order of things
[and] it must not complain if the 'representatives of Federal authority'
[Dawson] are among the sufferers."[1] In the same letter, Young reported
information from Robert T. Burton and Robert J. Golding, who both
accompanied Dawson from the Weber River to Fort Bridger. Dawson
somehow "entertained none but the best of feeling towards the Citizens of Utah, and did not attack them for the maltreatment he had
received . . . but only to those who perpetrated it." Young cautioned Bernhisel, "It is not known how Gov. Dawson will represent us in the east."[2]

"Dawson cannot do us any harm," answered Bernhisel after contacting the Indiana delegates, who, on hearing the Mormon allegations, seemingly sensed blood in the water. "[Now] not a single member . . . speaks well of him," Bernhisel wrote, "and it is thought that he ought never to have been elevated to that office."[3] However, the *New York Times* had a different report: "There are those here who think that [is] an incorrect estimate; for . . . a practiced, naughty man would have been too shrewd to make such a blunder as the one that used up Mr. Dawson."[4] When information reached Young's ears that some of the men inflicting Dawson's injuries had been killed, the prophet angrily gave his stamp of approval: "For thieves, cut-throats, liars, adulterers, and every foul and wicked person . . . [i]t is "time to cleanse the inside of the platter."[5]

Voting at the mass meeting for electing constitutional convention delegates was unanimous, as usual. Legislators also "unanimously" elected territorial officers, and in January they drafted a constitution for the State of Deseret. The "Ghost Government of the State of Deseret" meeting was repeated every January for nine years, each time passing the same legislation its members then passed while sitting as the bona fide Utah Territorial Legislature. This was as being "at once pitiful and inspiring, tragic and ridiculous" because the "Saints' eyes were on heaven," but happenings on earth were not seen.[6]

Rain made voter turnout low for ratifying the constitution for the desired state of Deseret, yet it received a unanimous vote. Considerable enthusiasm was needed for a voter to walk miles "through slush to tender his vote, when that vote could in no wise affect a result," since there was no opposition, explained the *Times*.[7] The candidate list was not a republican one: only a single candidate, Brigham Young, appeared for the office of governor; only Heber C. Kimball for the office of lieutenant governor; and only John M. Bernhisel for the office of representative to Congress. One name only was entered for each county's representative to the lower house, and one name per county to the legislature's higher house.[8]

Young insisted: "If the General Government is not disposed to receive us into the family of States we still have a right to be governed by the Constitution of our own choice, and this according to the constitution of the United States and the declaration of independence [*sic*]."[9] Young held that the Constitution made no provision for government to appoint, organize, and control territorial officers and laws. He was sustained by malleable Judge Kinney: "It has been seriously contended by able jurists, that there is no authority given to Congress by the Constitution to organize these Territorial governments. . . . [T]he best way to . . . remedy the difficulty, is to exchange them for State governments."[10] James Duane Doty sided with the Mormons, saying that if a state's constitution is "republican," then its citizens "have the right . . . to put an end to their Territorial servitude."[11] Doty had received Mormon approbation when he "entered at once upon the duties of his office" with a better understanding than that of his predecessors, but a warning was sounded: "If he does not profit by the examples of those who came before him he will be unwise."[12]

The *Times* asked, "Are we [in Utah] a Territory or are we a State?" and then described the present situation: "We have a Territorial organization, and we have a State organization. We have a Territorial Acting Governor, and we have a State Governor beginning to act. We have a batch of high civil officers appointed by the National Government, and we have a corresponding batch of high civil officers elected by the 'sovereign people' of the 'State of Deseret.'" The *Times* surmised that "the questions of 'to be, or not to be,' and what to be," had great importance.[13]

The highly regarded *New York Post* was blunt about the simultaneous existence of incompatible systems. With Young seated as the governor of the State of Deseret and Ashley's bill for the punishment of polygamy passed, the *Post* declared, "Here is a conflict at our doors." Mormons were demanding "immediate admission into the Union, while Congress declares their fundamental system [polygamy] a crime." Because the Mormons wished "to supersede the territorial form of government," the federal government would have to choose "between the admission of Mormons" and the "forcible suppression" of a rebellion. Although Mormon leaders had once given in to "Federal power," but they now seemed "ready to re-enter the lists [of call to military service] and stand by the doctrine of 'State rights.'"[14]

Young moved to several threats. On July 6 he spoke in the Bowery: "The Congress of the United States have lately passed a law to punish polygamy. . . . In doing this, they have undertaken to dictate [to] the Almighty . . . and those who handle edged tools, unless they are skill-ful, are apt to cut their fingers; and those who hand out insult to the great I Am, . . . are apt to get more than they have spoken for."[15] Young warned that before the States make "war upon us they could consider that probably the Mormons would burn everything up, cut down the telegraph lines," and "it might be worse for them this time than it was last."[16] On January 6 he had said, "If they undertake to install their officers here at the point of the bayonet as they did in 1857 they will not fare as well," for federal officers "would defile every bed in this ter-ritory." Lt. Col. Edward J. Steptoe was in Utah for that purpose, Young declared. He warned a young lieutenant, "Stop your present course, or I will kill you so help me God; I will cut your damned throat. You may tell it to your brother officers that if they infringe upon us we will kill every devil of them."[17] James Ferguson warned his wife of Union sol-diers: "Their very look is a basilisk's that devours and kills, and the air they breathe is poisonous. Oh, my Jane, won't you teach my little ones to hate them and walk and talk with none but those that God allows?"[18]

In the Tabernacle, Young repeated that if the federal govern-ment "should be so unwise as to again attempt to oppress us" and sent "armies" to Utah again, "they will find the road up Jordan a hard road to travel."[19] The *Deseret News* framed the position of the Mormons: if "admission into the family of States should be refused, they *feared not the consequences* of throwing off the Federal yoke and assuming the right of self-government."[20] The *Times* wrote that Mormon leaders remained steadfast: "The resolution appears to be unbending to put an end to the territorial form of government, Congress pleased or displeased."[21] Support came from southern Utah colonies, as Calvin C. Pendleton of Parowan wrote: "Many of us feel that 'Live or die, sink or swim, survive or perish, we are for the Constitution' . . . and dare risk the consequences."[22]

Young prayed publicly "in the name of the Lord Jesus Christ" that *only* those who "persecute thy saints and people" should "be wasted away, and removed" and that authority should "pass into the hands of the just."[23] Should his words find their way to Washington, he added: "We mean to sustain the Constitution of the United States and all righteous laws. We are not . . . treasoners, secessionists, or abolitionists. We are neither negro-drivers or negro-worshippers. We belong to the family of heaven, and we intend to walk over every unrighteous and unholy principle."[24] In the *Millennial Star,* Young eschewed modesty regarding the status of the Mormons, "for we are . . . the ambassadors of the Almighty and messengers of salvation to the children of men."[25]

Non-Mormons in Oregon observed that Mormon leaders "have pursued a policy to drive off the officers of the General Government, . . . formed a constitution, and . . . given notice that polygamous Utah must be admitted into the Union as an independent State, or that she will remain out of the Union as an independent nation."[26] Young was courting secession, rebellion, or war, and his followers were obedient, even enthusiastic.

Young claimed that Utah owed no tax, because all land remained legally the possession of the federal government. He was correct that land had not been cleared of Indian claim, federally surveyed, or purchased from the U.S. government.[27] The *Times* treated Utah's war tax payment sympathetically, stating that it was a formidable burden for a territory "remote from the ordinary avenues of trade," where local commerce produced "but little cash," which went "with remarkable celerity into the hands of the merchants."[28] George A. Smith insisted that "there is so little cash in circulation among us," overlooking thirty thousand dollars spent in February for "machinery."[29] Nonetheless, the legislature abolished county and city taxes and raised the amount due the federal government by levying a one percent tax on all property previously taxed by the territory. Utah petitioned Congress to remit Utah's quota, but this was denied and the tax of nearly twenty-seven thousand dollars was paid. The *Times* explained that much of the money was raised by Mormons who had taken over the whiskey trade, collecting fees for both liquor licenses and the liquor stalls.[30]

The constitutional convention's plea, coauthored by five prominent Mormon leaders, focused mainly on attaining statehood but also articulated a concern for public welfare, usually missing from their fiery condemnations: "We wish to preserve an asylum of peace, where, when you get tired of war, you can lay down your arms and repose in safety." Utah's nonparticipation in the war could benefit the ravaged nation, for the Saints would "cultivate the earth . . . that when famine presents his gaunt visage, and sweeps desolation over the land," the Mormons would have "means on hand to administer to your necessities," when the "paraphernalia of war shall have expended itself in fruitless efforts."[31]

Stephen Harding—A "Chosen Vessel of the Lord"

Stephen Selwyn Harding was tapped by Lincoln as Dawson's successor for Utah's governorship. Born and raised in Palmyra, New York, Harding had visited his hometown in the summer of 1829 and was brought into personal contact with several of the earliest members of the nascent LDS Church, including Joseph Smith, Sr., and his wife, Lucy Mack Smith ("Mother Smith"); Joseph Smith, Jr.; Oliver Cowdery; and Martin Harris. From that visit, he gained insight into the religion's origins that was unique among all federal appointees to Utah Territory.

The eldest son of thirteen children born to David and Abigail Hill Harding, he was twelve when the family emigrated to Ripley County, Indiana. At age sixteen, with only nine months of formal education, he began teaching school. He entered the study of law in the office of William R. Morris of Brookville and, by age twenty, was licensed and opened a law office. In competition with older and better-known lawyers, his practice in Richmond was not successful. Fall in 1828 found him on a New Orleans–bound Mississippi steamboat to take charge of property for a client. With letters of recommendation from prominent Indiana lawyers to former Arkansas governor James Miller, Representative. Henry H. Gurley of Louisiana, and Louisiana governor Henry Johnson, he sought opportunities for practice.[32] A lifelong opposition to slavery was born in the human markets of New Orleans and ended any interest in moving south: "I witnessed scenes . . . not fit to be named among Christians. And yet, the buyers and sellers in this human shambles could be found . . . often-times at a Christian Church!" Harding was reminded of Thomas Jefferson's view on the consequences of slavery and paraphrased his remembrance as "'I tremble for my country when I consider that God is just, and that His justice will not sleep forever.'"[33]

In 1829 Stephen Selwyn Harding encountered several men
in Palmyra, New York, who would soon became founders
of the LDS Church. During his tenure as Utah's governor,
his relationships with Mormon leaders in the territory
were abrasive, and he was threatened with death or forced
removal from office. Used by permission of the Utah State
Historical Society.

Eight unproductive months found Harding down to his last dollar;
he financed his home passage by clerking on an upriver steamboat.
Once home, he decided to visit family living in Palmyra, while admitting, "I had never heard of Mormonism by that name." In a newspaper, he had chanced upon "an account of the finding of a book of
metallic plates, in the neighborhood of Palmyra." However, he said,
"in trying to recall the identity of Joseph Smith, the alleged finder
of the plates, I had only a dim recollection."[34] Writing to his cousin
Pomeroy Tucker, Harding recounted, "Upon my return to Palmyra
and learning that Martin Harris was the only man of any account, as

we say in the West, among all of his near associates, it was but natural that I should seek an early interview with him. I found him at the printing office of the Wayne County *Sentinel* . . . where the *Book of Mormon* was being printed. He . . . expressed great pleasure at seeing me."[35] In another letter to Tucker, Harding gave details of his Palmyra visit: "I went with Joe Smith . . . to his father's house, in company with Martin Harris and Oliver Cowdery, for the purpose of hearing read his wonderful 'translations' from the sacred plates." Harding reminded his cousin, "I was in the printing-office with yourself, and also the three pioneer Mormons named, when the proof-sheet of the first form of the book, including the title page, was revised by you. A corrected impression of it was passed around to the young prophet and his attendant disciples, all of whom appeared to be delighted. . . . By consent of the brotherhood, you finally gave this 'revise sheet' to me as a curiosity."[36]

Mother Smith told Harding that he had appeared in her dreams; she repeatedly questioned Harding as to whether he had dreams, until he relented and gave her a response. To her and Martin Harris he told a false story that he had experienced a dream but could not reveal its contents. Harris repeatedly troubled Harding about the contents of the dream, until Harding "proceeded to relate a wonderful dream—that never was dreamed—during the course of which he took occasion to describe some characters that had appeared to him on a scroll—presenting some of them with a pencil, a mixture of stenographic characters and the Greek alphabet, rudely imitated."[37] Seeing the characters Harding had drawn, Harris fell to his knees, speechless, but on recovery replied, "O Lord, God! the very characters that are upon the plates of Nephi!"[38]

Calvin Stoddard, the husband of Joseph Smith, Jr.'s sister Sophronia Smith, was an early believer in Smith's religion but did not have the conviction to preach until benefited by a joke played by Harding and one Abner Tucker. At midnight the two went to Stoddard's house, awakening him with three heavy blows on the door, then intoning in a stentorian voice, "The angel of the Lord commands that before another going down of the sun thou shalt go forth among the people and preach the gospel of Nephi," on pain of death and his ashes thrown in the wind. By morning, Stoddard was preaching door to door in "full faith."[39]

About to board an Erie Canal packet boat to Buffalo, en route back to Indiana, Harding was met by Harris and Cowdery, who said that he was "a chosen vessel of the Lord" and that they must "pursue" him. Harding wrote that the two men informed him of the angel's commands that "I must remain in Palmyra until the printing of the *Book of Mormon* was completed . . . [and then] go to the city of London and there remain until the Lord would inform me what to do." When asked how this would be financed, Harris answered, "The Lord will find the money. The *Book of Mormon* will sell for thousands and thousands of dollars, and I can furnish the money any day." Years afterward, Harding wrote, "Many times . . . have I asked myself: 'What if I had accepted the apple plucked from the tree of knowledge of good and evil, crucified my own sense of honor and manhood, and sold myself to the devil of ambition!'"[40] Harding concluded that "the intellectual forces" of Joseph Smith, Jr., had been "greatly underrated," but that "in deception and low cunning he has no peer." While living among Utah's Brighamite Mormons, Harding made no reference to these illuminating experiences with the founders of the Church of Jesus Christ of Latter-day Saints. However, the Saints knew of Harding's Palmyra visit and of the *Book of Mormon* title page he donated, for years later he wrote, "After my appointment as governor was known" the people "heard a thousand times from bishops and elders that the hand of the Lord was in it."[41]

Passing into the Land of Shadows

Harding returned to Indiana, opened a law practice in Versailles, and in October 1830 married Avoline Sprout of Chautauqua County, New York. He joined the Liberty Party, running twice for election as Indiana's lieutenant governor. In 1848 he attended the National Free Soil Convention and became sought-after as an ardent abolitionist speaker. Anti-slavery led him to make his home in Ripley County, fifteen miles from the Ohio River, as a way station for fugitives on the Underground

Railroad. Male slaves were hidden in his basement, while women and children were hidden in the upstairs bedrooms or in the false ceiling on the second floor.[42] Biographers emphasized his three passions: temperance, abolition, and opposition to polygamy. Etta Reeves French observed, "Harding always felt that Mormonism was a hoax and welcomed the chance to vote against polygamy in the election of 1856."[43]

In February 1860, Harding was appointed to the Indiana State Republican Committee. He wrote to his family in early 1862 that his friends in Washington were urging his appointment, and on March 14 he called on Bernhisel to say he had been promised Utah's governorship.[44] Among his supporters were Indiana's Schuyler Colfax and George W. Julian, who presumably judged him able of bettering Dawson's stay.[45] Secretary of War Edwin Stanton, concerned with Indian dangers on the Overland, furnished a company of cavalry to guard Harding's travel. En route to join his military escort, Harding wrote his longtime friend George Julian of the difficulties he anticipated: "I am about to pass into the land of Shadows—where strange people, with a stranger religion, await my coming." Referring to Representative Justin Morrill's pending anti-polygamy bill, Harding foresaw its adverse impact: "Following its passage, matters will be very much complicated in Utah and my position be rendered much more difficult— Yet the law in itself is right . . . [but] at this time only evil will result from its passage."[46]

Harding was joined by his son Attila, who had recently served in Missouri with the Twenty-sixth Indiana Infantry.[47] They and the escort passed the night of July 4 on a mountain spot where they estimated the snow depth at thirty feet in some of the gullies. After Fort Laramie, their escort reduced to fifty dragoons, Harding saw the bloody site near Sage Creek where Indians had recently slaughtered two men. Nearing Salt Lake City, Harding was met at Kimball's stage station by Acting Governor Frank Fuller and Superintendent Doty. Quarters awaited at the Townsend House.

Harding wrote of the next day: "Brigham Young and his 1st Counsellor Gen'l Wells, called in his <u>carriage of state</u> with beautiful matched horses to be introduced to me at my rooms. . . . It is the first time that the Great Prophet and his minister ever paid such honor to a Federal

Governor.⁴⁸ I understood at a glance . . . and was most gratified that they called. They staid [*sic*] about an hour, and I must say that Brigham Young is a great man. He invited me to call at his office at my pleasure." Overconfident, Harding added, "I know exactly how to deal with ~~him~~ such a man,—that is, I will be Governor, and he may be Prophet and Priest."⁴⁹

No stranger to protocol, Harding wrote a request to Young: "The Governor desires to pay his respects to President Young at his office tomorrow afternoon at 3 o'clock, or at some other hour if agreeable." The visit took place on July 17, as suggested.⁵⁰ George A. Smith's after-meeting comments to Hosea Stout were less than ingratiating: "The governor tells me he hopes we would take as good care of him as he did that paper [the title page of the *Book of Mormon*]. I told him we should certainly do it for he had placed it in a box where the rats could get access to it, and we would not do worse than that."⁵¹

When no place had been afforded him in the Mormon celebration of July 24, Harding made it known that he would leave the city, and "presto change," the next morning, he received a complimentary ticket to the evening's ball. Young announced at the gathering, "Ladies and gentlemen, I have the honor of introducing to you Gov. Harding who is an invited guest." Afterward, Harding was introduced to the dozen or more of Young's wives and "in particular to his youngest and handsomest one, and to her sister, also his wife," whom Young desired to be his "partners for the occasion." Harding said he thought Lucy, "the favorite one as the saints say," to be among the "prettiest women that I have seen in a long time" and a dance partner who "knew all the 'cuts and calls.'" Harding astutely observed that as Young moved about, "many middle aged persons, women in particular, reached out their hands and touch[ed] his garments, as the women of the period when Christ was on earth, touched the 'hem' of his garments."⁵² Harding's not questioning the excesses of his welcome, his easy manipulation by the Mormon elite, and his apparent ignorance that all his letters and telegrams were read are surprising for one experienced in political intrigue.

In the city a month, Harding innocently wrote home to his son Selwyn, "I have been making many friends . . . [and] my speech at their celebration of the 24th July has acted like a charm on them." He reported,

The Bowery, near the temple site in Salt Lake City, provided shade for the Saints during sermons by Mormon leaders. Used by permission of the Utah State Historical Society.

"[Many say] that God inspired me to say what I did on that occasion, or I never could have spoken so much in so little."[53] Saddened that he could not attend his daughter's wedding, he found comfort in "discharging great and solemn duties to our Common Country now in need of the service of the best of men." Harding pictured himself as "[a man] in the midst of a powder house with his hands full of matches," adding that "unless he is very careful he might let one drop and the consequences might be dreadful." Although noting that Mormons "come to me almost every day and tell me they must look to me for protection," their leader's speeches were "so defiantly against the Government" that he had "refused to attend the Bowery for two Sundays."[54]

Spreading to the Banks of the Rhine

As war entered its second year, Spain, France, Mexico, Great Britain, and Russia—all with vital interests in North America—watched carefully. Mormons continued asserting that the Civil War would metastasize to Europe. Young preached, "The people in the States have violated the Constitution in closing their ears against the cries of the oppressed [Mormons], . . . and now war, death and gloom are spread like a pall over the land, which . . . will sooner or later spread all over the world."[55] George Q. Cannon, Young's trusted head of LDS affairs in Europe, warned that "the nations of Europe will . . . get their part in due time."[56] Cannon, as "an Apostle of Jesus Christ," served England an ominous prophecy: "In the name of my Master, . . . England will suffer and mourn even as America is now doing, and as all other nations shall do unless they repent and receive the message that has been sent unto them. They shall weep tears of blood and bewail in bitter anguish the miseries which they shall be forced to endure."[57] Orson Hyde's predictions were similar: "Many nations will be drawn into the American maelstrom . . . [and] when the demon of war shall have exhausted his strength and madness upon American soil, . . . he will remove his headquarters to the banks of the Rhine."[58] Young advised Cannon that at any sign of "the beginning of war between England and the Northern States," Mormon leaders should "make their escape to some port in the States or Canada."[59] However inconsistent with Kilkenny cat prophecy, the *News* urged action "before England, France, or other European powers may . . . take a hand in the fight."[60]

The U.S. military realistically weighed foreign involvement. Brig. Gen. George Wright, in San Francisco, assured Leland Stanford, California's governor, that "in case of a war with a maritime nation . . . the enemy would most certainly be directed to this city, the great entrepôt of our possessions on the Pacific coast." At Fort Point and Alcatraz Island, 140 heavy guns were in position at commanding points. "Batteries can readily be thrown up," Wright predicted, "and with such naval force as can be concentrated in the harbor it is believed that this city would be safe."[61]

Mr. Morrill and Two Elephants in the Room

In Utah, polygamy was an elephant unrecognized in the room, but nationally it received increasing attention and criticism. In the legislature, Young and others spoke on their right to statehood while avoiding mention of polygamy, yet the two subjects were increasingly intertwined. Justin Morrill's bill "to punish and prevent the practice of polygamy in the Territories of the United States" passed the House in April and the Senate in June. Only two senators—both from California—spoke against it, fearing that Mormons would retaliate by cutting transcontinental communication and travel, thereby isolating California, as in 1857.[62] Only a year earlier the *San Francisco Bulletin* charged that "Mormons wield complete sway over the Indians on a portion of the Overland Mail route," adding that "whenever these fanatical people have dared to exhibit their revenge against the 'gentiles' they have not failed in doing it."[63] Still, the *Bulletin* was not pleased with its state's senators: "California will scarcely be thankful to her Senators for putting her against the rest of the Union in their abhorrence of and protest against polygamy."[64] The *New York Times* was against the bill, although for a reason that had nothing to do with polygamy: "Better have no law upon the statute book . . . than let it lie unexecuted, to teach contempt for all law, and demoralize the people." According to the *Times*, the law could not be enforced because Young "exercises a control no less absolute than that of the strongest military despotism on earth."[65]

John Wilson Shaffer, who was familiar with the Mormons and would become Utah's governor in 1870, wrote to the *San Francisco Bulletin*, predicting that the Morrill Act would "remain substantially a dead letter" unless the Mormons were to forget the lessons of 1858 and "begin to drive out the federal officials, incite the Indians against Overland emigrants, or outrage Gentiles living in their midst." Should this happen, the *Bulletin* believed, "the administration could enter upon no policy of war that would be half so popular, as one in which twenty-five thousand of the veterans from the fields of Shiloh and Richmond should be employed in removing polygamy from within our borders, no matter what the costs."[66] Without funds for use in enforcement, with Washington occupied with the agon engulfing the nation, Morrill's law was, in fact, ignored. As the *Times* predicted, Mormon leaders were emboldened.

In July, Bernhisel presented Hooper and Cannon to Secretary of State William H. Seward as Utah's new "senators from Deseret." Seward indicated that population size was subordinate to "other considerations" preventing Utah statehood. Missouri's John Phelps identified the other elephant, reminding Bernhisel of the "atrocious affair" of the "horrid Mountain Meadows massacre." Bernhisel lamented that the killings were continuing "to do us as a people incalculable injury, and will prove a serious obstacle to our admission into the Union as a sovereign and independent state."[67] The tumult of a massive war effort, and the triplet of small population, plural marriage, and remembrances of mass murder, were all against them. By mid-1862, Utah's quest for statehood with its carefully worded constitution, whose creation ended the political career—and almost the life—of John W. Dawson, remained ignored in the desk of Ohio representative James M. Ashley.

The Finest between the Missouri and San Francisco

By will and determination, Young led his people to wrest from Utah's arid lands the means to feed and house themselves. Now he moved to create a center for entertainment and culture, one unequaled within hundreds—even thousands—of miles. Young's interest in theater began in the Nauvoo period, when he, Erastus Snow, and George A. Smith took part in plays in Joseph Smith, Jr.'s dramatic company. Young's plans for a "new" theater for Salt Lake City were publicized in February 1861, and construction soon under way. It would exceed the Tabernacle in size and accommodation, having rock walls, "exhibit pit, boxes, and galleries—where the neither poor nor rich, the 'upper ten' and the 'gods' can severally shine, according to their rank and pockets."[68] December 1861 found "the theatre [roof] covered in" and the interior "the scene of hasty finishing exertions."[69] Built on a lot owned by Young at the corner of State Street and First South, the theater was projected to cost at one hundred thousand dollars or more by completion, and "for that outlay," the News said, "we are again indebted to President Young."[70] Although it was not fully finished, a "select audience" of LDS officials, and men who had worked on the building were welcomed with their families at the inauguration on March 5, 1862. A crowd of 1,200 to 1,500 people filled the building for a play and dancing.[71]

"Brigham's big theatre continues well filled twice a week," the Times stated, adding that "for two hours before the curtain rises, the people

Brigham Young's illustrious Salt Lake Theatre, under construction circa 1862. It was judged the finest such structure between the Missouri River and San Francisco, and its performances were lauded. Used by permission of the Utah State Historical Society.

are there, and in another hour the house is comfortably filled." The institution was patronized by "all the patrician and plebeian blood of Mormondom alike," said the *Times*.[72] Young remarked that he preferred humor on the stage, admitting, "There is enough tragedy in every-day life."[73] In mid-October, "carpenters, plasterers, and painters" were busily readying the theater in time for "the festive season."[74] In November, Young contacted Thomas A. Lyne, then of Denver, with whom Young had previously had experience in the theater. A prominent actor from Philadelphia, Lyne had played in Joseph Smith's dramatic company in Nauvoo and was vastly popular, never failing to draw enthusiastic audiences.[75] When Young wrote to Lyne, he noted that the theater's reliance on amateurs "will preclude my entering into any [financial] arrangement with you." However, many young people "would be pleased to take lessons in elocution," he suggested, and "in this way you might do comparatively well."[76]

"The theatre is rapidly approaching a serviceable completion ... and the 'Deseret Dramatic Association' is exceedingly busy with rehearsals," the *Times* reported in December.[77] On Christmas night, 1862, John T. Caine took the stage, saying, "For all the grandeur of conception, magnificence of design and beauty of execution, which characterize everything that surrounds us here tonight, we are pre-eminently indebted to him who is ever foremost in every good work, the patron of the fine arts, the friend of the industrious talent, and in the fullest and broadest sense the first citizen of Utah."[78] Young would certainly have basked in the warm applause that followed.

Shiloh Takes Johnston

The Saints congregated in the Tabernacle on the first Sunday in April for their customary spring conference. Young repeated his often used condemnation of those "who are now destroying each other, but who were once united in taking from us our homes and possessions, and winked at the shedding of the blood of our best men, . . . and sisters, of our fathers and mothers, of our wives and children." Blood would soon flow as rivers, "for the press is only just beginning to come down upon the ungodly."[79] As these words were spoken, a ghastly event was unfolding at Pittsburg Landing on the Tennessee River, more than 1,600 miles from Salt Lake City. Some forty-nine thousand men under the command of Ulysses S. Grant joined in battle against fifty-five thousand troops of the ranking military leader of the Confederacy, Gen. Albert Sidney Johnston. A substantial portion of Grant's men had seen battle at Fort Donelson, while the Confederates were largely untested. Johnston initiated the encounter, surprising Union forces, planning to drive them northward into the swamps of the Snake and Owl Creek rivers. Confederates were decisive on the first day, but at great human cost, including the death of General Johnston, when he ignored the bullet wound that had transected the popliteal artery behind the knee, causing hemorrhage that proved fatal. On the following day Union forces strengthened, regrouped, and prevailed, in what became the bloodiest battle in United States history up to that time, with thirteen thousand Union casualties and nearly eleven thousand for the Confederates. The bloodbath became known as "Shiloh," a name some scholars contend comes from the Hebrew, referring with tragic irony to a "place of peace." At the end of a general update on the war, the *News* blandly noted—without judgmental or editorial comment—that "among the slain . . . was Gen. A. S. Johnston, late commanding the Department of Utah."[80]

The prewar writings of journalist and infantryman Ambrose Bierce were sympathetic to the Saints and critical of the treatment levied on them. A survivor of the Ninth Indiana at Shiloh, he left his personal account, with its subtle handling of euthanasia and its vivid images:

> Dead horses were everywhere; a few disabled caissons, or lim-bers, reclining on one elbow, as it were; ammunition wagons standing disconsolate behind four or six sprawling mules. Men? There were men enough; all dead, apparently except one . . . a Federal sergeant, variously hurt, who had been a fine giant in his time. He lay face upward, taking in his breathe in convulsive, rattling snorts, and blowing it out in sputters of froth which crawled creamily down his cheeks, piling itself alongside his neck and ears. A bullet had clipped a groove in his skull, above the temple; from this the brain protruded . . . in flakes and strings. I had not previously known one could get on, even in this unsatisfactory fashion, with so little brain. One of my men, whom I knew for a womanish fellow, asked if he should put his bayonet through him. Inexpressibly shocked by the cold-blooded proposal, I told him I thought not; it was unusual, and too many were looking.[81]

While thousands of corpses were still not buried at Shiloh, Young wrote to his friend and counselor George Q. Cannon that "Peace, prosperity, content, and good works continue on the increase in the 'Mountain Home' of the Saints, and our God is abundantly blessing His cause and people."[82]

Civil War Dead Unqualified for Heaven

Three months after Shiloh's carnage, Heber C. Kimball, of the First Presidency, proclaimed that the thousands of Civil War dead could enter heaven *only* by becoming a Latter-day Saint. According to Kimball, the war's victims became disembodied spirits "unprepared to enter the presence of God." However, Mormon men, holding "the same priesthood that Christ and the Apostles held," would now "become the saviors of men on earth and in the spirit world." Kimball continued: "Therefore the thousands slain in the present war are not without hope. It is our calling to preach life and salvation to them even in another existence.[83]

Although it has been publicized in recent decades, the theological tenet of the Mormon faith that offered membership in God's one and only true church by proxy baptism after death was not widely known in 1862. To non-Mormons in the war's years, Kimball's expression may have seemed a variant of the Mormons' claim that those killed in the war were due special punishment, for they were stained with the "blood of the prophets."

One hundred thirty years after Kimball's assertion, Thomas S. Monson, then the second counselor in the LDS Church First Presidency, celebrated the news that some of the Confederate dead could receive the LDS temple rites that would allow heaven's blessings. Monson had received a letter from William D. Taylor, a Canadian and Mormon living in the South who had worked for years at the task of "extraction"— that is, the compilation of identifying information of the long-dead, for submission to LDS temple authorities. Under Mormon theology, members have an obligation to perform proxy baptism and vicarious temple ordinances, not only on behalf of Civil War veterans, but for *all* humans who have lived. The practice does not require approval by surviving descendants, since it is believed that those existing in afterlife may accept or reject the action. Taylor's letter to Monson proudly reported: "We have sent for temple work just over 101,000 names. . . . I exult when another regiment is . . . ready to be sent to the temple, and my soul is pained when the information . . . is insufficient for a soldier's work to be submitted."[84]

Hundreds of thousands of Civil War dead lay in graveyards—named or unknown—after rites by their Baptist, Methodist, Presbyterian, and Catholic officer or their Jewish rabbi. Half of the war's dead were never individually identified. A soldier might pin to his shirt his hastily written name on a scrap of paper, but no name tags were issued. There was no official next-of-kin notification. Unknown thousands were never buried, their body parts feasted on by animals, their bones scattered. Thousands lie anonymous in mass graves, honored simply by why and where they fell. Descendants of those of the Grand Army of the Republic, the Sons of Confederate Veterans, and the United Daughters of the Confederacy might be angered by the condemnation that their Civil War ancestors were considered unfit for God's presence in heaven and would remain so until baptized as Latter-day Saints. They may be incensed at the present-day temple work that has not been requested or authorized, just as Jews have been by unauthorized LDS baptisms of those who died in the Holocaust, who are also—by Mormon doctrine—as yet ineligible for an exalted level in afterlife until they become Mormons.[85]

Utah's Volunteers during the Civil War

The troops remaining at Camp Crittenden departed Utah Territory in July 1861, leaving no U.S. military presence to deal with Indian violence or to protect the non-Mormons of Utah's populace. The vacuum resulting from their exit brought about Utah Territory's one and only contribution of manpower in the Civil War.

For ninety days in 1862, one company of cavalrymen guarded the Overland Trail and the telegraph lines and discouraged Indian depredations by their presence. These militiamen neither saw nor engaged Confederate troops or Southern sympathizers; they did not engage any Indians, although a number of whites had been killed and mail stations attacked prior to their deployment. The only casualty was one cavalryman who drowned while fording a river on horseback.

On April 14, Young angrily wrote to Bernhisel, "I am informed that a telegram has been forwarded from here over the signatures of

[Acting Governor] Frank Fuller, [Judge] J. F. Kinney, and six others, not one of whom is a permanent resident in this Territory, to the Secretary of War, asking him to authorize James D. Doty, Superintendent of Indian Affairs, to raise [troops] and officer[s for] a regiment here for three months, or until U.S. troops can reach here, under the general allegations that the property of the Overland Mail Company and the settlers are in danger from the Indians." Young did not explain his acquiring the April 11 private telegram but said, "So far as I know, the Indians in Utah are unusually quiet. . . . Besides, the militia of Utah are ready and able, *as they ever have been*, to take care of all the Indians within our borders, and are able and willing to protect the mail line, if called upon to do so."[86] This assertion is very different from Young's September 1857 statement claiming the helplessness of Utah's militia in securing safe passage of the Baker-Fancher emigrant train through Utah, when he had pronounced that "*the Indians we expect will do as they please.*"[87] Offended that territorial officials would act without his approval, Young repeated his opinion expressed in the previous day's mail: "I have made many inquiries of reliable persons well informed on these points, and . . . no depredations have been committed by Indians upon the mail or any mail station this side of the Rocky Mountains."[88] In his letter to Superintendent of Indian Affairs William P. Dole, Doty's retort that Young's observations were "without foundation in truth" did not strengthen Young's regard for the new appointee to Utah.[89]

The response of Lt. Gen. Daniel H. Wells on April 24 proved that Young was incorrect in denying hostile Indian acts.[90] Summoning one Joshua Terry, Wells wrote, "Owing to reported disturbances with the Indians at Green River and on the Sweet Water it has been deemed advisable to send an escort with Col. Hooper and others who are going to the States. . . . [A] detachment of twenty men has been made to go under Col. Robert T. Burton to be ready to start tomorrow . . . with horses and the necessary rations for 30 days." Wells said simply, "We depend upon your going."[91] Burton's instructions were to protect Colonel Hooper, Gen. Chauncey W. West, and Judge Kinney "as far as it may be deemed necessary." Hooper and West carried copies of the proposed state constitution and other papers relating to statehood.[92] Wells added, "There must not be any drinking of spiritous liquors, neither swearing or abusive language . . . , and treat every body with courtesy and prove there is no necessity of trouble with the Indians when white men act with propriety."[93]

Wells also ordered the support of Lewis "Uncle Jack" Robinson, the Nauvoo Legion's quartermaster general at Fort Bridger: "The Station Keeper at Greenriver has been killed, . . . two Coaches on the Sweet Water had been set upon by Indians, six men wounded and Stock, Mail of Coaches lost." With Hooper and West headed east, Wells wrote, "it is proposed that we send an escort of some twenty men . . . and we think you had better come and go out to Green River with your men as soon as possible."[94]

Brig. Gen. Lorenzo Thomas, U.S. adjutant general—very familiar with the Mormons from the 1857 Utah War—proposed several measures to secure the Overland mail and travel near and in Utah. He considered the proposal of California's Senator Milton Latham that Brigham Young raise a company of one hundred mounted men to protect the mail, the route, and the telegraph line from Indian depredations and to recover the stock and property of the mail company. With telegraphic communication and Young's "influence over his own people, and over the Indian tribes around," Thomas recognized this plan as "the most expeditious and economical remedy to the obstructions to the mail route." However, Thomas noted that because Young was "not a functionary recognized by the United States Government, . . . a requisition for volunteers from Utah should be made upon the Governor of the Territory."[95] But four days later a telegraph message reached Brigham Young by order of the secretary of war: "By express direction of the President of the United States you are hereby authorized to raise, arm, and equip one company of cavalry for ninety days' service . . . to protect the property of the telegraph and overland mail companies in or about Independence Rock, . . . and will be continued in service only till the U.S. troops can reach the point where they are so much needed." Thomas cautioned, however, that "*it will not be employed for any offensive operations* other than may grow out of the duty hereinbefore assigned to it."[96] Young immediately ordered Wells to the ready. Young's propensity for managing detail is found in his instructions to Lot Smith: "Be kind, forbearing, and righteous in all your acts. . . . Let there be no card playing, dicing, gambling, drinking intoxicating liquors, or swearing. . . . Ever be kind to your animals and give them the best care . . . and be ever on the alert that they neither stray nor are stolen from you. . . . A liberal use of molasses will be more healthy than too freely partaking up salt meat. . . . [B]uild a good storehouse, in readiness for the supplies."[97]

According to the *News*, the request for military volunteers "was responded to with that alacrity that has ever characterized Governor Young and the citizens of Deseret when their services have been required by the Government, either to fight the battles of their country or to protect its citizens." This contrasted with the Mormons' frequent contention that they had been *forced* to provide troops in the 1846–67 Mexican War.[98] Doty, one of the six whose telegram requested the troops, risked Young's wrath with another letter to Superintendent Dole, complaining that "the President having conferred upon him [Young] the authority to raise troops and withheld it from the officers of the United States" had resulted "only in increasing his [Young's] power in this country and not that of the United States."[99] Doty's letter exemplifies the backstage antipathy between Doty and Young that has received little attention in earlier accounts. It would worsen with time.

The *Roster of Union Soldiers* lists ninety-five men serving in the Lot Smith Company.[100] The names of the seventeen officers were published in the *Deseret News* on May 7, together with names of two farriers, two musicians, one saddler, and one wagoner, exactly as authorized.[101] Each man was required to furnish his firearms and mount; ten baggage wagons and four wagons carried supplies and food. The *New York Times* correspondent cast a discerning eye on the gathering cavalrymen: "[They were a] fair mixture of elderly and young heads, rough-and-ready looking fellows, not a martinet in the Company, inured to labor and mountain life, rough riders up and down the mountain, and most of them passionately fond of horseflesh, with probably a slight sprinkling of experienced soldiers from European armies . . . [and] a considerable proportion of fair shots and some dead ones in the Company. The arms—rifles of many kinds—Sharpe's, Yeagers, Mississippi and European. The horses, mostly California and Indian, some . . . Rosinantes."[102]

Lot Smith's company arrived at Fort Bridger on May 11, "all safe," the *News* reported, adding: "[It] will soon reach the most eastern point on the route indicated by the order requiring the service. The most timid can now pass that way with much safety."[103]

Burton reported by telegraph on his twenty cavalrymen guarding Hooper and prominent Mormon Chauncey West: "We have seen no Indians on the route; found all mail stations from the Green River to this point [Deer Creek] deserted, all stock having been stolen or removed and other property abandoned to the mercy of the Indians or white men. We found at the Ice Spring station . . . a large lock mail—twenty six sacks, a great portion of which had been cut open and scattered over the prairie. Letters had been opened and pillaged, showing conclusively that some renegade whites were connected with the Indians in the robbery." Burton reported he had not been able to identify those responsible, but some among the marauders "spoke English plainly" and one spoke "the German language."[104]

The Stars and Stripes were raised at Fort Bridger to greet Smith's command as it entered to celebrate the Fourth of July.[105] On July 19, Indians struck one of the oldest ranches of the Wasatch Range, only six miles from Bridger, netting one hundred horses and mules. Smith and sixty-two men were shortly in the saddle, to pursue and punish.[106] They tracked for eight days—going north to the Snake River valley, near the Three Tetons, almost three hundred miles from Great Salt Lake City. With spent horses, food supply dwindling, they returned without firing a shot at Indians or rebels. Their one fatality was twenty-two-year-old Pvt. Daniel McNichol, of Bountiful, Utah, who drowned while crossing the flooding Lewis Fork of the Snake River.[107] On August 6, Young wrote, "A part of Cap. Lot Smith's command have come in, their 90 days having expired, and the remainder are daily expected, they having made a detour . . . in pursuit of some horse thieves."[108] Burton's cavalry returned "in excellent health" on June 1, after encountering one small band of Indians and confirming that some mail plundering was by "white Indians."[109] The *News* praised Smith and his men, for "they all did their duty and nobly comported themselves."[110]

On August 24, Stanton authorized Gen. James Craig at Fort Laramie to raise one hundred men for cavalry service and to reenlist Lot

"White Indians" were more feared than their Native counterparts in attacks on Overland Mail and emigrant trains. Photo by G. E. Anderson, taken near Springville, Utah, about 1896. Used by permission of Will Bagley and the Prairie Dog Press.

Smith's troops for an additional ninety days of service.[111] The news of Young's refusal of this request came by way of an August 25 dispatch by Craig to Gen. Henry Wager Halleck, reporting Harding's conversations with Young. Craig telegraphed, "Harding . . . in dispatch of to-day in relation to re-enlistment of Mormon troops, after saying he had interview with Brigham Young, closed the dispatch as follows: 'You need not expect anything for the present. Things are not right.'"[112]

Harding's cautious brevity is explained in his letter four days later to Secretary of State Seward:

I dare not put this communication in the common mail bag, but send it by secret express. I shall have to ask one favor at your hands,—this communication must be only for your eye and that of the President. It must not be placed on the files of your office. My reasons for saying this are cogent. ~~My life would not be worth a "pins head" if the Powers here should learn its contents.~~ . . . It is my deliberate opinion that no communication from this Department to the General Government can be sent from this point, through the P.O., without danger of its contents being known here, at "Headquarters" by which I mean the power that rules the people here with an absolutism scarcely to be credited by those not in a situation to see and hear for themselves.

Young's refusal to re-recruit Mormon troops was part of the evidence that added to Harding's judgment of Mormon disloyalty to the federal government. Harding added that Young and others were "constantly inculcating in the minds of the crowded audiences . . . that the Government . . . is of no consequence, that it lies in ruins." They taught that Joseph Smith's prophecy was being fulfilled, that fighting will consume both sides in the war, that "the Saints are to step in and quietly enjoy the possession of the Land, and also what is left of the ruined cities and desolated fields." In the Bowery were those "who 'chuckle and wink' at each other when some disastrous intelligence reaches us concerning the great army of the Union," and "not one word, not one prayer, has been uttered or offered up for the success of our cause." If the language coming from the pulpit in Utah were to be heard in "any of the States, . . . the Provost Marshall would soon take charge of the individual."[113] Harding asserted that the *Deseret News* "pretends to publish verbatim the remarks of Brigham Young" but that "all such sentiments . . . are studiously kept out of print." For Harding the question was not what Young and his followers would *do to sustain* the present government but "what they will not do to destroy it." Harding did not endorse further enlistment of Utah militia, insisting that weapons should not be placed in the hands of people who might turn against the government at any moment.[114]

On August 25, Young telegraphed General Thomas: "Harding has received a telegram from Brig. Gen'l Craig, at Laramie, for the re-enlistment of Captain Lot Smith's company and their being marched to Laramie. Please inform me whether the Government wishes the

militia of the Territory of Utah to go beyond her borders while troops
are here from other States who have been sent to protect the mail and
telegraph property."[115] MacKinnon identifies the catch-22 absurdity
into which Young had placed himself: he was unwilling to recruit Mormon troops because troops were headed to Utah from California, and
troops were headed from California because Young would not furnish
troops in Utah.[116]

The *New York Tribune* outlined Young's reason for refusing an additional tour: "the 'boys' were busy with their harvesting, and . . . he did
not think they would be willing to do anything more in the military
line until they should see a pile of 'green backs.'" To Young's allegation that "Government is going to pieces on the principle of the
Kilkenny-cat fight," Harding's response was blunt: "I prophesy against
your prophesy. These difficulties will be settled, and there will be more
cats left than ever were heard of in Kilkenny."[117]

The Out-and-Back Trains

Cannon wrote from Liverpool, "Our emigration from Europe this year
will in all probability exceed 3,000 souls. It is cheering . . . to see so
many breaking loose from Babylon and misery, and it has the effect
to stir the Saints up to diligence."[118] Organizing disparate elements
of the process began in February, when both Joseph Watson Young
and Horace S. Eldredge were appointed to take charge. Assurances
to the Saints in Great Britain that the passage to Utah would be safe
had the same ring of those made to the Saints of the ill-fated 1856
Willie and Martin handcart companies. According to the *Millennial
Star*, "Affairs in the States [the Civil War] should not be any reason for
those who have means delaying their departure . . . but should rather
be an incentive to them to gather to Zion as early as possible," for "the
dangers and difficulties of the journey will be lessened to them . . . who
faithfully keep his commandments."[119]

By mid-April three hundred wagons and teams were ready to
depart Utah, whenever trail conditions allowed. Each man of the
First Presidency financed a private team for personal purchases.[120]

Hiram Clawson wrote the contract particulars to Edward Creighton, in Omaha: "For 375 oxen, 40 wagons and outfit of wagon covers, bows, yokes with bows, chain tents, cooking utensils and tools. Ten Thousand five hundred dollars."[121] Additional purchases nearly doubled the bill, for Young wrote to Eldredge in June, "I have forwarded to you $19,000 in gold by [name missing], and $590.00 in drafts with Senator Hooper."[122] Noteworthy: Gold was available for freight and emigration expenses but not for Utah's war tax.

The *Times* printed that Salt Lake City "has been thronged with innumerable ox teams and covered wagons . . . fitting out for the Missouri River, to return . . . with freight and souls of the Mormon immigration." The article continued, "The teams are from all parts of the Territory, from four to eight yoke per wagon, the wagons of good and moderately light kind, chiefly Chicago make, and the oxen invariably young." With each team "well armed and provided," and each wagon carrying eight to ten hundred pounds of provisions, chiefly flour, the teamsters and immigrants would be well fed as they returned.[123]

Six Mormon trains started eastward by May 19. Young wrote to Eldredge, in New York City, that on the way were 244 wagons, 2,080 oxen, 267 teamsters, 26 guards, and over 70 tons of flour. Eight private emigrant companies, at least six commercial companies, and six for the transport of the poor were tallied for the 1862 season. Young reported that the year's immigration "will probably reach nearly 5000" and that "much woolen, cotton, and other machinery will be brought."[124]

There Is Not Room for Two Caesars

Condemnation of apostates by Jedediah M. Grant and Brigham Young marked the 1856 Mormon Reformation, but violence against apostates did not end with cooling of the reform fervor. William Kirby, formerly of Yorkshire, England, learned this firsthand when he decided to leave Payson, Utah, after two winters and a summer in Zion as a convert. Before departing, the Kirby family stopped in Ogden to collect money owed him by a brother and sister Ledgway. On hearing that the family was leaving, Sister Ledgway chose to leave with them, causing tension between herself and her husband, who—unknown to the Kirbys—reported the matter to LDS Church authorities. William Kirby wrote of the experience:

> While I was hitching up my team to leave, a remark from a stranger passing by to Bro. L. [Ledgway] spoke volumes to myself. . . .
> "Is that apostate going to leave?"
> "Yes," Bro. L. answered, "He is all right; everything is right."
> "Well," said he, "He had better leave, or we will help him."
> "He is all right; that is all right," remarked Bro L.
> By these remarks I knew there was a storm gathering . . . and that Bro. L. was now doing his utmost to save me. . . . I had heard the highest priesthood in the church admonish the brethren to cut the apostates off from the church under the chin, or a little below the whiskers, at the same time drawing his finger across his throat. I had learned by this time . . . what they were capable of doing. [125]

The exit of the U.S. military under Col. Philip St. George Cooke began a fourteen-month interval when objectionable non-Mormons, and especially apostate Mormons, were in greater than usual peril. An ominous prediction of "fatal resistance" was contained in the title of a *Deseret News* article decrying a June outbreak of "lawlessness." Some "outlaws" had congregated at South Weber, where they were engaged in the "first armed resistance" to Utah Territory's laws. These "desperadoes" were "providing themselves with arms," the *News* contended, and "some of the band . . . made threats of using them."[126]

The events leading to more than four hundred men and women gathering in a primitive enclave near the Weber River had begun several years earlier with a man named Joseph Morris. Today's mental health experts, using *Diagnostic and Statistical Manual of Mental Disorders*, might diagnose Morris with a post-traumatic stress disorder or some degree of functional psychosis.[127] But hundreds of his contemporaries saw him—as he saw himself—a visionary, a new prophet of God who was to supersede the false, failed prophet Brigham Young.

As a solitary apostate, Morris was harmless, but by June 1862 he had nearly five hundred baptized followers with an equal number anticipating baptism.[128] "The news spread throughout the Territory that a new prophet had arisen who had been denounced by the Church, which led many to inquire into the matter. . . . Thus the membership continued to increase."[129] Apostasy carried risk at all times in Utah, but the organized apostasy of large numbers in the absence of any U.S. military proved particularly fateful. Although Morris's followers had no criminal motives in "providing themselves with arms" and were frightened amid the controversy engulfing them, being armed contributed to their tragic downfall.

Born in England to a poor family of farmers, Joseph Morris and five siblings lived impoverished lives. Having little schooling, he worked as a farmer, a servant, and a coal miner. A cave-in left him partially disabled with back and knee problems. According to his brother George, he was baptized into Mormonism, whereupon he "became very zealous and received the Gift of Tongues." Shortly after joining, he "was very severely burnt . . . in the coal mines and suffered great torture while recovering." His suffering "affected his mind very much," his brother recounted, and Joseph "began to feel very self-righteous and that he was in very high estimation with the Lord." He emigrated in 1842, spent several years in St. Louis working on riverboats, and "became very flighty and visionary in his mind . . . dreaming wonderful dreams, seeing visions and getting revelations." In Pittsburgh he "succeeded in establishing himself as President of the [LDS] Branch . . . [and] studied the scriptures a great deal," becoming an LDS scriptorian who "spoke with great earnestness and fluency." Arriving in Utah in 1853, he was accompanied by his wife, Mary, and one child.[130]

Some descriptions of Morris included phrases like "indolent and indisposed to labor" and "eschewing farming in favor of prayer and cogitation," from which he earned a reputation "as a fanatic ne'er-do-well." His public criticism of some Mormon doctrines and local church leaders led to his censure and removal from church assignments.[131] Convinced that he was destined to supersede Young, Morris began a series of letters to Young. From a difficult-to-read, rambling, obtuse October 1858 letter, biographer C. LeRoy Anderson clarifies Morris's message:

Young's authority to act was null, and only he—Morris—could reinstate Young to his former role. There should be a separation of the prophetic role and the administrative role; the former should be Morris, and the latter should remain with Young. Young's materialism was condemned, as was his taking multiple wives. A similar letter followed in January 1859, charging that Heber C. Kimball had "commited [sic] a grievous sin" and was to be replaced with a Morris appointee, one John Banks.[132] George A. Smith was named as the "real" leader of the LDS Church and was the alleged instigator of the Mountain Meadows murders.[133] From February to September, additional Morris letters came, some asking for a personal meeting to make his plea of being called by God.[134] By August 1860, Morris claimed he had received four revelations. Twenty-two more would come by November 13. Morris irretrievably crossed the line with his revelation of September 6, which announced the demotion of Brigham Young and berated Heber C. Kimball: "Behold! Verily I say unto you, my servant Joseph [Morris], . . . I have chosen you to stand at the head of my Church, as the Prophet, Seer, and Revelator . . . [and] you shall take my servant Brigham to be your first counselor. . . . As concerning my servant Heber, I, the Lord, am not well pleased with him; for he has committed a grevious [sic] sin against me."[135] According to C. LeRoy Anderson, an audience with Young took place in the summer or fall of 1860, but Young most likely "rebuffed" Morris. Morris established a relationship with brothers John and Richard Cook, to whom he "unfolded the great and precious things which the Lord had revealed to me." Morris's final letter to Young, dated December 21, concluded: "I have now said and done all that I could do for you, except you will humble yourselves and comply with the Lord's request. . . . There are but two ways before you. You must take either one or the other of them; the one leads to death, and the other leads to life."[136] But Morris was writing his own fate, not that of Brigham Young.[137] The assessment of William Adams Hickman was correct: "There is not room in the . . . empire for *two* Caesars."[138]

By early 1861, Morris—deluded, inspired, or both—had accumulated a large following. Increasingly they received the attention of mainstream Mormon leaders, until February 11, when Wilford Woodruff,

John Taylor, and others convened a local meeting to investigate the apostasy of Morris and fifteen others.[139] Woodruff asked Richard Cook to explain his view of Morris and his teaching and revelations. Cook's response was lucid, well spoken, and composed, far from the "enfeebled intellects" of semidemented status cited by some historians as the caliber of Morris's adherents.[140] Cook assured Mormon leaders: "I have never taught . . . anything but what was sound doctrine . . . only that which was moral and led to good, . . . and I boldly defy anything to the contrary. . . . Joseph Morris [is] a man with whom I became acquainted when I was a traveling Elder, some 16 or 17 years ago. My brother, John, and myself have known him at intervals from that time unto the present, and we never have known him to be anything but a hard working industrious and moral man." When Woodruff pressed Cook about and whether he believed Morris's revelations, Cook's responded emphatically, that "every revelation that he [Morris] has received is consistent with those which have been given . . . and his pretensions to being a prophet can be as easily sustained from the Bible and Book of Covenants, as the pretensions of Joseph Smith ever was." Cook continued: "I do say before men, mortals and immortals, angels and devils, that I do believe in his revelations. . . . I believe them because I have read them, and because I have prayed and have asked for the light of the Holy Spirit." Cook moved to the level of undeniable apostasy, when he said, "Am I satisfied with the Presidency of this Church? I answer, No! . . . I want a man that can receive the word of God . . . who can say 'Thus saith the Lord.' . . . We have been led for years by a man who could receive no more revelation from God than any other sectarian minister, he has not received a particle of revelation."[141] As T. B. H. Stenhouse phrased it, "Morris abounded with revelations. . . . Brigham had been barren—Morris was overflowing."[142]

When Woodruff called on Joseph Morris to confirm Young's place as the one and only prophet of God, he was unequivocal: "Brigham is an apostle" ordained by Joseph Smith but "I tell you in the name of the Lord God of Israel, that he is not a prophet of the Lord; the Lord never called him to such a place."[143] When asked if there was a prophet among them, Morris replied, 'I am by right of my heirship, prophet, seer and revelator to the Church of the Latter Day Saints."[144]

Woodruff concluded, "I am sorry that Bro. Cook and the others have got into the dark, and holding the views that they have we cannot fellowship them in this Church." From the audience a Mormon, one brother Watts, called for Morris to be "cut off under the chin" with a motion of drawing his hand across his throat, reminding those present of the blood atonement that Young, Jedediah Grant, and others had proclaimed as the punishment for apostasy.[145] Woodruff and Taylor disapproved Watt's words.[146] Woodruff instructed all wishing to follow Morris to give their names. Morris and fifteen others did so. John Taylor moved that all be excommunicated from LDS Church membership. Seconded by Woodruff, the motion carried unanimously.[147]

On April 6, 1861, six men—Joseph Morris, John and Richard Cook, John Firth, William Kendall, and Nathan Byrne—formally organized the Church of Jesus Christ of the Saints of the Most High.[148] On May 11 a revelation told Morris to gather his people along the Weber River, at a place formerly named Kington Fort.[149] By June, John Banks and fifteen men had been ordained as apostles and presidency.

Young and LDS leaders claimed they took little interest in the disturbances of Joseph Morris. However, at least ten discussions concerning him took place in Young's offices or in other venues between July 1861 and the end of February 1862. On July 25, 1861, "Young had conversation with his Br. Joseph about . . . that Morris the crazy prophet [who] would give fight to this people if his numbers were strong enough.[150] On August 25, "Young attended the Tabernacle and spoke at both services. He proposed that some Morrisites should be cut off the Church."[151] On September 17, plainsman and deputy marshal Judson Stoddard reported to Young and Heber Kimball a long list of the recent teachings and criticisms of Morris and Banks: Young was a fallen prophet, for he had "descended to the meanness of trading" instead of building a temple; Banks found fault with Young's handling of the handcart companies and their sufferings, with his forming the X.Y. Company for federal mail transport, with his building of the rock wall round his house, with his "forming confederacies to destroy men" and sending out spies and secret emissaries, and with the oppression of the people through the greed of their rulers. Morris had recently gone so far as to predict God's destruction of Brighamite Mormons.[152]

On October 8, Young heard Apostle Orson Hyde speak of the Morrisites, particularly John Banks and Thomas Parsons, who "vilified the characters of the Best men in the Church." Faithful Mormon Peter Maughan warned that Morrisites "must speak the truth."[153] Bishop John Hess informed Young on October 31, "the crazy man Morris with some of his followers had paid their fine for refusing to attend Military duties."[154] On January 8 of the new year, another Mormon leader, Ezra T. Benson, "mentioned that Joseph Morriss [sic] the crazy prophet had said that these light Snows was an evidence of God's favor to them in their unsheltered state."[155] Young asked John T. Caine on January 13 "to read the last revelation of the crazy man Joseph Morris."[156] Two brethren called on Young on January 25, reading from their notes the "speeches and revelations of Morris the crazy Man."[157]

John Banks, while naming Morris as his followers' inspirational prophet, was particularly influential in the group's rapid growth, serving as the Morrisite orator.[158] His message of urgency, that Christ's second coming was near, attracted new members. Other progressive tenets included communal ownership of property, which appealed to many who were very poor; condemnation of racial discrimination; and the granting of priesthood authority to women. Of the Morrisites' criticisms of Young's leadership, the most important was the Morrisites' opposition to taking multiple wives.[159]

Some of the Morrisites at Kington may have feared the atonement by death promised to apostates; others placed their faith in a millennial ending. But all who gathered there were ill prepared for siege of their compound. Destitute of food and supplies and facing increasingly strained relations with neighboring Brighamite Mormons, they acquired arms, a fateful act. Morris required his followers to consecrate their properties to the general good of the church and to him as trustee-in-trust. Believing the end imminent, individual wealth and property, even crop harvesting, became inconsequential. When some of the Morris prophecies failed, the faith of several waned; they wished to leave and wanted their property returned. Dissension arose over the ownership and value of donated material, and lawsuits erupted.[160] One William Jones requested that his wagon and oxen be returned, but Morrisite leaders refused this. When Jones enlisted two men to help him retake his former property by force, they were jailed at Fort Kington. Justice Kinney issued a writ for their release May 22. Territorial marshal Henry W. Lawrence saw that the situation portended violence, wanted no part in it, and left the territory; therefore Judson Stoddard, the plainsman and deputy marshal, did so.[161] The Morrisites refused the writ; like Young, they obeyed a higher law. On June 10, Kinney ordered the arrest of Morris and his three principal followers. After receiving Young's imprimatur, Kinney addressed another writ to both the absent Lawrence and "acting marshal" Robert T. Burton. The designation of Burton as "acting marshal" overlooks the relevant fact that he had returned only ten days earlier, after sixty days in the saddle as the Nauvoo Legion "Colonel Burton." During that time, he had guarded the stage transporting the Nauvoo Legion's Gen. Chauncey W. West, who had participated in Morris's excommunication and had earlier headed a manhunt party that barely missed killing Morris.[162]

On June 10, Governor Fuller issued an order for Burton to call a posse comitatus to enforce the writ. Two companies of militia from Salt Lake County, two from Davis County, and one from Weber County were joined by some five hundred other volunteers, resulting in an army estimated at one thousand men, along with three cannons, that converged on the morning of June 13 on the bluffs above Fort Kington.[163] Nonviolent isolation of the destitute Morrisites at a place where hunger would lead to early capitulation was apparently not considered. Controversy and contradiction plague the Mormon and Morrisite accounts of the happenings of the next three days. Unquestioned is that cannon fire from the Mormon militia was used on the Morrisite group, which included women and children. Cannons and small arms firing both from the militia's massed infantry and sharpshooter groups and from the Morrisites resulted in eight deaths, two militiamen and six Morrisites.[164]

Claiming multiple revelations each day, Morris insisted that God would miraculously intervene at any moment and wipe out those opposing him and his people. For the Morrisites—outnumbered, inadequately armed, and relying on divine deliverance that did not come—the outcome turned tragic. On day three, it was apparent that this was an LDS Church mission—not a civic mission—when Burton told the Morrisites he wanted "no more of their 'damned apostacy'" and commanded them, "in the name of the Lord Jesus Christ," to give up.[165] After a white-flag surrender, Burton rode into the campsite and allegedly said, "I do not know how you have escaped as well as you have done." Morrisite history claims that five thousand cartridges and a hundred cannonballs had been fired.[166] Morris is said to have grasped the bridle reins of Burton's horse to avoid being run him down, when Burton "personally shot Morris to death with a revolver at close range."[167] John Banks had received a gunshot wound in the neck. He died not long after, either from his wound or after being pithed or poisoned by militia surgeon Dr. Jeter Clinton.[168] Two Morrisite women, Isabella Bowman and Mrs. O'Hagg, a second protestor, were killed at this time.[169] Morrisite eyewitnesses asserted that Burton himself killed the two women with his handgun, but he "denied it to the end of his days."[170] Burton's own version of the deaths, taken from the Wilford Woodruff record, is less certain: "I ordered Morris to stop several times & followed him up. I had no arms but my revolver and as He would not stop I stoped [sic] him with my revolver. . . . Two women were shot at the same time which I very much regret but it could not be helped."[171] Stenhouse laid out the basic logic: "If General Burton did not shoot Banks and the women, then was he under obligation, as commander of the militia and chief deputy-marshal, to have brought the murderers to justice. Nothing of this kind was done, nor did the Chief-Justice or the acting-Governor make any inquiry."[172]

As with Mountain Meadows, nearly two decades passed before a grand jury investigated and brought criminal charges related to the killings. In July 1877, Burton was arraigned and his bail set at ten thousand dollars. Witness Samuel D. Sirrine recanted his decision to testify of Young's involvement or about whether Burton had killed Isabella Bowman, and he returned safely to San Francisco.[173] The report of the 1877 investigation, published in the *New York Herald*, read in part: "The evidence . . . by the principal witnesses . . . shows that Brigham Young's orders were that neither Morris nor Banks should not be [*sic*; read: should be] brought back alive."[174]

Ten days after the attack, Young forewarned Bernhisel to prepare for questions regarding Kinney and Fuller that might arise in

Washington. Entrepreneurs James Monroe Livingston and Ben Holladay were in Salt Lake City at the time of the Morris episode and made "some very harsh expressions about the operations" taking place and "threatened to expose Judge Kinney and Acting Governor Fuller," Young wrote, adding, "Should you meet Mr. Livingstone in Washington, and he undertakes to carry out his reported threatenings, please ask him . . . what could he know, in the few days he was here . . . and how could he determine correctly the line of truth."[175] Holladay had come to be on warm terms with Young, assisting with securing payment for the services of Lot Smith and Burton.[176] However, Young held no trust in what Livingston might say.[177] Young's caution to Bernhisel stands as additional evidence against Young's alleging disinterest in the Morrisite affair, as does historian Orson Ferguson Whitney's contention that Young "was very much averse to the execution" of Kinney's writ.[178]

Bernhisel assured Young about Livingstone, "I very much doubt whether he will ever lisp the matter at any of the Departments of the Government, and if he should, it will avail him nothing. His influence there is very limited, and the President is solemnly sworn to see the laws faithfully executed, and the law in this as in every other case was executed by agents of his own appointment."[179] Three days after the hortative to Bernhisel, Young raised new allegations of Morrisite moral transgressions. Asserting that Morris and his followers "hired a large barn, and invited spectators to see them . . . in a state of perfect nudity," Young remarked, "But probably the most nonsensical, low filthy, groveling, idiotic, insane system . . . that ever was subscribed to by mortal folly, is that which has been fostered on the banks of the Weber."[180]

The bodies of Morris and Banks were displayed to the public in Salt Lake City. "The robe, crown, and rod of the former [Morris] being laid in mockery by his side, and his fate regarded by the saints as the just punishment of one who 'had set himself up to teach heresy in Zion, and oppose the Lord's anointed.'"[181] The News did not announce the display of the bodies and omitted labeling surviving Morrisites as heretic-apostates, but it allowed them only as a "band of law-breakers" to whom "strict justice will be meted out."[182] Morrisite men who had allegedly borne arms against the posse appeared before Judge Kinney on June 18. Richard Cook was fined fifty dollars for contempt; Peter Klemgard and Christian Nelson were sent to prison; and the remainder were placed on bond to appear later. Nine months later, in March 1863, seven Morrisites were convicted of second-degree murder and given prison sentences of ten to fifteen years; two were acquitted, and the remainder fined one hundred dollars each.

Harding explained the next events in his 1871 letter to journalist John H. Beadle. Petitions for unconditional pardon of the Morrisites were submitted by all the non-Mormon federal officials, including the two federal judges, joined by all the officers at Camp Douglas. "Not a Mormon signed them; but several called . . . always after dark, and by the back way, to say that they hoped mercy would be shown . . . but they dared not let it be known," Harding wrote. Mothers and wives of the convicted "came and fell on their knees and begged with tears and sobs that I would show mercy to their sons and husbands." Mormons made "angry threats," and Harding reported that "Bishop Woolley came to urge me against it [issuing a pardon], saying he could not answer for my safety in case I pardoned those men."[183] Three days later, Harding issued a "full and perfect pardon" to all convicted. Supreme court justices Charles B. Waite and Thomas J. Drake, by this time under the same threats of expulsion as Harding, both courageously supported the pardon.[184]

In a face-to-face meeting, Young asked Harding, "Don't you think . . . that a Government administered by one man . . . appointed by God, would be far better than a Government of the United States?" Harding answered with a stinging allusion to Morris: "The only question would be to know what man the Lord has chosen. . . . It is only a short time since some of your followers set up a new Prophet . . . thus creating schism in the church . . . and the death of several men. So you see that opposing factions may arise as well among this people as elsewhere.'"[185] The Morrisite apostate affair made clear that Utah's government was not republican and that Brigham Young brooked no competition, especially from apostates.

Spicy and Exciting Events

The *Deseret News* often placed Civil War news in its back pages, but dedicated readers remained well informed. Two reports of the spring battles just outside Richmond are examples: "The operations of the civil war . . . are far more destructive of life than generally supposed. The number of the killed and wounded in battle, although far greater than has been announced . . . is acknowledged to be but small in comparison to the number of those who have died of disease and from other causes." Figures were cited for the Eleventh Maine Infantry, which started with 850 men, then lost 100 to typhoid while in Washington. Many hundreds fell from starvation and exhaustion while repeatedly marching forward toward Richmond, then retreating eastward on the Richmond peninsula. At the May 31 and June 1 battle of Seven Pines, in Henrico County, only 180 were fit for duty. Of the 90 who were in action, nearly all were killed or wounded.[186] Lt. C. C. Baker of the Second Michigan Infantry wrote to his mother of this battle: "You can scarcely get your feet on the ground between the bodies of the dead. They lie four and five, and in some few places more than that deep, of dead and wounded. . . . [I]t will take three or four days yet to bury them all. . . . We numbered some 3,500 men when we were at Yorktown, but now there are only 1,130 in the whole four regiments; ours, only 410. . . . Another battle will wipe us out."[187] The evacuation of more than three thousand wounded began the night of June 1: "Surgeons packed living and dead like freight into boxcars with nothing to ease the jolting and bumping; but this was only the beginning of the inferno." Those who carried "the shattered and shrieking" onto waiting hospital transport ships were "banging the stretchers against pillars and posts, and walking over men just to dump the wounded anywhere."[188]

The level of Union and Confederate unpreparedness for the enormous butchery that marked 1861 and early 1862 invites comparison: "Armies the world over were probably worse provided in 1860 with medical and surgical resources than European armies had been when Napoleon's wars ended in 1815; the standard had deteriorated. The work of Pasteur and Lister lay . . . well in the future. Almost every

abdominal wound meant death. . . . The North systematically prevented shipments of drugs and surgical instruments to the South, a
piece of barbarity which did not shorten the war by a day, but on the
Confederate side added greatly to its sufferings. . . . So rudimentary
was the knowledge of hospital sanitation that surgeons marveled when
tent hospitals, open to the clean winds and sunshine, proved healthier
than wooden buildings with dirty walls and filth-soaked floors."[189]

Only among the Mormons could be found explanations that
placed the blame for the war's horrors on the failure of the nation's
people to accept the Saints' unique theology and their claim to be the
only church holding God's authority. "The present internecine struggle in America . . . shows in the clearest possible light how far men can
wander from consistency and truth, in matters of religion, when bereft
of the light of revelation, and guided by their own conceptions. . . .
If ever a warning lesson more impressive than another was given to
man, . . . it is afforded in this American struggle"—so said the *Millennial Star.*[190]

Young's letter to Confederate spy and Mormon Walter Murray Gibson in the Hawaiian Islands suggests no empathy held for the suffering outside Utah: "Home affairs have continued in their accustomed
grooves of peace and prosperity, without being jostled by those *spicy
and exciting events now characterizing news from the East.*"[191] The relatives
of those who fell in 1862, including the men lost at Seven Pines, would
not have been pleased to hear that their loved ones' sufferings and
deaths were merely "spicy and exciting events" to one who proclaimed
himself the earth's *only* "Ambassador of Almighty God."

Soldier of the Overland versus Lion of the Lord

P. Edward Connor, the fiery Irishman who came to Utah by way of his
military assignment to Missouri before the Mormons left for Nauvoo,
the Mexican War, then California and the U.S. Army's Department
of the Pacific. He challenged Brigham Young's dictatorial power in
Utah Territory as few others dared. Historians claim that the two never
met face to face. During his years of commanding military units from

headquarters only three miles from Young's home in Salt Lake City, Connor spoke fearlessly against Utah's theocracy and its disloyalty to the federal government. He earned distinction as the preeminent soldier of the overland, established a newspaper for non-Mormons, and provided non-Mormons with security and safety unmatched previously. Connor recognized that only through the influx of non-Mormons could control of Utah by LDS theocracy be diminished, and his efforts to attract industry led to his title as "the Father of Utah Mining."[192]

"Treasonable designs" of disloyal citizens on the Pacific coast roused many loyal citizens in the area to appeal to Gen. George Wright for action. As the head of the Department of the Pacific, Wright ordered military commanders to arrest and hold "all persons against whom the charge of aiding and abetting the rebellion can be sustained," adding that "under no circumstances will such persons be released without first subscribing the oath of allegiance to the United States."[193] Col. P. Edward Connor was very aware of the vigor of the secession element, for his life had been threatened many times for his strong pro-Union stand while living in Stockton.[194] In this charged atmosphere he was named to march California Volunteers to Utah.[195] Connor delayed, needing one hundred men to fill his companies. Departure was also held off by deep snow in the Sierra. Not until mid-June would he be able to cross with troops and supplies.[196]

Moving federal troops into the only state or territory that contained none was seen by the editor of the New York Times as needless provocation of the Mormons toward war. With no Confederates known to be there, with Indian reactions to white encroachment no worse than usual, with Young claiming he could handle the Indians, and with the Mormon leader allegedly swearing "unflinching fealty" to the parent government, the editor asked, "What are these troops needed for in Utah?" Oh, yes, there was that "little cloud of mischief" that Mormons had established an independent state and government without authority or permission, but such problems could be "easily settled" by legislation or cutting the territory into pieces and dividing it among adjacent territories run by non-Mormons, according to the Times.[197]

Arriving in Stockton, Connor found eight hundred troops at Camp Halleck. The regiment was said to be a "very efficient force," according the *News*.[198] General Wright inspected Connor's camp in late June and reported: "The arms, clothing, and equipments were in high order. The industry and untiring zeal and energy of Colonel Connor is manifest throughout. He has a regiment that the State may well be proud of." Four artillery pieces would go with Connor to Utah.[199]

John Alexander Anderson—the son of William C. Anderson, who established the first Presbyterian ministry in San Francisco—was himself the minister of the Presbyterian flock in Stockton, where he had labored since 1857 and had erected a handsome church building. Elected by the California legislature in 1860 as a trustee of the Stockton State Insane Asylum, John Anderson worked closely with famous Unitarian preacher Thomas Starr King for reforms and correction of abuses in the asylum system.[200] Anderson was appointed by Colonel Connor in June as the regimental chaplain of the California Volunteers. Anderson's position may have been as much sought-after as by appointment, for only two months before, Reverend Anderson preached a "Union sermon" that offended one of his Southern-aligned members, and the two entered a "terrific pugilistic encounter" with "smashed chairs and tables," until "finally Anderson wore the deacon out."[201] More an ardent Unionist than an abolitionist, Anderson had another physical encounter while in Utah: "Porter Rockwell, the 'destroying angel' of the Mormon church, got after him for his denunciations of the disloyal statements of Brigham Young and the church. The 'destroying angel' took water—he was up against a buzz-saw."[202]

Concerned with the welfare of his soldiers, Anderson appealed to the people of California to supply the volunteers with books for a unit library.[203] The volunteers also received a three-hundred-person canvas chapel tent, a gift to Anderson and his troops from his father's congregation in San Francisco.[204]

Anderson remained with the California Volunteers through their march to Utah, shared their nightmarish midwinter march to Bear River, and remained with his flock in their January 1863 battle there against the Shoshonis. Two months later, he retired from the volunteers, becoming California's correspondent and representative to the United States Sanitary Commission. His first assignment was as relief agent with the Twelfth Army Corps, who became defenders of Culp's

John Alexander Anderson, a minister from Stockton, California, and chaplain of the Third California Volunteer Infantry, was with P. Edward Connor at Bear River and served as a relief agent of the U.S. Sanitary Commission. His postwar career was highly distinguished. Courtesy California History Room, California State Library, Sacramento, California.

Hill at Gettysburg. In 1864, when Grant began moving toward Richmond, Anderson was made a superintendent of transportation, in charge of six Union steamboats. At the campaign's closing he served as assistant superintendent of the Canvas and Supply Department at Philadelphia and edited the *Sanitary Commission Bulletin*.[205] As late as fall 1864 he was warmly remembered by Camp Douglas's Charles Hempstead: "We learn that the late Chaplain of the 3rd Inf'y, C. V., has left New York for Petersburg to tender his services to the Government. Dr. Anderson will ever remain dear in the hearts of the officers and soldiers of this command. To know him was but to love him. So noble, so good, so pure and so patriotic. He was ever the soldier's friend. His affable smile and kind expression is with us in dear remembrance. He goes now to the front where many a comrade in the Army of the Potomac will be by him cheered and blessed."[206]

At his enlistment, Anderson was also the special correspondent of the *San Francisco Bulletin* and wrote of Utah matters even after his appointment to the Sanitary Commission. During the war he wrote for other San Francisco newspapers, sometimes under the name "Hackatone."[207] A classmate of Benjamin Harrison while a student at Miami University, he breakfasted—at their invitation—many Sunday mornings while in Washington with President and Mrs. Harrison at the White House. Anderson's life beyond Utah and the Civil War continued with distinguished service as the pastor of the Presbyterian Church in Junction City, Kansas, in 1868.[208] Appointed president of the Kansas State Agricultural College in 1873, he also served six terms in the Kansas House of Representatives. His last service was as consul general in Cairo, Egypt.[209]

Mormon reports exaggerated the number of Connor's volunteers, describing their march from California: "The pompous procession is expected to consist of one thousand infantry, five hundred cavalry, a field battery, one hundred and fifty contractor's wagons and seventy army wagons, besides the officers' ambulances and carriages for their families who accompany them. . . . [S]everal hundred head of cattle are to be driven in the rear of the procession. The Indians will of course be tremendously scared, and horse-thieves, gamblers, and other pests of community wondrously attracted."[210]

July's heat was felt before Connor crossed the Sierra to establish a post at Ruby Valley, Nevada. Col. Columbus Sims, with two companies of the Second California Volunteer Cavalry, was ordered to join Connor on the eastern slope.[211] By July 25, Wright wrote that Connor was making good time, probably having reached the vicinity of Carson City, but according to Van B. De Lashmutt's diary, the men found Lake Bigler—now Lake Tahoe—on that day, where Connor and others went sailing on "the prettiest lake they ever saw."[212]

By August, Connor had established the District of Utah at Fort Churchill, Nevada Territory, and here charged that he had been "credibly informed" that there were those in Utah and Nevada who were "endeavoring to destroy and defame the principles and institutions of our Government." Lincoln had directed that all who made treasonable sentiments against the government were to be arrested and confined, at least until they had taken the oath of allegiance. "Traitors shall not utter treasonable sentiments in this district with impunity, but must seek some more genial soil, or receive the punishment they so richly merit," ordered Connor.[213]

Connor arrived at Ruby Valley on September 1 but left by stage for Great Salt Lake City on September 5, arriving four days later. For two days he reconnoitered, dressed in mufti, no doubt selecting a site for his troops. If he thought to pass unnoticed in ordinary dress, he was mistaken; his visit was noted in the *News:* "Col. P. E. Connor . . . arrived in this city yesterday. . . . [He] took a stroll about town and looked around with an air of familiarity."[214] Connor returned to Fort Crittenden, then left there on September 11 to return to Ruby Valley. John Anderson wrote to his parents from the trail, east of Ruby Valley, that he was recovering from "Panama fever" and that "Mrs. Col. Connor sent me a couple of fine apples which was very great luxuries." Of Connor's report on Salt Lake City, Anderson commented, "The Col. was hugely disgusted with Mormonism . . . says they are a pack of secessionists & villains: federal officers [have] no possible power or respect."[215]

Connor had several earlier exposures to the Mormons, and his opinion of them came from more than his recent two-day visit. During his service with the First Regiment of Dragoons, he was a "spectator" to the happenings in Clay and Daviess Counties in Missouri and at Nauvoo and likely read the newspapers that reported on Mormon troubles, on Joseph Smith's presidential candidacy, on the stories of polygamy circulating in 1842, and on the attempted murder of Missouri governor Lilburn Boggs by Orrin Porter Rockwell. While living in Stockton, he was aware of the scathing condemnations of the Mormons in 1857–58 by the *San Joaquin Republican*. To its editor, Young was "'the arch imposter, tyrant, and debauchee,'" and the Mormons were "living in a moral and social state so revolting . . . so repugnant to the moral sense of the whole nation, and so subversive of the foundations of republican government" that a U.S. Army force should "bring them to heel.'"[216] Southern California was a hotbed of anti-Mormon sentiment stemming from the Mountain Meadows murders, as confirmed by Mormon elder William M. Wall's report of threats against his life.[217] Any forces sent to subdue the Mormons, widely considered guilty of the mass murders of the Arkansas travelers, should include men from California, insisted the editor.[218]

Connor's report to Drum covered three issues: preparations for the march of his command from Ruby, the treasonous state of the Mormons, and the location of the camp he would create on his arrival. Of the first he wrote: "The country between this point and Salt Lake is an alkali desert, scarce of wood and water, but I have made such arrangements as will enable me to take my command over with comparative comfort." Of the second matter his observations were hypercritical:

It will be impossible for me to describe . . . the enormity of Mormonism; suffice it, that I found them a community of traitors, murderers, fanatics, and whores. The people publicly rejoice at reverses to our arms, and thank God that the American Government is gone, as they term it, while their prophet and bishops preach treason from the pulpit. The Federal officers are entirely powerless, and talk in whispers for fear of being overheard by Brigham's spies. Brigham Young rules with despotic sway, and death by assassination is the penalty of disobedience to his commands. I have a difficult and dangerous task before me, and will endeavor to act with prudence and firmness.[219]

Crittenden, the former camp site of Johnston's troops was unacceptable for several reasons, including a price of fifteen thousand dollars, and Connor wanting to be "within striking distance of the heart of Mormondom." Crittenden's "only asset was good grazing ground."[220] Connor sought his superior's permission to locate much closer to Great Salt Lake City: "It is on a plateau about three miles from Salt Lake City; in the vicinity of good timber and saw-mills, and at a point where hay, grain, and other produce can be purchased cheaper than at Fort Crittenden. It is also a point which commands the city, and where 1,000 troops would be more efficient than 3,000 on the other side of the Jordan." It was obvious that Connor visited with Judges Drake, Waite, and Titus and with Governor Harding during his scouting tour of the city, for he added, "Federal officers . . . beg that I will locate near the city. The Governor especially is very urgent in the matter." Connor's request was approved, for it best offered "the protection of the Overland Mail Route and the *execution of the laws of the United States*."[221] This information had not yet been given to the troops or communicated to the Mormons, but from their own intelligence sources, the Mormons knew that the California troops would not winter at Crittenden. Connor's location constituted a painful abscess that would fester with Young and Mormon leaders for years.

California's volunteers were well informed by the *Sacramento Daily Union* of the humiliating second Union defeat at Bull Run on August 28–30, and then of the Union victory at South Mountain in mid-September. They read of September's battle at Antietam, the first major battle on Union soil, with fighting was "so intense and sustained . . . , a man recalled, that . . . in his mind's eye the very landscape around him turned red."[222] This bloodiest day in American history counted more than one hundred thousand souls engaged in the hellish fighting, of whom more than twenty-three thousand fell in Union and Confederate lines. Four days after the battle, "two thousand wounded had received no attention." Doctors searching "among heaps of putrefying dead for men clinging to life" would hear the cry: "'Doctor, come to *me;* you look like a kind man; for God's sake, come to *me.*'" Dr. William Quentin Maxwell, the historian of the U.S. Sanitary Commission, declared, "Let anyone who would understand what a great battle means, not in cheap pageantry and empty glory, but in agony and despair, *hear these words* himself."[223]

Battle reports were devoid of this wrenching intimacy, and the war-innocent of the Third California Volunteer Infantry grew restless at Ruby Valley, naive in wanting "to see the elephant."[224] Wounded in the Mexican War, Connor knew firsthand the grisly aspects of combat, but he understood his men and represented their wishes—even his own—in a request to General Halleck that they be sent into battle, for "the men enlisted to fight traitors, and can do so more effectually than raw recruits." The regiment, he said, was "well officered and thoroughly drilled" and was "of no service on the Overland Mail Route, as there is cavalry sufficient for its protection in Utah District." Anticipating disapproval because of cost, the men offered to "authorize the paymaster to withhold $30,000 of pay now due" if they could be ordered east. "If the above sum is insufficient we will pay our own passage from San Francisco to Panama," promised Connor.[225] He also informed the *San Francisco Bulletin* that "700 hearts camped in Ruby Valley pulse vigorously with the patriotic desire to serve their country in shooting traitors instead of eating rations and freezing to death around sage-brush fires."[226]

Chaplain Anderson published news about the volunteers as they trekked. He understood that infantry was less useful in Utah and included in his October 15 report a jovial semiprayer that General Halleck would "be in a good humor" when their dispatch pleading to be sent east arrived. The chaplain continued: "May he just have eaten the biggest kind of good dinner; may he just have lit the best Habana [cigar] in all America; . . . may the Third have a chance to shoot seceshers, and pat Uncle Abe Lincoln on his long back for that slavery proclamation! Amen!"[227]

A company of forty emigrants from Warren County, Iowa, were attacked along Sublette's Cut-off on August 26, with three killed and the loss of all stock and supplies. The train captain and his wife and daughter were shot; all died shortly after reaching settlements in the Bear River area. "All the white folks are deserting the Northern routes— mountaineers, ferrymen and emigrants—as life and property are now so very uncertain," claimed the *New York Times*.[228] Twelve emigrants were killed near Gravelly Ford on the Humboldt, apparently by Indians, but rumor said whites were involved.[229] In response to the situation, Connor wrote to Drum: "Indians murdering emigrants on the Humboldt. Will attend to it."[230] Instructions issued to Maj. Edward McGarry at Fort Ruby were a presage of Connor's dealing with Indian aggression throughout his military tenure: "[E]xamine every valley or place where . . . hostile Indians are congregated, whom you will capture; but if they resist you will destroy them. In no instance will you molest women or children. If . . . friendly Indians deliver to you Indians who were concerned in the late murder of emigrants, you will . . . immediately hang them, and leave their bodies thus exposed as an example of what evil-doers may expect while I command in this district." Of the rumors that whites, secessionists or Mormons, were involved in the Indian attacks, Connor further ordered: "If you should discover such a band you will take them prisoners and convey them to headquarters near Salt Lake, but if they should resist you will destroy them without mercy."[231] Confirmation of Mormon involvement in the Humboldt attacks came in Capt. Albert Brown's letter telling Drum of "Mormons keeping ferries in the neighborhood of the Indian troubles," selling ammunition and arms to the Indians and informing them of "any trains worth robbing."[232]

Connor anticipated needing cash on arrival in Utah and wrote of this to his superior officers. He feared that Young might use a lack of cash as an excuse for refusing to supply the troops. Merchants had already inflated the price of goods, but the increased costs were also hurting Utah's population. Young called a meeting of the Saints in Payson, Utah, "to enter into some arrangements to lower the present high prices of goods, and by combination to drive from our midst all foreign merchants."[233]

Connor left Ruby Valley with his troops on October 2. Their eastward course followed the 1859 course laid by U.S. topographical engineer Capt. James A. Simpson, on a route that saved more than two hundred miles between Carson and Camp Floyd.[234] Carrying extra water, Connor traveled the alkali expanse at night, anticipating good water at Simpson Springs and Rush Valley, the last stop before Camp Crittenden. Anderson, referring to the site to be selected for their Utah camp, wrote, "The Commander [Connor] . . . has a fashion of keeping his own counsel, and what he has determined upon will not be discovered till the order to halt is given." Anderson also admitted, "What we are sent here to do, how it is to be done, and the effects of doing it, are all riddles."[235] Twenty miles were covered the next day, and on October 17, from the dilapidated remnant of Camp Crittenden, Connor telegraphed this Spartan message: "Have just arrived; will cross the Jordan [River] tomorrow."[236]

Anderson was surprised when the colonel, "who rarely makes a speech, made two today within an hour." Connor warned that they were coming among a people whose customs were different but who must be treated with the same courtesy and justice afforded to their own people. No soldier could leave camp without a written pass; Connor rode the line, saying that he had no complaint to make and was heartily proud of them, but only spoke because the "circumstances not proper to be mentioned"—presumably referring to threats of Mormons' armed resistance—required the strictest discipline. As he finished, Connor's men gave him three rousing cheers.[237]

Anderson filled in speculation regarding the Floyd-Crittenden site. Connor had been solicited by Overland Mail Company representatives who had purchased the former campsite; they would restore it, pocketing big profits. The approach of winter leaving little time for construction, the apparent resolve of the Mormons not to allow establishment of a site closer to town center, and the relatively small number of troops all made Crittenden a logical choice. Rumors of armed resistance at crossing the Jordan River may have been credible or may have had the hope of forcing Connor to use the Crittenden site. The *Times* treated the matter lightly: "Quite a number of sharp persons . . . have, for a week or so, been gathering . . . salable notions . . . at Fort Crittenden, with the idea of making a good thing out of the California volunteers"; however, the colonel passed the "expectant venders and stores with one night's short visit."[238]

Rumor circulated of a five-thousand-dollar bet against the troops successfully crossing the river. Another held that proximity to the Mormon central city would be forcibly resisted. Connor prepared by ordering thirty rounds of ammunition issued to each man, and a pair of six-pound cannons were appropriately supplied, as was a twelve-pound mountain howitzer.[239]

Chaplain Anderson, who seriously believed they would meet armed opposition, wrote, "If our troops are to march on United States territory wherever Government sends them, then those who resist their march because of polygamy, are as really traitors as those who resist because of slavery." He explained that "the river Jordan will be as acceptable to us as the river Potomac, for we shall be fighting for the same precise principle—the flag and national existence," and that "should annihilation be our fate, . . . the belief that our countrymen would think of our graves as they do of those in Virginia, and that the Union men of California, our old friends, would swarm forth by the thousand to avenge us—such a hope and belief would nerve us for death."[240]

On Saturday, October 18, the command camped on the west side of the River Jordan near "the point of the mountain."[241] Early on Sunday, preparations to move out were in the making. Reverend Anderson found Connor seated on a log, "calmly engaged in loading his revolvers and playing with his toddling child [Maurice]."[242] Surgeon Reid urged all hospital patients able to carry a musket to do so. When artillery Lt. Francis Honeyman asked Connor about canister for the twelve-pound howitzer, the reply indicated where and when Connor anticipated opposition: "Not to-day; but tomorrow do so."[243] About two o'clock that afternoon, the Jordan was crossed, using the bridge "below the mouth of Little Cottonwood" canyon; they camped nearby.[244] As Connor had anticipated, no opposition was encountered.

The volunteers were still in shadow at the reveille on Monday morning, for the already snow-touched Wasatch peaks blocked direct sunlight until later hours. Vivid orange, yellow, and red had begun to appear in the trees and scrub oak bushes of the mountain's approaches, and in morning's reflected light, colors were fully saturated. The northward march of seven hundred troops resumed on the course of present-day State Street—while Anderson worried that "it was in their [the Mormons'] power to vastly outnumber and in all probability annihilate us." Two miles out, halt was sounded; the column formed with a cavalry guard and Colonel Connor in the lead, then the brass band, the light battery, infantry, quartermaster, and commissary, with a final rear guard of more infantry.[245] The sidewalks of Great Salt Lake City's main thoroughfares were lined with women and children; the doors, windows, and rooftops were occupied by spectators. They passed to Emigration Square and the grand theater. The silence was eerie, as "Not a cheer, not a jeer greeted us."[246]

Brigham Young was not present in the city, for he and his camarilla left on October 17 for a visit to Cache Valley colonies. This avoided an awkward confrontation, but if Connor knew of Young's absence from the city, he left no record of it, and his preparations to meet resistance were nonetheless thorough.[247] The troop column turned east on First South Street, stopping at the residence of Governor Stephen Harding. Connor gave the governor the salute due him, introduced his troops, and received Harding's response:[248]

> I am conscious . . . that your mission here is one of peace and security. . . . God bless you, and God bless the flag you carry; God bless the government you represent; and may she come out of her present difficulties unscathed; and may the fiery ordeal . . . purge her of her sins; may her glorious institutions be preserved . . . from the . . . calamities through which she is passing. I suppose you will be encamped somewhere . . . a short distance of this city. I believe the people you have now come amongst will not disturb you if you do not disturb them in their public rights and in the honor and peace of their homes. . . . God being my helper, I will be with you to the end, and to death.[249]

When Harding finished, Connor took his command to an expanse elevated above the valley floor; they encamped near a spring between Red Butte and Emigration Canyons. To the Mormons' dismay, Connor made this location permanent, designating it as Camp Douglas.[250] The camp was a square, with each side two miles in length, containing about 2,560 acres.[251] Contrary to rumors, the distance between Camp Douglas and Young's residence exceeded the range of the best cannons then possessed by both sides—1,500 to 1,800 yards.[252] Three weeks later Connor reported in detail to the U.S. adjutant general the reasons for selecting the campsite. Three miles east of Great Salt Lake City, which had a post office and a telegraph office, the camp was located on "an elevated spot which commands a full view of the city and the Great Salt Lake and Valley, with a plentiful supply of wood and water in its vicinity, and in the neighborhood of numerous quarries of stone adapted to building barracks." It was near the divergence of three roads to California, two to Oregon, and the great Overland Mail Route to the east.[253]

Young responded to the camp's placement by organizing a scheme to prevent Mormons from associating with troops. Each ward of the city was to designate thirty-six priesthood men as policemen, to watch other Saints "day and night until they learned what they [the Saints] were doing and who frequented their houses." Any women visiting Camp Douglas, "no matter under what pretense," were to be cut off from the Church. Each ward was to form a committee to set standard prices for all trading with the camp. The bathhouse was taken down to deny "loose characters" a meeting place for "their wicked purposes."[254] Young claimed, incorrectly, that Connor had started with 1,600 men, expecting "they will dwindle to 300 by next spring." Young's measure of Harding was crude and emphatic: "If you were to fill a sack with cow shit, it would be the best thing you could do for an imitation."[255] The *Deseret News* carried advertisements for purchase of hay, potatoes, beef, and other staples needed at Camp Douglas, where an oath of allegiance was required from each seller.[256]

At the Camp Douglas flag raising, Harding again criticized Young's loyalty. Describing the flag as "a beacon light of hope to the downtrodden millions of earth," he said, "Who is so craven as not to defend it, or who so traitorous-hearted as not to love It? If any there be, who calls himself an American citizen, may blindness smite his vision, for his soul is as 'black as hell whereto it goes.'"[257]

In a personal letter to a friend, Harding wrote, "Young has found he cannot use me. . . . All manner of traps have set for me, but I am a rat that don't bite, at least in the old fashioned Dawson trap."[258] Proof that Harding's mail of the day was read was supplied that evening. He and his son "Till" were together in the sitting room of his residence when a live cat was thrown through the window. The two men rushed to the street, but the thrower of this living "rat trap" had fled.[259]

November passed with troops working to complete quarters ahead of winter weather. Each unit was thirteen square feet, dug five feet deep into the earth, and covered with a tent. Installation of a bake oven furnished by the Masons, as well as construction of ditches, a hospital building, quartermaster and commissary structures, and officers quarters, were all under way. Axmen cut trees faster than fifty teams could haul them away. Two miles distant, another force quarried "a fine variety of sandstone."[260] "The discipline of the troops is excellent," wrote Anderson, for there had been "but two desertions to record during the last two months."[261]

In the *Sacramento Daily Union*, correspondent Stenhouse, writing under the name "Liberal," gave credit to Chaplain Anderson for setting the demeanor of the camp. He was "in our streets yesterday, with coat off " and was working "with his half dozen volunteers fixing up his lightning line of communication between Camp Douglas and our central office that unites the Pacific and Atlantic." The *Union* gave its assessment of the chaplain: "[He] is a hard sense fellow, with as hard working hands as any man in camp. He preaches when he likes, says what he has a mind to, and asks no odds of anybody. Of course he couldn't live without driving a quill, and digging at the honorable profession of a correspondent." Not only had Anderson "laid out Camp Douglas" with "line and level," but he had also built the telegraph line and "acquired sufficient experience with the [telegraph's dot-dash] key to entitle him to the position of camp operator." Stenhouse added, "I confess to a great partiality for a working parson. . . . 'Liberal' gladly shakes hands freely with Anderson, and wishes him all the success he aims after in the rostrum, the field and the press."[262]

The *Times* reported that "the snug sum of $74,000" was distributed in pay to the volunteers, and thus Salt Lake City's storekeepers were "doing a heavy business": "The stores are thronged most of the day, and 'green-backs' are more plentiful than blackberries in this Territory. As a general thing, however, the peace and quietness are remarkable, considering so much money is stirring in such a small place."[263] That Utah had become immensely rich by war was attested to by the *Times*: "Millions of gold were spent and Brigham Young is perhaps now one of the richest men on the continent." The *Times* noted that, as Joseph Morris had claimed, "riches have . . . hardened Brigham's heart, made him worldly-minded, and careful to keep his treasures."[264]

Concern arose over the "new species of currency" that appeared in conjunction with the paymaster's visit. It was "promises to pay" currency, or "shinplasters," the *News* pronounced, adding, "We hope that no one will be so foolish as to receive them in exchange for any thing of value, for if they do they may expect to be bitten to the full extent of the expressed fraud."[265]

The rumor circulating of six men mining gold in City Creek canyon only miles from downtown Great Salt Lake City caused Chaplain Anderson to reflect on Young's often publicized opposition to Mormons mining in Utah. Anderson wrote that Young "saw far more clearly and sharply than ordinary thinkers" the loss of control and the social change that would follow inroads by miners and mining Anderson predicted, "Just what '49 did for California would the discovery of gold would in '62 do for Utah; and the difference between San Francisco in '50 and San Francisco in '60 might prove to be an approximately fair criterion of Salt Lake's growth." Confident that Utah's mountains held metal ore, non-Mormons asked Connor "whether he would give protection . . . in case gold should be found." Connor assured them, pointing out that, regardless of Mormon practices, "no lands in this Territory . . . have ever been deeded away by Government, and hence, as those lands are usually free to all citizens of the United States, the colonel assured them of protection."[266]

It would be understandable that Connor's arrival with seven hundred soldiers, the trip to Cache Valley, the rumors of gold in City Creek canyon, and the almost daily arrival in the city of emigrant trains from Nebraska might keep Young overoccupied. However, Stenhouse's report in the *Sacramento Daily Union* cited another demanding project: "Two hundred and fifteen men with their families were called upon on Sunday to go to the cotton country. The names were read out in the Bowery . . . , and in the evening the 'called' were assembled in the Tabernacle to receive instructions." These October Saints would join the three hundred from the previous year. "The importance of this southern move seems to have taken hold of the chiefs, and nothing is to be neglected," wrote Stenhouse, adding, "Curious folks, the Mormons. No community in the world would 'get up and git' in this style, at the direction of any leader; but they do it here, and fortunately see salvation in obedience."[267]

Allegiance to Southern causes was especially true for the families sent to raise cotton; among them were many former Southerners. In his account of life in the cotton mission, Mormon elder George Armstrong Hicks recalled, "The old settlers . . . were all southerners and southern sympathizers. There were but two Union men . . . myself and an old friend from Nauvoo by the name of John P. [Peck] Chidester."[268]

Hicks described three cotton mission men—Robert Dockery Covington, Albert Washington Collins, and Robert Lewis Lloyd—for their support of the Southern cause and their reprehensible conduct before joining the Mormons. Covington, a North Carolinian by birth, moved to Mississippi, where his family owned a large cotton plantation with many slaves. Although he was "a strong Mormon" and appointed as the local LDS bishop, "he could scarcely read or write . . . and was a strong Rebel sympathizer and rejoiced whenever he heard of a Southern victory." Collins, first counselor to Covington in the bishopric of the settlement of Washington, near St. George, had been born in Georgia but near Covington's place in Mississippi, where his family also owned a large cotton plantation. The two were interconnected by marriage, and both were overseers. Hicks reported that Collins frequently related in lurid detail his whipping of male slaves, killing at least one with a particularly severe beating. Of his female slaves, Collins said, "He had had sexual intercourse with all but one, and that one was married to a young man. 'I had tried her several times,' . . . and she always refused, but that only made me the more determined." Collins whipped the husband and then "marched the gal off to a little grove," where he raped her and then whipped her. The third man, Lloyd, was born in Tennessee and joined the LDS Church in Texas, where he was second counselor in the bishopric. "[Lloyd had] killed a man, and then fled the country and became a Mormon. With such a bishop and such a pair of councillors, one may imagine what kind of church government we had in [the small settlement of] Washington [City]."[269]

Ranking Mormon official Erastus Snow traveled to Washington County in late 1861 to select a townsite in anticipation of the arrival of the Mormon men and families called in the prior October conference. Snow "expressed his sorrow at finding disunion prevailing" between Union and Confederate supporters. To counter this, he informed his Saints that a gathering would be held on January 6, 1862. At this mass meeting, "patriotic demonstrations exhibiting love for, devotion to, the Union, and solemnly protesting against its dissolution, were enthusiastically manifested." The Honorable Joseph Orton felt moved to express "himself in spirit-stirring appeals to the patriotism of the assemblage." According to James G. Bleak, historian of Utah's southern mission, "[Orton] was repeatedly interrupted by the most hearty applause of his hearers. His sentiments and the plaudits of the people were calculated to strike terror to the hearts of the promoters of disunion and fratricidal war."[270] Bleak's report confirms that of others who asserted that a significant element existed among the Mormons, in numbers unstated, who supported and promoted disunion and war. By March, attitudes mellowed, at least superficially, for Snow reported that "peace and contentment seem to prevail among the Saints."[271]

Connor had been in Utah Territory sixty days when he reported to his Pacific coast superiors the major issues that had developed in this brief time: Young, "his satellites," and William Alexander Carter, agent of the Overland Mail Company, along with other "agents and contractors," had "constantly worked to separate this command." Young had openly sought to "drive me away from here before spring." Carter did not have "the interests of Government or the Overland Mail Company at heart" but instead worked "to make money out of the Government" and "to speculate upon the necessities of this command." Carter originated the rumor that one hundred head of cattle were stolen from Fort Bridger, circulating it "for the purpose of having troops ordered to that post" and away from Great Salt Lake City. "I am credibly informed . . . that Mormons have instigated the late attack by Indians on the telegraph station at Pacific Springs in order to draw my forces to that point," Connor wrote, adding, "Mormons . . . encourage depredations by the Humboldt Indians by purchasing of them property of which massacred immigrants have been despoiled by giving them in exchange therefor powder, lead, and produce." Connor also observed, "Young is making active preparations . . . to oppose the Government of the United States in the spring, provided Utah is not admitted into the Union as a State, or in case of a foreign war or serious reverse to our arms, . . . [and is] mounting cannon for the purpose of resisting the Government."[272]

The Union's most lopsided loss was experienced during December 11–15 at Fredericksburg, on Virginia's Rappahannock River. Eager for a Union victory to restore the nation's confidence, the unproductive Maj. Gen. George B. McClellan was replaced by Maj. Gen. Ambrose Burnside as the commander of the Army of the Potomac. Burnside's 114,000 troops were facing 73,000 of the Army of Northern Virginia under Robert E. Lee, Thomas "Stonewall" Jackson, and James Longstreet. From the Union side of the river, Burnside's 150 guns rained eight thousand projectiles into the city, to clear Confederate forces that were preventing construction of pontoon bridges to carry his troops across. "Rapidly the huge guns vomited forth their terrible shot and shell into every corner and thoroughfare," recalled one eyewitness. Union forces finally crossed the river, but Confederates repositioned, placing dozens of cannons atop Marye's Heights. Burnside's repeated frontal assaults were met by cannon and infantry from the heights. "A chicken could not live on that field when we open on it," a Confederate cannoneer bragged. In an hour, Burnside lost nearly three thousand men.[273] Confederate casualties were estimated at more than five thousand, but those of the Union amounted to nearly thirteen thousand. The disastrous results appeared in the *Deseret News*.[274]

Harding's proclamation of a day of "Thanksgiving and Praise to Almighty God" to begin the coming year of 1863 was published without editorial comment in the LDS press and ignored by the Mormon people. It read in part: "Plenty [has] poured out upon you. . . . Your granaries are full to overflowing; no scourge has fallen upon you, but the God of Peace has reigned . . . in your midst, while in other and fairer portions of the land, the Demon of the Civil War has driven his blood-stained chariot over desolated fields and deserted cities."

The governor chose January 1 as the day to give thanks for "all His mercies to us as a people" and asked that the people of Utah "manifest in a proper spirit our dependence on Him."[275]

In his December 10 address to the territorial legislature, Harding took on a different tone, calling the Mormons to patriotism: "It is the duty of every lover of human liberty and friend of republican institutions on this continent to stand by the government in its present trials. . . . [S]ince my sojourn amongst you I have heard no sentiments, either publicly or privately expressed, that would lead me to believe that much sympathy is felt by . . . your people in favor of the government . . . , now struggling for its very existence." He then launched a polemic, moving from censure to a scathing criticism of polygamy, calling it an "anomaly throughout Christendom" and adding the lurid charge that "a mother and her daughters are allowed to fulfil the duties of *wives* to the same husband." Harding invoked language very similar to that which would later be heard in the U.S. Supreme Court ruling: "When religious opinions . . . pass from . . . *mere sentiment* into *overt acts*, . . . [they] must conform to those usages established by law." Stenhouse called Harding's speech the "tocsin of war" as the legislators silently stared at the floor and grit their teeth on "hearing their faith condemned."[276]

Passing to other sensitive issues, Harding noted that considerable money had been approved for the militia but none for public schools, and he recommended the reverse. He admitted, despite being the commander in chief of the militia, he knew nothing of it and had not received any report from Lt. Gen. Daniel Wells.[277] The legislators and Young fumed, refusing the protocol of publishing Harding's address. Of twenty pieces of legislation passed, the governor vetoed fourteen.[278] Harding soon would join the ranks of Utah's banished federal appointees and would make sour Stenhouse's earlier assessment: "I have seen Brother Stephen S. Harding and . . . set it down that he is going to remain longer than Dawson."[279] Harding's stay outlasted Dawson's, but Harding was equally despised, if not even more so, by Young and the Mormon leaders.

The end of 1862 found Utah striving for statehood, on the cusp of rebellion, barely avoiding the conflict pending at its doors, profiting by the circulation of federal monies, and enjoying culture and humor in the finest theater in West, with its Saints safe in their mountain home, removed from the carnage afflicting those loyal to Union and Confederacy.

Chronology
1862

January 4	Acting Governor Frank Fuller writes Albert Perry Rockwood in answer to the legislative committee investigating why Governor John W. Dawson left the territory.
January 8	Dawson reaches Fort Bridger, writes of his attack by Mormons.
	Mormon legislature continues planning for independent statehood. Nominates and unanimously "elects" the "Ghost Government of the State of Deseret," with Brigham Young as governor, other ranking Mormons to state offices, and George Q. Cannon and William Hooper as delegates to Congress.
	Mormons leaders express strong objections to federal appointees from outside Utah Territory.
	Utah's Civil War tax of $29,982 is paid through a special real estate assessment and whiskey taxes.
	Civil War is predicted to involve destruction of Great Britain, Europe, and Scandinavian countries.
January 20–22	John Bernhisel shows affidavit about Governor Dawson's alleged behavior in Utah to Washington senators and representatives and to President Lincoln.
January 29	Dawson arrives at Fort Laramie.
February	Preparations begin for 300 wagons of out-and-back emigrant teams.
February 11	Joseph Morris and fifteen others are excommunicated by Wilford Woodruff.
February 19	Dr. Robert Arthur Chambers writes President Lincoln about promises made to him in Utah for a federal appointment.

March 5   Salt Lake Theatre opens, with packed performances of a full season of entertainment.

April 6   Battle of Shiloh is fought, with the death of Gen. Albert Sidney Johnston.

Joseph Morris and others form the Church of Jesus Christ of the Saints of the Most High.

April 14   Telegram is sent by Judge John Fitch Kinney and six others, asking the secretary of state to authorize Superintendent of Indian Affairs John Duane Doty to raise a regiment for protection of the Overland Mail Company from Indian attacks.

April 24   At Acting Governor Fuller's request, Gen. Daniel H. Wells activates Col. Robert T. Burton and twenty cavalrymen to protect an eastbound stage carrying William Hooper and Chauncey W. West.

April 28   Young is authorized to raise a company of men for federal service in protecting the mail and overland travel and calls Capt. Lot Smith into service.

Anti-bigamy Morrill Bill is debated in Congress and passes on June 3, despite objections such as those from California and the *New York Times*.

May 11   Lot Smith and his company arrive in Fort Bridger.

May 19   Six outbound emigrant trains leave Utah, bound for Nebraska.

May 22   Judge Kinney issues a warrant for the release of those imprisoned at Fort Kington.

May 31   Eleven thousand casualties at the Battle of Seven Pines are considered "spicy events" by Young.

June 10   Judge Kinney orders the arrest of Joseph Morris and others.

June 11   "Acting marshal" Robert T. Burton is ordered to form a posse comitatus of the militia to enforce the writ.

June 13	More than one thousand troops of the Nauvoo Legion under Colonel Burton begin cannon and small arms fire on Morris and several hundred apostates at Fort Kington.
June 15	Morrisites surrender under white flag; Morris, John Banks, and two women are killed.
	Bodies of Morris and Banks are put on public display in Salt Lake City.
July 7	Recently appointed governor Stephen S. Harding arrives in Salt Lake City.
July 12	Col. P. Edward Connor and company begin their march from California to Utah.
July 19	Captain Lot Smith leads a chase of Indians into Snake River valley but fails to find them.
August 1	Colonel Connor reaches Fort Churchill.
August 6	Capt. Smith and company return to Salt Lake City.
August 24	Young refuses a request for the extension of service of Lot Smith's company and again refuses to send military forces into Civil War.
August 27	General James Craig is authorized to reenlist Lot Smith's Utah troops.
August 28–30	Union forces sustain another humiliating defeat, at the Second Battle of Bull Run.
September 1	Connor and the California Volunteers reach Ruby Valley.
September 5	Connor leaves his troops at Ruby Valley and explores Fort Crittenden and the Salt Lake City area.
September 11	Connor leaves Fort Crittenden and returns to Ruby Valley.
September 14	Battle of South Mountain is fought in Maryland.
September 17	Battle of Antietam results in twenty-three thousand combined casualties.

September 21	Connor and the California Volunteers plead for assignment to the war zone, offering to pay their own way.
October 2	Main body of the California Volunteers leaves Ruby Valley, bound for Utah.
October 17	California Volunteers reach the remains of Camp Crittenden.
	Young leaves Salt Lake City on trip to northern settlements.
October 19	Connor and his troops cross the Jordan River, encountering no resistance.
	More than 200 Mormon families are called to emigrate south to grow cotton.
October 20	Connor and 700 troops march through the silence of Salt Lake City, and Governor Harding addresses them.
	Connor sets up a permanent camp in the foothills, about three miles east of the city's center.
October 25	Young returns to Salt Lake City from his trip north.
October 26	Young calls for thirty-six extra policemen from each ward of the city to spy on LDS members.
	Young rules that Mormons will fix the prices of all provisions purchased by Connor's troops.
November	California Volunteers construct winter quarters at Camp Douglas.
November 5	Oath of allegiance is required of all Mormons who sell goods to troops.
November 12	Live cat is thrown through the window of Governor Harding's house.
December 3	Governor Harding declares January 1 to be celebrated as a day of thanksgiving, but his declaration is ignored.
December 10	Harding's address to the legislature of Deseret infuriates Mormons, who refuse to publish his speech.

December
11–15

Battle of Fredericksburg is the Union's most one-sided loss of the entire war.

December 20

Brigham Young and others, vexed by the proximity of Connor's troops, work to have them moved to Fort Bridger or another distant location.

December 24

Salt Lake Theatre is dedicated with an evening gala.

CHAPTER 5

Who Will Blink First? 1863

The supreme art of war is to subdue the enemy without fighting.

SUN TZU, *THE ART OF WAR*

Eyeball to eyeball, but neither side blinked. With Mormons intolerant of marplots, Governor Harding's status with the State of Deseret's legislature reached its nadir in January with his block of the territory's sixth attempt at a constitutional petition, just as Governor Dawson's status plummeted after his denial of their fifth.[1] "Legislators are on the checker board with His Excellency," was the *New York Times*'s description.[2]

The *Deseret News* reported the legislature's doings, but Harding's official but highly offensive speech remained unpublished. Ohio's Benjamin Wade arranged for the Senate Committee on Territories to print a thousand copies and send it to Utah for distribution. Wade commented that Utah's theocracy was headed by one who "is the only real power acknowledged."[3] Harding wrote Secretary of State William Seward of the failure to publish his gubernatorial message, adding, "No individual outside of this Territory, can form a true opinion the state of society here." Only firsthand could the control "wrought, by a cunning almost supernatural, on the superstitions of an ignorant, credulous, and dependent people" be understood. "Every art and appliance was made use of to win me over to the interest and schemes" of Brigham Young, Harding explained, "but when he discovered that this was impossible, he commenced his work of slander and defamation, and . . . sent to every settlement in the Territory reports the most false and scandalous, . . . to make my stay here so unpleasant that I would voluntarily resign."[4]

The *Times* cautioned: "A pamphlet must issue from Nevada, California, or elsewhere, if the masses of Utah are to receive official information of the sentiments of the Governor. . . . The country cannot afford . . . to inaugurate anything that may lead to another series of [war's] blows."[5] Sharing the same concern that ill will would progress to open conflict, Harding issued Order No. 1 on January 20, calling on Daniel Wells to supply duplicate records of ordnance held by the militia. Harding's February 3 letter to Seward pointed out, "[Young] is procuring arms and heavy ordnance. . . . [H]e is at this time secretly manufacturing shells and solid shot, cartridges, and a new weapon. . . . I have been able through secret service to learn that his arsenal is full of new and efficient small arms equal . . . to those used by the Government."[6]

Wells's reply to Harding's request for a full report was illuminating, especially in comparison with James Ferguson's outdated fourteen-page report of 1858 to Young, which listed more than 2,000 rifles; more than 1,000 muskets; nearly 300 revolvers; 1,500 pounds of powder; and more than 3,000 pounds of lead. Wells gave no such pandect to Harding, courteously noting that the information on armament held by the Legion was not his business to know. Although federal law named him its commander, virtually nothing in its arsenal was property of the federal government: "Strictly speaking there are no arms or ammunition . . . belonging to this Territory. In 1851 Judge Perry E. Brochus for his protection across the plains was furnished by the department one brass 12 ponder [*sic*] mountain Howitzer. . . . If this can be said to belong to the territory it is the only ordiance and ordanices [*sic*] stores . . . that I have any knowledge of coming under the purview of your Excellency."[7] By any name—Nauvoo Legion, Standing Army of Israel, or Utah militia—this was a private army whose armament was owned by individuals, by those under the theocracy, all at Young's de facto control.

President Lincoln signed the Emancipation Proclamation as an executive order on January 1, freeing more than three million of the

Officers of the Third Regiment of Infantry of the Nauvoo Legion, part of the
seven-thousand-man private army of the Latter-day Saints in Utah.

four million slaves held in states then in rebellion against the Union,
in areas where the rebellion had been suppressed. The U.S. Army and
the executive branch of the government were ordered to treat as free
all those enslaved in ten states and in Confederate areas occupied
by Union forces. This was widely celebrated, but in some Southern
states, armed and mounted patrols were formed to prevent mass slave
uprisings. The situation was acute in border-state Kentucky, whose
slaves misunderstood and thought they too had been freed.[8] The *News*
declared that the proclamation was not a harbinger of benefit to millions but rather "will bring about a literal fulfillment of certain predictions of the prophets."[9]

Mormons were facing problems on several fronts. While Representative James M. Ashley of Ohio prepared a bill for the admission of
Utah Territory into the Union, it also prohibited polygamy. In Young's
January message to the State of Deseret, he found in Ashley's enabling
acts for Nebraska, Colorado, Utah, and Nevada a "wise abandonment"
of strict requirements regarding population, insisting statehood should
rest solely on the "capacity for self-government and its Republican
form of Constitution." This was a careful stringing of words, because

The Third Regiment of Infantry formed in a skirmish line.

a "republican government," as defined since 1787, did not exist in Utah.[10] James Madison's federalist paper specified two basic elements of a republic: the government "derives all its powers directly or indirectly from the great body of the people"; and second, "is administered by persons holding their offices . . . for a limited period, or during good behavior."[11] In the Federalists' view, "Men are not to be trusted with power, because they are selfish, passionate, full of whims, caprices, and prejudices."[12] Also relevant was Thomas Jefferson's letter that laid out the intent of the constitutional amendment regarding religion: "I contemplate with sovereign reverence that act of the whole American people which declared that their legislature should 'make no law respecting an establishment of religion, or prohibiting the free exercise thereof,' *thus building a wall of separation between Church & State.*"[13]

Other vexations included Judge John Cradlebaugh's planned speech against Utah's admission, "in which some astounding disclosures will be made in regard to Brigham Young and his church operations."[14] Reimbursement for the service of Col. Robert T. Burton and his twenty men, and that of Capt. Lot Smith and his company, remained unpaid.[15]

Young worked all options for Col. P. Edward Connor's removal from the four square miles claimed to be within the city limits.[16] Connor set the camp's size in part to maximize the distance between troop quarters and the houses where "Bacchus and Venus hang out their colors," observed the *Times*.[17] Bernhisel wrote of instructions sent by Secretary of War Edwin M. Stanton to Connor to relocate, but if the order reached Connor, it "has not yet produced any motion," Young responded.[18] Mormon leaders wished Connor to be at Fort Bridger or at a farther distance.

The push for Connor's removal was addressed by Harding in a letter to Seward, naming Frank K. Cook, the assistant treasurer of the mail company, as bringing the influence of the Overland Mail to the fight for relocation. The Overland, dependent on Young and Mormon suppliers for hay and grain for their animals, could save thousands of dollars by not having to compete with the U.S. Army.[19] Overland's Hiram S. Rumfield "laid down a policy of friendliness to the Saints," and in their correspondence "you will find almost no criticism of Mormon leaders or Mormon policy."[20] Cook, stationed in Salt Lake City, wrote severely disparaging letters regarding another Mormon irritant, Harding. Cook's letter to Overland treasurer A. J. Center in New York City said that Harding "is working by all the arts of his ambitions . . . to bring the Gen'l. Gov't into collision with the people of Utah." Harding, Cook wrote, "has rendered himself unnecessarily offensive to this community by the bitterness of his attacks upon their social and political sentiments, and by the peculiarity and arrogance of his manner, and has made the whole people feel . . . that the Administrations are hostile to them." According to Cook, it was not Young who was threatening conflict, as Connor claimed, but Harding who would involve his country in an unnecessary war.[21] Cook's letters were influential in bringing about Harding's removal. Rumfield sided with Cook against Harding and Connor, stating, "The embroglio between the Mormons and Governor Harding . . . is seething like a volcano just before eruption. . . . Unfortunately, Col. Connor and his command, are enlisted heart and soul in the cause of the unscrupulous and blood thirsty Governor." Rumfield also asserted that Doty and others were "unremitting in their endeavors" to provoke hostilities, and he urged authorities at Washington to recall Harding at once.[22]

Harding wrote Seward again on April 11, reinforcing Connor's position that northern raids were induced to draw Connor out of Utah. Living amid a hostile seven-thousand-man private army, Harding assured Seward that, without Connor's protection, the territory would quickly "be relieved of my presence." The best way to identify officials performing their duties most effectively would be to scan the list of those men Mormons wanted removed, Harding advised Seward.[23]

Starting as a Battle—Ending as a Massacre

What happened near an ice-filled river in January 1863 must be placed in context. Deprivation and hunger fueled the several Indian attacks of 1860–63 along the Humboldt, the Snake, and the Oregon Trail.[24] "The rapacity of the Indians . . . was born of sheer necessity," Doty's biographer emphasized. Their lands were increasingly being taken by white men, their food sources destroyed, and "steal or starve" became their options. Neglect by both territorial and federal governments and dismal conditions of Native Americans faced Doty and Connor on their arrival.[25] Doty requested $68,500 to meet the requirements of Utah's Indian affairs. Of his predecessors—though he did not name Brigham Young—he charged: "No definitive action had been taken, no tribal land titles established, no treaties of cession negotiated. Appropriations had been niggardly."[26] Despite pleas from December 1861 to July 30, 1862, Doty and his staff received no salaries, and no funds for distribution to Indian groups. Not only was the requested increase in funds denied, but they were cut further to the bone, at $10,500. After expenses only $5,000 remained for goods and clothing for the Indians. Faced with insufficiency, Doty sent Agent F. W. Hatch home to Michigan.

In January, Connor learned of the winter encampment on the Bear River of a large body of Shoshonis and a smaller number of Bannocks under the command of Chief Pocatello who were believed responsible for the Humboldt attacks and those recently in northern Utah. U.S. marshal Isaac L. Gibbs came from Judge John Fitch Kinney's office to Connor with instructions to arrest Shoshoni chiefs Bear Hunter,

Sanpitch, and Sagwitch for the recent murder of one John Henry Smith. The three were to be delivered as prisoners to court in Salt Lake City, according to conventional accounts. Chaplain John Alexander Anderson's account in the *San Francisco Bulletin* gave different details: "[It] was not because Judge Kinney had issued warrants . . . but because . . . Connor was receiving such details of the robberies and murders practiced on American citizens as compelled him to take measures for the punishment of the criminals." Connor's plan had two important ends. Clearly he aimed to stop Indian attacks on emigrants and citizens. Additionally, it would deprive Young and the Overland entrepreneurs of reasons to have the troops removed from their established, preferred site at Camp Douglas. Connor assured Gibbs that he was not needed, for "it was not my intention to take any prisoners."[27] Severe punishment had been set as official policy by the Department of the Pacific in April 1862. Wisconsin's James R. Doolittle, of the Senate Committee on Indian Affairs, held that Indian tribes were a dying race destined to be conquered by superior whites. As eradication became policy, he advocated placing Indian Affairs under the War Department.[28] In the fall of 1862, Connor ordered harsh actions against those responsible for the Humboldt attacks, and his plans against the Shoshonis were similar.[29]

Connor did not explain hiring the expedition's guide, the taciturn Mormon trail-tough, enforcer, and Young's agent and killer-on-command, Orrin Porter Rockwell. Connor had signed on "Port"—despite unswerving loyalty to only Young—for five dollars per day.[30]

The winter timing was purposeful, for Indians would concentrate at the hot springs at Bear River—or "Boa Ogoi," as they named it—"for the Warm Dance to hurry along the spring," rather than scattered in hard-to-find bands across thousands of miles of landscape well known to them. Connor envisioned secrecy, but Bear Hunter was warned.[31] Before troops left the grounds of Camp Douglas, the *Deseret News* reported that the Shoshonis were already entrenched with "breastworks," gun placements, and "rifle pits" preplanned. The *News* did not reveal the source of its information or the time when the Shoshonis constructed their defense works.[32]

Connor's first move was a feint. Sixty-nine men, fifteen baggage wagons, and two howitzers of the California Third Infantry started

January 22 under Capt. Samuel W. Hoyt, allegedly to protect grain ship-ments in Cache Valley. Traveling slowly in daytime, men seemed to be on a routine mission. Two days later, Connor started with his main force of 225 cavalrymen, each armed with forty rifle rounds and thirty pistol rounds.[33] Traveling at night, Connor hoped to conceal the expedition's strength and intention. Anderson explained that Hoyt's group was meant to appear no match for an Indian band whose size was estimated as up to seven hundred men. Anderson thought that the vigilance of the Indians was "slackened," so "they failed to notice the movement of the cavalry," but he added, "All along the march Col. Connor had been diligently lied to by interested parties, who assured him that the Indians had left their camp and dispersed through the hills."[34]

Infantry and cavalry united at the village called Mendon, where Connor ordered a night march of sixty-eight miles to Franklin, with temperatures "so cold that whiskey rations froze in the canteens."[35] Capt. Charles H. Hempstead's version of the march first appeared in his 1864 oration: "The shrill north wind . . . [froze] every rivulet and stream. The moistened breath freezing as it left the lips, hung in minia-ture icicles from beards of brave men. The foam from their steeds stood stark and stiff upon each hair. . . . The sufferings of that night-march of 68 miles can never be told in words."[36] Connor described the march as "awful beyond description," with at least seventy-five men with frozen or near-frozen extremities.[37] "As daylight was drawing near," Hempstead continued," it was necessary . . . for the mounted men to pass on, leav-ing the footmen to follow as rapidly as possible. [As the sun rose,] . . . the smoke of the wigwams . . . was discovered slowly rising from the dense thicket of willows in a ravine on the opposite shore. . . . Between the combatants ran and roared the treacherous current of the rapid stream, filled with floating ice."[38] Crossing the river "with great diffi-culty," the troops started to cross an open plain of one-third mile, but meeting intense fire, they stopped and fought dismounted.[39]

Hempstead confirmed that advance warning and expert instruc-tions on construction of defenses had been received by the Indians: "The position was one of the strongest natural defences which it is pos-sible to conceive, and its selection betokened *a degree of skill on the part of the Indian braves, not to have been expected.* It was . . . almost impregnable to assault while a dozen defenders remained."[40] Historian David Bigler was more specific, stating that if Connor "feared the enemy might get away, he was soon relieved of this concern," for he was in "a carefully laid trap that found his force outnumbered by at least three to two," with the Shoshonis in an "almost unassailable position in a ravine some forty feet wide, six to twelve feet deep."[41] Connor's official report noted that the Indians "had constructed steps from which they could deliver their fire without themselves exposed."[42] Superintendent Doty reported that the Indian camp "was filled with provisions, bacon, sugar, coffee, and various other articles," suggesting that white men—Mormons—had been the source of much of the camp's supplies.[43]

In her 1976 account, Mae Timbimboo Parry, the granddaughter of Chief Sagwitch, related that "a white friend of the Indians came to the camp and told them that the settlers of Cache Valley had made plans to get rid of the Northwestern Shoshones and . . . had sent an appeal to Colonel Connor to come and settle the Indian affairs once and for all." If true, this warning may have led to the construction of a near-lethal surprise for Connor and his expedition.[44] John A. Anderson, on the scene in the dual capacity of chaplain and newspaper correspondent, said in his *San Francisco Bulletin* report: "If the [Union] engineers had labored sedulously, a better breastworks could not have been devised."[45] One Cache Valley Mormon, Henry Ballard, left a puzzling message in his use of uncertain pronouns: "The Lord raised up this foe to punish them without us having to do it."[46] Did Ballard see Connor's volunteers as their foe, as Bigler interprets, or did he mean the Indians were the Mormons' foe?

Connor was behind his cavalry, and when he arrived on the field, he "found that Major McGarry had dismounted the cavalry and was engaged with the Indians, who had sallied out of their hiding places on foot and horseback, and with fiendish malignity waved the scalps of white women and challenged the troops to battle."[47] In his handwritten report, Connor added that "many of the warriors sang out: 'Fours right, fours left, Come on, you California sons of b——s."[48] McGarry's field decision—rash or reasoned—to mount a cavalry assault across an open field against an entrenched and well-armed enemy came close to bringing the expedition down in defeat. In a short span of minutes most of the deaths and casualties were inflicted on the volunteers.[49] Anderson wrote, "Little is it to be wondered at, that the 300 to 350 picked warriors, armed with the best of American rifles stolen from slaughtered emigrants or bought from Mormon and other traders, . . . [and Indians being] experts in use of that weapon felt amply secure against the attack." Connor salvaged the situation, thanks to the swift response by McGarry and his twenty men to Connor's order to scale the hills on the Indians' left and dismount, in order to flank the main body of Indians from a high ground, less vulnerable position. As this maneuver was unfolding, Hoyt's infantry arrived, delayed by not finding a local Mormon guide who could reveal a fording site. Infantrymen, using cavalry horses to make the river crossing, aided McGarry in the flanking of the encampment. Anderson praised surgeon Robert E. Reid, who "instead of cooly smoking his pipe in the background and contemplating the polish of his saws, as is the custom of the profession, acted as an aid to the Colonel, until the wounded began to appear, when he rolled up his sleeves and soon became red with the blood of the poor fellows, so many of whom are indebted to him for their lives."[50]

An uncertain but significant number of women and children died at Bear River, caught up in the chaos and frenzy of the melee that ended the battle.[51] In his anniversary oration, Hempstead did not "rehearse the bloody details of the hand to hand conflict in the ravine, among the tangled willows; in, out, through and over the smoking remains of the 70 lodges there found and one by one destroyed."[52] The total number of dead Indian men is uncertain, with estimates covering a wide span. A figure of 250 seems to have a general agreement among the many writers who have attempted the tally. Whatever the exact number, Bear River was among the most deadly actions recorded in the history of the U.S. forces against the indigent people.[53]

The number of dead and wounded among the volunteers is well documented. Twenty-two enlisted men—most of them Catholic—and one officer, an apostate Mormon and a Freemason, Lt. Darwin Chase, died.[54] The *Alta California* tells of their funeral services: "Sixteen coffins lay side by side in the Quartermaster's storeroom, there the dead were visited by their surviving comrades. . . . [T]he entire command formed in procession and escorted the bodies to the military grave-yard." Chaplain Anderson officiated, and three volleys saluted the fallen as they were laid in their graves. Chase, a Royal Arch Mason, received an interment ceremony from the Masonic fraternity members of the command and from the city. Frank Fuller, territorial secretary, officiated as Worshipful Master, and Colonel Evans of the Second Cavalry as Marshal. Justice Kinney and U.S. marshal Gibbs walked in the procession, which totaled some twenty Masons.[55]

At least seventy-five men suffered cold injury to their extremities. Almost a month after the battle, Connor reported there were ninety men sick in quarters and twenty-two in the post's hospital, with four toe and two finger amputations.[56]

Historian Brigham Madsen concludes that the first hour of the Bear River attack was a battle; the second and third hours became a massacre with an uncertain—but large—number of women and children killed. Since intent is rarely discernible to the historian's search, the final hour could be labeled either a brutal slaughter or the compassionate ending of the suffering of the mortally wounded, or some admixture of both.[57] Neither Connor nor Anderson left information that would answer this troubling question.

Researcher and novelist Kass Fleisher insists that the after-victory actions of the volunteers require revision of the event's title to "the Bear River Massacre and Rape."[58] From Fort Hall and the Shoshone-Bannock Tribal Museum visits, and interviews with several of those knowledgeable, including Mae Timbimboo Parry, Fleisher examines the evidence for and against rape accusations made by Cache County Mormons. In a letter to Young, Peter Maughan cites James Henry Martineau's having heard from Israel J. Clark, who heard "from the squaws," that soldiers "commenced to ravish the Squaws which was done to the very height of brutality" and that "some were used in the Act of dying from their wounds."[59] A report arose from another Mormon man, Samuel Roskelly, who like Martineau and Maughan was not present at the battle but claimed that Shoshoni women had voiced similar charges. Fleisher concludes that the "ordinary men" of the California Volunteers were not immune to the culture of violence and exploitation of women that pervaded military society. She posits that in intense inebriation of victory and power, the women were ravished, but she does not note that 50 percent of the Third Infantry were a cut above "ordinary men." As active members of the Garrison Lodge of the Good Templars, they were dedicated not only to temperance but to probity, to "brotherly love, honesty, and obedience to law," and to a "reformed world order based on human equality of race, gender, and class," while living according to moral standards higher than ordinary.[60] Unacknowledged is the LDS partiality of Cache Valley men voicing the accusations. They knew of Young's anger over the presence of the volunteers at Camp Douglas and would supply Young with a tool that could hasten their relocation. Allegations of rape of the women or of barbaric dispatch of the wounded are absent from Mae Timbimboo Parry's written account. Parry finds fault Connor's failure to offer Bear Hunter an opportunity to give up the guilty men, adding also the charge that this chief was tortured and killed by ramming a red-hot bayonet from one ear to the other.[61] In answer to Fleisher's 1998 direct question regarding rape, Parry answered, "'That's one thing I have never, never heard my grandfather or some of those people, come along and talk about this. I have never in my life heard them say the soldiers raped the women. Never. I was surprised when I read Madsen's account of that, saying that the women were raped by the soldiers, because that was never mentioned by the Indians. And I don't think it's true.'"[62]

Major McGarry's decision to charge is claimed as evidence that Connor lacked control of his men. McGarry, experienced in fighting Indians, was out of contact because Connor was not yet on the field, and with his unit already under intense fire, McGarry made the decision it was his to make. That his order proved costly in lives lost and injuries can be criticized, but his actions do not equate with officers and men running amok, raping. No record has been found that Orrin P. Rockwell—Young's man on the ground—carried accounts of rape to his leader. Had Young been able to credibly report that rape was witnessed, either by Rockwell or by non-Mormons living near Bear River, he would have immediately seized such information to accomplish the removal of Connor and his volunteers. The account of the fighting by Mormon journalist T. B. H. Stenhouse in *Tullidge's Quarterly Magazine*, cited by Newell Hart in his book, does not mention rape. Neither rape nor desecration of the wounded is consistent with the character of P. Edward Connor and with the discipline he instilled in his volunteers from the very early days of their formation. Hart's report includes a quote from the *Stockton (Calif.) Daily Independent* that Connor gave explicit orders that women were not to be harmed.[63] All that is known of the moral fiber of Chaplain and Good Templar John Alexander Anderson, who was a noncombatant at the site, indicates that had he witnessed—or heard reported from credible sources—instances of rape or other barbaric acts, he would have published that information in his accounts or in his later private papers.

The facts of the physiology of erection also puts at serious question the accounts of Indian women being "ravished" by the soldiers. The men were extraordinarily cold, having been in temperatures far below freezing for four to five hours. Many had frozen hands or fingers, unable to feel the cartridges they placed in their weapons; ears—and other peripheral appendages—were insensate. Winter-weight trousers, soaked from fording the ice-filled river, froze solid in the subfreezing air. Under these extreme circumstances, rape would have been almost impossible, unless the claims made were in reference to the use of foreign objects. The allegations did not reach such lurid detail.

Accusations of wrongdoing also flowed from the non-Mormons against the Mormons. Harding claimed that "Mormons were daily in the habit of visiting the camps of the [Indian] band . . . and were enabled to pass through their country with safety where a Gentile would have been robbed and murdered without mercy."[64] Harding's opinion adds to those suggesting that Mormon agents had opportunity to advise the Indians on the construction and placement of defensive structures. Connor said that in the march from Camp Douglas "no assistance was rendered by the Mormons, who seemed indisposed to divulge any information regarding the Indians." Connor confirmed Anderson's observation that the Bear River natives were "well armed with rifles and . . . plenty of ammunition."[65] An April article in the *San Francisco Bulletin* reported what correspondent Anderson "has discreetly said nothing about": "The most unconscionable claims were put in [for] the most trivial services, and . . . the Saints had certainly studied the multiplication table to some purpose." Regarding the Mormons who helped escort the wounded and the men with frozen extremities to Camp Douglas, the *Bulletin* noted that "for every pony taken from the Indians, there were at least two claimants among the thieving, cowardly denizens," who also had to be "watched closely to prevent their stealing the very victuals from our famished men." When portions of the ambulance harnesses were stolen, Rockwell arranged their return, "for even he did not consider this quite the 'squa thing,'" a local idiom for "that which is right."[66]

Rockwell's participation in the mission has received little questioning. At what point did he apprise Connor of the advance preparations by the Shoshonis for the attack? Why did this mountain-wise, experienced plainsman not insist that Connor use sleds drawn over the snow, rather than wheeled wagons and cannons? Rockwell quickly implemented this method to transport wounded after the battle. Why was Rockwell not able to find a guide among the local Mormon people to identify the river's fording locations where Hoyt's foot soldiers could cross? The report by the *Sacramento Union* praised only Rockwell's actions after the battle, when "he exerted himself in behalf of the soldiers, causing the inhabitants to furnish sheets and contribute such delicacies as the wounded required."[67] Rockwell drove the carriage that returned Connor to Camp Douglas after the battle, but Connor's records do not clarify Rockwell's responsibilities or address his apparent failures. Historians Charles Kelly and Hoffman Birney claim that "the fighting Irishman took care that the Mormon spy did not receive any valuable information," and they note that Rockwell took "a liking to the bluff soldier," even admitting to his attempt on the life of Governor Boggs. Rockwell may have admired Connor and transferred some of his affection from Young, but it helped—according to Kelly and Birney—that Connor paid in cash, which as "far as history knows" Young never did.[68]

Strategists criticized Connor for the number of Bear River casualties, but the victory resulted in his promotion on March 29 to brigadier general.[69] The *Deseret News* account was guarded, filled with double meaning: "He is a brave soldier who will yet honor the appointment. . . . We congratulate him upon his promotion and wish him all the good fortune that an honorable soldier can desire; and if he keeps clear of politicians and wire-workers, we have no doubt that his own 'back bone' will carry him [away from here?] where the country can appreciate him."[70]

The outcome at Bear River erased the major reason cited by Young and the Overland businessmen for the California Volunteers to be removed from their base at Camp Douglas. Connor would stay and continue his watchful eye on Mormon doings. The *San Francisco Bulletin* addressed Utah's allegiance: "Could the press of California know the amount of disloyalty of the copperhead stamp vended by the Church leaders in this territory [Utah]," of which their news journalists in Salt Lake City were aware, there would be "immediate concern."[71]

On January 29, 2013, more than two hundred members of the Northwestern Band of the Shoshone Nation traveled through snow on treacherous roads to commemorate the 150th anniversary of the battle-massacre. They met at the historical marker three miles northwest of Preston, Idaho, where the recently discovered names of forty of those killed in 1863 were ceremoniously read by eleven-year-old Brooklyn Timbimboo and her grandmother Patty Timbimboo-Madsen. The remains of two teenagers killed at the battle were returned to the tribe from the Smithsonian Institution. "Two eagles—one of them clearly a golden eagle—circled the nearby killing field during the ceremony," wrote Kristen Moulton in her *Salt Lake Tribune* report.[72]

Indian Tensions Cooling, Politics Heating

As tension with the northern tribes abated following Bear River, the political invective worsened. Harding wrote Seward of the "peculiar element of disloyalty and religious fanaticism in Utah." with Young making his people believe that "the only rightful authority to govern rested in his hands." Young was "aiming if not at universal empire on this continent at least in this Territory."[73] Harding's letter to Gen. George Wright disclosed real fear at the prospect that should Connor "be called elsewhere with the troops," non-Mormons loyal to the government "would not be safe . . . in the city." Rather than removing Connor, the government should strengthen his troops by "at least two additional regiments as soon as possible," he urged.[74] Only two weeks after the Bear River venture, Connor again wrote to Col. Richard C. Drum:

> The Mormon creed . . . winks at murder, pillage, and rapine, and is the very embodiment of hypocrisy; mocks at God and insults the nation. Civil law is a perfectly dead letter in the statute books. . . . The people, from Brigham down to the very lowest, are disloyal almost to a man, and treason, if not openly preached, is covertly encouraged and willful and infamous misrepresentations as to the intention of the Government toward this people constantly made under the specious guise of heavenly revelations. . . . Brigham has been engaged in mounting cannon, ostensibly for protection against Indian depredations, and by this means has placed himself in a position of formidable importance as an enemy. He has fifteen cannon, 9, 12, and 24 pounders, ready for use, and workmen have been engaged for a long time past in manufacturing fixed ammunition of every description, and I truly believe only awaits a serious reverse to our arms, or a foreign war, to break out in open rebellion.

Connor recommended dividing Utah into four parts, adding each to an adjacent territory, declaring martial law, and adding three thousand additional troops, with "three pieces of heavy ordnance."[75] Receptive to the warning, Colonel Drum reacted by ordering the California Third Infantry Volunteers, then at Sacramento, to prepare and proceed early in the spring to join Connor.[76]

While Connor was writing his alarming message, Harding and Judges Charles B. Waite and Thomas J. Drake were increasingly coming under fire. In early March, Young drafted a letter to President Lincoln that blamed the "foolish, uselessly expensive and impolitic location" of Camp Douglas on the influence of Harding, who furthermore has "steadily and industriously written and spoken against the peace and welfare of this Territory." Harding would have had little impact "had he not succeeded in gaining the assistance of Associate Justices Waite and

Drake." Their actions, Young emphasized, "well nigh sufficed to bring on a collision between the citizens and the troops in Camp Douglas." At letter's end, Young threatened war if certain demands were not met. Should the three officers named "be continued in office beyond the lapse of a reasonable time" and should the troops not be ordered out of Utah, or "should steps be taken to reinforce them in their present locality," then he could not avoid concluding "that war upon Utah is determined." Fortunately, the letter was not mailed.[77]

On March 3, Saints crowded the Tabernacle to hear Albert Carrington read Harding's message to the legislature. "There was one deep feeling of contempt manifest for its author," the *News* commented. It was reported that Harding, Waite, and Drake had secretly prepared a bill to be sponsored by Illinois senator Orville H. Browning. To Mormon leaders its provisions were unacceptable: the jurisdiction of the probate court was limited to the probate of wills and the appointment of guardians. Only the U.S. marshal held the authority to summon jurors. Theocracy's ultimate security, its private army—the Nauvoo Legion— was threatened by granting to the territorial governor the sole authority "to appoint and commission *all* militia officers . . . and remove them at [his] pleasure."[78] In remarks to his followers, Young urged lawlessness: "'This man, who is sent here to govern the Territory—man, did I say? Thing, I mean; a nigger worshiper. A black-hearted abolitionist . . . and these two things I do utterly despise.'" Young asked, "'Do you acknowledge this man Harding as your Governor?'" Voices were heard responding, "'No; you are our Governor.'" Next he asked, "'Will you allow such a man to remain in the Territory?'" Voices from the congregation replied, "'No; put him out.'" Then Young pronounced, "'Harding and Drake and Waite must leave the Territory. If they will not resign, and if the President will not remove them, *the people must attend to it.*'" Describing Drake and Waite as "'tools for the Governor,'" Young predicted that these judges "'would have the marshal choose juries of cutthroats, blacklegs, soldiers, and desperadoes of California.'"[79]

John Taylor, Jeter Clinton, and Orson Pratt, Sr., were appointed as a committee to force Harding, Waite, and Drake to resign and leave the territory. Harding answered, "'I came here a messenger of peace and good will to . . . discharge my duties. . . . It is in your power to . . .

shed my blood, but this will not deter me from my purpose.'"[80] Drake, having been accosted in the street and threatened with death, replied to the elders with exhortative spirit: "I deny that you have any cause for such conduct toward me. . . . Your resolutions are false. . . . Go back to Brigham Young, your master, . . . and tell him that I neither fear him, nor love him. nor hate him, but that I utterly despise [him]. . . . [T]ell him . . . that I did not come here by his permission, and that I will not go away at his desire." Drake continued, "I tell you if you . . . attempt to interfere with my lawful business, you will meet with trouble . . . you do not expect."[81]

On March 3 the militia's ordnance was moved to Young's property and guarded by a large body of armed Mormon men. Connor reported to Drum that Mormons were again "engaged in preparing ammunition and cannon" and that "their foundry for some weeks past has been used for casting cannon-balls," adding that they "loudly assert that I shall not be reinforced, and that if the attempt is made they will . . . attack me" with five thousand men and "cannon of heavier caliber than mine."[82]

Young's March 7 letter to Col. J. M. Rossé, the officer who had allegedly been commissioned by Lincoln to investigate the charges made by federal officials, declared the charges fraudulent: "I have never . . . thrown any impediment in the way of the execution of the laws of the U.S.; and . . . shall at all times be at the service of the civil authorities to assist in the execution of the laws. . . . [T]he inhabitants of this whole Territory, will sustain the Constitution and laws of our Government to the uttermost, as we have ever done. . . . [A]ny and every law for the government of the people of this Territory shall be executed without any hindrance whatever."[83] Connor stated that Rossé was an imposter, a Southern emissary meeting privately with Brigham Young. Connor arrested Rossé but, on finding no paperwork in his possession to ensure a conviction, released him.[84] The next day, Young reiterated his earlier refusal, that should the "present Administration . . . ask us for 1,000 men, or even 500, . . . I would see them damned first." Heber C. Kimball joined in, announcing, "'We can defy the whole Federal Government.'" And the congregation replied, "'That's so! We can.'"[85] Mormon apostates wanting to leave the territory came to Connor daily, seeking protection for their lives and property, the colonel wrote to Drum.[86]

When Young heard cannon fire from Camp Douglas on March 9, he raised the alarm, and 1,500 men quickly assembled at his residence, readying two cannons. Connor judged that Young was "trying to provoke me."[87] From Sacramento, Wright warned Connor, "Be prudent and cautious. Hold your troops in hand. A day of retribution will come."[88] Wright informed Washington that "as soon as the roads are passable, I will throw forward [as reinforcements] the residue of Connor's regiment and such other troops as can be spared." Two weeks later Wright updated his superiors: although the excitement provoked by Young had settled somewhat, "yet I am fully satisfied that they only wait for a favorable opportunity to strike a blow against the Union."[89]

Washington was also receptive; General H. W. Halleck telegraphed Wright on March 9 to say, "Prepare to re-inforce Colonel Connor as early as possible. The Secretary of War authorized you to raise additional troops for that purpose in California and Nevada." To Connor, Halleck wrote, "All arms and military munitions intended for use against the authority of the United States are liable to seizure. You will exercise your discretion in regard to making such seizures. You will be cautious and prudent, but when you act, do so with firmness."[90]

Disloyal Acts

Connor's contention that sufficient disloyalty existed for open war to unfold did not arise a priori. It formed from evidence from the sources on which military leaders rely: the written after-action and verbal reports of line officers, such as those of 2nd Lt. Anthony Ethier, Capt. George F. Price, 1st Lt. Francis Honeyman, and Col. George S. Evans.

Lieutenant Ethier left Camp Douglas with twenty-five cavalrymen on March 26 with orders to search for hostile Indians in the vicinity of Skull Valley and Cedar Mountains, southwest of Salt Lake City. After five unremarkable days he made contact with what he later learned were about one hundred of Little Soldier's band.[91] With his horses debilitated from traveling two hundred miles with little rest and forage,

Ethier stopped at Camp Crittenden. Seeing several Indians exiting a nearby small canyon, he executed a creative plan. Packing thirteen men into a commandeered mail coach and finding mounts for eight men, they caught up with the Indians at Cedar Fort. There, Ethier stated, Mormons "wishing to see my party destroyed, gave me false report as to the position of the Indians and . . . to their numbers." Ethier acted on his own assessment, "which I firmly believe saved my party from destruction." Ethier reported that "the Mormons were . . . not farther than 100 yards from the Indians," but "not a shot was fired at them." Then, he said, "while I was not more than 100 yards from the fort" a Mormon rode off toward the Indians, "meeting several of them on the trail . . . where they held conversation in plain sight of me." Ethier continued, "I then being satisfied that there was treachery, returned to Camp Crittenden," and he reported the happening to Connor.[92]

At one o'clock in the morning, Capt. George F. Price headed fifty-one cavalrymen to reinforce Ethier. They met near noon at Crittenden. The combined force traveled south, crossing into Utah County, to the town of Spanish Fork, where they were "assured that no Indians had been seen for ten days."[93] Shortly after this deception, two Indians were spotted in the settlement.[94] A scouting party followed them into Spanish Fork canyon. With little daylight remaining, Price's men mounted quickly. At the canyon's mouth they found upwards of fifty Indians positioned along the canyon's small river. Dividing his force into three units, one on each side and the third led up the center by Price. Meeting "a brisk fire," the cavalry continued up the canyon until forced by darkness to withdraw, still under fire. When they returned to the canyon the next morning, the Indian group was gone, headed south.[95]

In response to hostility proved by these encounters, Connor sent Lt. Francis Honeyman and five artillerymen from Camp Douglas on the morning of April 11 with a howitzer and ammunition concealed in an ambulance. Their instructions were to proceed to the town of Pleasant Grove and await Colonel Evans's arrival or further orders. Reaching this city, Honeyman "put his animals up in a corral of one of the Mormon settlers." At six o'clock that evening, "some 100 Indians came rushing down upon the town." Hiding behind city fences, and haystacks, they fired at the troops, who loaded their cannon and took refuge in a small adobe building. After the concussion of firing only two howitzer loads, the fragile-walled structure was in danger of collapse, and use of the cannon abandoned. Indian gunfire continued "until 8 o'clock at night, literally riddling the door and windows, but fortunately without killing or wounding any one in the building, although the stovepipe, pans, plates, and almost everything in the house except the men received a shot." The Indians made off with the soldier's provisions, blankets, and government animals. Evans expressed outrage that some "100 or 150 white men (Mormons)" merely watched as "in the broad daylight 75 or 100 savages . . . attempt[ed] to murder six American citizens," and none of the Mormons lifted a hand to help them. "On the contrary," Evans said, "they stand around the street corners and on top of their houses and hay-stacks complacently looking on, apparently well pleased at the prospect of six Gentiles (soldiers) being murdered."

Honeyman claimed to have "prima facie evidence" that Mormons and Indians formed a partnership, thinking that the ambulance carried saleable goods, the party would be killed, and the spoils divided. Evans and Honeyman, together with forty-seven men under Lieutenant Ethier and forty-nine under Lt. C. D. Clark, left Pleasant Grove to search for the band that had attacked, but were initially unsuccessful. Evans reported, "The statements of the Mormons in regard to the Indians were premeditated lies . . . for the purpose of misleading me, and giving the latter time either to get away or prepare for battle." Learning that the Indians had returned to the area of Spanish Fork, Evans pursued them but was informed by one of his soldiers posing as a Mormon "that one Potter, a Mormon, had gone into the cañon to notify the Indians of my approach, of the number of men I had, &c,, and that there were other Mormons . . . to give the Indians notice of my every movement." Practicing "a little deception on the Mormons," Evans was able to engage the Indian force of about two hundred, and with cavalry and howitzer killed "about 30 warriors . . . and wounded many more," retaking much of Honeyman's matériel.[96] Citing Evans's report, Wright wrote to Washington, asking that "the conduct of the Mormons" receive particular attention, for "it was only a continuation of their perfidious acts which commenced when our troops arrived in Utah."[97]

Unbending Federal Officers

Each successive "David," while hoping to fare well in Utah, found no slingshots there and learned quickly that only those bending to the will of the panjandrums of Mormon theocracy could long remain. Cradle-baugh, Henry R. Crosby, Henry Martin, R. P. Flenniken, and Dawson each held to rational conclusions to which evidence had led them, and all were gone. The new "Davids"—Harding, Waite, and Drake—were equally observant; therefore, by the spring and summer of 1863, they too were headed for removal.

After Harding's address to the legislature was read in the Taber-nacle, Young commented that "the bread is buttered, but the poison is beneath," and received a supporting "Hear, hear" from the congre-gation. Young told his audience that Harding, with Judges Waite and Drake, were scheming for "the establishment of a military government over the Territory, in the hopes of goading on the people to open rup-ture with the general Government," and if they succeeded, "then, they would call out that Utah was disloyal!"[98] According to Young, Hard-ing had promised that if he became "obnoxious to this people," he would leave the Territory. Young said that such words "were a mix-ture of froth and blarney from beginning to end." Young then told his congregation, "As we are accused of secession, my counsel . . . is to secede, [but] what from? From the Constitution of the United States? No. From the institutions of our country? No. Well then, what from? From sin and the practice thereof."[99] Young preached that Mormons would also secede from miscegenation: "Shall I tell you the law of God in regard to the African race? If the white man who belongs to the cho-sen seed mixes his blood with the seed of Cain, the penalty, under the law of God, is death on the spot. This will always be so."[100]

With Waite, Drake, and himself subjected to mass meetings and petitions for their recall or withdrawal, Harding asked Seward to inform Lincoln that "no man can be popular with Brigham Young who holds a

Federal office, unless he can be used to advance his own personal ambition." Should U.S. troops be withdrawn, "no man can live securely in this Territory, who has become obnoxious to Brigham Young."[101]

Connor wrote Lincoln that "there is no good and true cause for the removal" of Harding, Drake and Waite, who had been endorsed by more than thirty Camp Douglas officers. These three men "have been true and faithful to the Government," Connor said, "and fearless in the discharge of their duties." He continued: "[They have] regarded the rights of all, attended to their own affairs, and have not disturbed or interfered with the affairs of others, outside of their legitimate duty to the Government; and *in all their conduct,* . . . [they have] demeaned themselves as honorable citizens, and officers worthy of commendation by your Excellency, our Government, and all good men."[102]

If Mormons could not force Connor's removal, they could prevent him from living among them by redlining him from rental of living quarters in Salt Lake City. After six months in the territory, Connor had "been entirely unable to obtain a house for love or money." It is an anomaly reported a San Francisco newspaper that "a Brigadier General of the United States cannot rent even a shanty in a city of 10,000 people . . . among a population who claim to be loyal."[103] In April, Connor and his family moved into a house vacated by Harding; they remained there until February 1864, when Camp Douglas quarters were completed.[104]

In January, Brigham Young married Amelia Folsom, thirty-seven years his junior, in what was described as a marriage out of love. It was his first marriage in seven years and done within months of the passage of the Morrill Act. Harding, Drake, and Waite were outraged and reported the marriage to Lincoln on March 6.[105] It was not by chance that Judge Kinney issued a warrant for the arrest of Young and his two counselors for violation of the Morrill Act. Because these leaders had been charged, it could then be argued that justice was done in Utah, that Utah was compliant, that Connor and troops were unneeded. The *New York Herald* and the *Times* agreed: the arrest order by Judge Kinney was an arrangement agreed upon to test the constitutionality of Morrill and create the impression that there was no resistance to judicial process in the territory.[106] The tepid reaction of the *Deseret News* to actions ordinarily met with vitriol is telling: "An immediate response [by Young] was made . . . by the prompt appearance before the Judge Kinney." The *News* found no fault with Kinney, for "it is his duty to magnify all constitutional law, as we trust it will ever be the pleasure of the people to submit to and obey."[107] The *Springfield (Mass.) Republican* dismissed the risk that Young's arrest would result in another national conflict: "[The] heroes of the harem show fully as much sensitiveness in regard to their 'peculiar institution' as the slaveholders do." The editor added, "We have one little rebellion on our hands, it is true; but we ought to be able to attend to 40,000 Mormons also."[108]

Harding further compounded Saints' anger when on March 31 he issued a "full and perfect pardon" to the eighty-five Morrisite men charged for resisting the law and to seven men for second-degree murder at the apostate affair at Fort Kington.[109] Harding's decree came only three days after the grand jury convicted the Morrisites in Kinney's court. Mormon grand jurors in the Third District Court likened Harding to "a pestiferous cesspool in our district, breathing disease and death."[110] "Persecution ran high" against the Morrisites after Harding's reprieve, and many of them—with their families—moved to Connor's protection on the grounds at Camp Douglas and were employed in building the camp.[111] Many remained until May, when Connor's escort took them safely to Soda Springs.

The *San Francisco Bulletin* gave support to Harding: "The innuendo, so industriously circulated by Mormon emissaries, that the Governor of the Territory and others are endeavoring to foment trouble with them, is utterly and unqualifiedly false." The Mormons had only been asked "to obey the law of the land."[112] Among the Saints' "emissaries" were cabinet member and postmaster general Montgomery Blair, the Kane brothers, and the *New York Tribune*'s Horace Greeley. Carrying letters of introduction by Senators James W. Nesmith of Oregon and Milton S. Latham of California, T. B. H. Stenhouse met privately with Blair, urging help with the removal of Drake, Waite, and the volunteers. He next traveled to Philadelphia to see Gen. Thomas L. Kane and younger brother Robert "Pat" Kane. Surprised to learn of Utah's troubles, Thomas Kane offered that he "had a friend in the cabinet" who looked after Utah's interests. Thomas asked Robert "to see Judge

Titus & to post him on Utah men & to put him straight." Stenhouse wrote to Blair, disputing the action reports of Ethier, Price, Honeyman, and Evans and asking Blair for "his best influence" to leave to the Mormons the security of the Atlantic-Pacific highway. On July 1, Stenhouse wrote to Horace Greeley, asking him to influence the secretary of war and Postmaster Blair, "with whom he is very intimate," on Connor's removal and to "let the [Mormon] troops of the territory be entrusted" with Overland security, "*with their own officers.*"[113]

Catherine Waite credited Harding with "a high degree of moral courage" required to perform anything "offensive to 'the powers that be' in the Holy City," adding, "Every attempt was made to seduce him from the path of duty, not omitting the same appliances [of sexual entrapment] which had been brought to bear upon Steptoe and Dawson."[114] Harding visited Lincoln, personally submitting his resignation, but Lincoln would not accept it until he could offer a better position. Harding left Utah on June 11 and was shortly appointed consul to Chile, but on the eve of his departure to that place, his wife was taken ill, and "he could not leave for duties so far distant."[115] Lincoln then appointed him to Colorado's supreme court.[116]

At its next meeting, Kinney closed Utah's supreme court, Drake declined further participation, and Waite resigned in disgust, moving his law practice to Idaho Territory.[117]

A Refuge for the Morrisites

The prediction was for twenty thousand 1863 emigrants traveling to destinations in Oregon, California, and along the Humboldt, including a significant portion who would head to Montana following the July 1862 gold strike at Grasshopper Creek–Bannack City and the May 1863 strike at Alder Gulch–Virginia City. Four-fifths of those attracted to these booms were openly secessionists. Every day trains of "two to twenty wagons" departed with supplies from Salt Lake City for destinations some 250 miles north, said the *San Francisco Bulletin*.[118] Knowing that this area was claimed by Chief Pocatello, the chief whose band had exited their campsite just before the Bear River battle, Connor planned to establish a deterring presence. An expedition for this purpose started for Soda Springs on the Bear River on May 5, with Capt. David Black's infantry company also protecting 160 Morrisites. Morrisites, apostate anathema to the Mormons, had been living on the grounds of Camp Douglas; many were destitute, but some "were able to furnish their own teams and wagons." Judge Waite's wife, Catherine, related that after the Morrisites were taken prisoners, their homes were searched and their possessions plundered.[119] Connor's report to Colonel Drum confirmed this: "'The Mormons have stripped them of almost everything they possessed, and they are consequently very poor, but they are industrious."[120]

Three members of the Soda Springs party deserve special notice: Superintendent Doty, surgeon John King Robinson, and William Adams Hickman. Doty and Connor would jointly sign important peace treaties with some of the Shoshonis. In 1866, Dr. Robinson would be assassinated in a Salt Lake City street ambush because he challenged Mormon land ownership policy. Hickman, another of Young's sometimes myrmidons, was Connor's trail guard and would become one of many suspects in Robinson's October 1866 murder.

Out of Brigham City, Connor ordered two night marches, for he believed that bands of Shoshonis connected with those of Bear River were in the neighborhood and might be surprised and punished for recent attacks.[121] The troops found none but did meet with some 250 to 300 peaceable Shoshonis at the Snake River ferry.

Company H, Third Infantry, arrived on May 20, with their Morrisite settlers safe. A young woman, Emma Thompson Just, recalled the trip's pleasantries: "The hillsides were so green and flower-covered and the river so deep and blue. . . . The Creator must have designed it just for this little band: logs to build our houses; firewood to keep us warm; health giving waters to drink, streams full of fish and mountains full of game."[122] On May 23 a military post of one square mile was established, placed under the command of Captain Black, and named Camp Connor. Each Morrisite family took a small plot of land; adequate housing was completed before winter. Capt. James Stuart, passing through on June 12, noted, "They [the Morrisites] have about twenty houses already built, and are busy building others. They expect a large train of their brethren to arrive in three days."[123] In a report, Connor wrote, "Having occasion to send an empty train to Carson for quartermaster's stores, I furnished to 150 Morrisites transportation to that point, and they have already safely arrived."[124]

Connor judged the Soda Springs area capable of agricultural productivity, but the weather ultimately proved defeating. Lula Barnard left an account of the dismal obstacles of wresting a livelihood from a place where freezing temperatures hit even on summer nights, and building fires did not save crops. "During the second winter," Barnard wrote, "more than half the livestock was lost by reason of extreme cold and lack of feed. Five successive grain crops were destroyed by freezing weather."[125] Hickman related a story of the region's cold. A whiskey canteen was hanging in a bush overnight; the first man taking a hit the next morning was sure sand had been added, but the particles were ice crystals.[126] Up to three hundred soldiers were quartered at Camp Connor from its founding in 1863 to its closure at February's end, 1865.

Friend for the Mormons

While Harding, Waite, and Drake were on the spit, roasting in the heat of demands for their ouster, John Fitch Kinney was openly ushered into theocracy's inner circle. That Kinney was to be enskied surfaced at the Morrisite trial when he said it was "probably the last time he should meet" in a judicial capacity. The *San Francisco Bulletin* described Kinney as "the special friend of Presidents Young and Kimball" and claimed, "[He] is regarded by the Mormons as their fast and true friend. It is even said that he has been baptized into the church."[127] A political move by the Republican administration caused the staunch Democrat to be replaced as Utah's chief justice by Republican John Titus of Philadelphia. Kinney's generous reward for years of biddable service, including the Dawson affair, was to be picked by Young as the first non-Mormon to represent Utah Territory's overwhelmingly Mormon population in Congress. At a meeting of some five thousand church members in Provo on June 27, Young assured Kinney's election by introducing him as "our next Delegate to Congress." Affirmation followed without opposition. Kinney responded with a long speech on democracy and "an intelligent and impartial review" of Utah's history.[128] Kinney made "stumping tours" throughout the settlements of Utah, all unneeded except to superficially acquaint the people with the candidate who would unavoidably receive a unanimous vote. As the *Times* wrote, "With or without these journeys, his 'calling and election' are equally sure."[129] On August 3, Kinney was "elected" as Utah's representative to Congress. Simultaneously, Albert Carrington became the mythical State of Deseret's representative to Congress, to stand ever ready should Deseret be admitted as a state.[130] By year's end, the man who had sent confidential letters to the U.S. State Department and attorney general, "amassed during the Pierce administration, . . . criticizing Brigham Young's influence on Utah's judicial and legal systems," now served at his bidding.[131] Forgotten or forgiven were Kinney's 1854 decision invalidating the territorial statute that forbade the citing of common law or precedent rulings, and his letter to the U.S. attorney general complaining that in Utah the priesthood laws were the only operative laws of the land.[132] Forgiven was Kinney's aid to Steptoe in carrying Mormon women to California. The same man, John Fitch Kinney, now stood before Congress and dissembled matters in Utah.

A Tourbillion of Arms, Blankets, Heads, Guns, and Knapsacks

Midsummer in Pennsylvania brought a dramatic turning point in the Civil War. By June those of the Army of Northern Virginia, commanded by admired tactician Gen. Robert E. Lee, were in high spirits, buoyed by December's victory at Fredericksburg and May's at Chancellorsville. Advancing into Maryland and into Pennsylvania brought opportunities not only for further military victories but also for weakening the resolve of the Northern public to continue a war immensely costly in lives and dollars. Fighting on Union soil might aid the efforts of Pennsylvania Democrats to sway Lincoln to end the war short of total military and civil capitulation. To the converse, Confederate invasion of Union soil would further motivate Union leaders and soldiers of the Army of the Potomac, for now they would be fighting for the security of their own lands and for the protection of their families.

Approaching was the battle of two massive armies in and around the small borough of Gettysburg, in Adams County. Gathering were some 160,000 soldiers, where more than 51,000 of them would be killed, wounded, captured, or missing, the largest toll for a single battle in the Western Hemisphere's history.

Brig. Gen. John Buford's cavalry opened the battle on July 1, pitted against a much larger infantry body coming in from the west, commanded by Confederate major general Henry Heth. Fighting dismounted on McPherson Ridge, Buford's cavalrymen were outnumbered by the Confederate infantry, but Buford's men were able to slow Heth's advance until Union major general John F. Reynolds arrived with the Iron Brigade, commanded by Brig. Gen. Solomon Meredith.[133] By the end of the day of July 1, Union forces, thanks largely to Buford's cavalry, had taken the high ground of Cemetery Ridge nearly to the promontories known as Big and Little Round Top. While these two forces battled, five to six thousand Confederate cavalry under Gen. J. E. B. Stuart were east of Gettysburg, trying to make effective contact with Lee's main body.

On July 2 the Confederate army unfolded en echelon attacks by parts of Gen. James Longstreet's and Gen. Ambrose P. Hill's corps, directed at Union forces on the southern end at "Devil's Den" and the "Peach Orchard." From late afternoon to darkness, the boulder-strewn "Wheatfield" changed hands at least seven times, with an estimated seven thousand casualties falling in an area the size of a football field. At Little Round Top, Col. Joshua Lawrence Chamberlain and his Twentieth Maine Infantry held their line. With ammunition exhausted, they repulsed the advancing Alabama units with a bold bayonet charge, saving the day. At the northern end, three hours of fierce Confederate assaults by Gen. Richard S. Ewell's Second Corps gave them the lower half of Culp's Hill on the eastern slope of Cemetery Hill.

By day three, Stuart's cavalry forces were attempting to flank the Union troops and attack them from the northeast, at the rear of Maj.

Gen. George G. Meade's forces. Meade was on the high ground of Cemetery Ridge, his attention focused west on the Confederate infantry on Seminary and Warfield ridges. Lee hoped to achieve a pincer action, with Stuart's cavalry attacking the northeast while the massed infantry under Longstreet and Maj. Gen. George Edward Pickett came from the southwest, to cut the federal line in half. Stuart's crack cavalry, including his First Virginia "Invincibles," the First North Carolina, and the Jefferson Davis Legion, met and were defeated by Union cavalry of the First, Fifth, and Seventh Michigan, the Third Pennsylvania, and the First New Jersey.[134]

Lee began his attack on Cemetery Ridge near noon with an intense artillery barrage. Confederate infantry then charged across three-quarters of a mile of open ground against Meade's presighted artillery and his prepared troops atop Cemetery Ridge. A disaster ensued, with many Southern infantry units annihilated, literally shredded by intense Union artillery and rifle fire. A 100 percent loss was sustained by University of Mississippi students who made up the University Grays of the Eleventh Mississippi Infantry. The Color Company of the Thirty-eighth North Carolina Infantry, and Company F of the Twenty-sixth North Carolina Infantry, also lost 100 percent.[135] Many Confederate men simply disappeared, their bodies so torn apart that reassembly of the fragments was not possible. Flesh, blood, and bodies became a whirling "cloud of . . . arms, heads, blankets, guns and knapsacks."[136] An estimated 7,500 Confederates were lost—in little more than an hour—during the massive infantry charge led by Confederate generals, including Pickett, J. Johnston Pettigrew, and Isaac R. Trimble. As Gen. Lewis Armistead led his Fifty-third Virginia Infantry into a break in the Union line, the Pennsylvanians re-formed. "'Men fire[d] into each other's faces not five feet apart," wrote Jacob Hoke.[137] The failure of "Pickett's Charge" to take the field sealed the battle.[138] The aftermath left a montage of grotesque: "Every house and barn in Gettysburg had been turned into an improvised hospital, where the haggard surgeons struggled to save the mangled wounded. Carpets and floors were awash in gore, walls were spattered with blood, and piles of amputated limbs were heaped outside the open windows."[139]

The groans and screams—the odor of blood, mixed with the fresh scent of the night, the grass, the trees—that slaughter-house! O well is it their mothers, their sisters cannot see them—cannot conceive, and never conceiv'd, these things. One man is shot by a shell, both in the arm and leg, both are amputated—there lie the rejected members. Some have their legs blown off—some bullets through the breast—some indescribably horrid wounds in the face or head, all mutilated, sickening, torn, gouged out—some in the abdomen—some mere boys—many rebels, badly hurt—they take their regular turns with the rest, just the same as any—the surgeons use them just the same.

Source: WHITMAN, "NIGHT BATTLE," 35.

The fourth of July was no holiday. Survivors saw twenty-two thousand wounded men who lay desperate on the fields in the summer heart. An estimated six million pounds of human and animal carcasses were strewn across the site, liquefying in the sun.[140]

The parallel universe in Salt Lake City featured "several balls" in celebration of Independence Day, chief among them the Union ball at the Salt Lake Theatre.[141] The *New York Times* described the event: "A temporary floor had been laid over the parquette, level with the stage, making a dancing floor over one hundred feet long. Three hundred and twenty-five tickets were issued at $2.50 each, which, with the 'additional ladies,' would probably bring a gross income of $1,000 for the night." Festivities began at five o'clock on July 3; a midnight meal was served, and dancing did not end until five in the morning of the fourth, with more than forty cotillions accommodated. "In short, everything is reported with *colour de rose*. The ball was the greatest thing of the day," the *Times* concluded, even though it left "every official or important body in the city . . . too wearied . . . to be ready for a midday's parade under the burning sun." Thus, rather than attending a

Reinterring skeletons at Cold Harbor, Virginia, where several days of battle in May 1864 produced forty-nine thousand wounded or dead. Library of Congress, LC-B811- 918 [P&P] Lot 4168.

parade, "all the folks in the city were at liberty to do that which was right and fitting in their own eyes."[142]

Some progress with the human detritus at Gettysburg had been made by July 16. On this day in Salt Lake City, a grand festival was held in the new theater for the surviving members of the "Pioneers of 1847" and the officers and soldiers of the Mormon Battalion. One hundred eighty-one of the original 500 men were present. Songs and toasts marked the occasion. Dancing and revelry for eight hundred attendees lasted from two o'clock in the afternoon to four o'clock the next morning, with several speeches by Mormon dignitaries and recesses spaced through the celebration.[143]

Connor, Doty, and Indian Treaties

As summer brought the war's turning point on the verdant hills of Pennsylvania, it also brought a crescendo of frustration to the commander of the District of Utah. The first week of June seemed auspicious, for Connor considered the Indian situation to be coming under control. He met with 650 to 700 Shoshonis near Fort Bridger and formed a peace treaty, and he found another 200 near Fort Hall who were friendly. However, by June 11 the tone of his letters to San Francisco changed dramatically as Southern Utes commenced hostilities: "Rumor says 1,600 of them in Mormon settlements south are on the way to attack me and destroy overland mail." He added, "Goshutes still troublesome. My force much scattered; should be doubled at once. I am surrounded by enemies, white and red."[144] A series of Indian raids along the Overland, with Utes gathering in threatening numbers, prompted letters from Connor to superior officers in late June. To Colonel Drum, he was precise: "Expedition from Bridger under Captain [Micajah G.] Lewis captured fifty of San Pitch's band. Captain [Samuel P.] Smith killed ten Indians Saturday last near Government Springs. Utes collecting in settlements south in large numbers, and threatening destruction to soldiers and overland mail. Have only sixty men for duty at Camp Douglas."[145] The next message was directed not only to Drum but also to the "President of the United States." Indian activity in Utah, Connor observed, was not from uncoordinated strikes of isolated bands but from the machinations of Young and LDS Church members. As Indians traveled through Mormon towns, "they were fed . . . by the people and . . . in some instances they sent . . . ahead to the next town to notify the bishop they were coming, and to have prepared a beef for them." They were boasting that "they would kill emigrants and break up the overland mail" and that they had "sufficient force to attack Camp Douglas and drive the military from the country."[146]

The Indians were said to exhibit "the reeking scalps they had taken from their murdered victims." This charge came in part from a letter written by a Mormon woman, Phebe Westwood, to her husband: "I have been to Salt Creek [Nephi] on a visit. . . . While I was gone the Indians captured another stage and killed two men. It happened about two miles this side [of] the ford of the River Jordan. They brought the scalps of the poor men they killed down to Salt Creek, and I saw them. . . . The bishop down there [Jacob G. Bigler] treated the Indians with tobacco and ordered the people to feed them, and it made me so mad that I pitched into them and told them what I thought of them."[147] Wood Reynolds, a participant in Dawson's beating, and Thomas O'Shawnessy were the victims in the attack described by Westwood. Grisly details appeared in the *Times*. Reynolds, the coach driver, turned off the road when approached by twenty-five Indians on horseback. Both men were quickly dispatched. According to the *Times*, "two ugly gashes four and seven inches long, appeared in the right side of Reynolds, from the larger of which his liver protruded." Scalps were taken, and the coach was thoroughly stained with the men's blood.[148]

Ute chief Tabby was revealed as responsible for the attack, in a June 23 letter from George Washington Bradley, polygamist and bishop of Moroni, Utah, reporting to Young on a meeting with several Ute chiefs in Sanpete County. Tabby admitted, "'I was leader of the war party that attacked the Mail lately and want you to know that I am sorry and ashamed to learn that a Mormon was killed in that affair, but now I am willing to listen to your counsel and do as you say, that is if the Soldiers will listen too, and quit seeking Indians to kill them.'" Tabby continued, "'We will take your advice and not molest the Mail Line nor Emigrants any more.'" Pete Berry, "an Indian who speaks good English," added, "'My Band are down South. . . . [W]e were intending to have made quite a business of the Mail Line etc, but will now listen to you, that is if General Connor will also listen: we feel good to the Mormons.'"[149]

Around the same time, Connor wrote, "That the presence of the military in this Territory is unwelcome to the hierarchy of Brigham Young cannot be doubted. It has to a great extent abridged his powers, limited his dictation, and secured protection to those whose persecutions cried aloud to Heaven." Connor acknowledged that "the authority of the Church is here recognized as supreme—above and beyond constitutions, laws, or regulations," with "a despotism so complete, so limitless, so transcendent," that it controlled the everyday details

Paiute Indians at a gathering in southern Utah. Used by permission of the Utah State Historical Society.

of life. Young's power was "supreme, made known and manifested through his apostles, bishops, and subordinates."[150]

Responding, Young spoke in the Bowery: "'As for those who Abraham Lincoln has sent here, if they meddle with our domestic affairs I will send them to hell across lots, and as for those apostates. . . . they will probably fall down and their bowels will gush out, or they will bleed somewhere else.'" Young's sermon was "remarkable for its innate treason, villainous hatred of the Government, and extreme vulgarity," Connor wrote to Halleck.[151] Connor noted that the Confederacy received the Mormons' "hearty sympathy merely because it is regarded as the appointed means of destroying the Government."[152]

There existed, said Connor in a June letter, a system of intelligence gathering such that "no secret military movement against hostile Indians can be undertaken without the latter [Young] becoming possessed of the number, time of starting, direction, equipment, &c." Connor ends his letter with the assessment that "the force under my command is entirely inadequate to the protection of the overland mail and telegraph lines and the several emigrant roads passing through the regions." He would be unable to cope with "the outbreak of armed treason liable to occur" if any serious Union reverse occurred in the East.[153]

In July, Wright updated Washington on the progress of reinforcements for Connor that were now beyond Fort Churchill, and he added, "The Second Cavalry and . . . the Third Infantry . . . have also been ordered to proceed at once to Salt Lake. The acting Governor of Nevada Territory informs me that he finds it impossible to raise infantry companies in that mining region, but . . . [could likely] raise two more companies of cavalry."[154]

Expeditions to the Shoshonis by Connor and Doty in the midsummer and fall months were very productive. Although Doty was made Utah's governor in June, he continued with his duties as superintendent of Indian Affairs, holding both posts for fourteen months.[155] The Overland Mail Company's twelve-thousand-dollar subsidy helped answer Indian demands when the twenty thousand dollars promised Superintendent Doty had not been allocated. Doty finally received those federal funds in midsummer. July 2 marked the establishment of a treaty with Chief Washakie's Eastern Shoshonis, providing a one-thousand-dollar annual annuity for ten years. On July 14 the Utes' Little Soldier met with Connor at Spanish Fork Reservation. On July 30, Chief Pocatello and ten bands of Northwestern Shoshonis agreed to a similar annuity. On October 1, 12, and 14, Connor and Doty made treaties with Western Shoshonis at Fort Ruby, a group of 350 Goshutes, and the Bannock and Lemhi Shoshonis at Soda Springs.[156]

Between July 2 and October 14, five delegations of Shoshonis, Goshutes, and Bannocks, representing 8,650 or more Indians—a number exceeding the population of Great Salt Lake City—signed treaties on terms set out by Doty and Connor. In late October, Doty wrote to his friend Alexander J. Center, of the Overland Mail Company, that "all routes through Utah were safe for travel."[157] Brigham Young did not participate in these treaties.

Connor praised the "indomitable bravery, activity, and willingly endured hardships" of the California column under his command.[158] Doty, politically astute, gave credit to *both* the military and the federal government. To General Wright he wrote, "Your troops have displaced the Mormon power over these Indians, and it [troop headquarters] is of great importance to Government at this moment that it be kept where it is for a year or two at least." Doty added, "There are reasons which cannot now be given why . . . Brigham Young does not desire the presence of troops either here or at any place in the Territory; but . . . it would be a detriment to the public service if this post should be abandoned." Doty presumed that Wright knew "that a military organization [Nauvoo Legion] exists among these people . . . expressly to be used to maintain the Mormon authority whenever it shall conflict with that of the United States."[159] As Doty pointed out, treaties "could not have been made without the aid of the appropriations made by Congress for this superintendency, which have been wholly applied to . . . restoring peace; and also to the presence of the military." Notably, Young was unmentioned as part of treaty making.[160] The *Times* added: "This treatment of the aborigines, as well as being more humane than the fire and sword method, will probably prove more economical and satisfactory."[161]

Thus far Doty had avoided the fate promised by Elias Smith, probate court judge and *Deseret News* editor: "If he shall give heed to unwise counsel . . . he may expect to be toasted, as was an unpopular dignitary a few years since, in the words of David, . . . 'Let his days be few; and let another take his office.'"[162]

"Pooder" for the Lord

Had Connor known that gunpowder was secreted in the returning wagons of the 1863 migration season, he would have acted. General Halleck had approved seizure of arms suspected to be for use against the authority of the United States. Authority came also from the July 1862 Second Confiscation Act, which gave military commanders broad authority "to punish Treason and Rebellion, to seize and confiscate the Property of Rebels," and to punish "any person [who] shall hereafter incite, set on foot, assist, or engage in any rebellion or insurrection against the authority of the United States."[163] Lincoln's suspension of habeas corpus and the liberal interpretation that military officers were allowed in judging treason were well and widely known.

In mid-1863, westbound emigrant train passengers, including those headed for California and Oregon, were ordered by Connor to swear an oath of allegiance before they were allowed to pass. Journalist Edward L. Sloan, traveling with the Daniel D. McArthur Company, wrote that the oath was applied at Fort Bridger to returning Mormon trains, which were searched for powder, arms, and weaponry.[164] Ebenezer Farnes, also with the McArthur Company, wrote: "There was a company of 'Mormon' boys . . . on horseback, and as all the Saints had been notified of the soldiers being on the road, they had disposed of all their gunpowder and these boys by a round about way brought the powder to Salt Lake City."[165]

In his recollections, David Dunn Bulloch, of the Samuel D. White Company, recalled a near catastrophe that occurred when he was eighteen: "Brother Charles Adams from Parowan had his three yoke of oxen on his wagon and an electrical storm came up and the lightning split telegraph poles and struck the hind end of the wagon, made a hole in the cover large as a hat and set the wagon on fire. He was loaded with 3400 pounds of powder, stoves, etc. We all ran to his rescue, pulled off the cover and used the emigrant cans of water we had along to drink to douse the fire. The lightning ran right through the wagon, along the tongue and killed five out of his six oxen and knocked him down. Had it struck an immigrant wagon many would have been killed."[166]

William Richardson, age thirty-four, of the Horton D. Haight train, recorded what happened when Captain Haight was taken for interrogation over the contents of his wagons: "The Mormons took 'the Wagon with the pooder' across Green River and into the mountains, unloaded 'the pooder into sacks & came back the next day.' . . . [W]hen troopers 'sarched all the train,' they 'did not find the lood of pooder.'" [167] William McLachlan's trail report of the John Wickersham Woolley Company corroborated Richardson's: "A company of brethren were sent out by President Young to Green River to meet the trains that had powder, as a company of U.S. soldiers were stationed near Ham's Fork to search the trains as they passed. There were 18 of the boys with mules from the City at Green River when we arrived." On the morning of September 24, they "left Green River with their mules loaded with powder from Haight's train." For September 25, McLachlan wrote: "This morning as we were driving up our cattle, 25 U.S. soldiers made their appearance and requested both aliens and citizens to take an oath of allegiance to the Constitution of the United States, which we did. He afterwards caused our captain, J. W. Woolley to take an oath that he had no powder or ammunition in his possession, only that necessary for his own protection and those under his charge."[168]

At least three of the fifteen Mormon emigrant trains of the season risked accident and federal arrest as they carried substantial amounts of gunpowder to Utah in the fall of 1863. The report in the *Times* suggested that the powder—in excess of personal needs—in additional companies was found: "The immigrants report that the detachment of C.V.'s [California Volunteers] at Ham's Fork overhaul the trains, make the folks take the oath of allegiance, and *confiscate their powder.*"[169] The total volume of illegal war matériel brought in 1863 is not known.

In October's LDS conference, Young embarked on a tirade over implements of war denied the Saints. "Who have expressed themselves as being unwilling that the Mormons' should have . . . a little powder and lead?" Young believed it was officers "sent here to protect the mail

Slavery is the cause of this terrible war, and it abolition is decreed by one of the parties of the war. I am with the abolition party in war as in peace. I discontinue my paper, because I can better serve my poor bleeding country-men whose great opportunity has now come, by going South and summoning them to assert their just liberty.

Let the oppressor fall by the hand of the oppressed, and the guilty slaveholder, whom the voice of truth and reason could not reach, let him fall by the hand of his slave.

Reason, argument, appeal,—all moral influences have been applied in vain. The oppressor has hardened his heart, blinded his mind, and deliberately rushed upon merited destruction. Let his blood be upon his own head.

SOURCE: EXCERPTED FROM "VALEDICTORY," BY FREDERICK DOUGLASS, FORMER SLAVE, ROCHESTER, NEW YORK, AS HE CLOSED HIS NEWSPAPER ON AUGUST 16, 1863, TO FIGHT IN THE WAR.

and telegraph lines, or to discover, if possible, rich diggings in our immediate vicinity . . . and to destroy . . . the identity of the Mormon community, and every truth and virtue that remains."[170] Hyperbole threatened reason: "I know what passes in their secret councils. Blood and murder are in their hearts, and they wish to extend the work of destruction over the whole face of the land."[171] Young declared, "Not less than one million men . . . have gone to the silent grave in this useless war." More vehemently he added: "What is the cause of all this waste of life ? . . . [O]ne portion of the country wish to raise their negroes or black slaves, and the other portion wish to free them, and, apparently, to almost worship them. Well, raise and worship them, who cares? I should never fight one moment about it, *for the cause of human improvement is not in the least advanced by the dreadful war which now convulses our unhappy country.* . . . Will the present struggle free the slave?"

Young's answer to that question was no, because "Ham will continue to be the servant of servants, as the Lord has decreed, until the curse is removed."[172]

Annihilating Theocracy's Baneful Influence

P. Edward Connor was familiar with how fortunes taken from silver mines of California had changed its economic and social fabric. That it could do so in Utah was apparent. The *Times* observed that gold dust was flowing from the Bannack and Alder Gulch mines in the north "in undiminished volume, and, indeed, faster than the merchants can supply 'greenbacks' in exchange." The rise in demand for provisions had "comfortably lined the pockets of many of the community, who, as might be expected of a people so generally destitute of dry-goods and groceries as are the Utah folks, have straightway run off to the stores to replenish their scanty wardrobes and ungarnished cupboards." Consequently, some merchants had "taken [in] from five hundred to fifteen hundred dollars daily."[173]

Connor moved to expand the role of his command. His letter to Drum in late October summarized his position. Two ways were open for striking at theocracy's root, for "annihilating its baneful influence." First was a tough military policy, as he had used with the Indians, "punishing with a strong hand every infraction of law." A "wiser course," Connor admitted, was to attract "large numbers of Gentiles" to live in Utah and thus change the territory by attracting a "hardy, industrious, enterprising population." The "discovery of gold, silver, and other valuable minerals" presented, in Connor's view, "the only prospect of bringing hither such a population." Connor was not asking permission but informing his commanding officers of actions already taking place. His officers had instructions for "men of their commands to prospect the country in the vicinity of their respective posts, whenever such course would not interfere with their military duties." With the opening of mines, "the Mormon question will at an early day be settled . . . without the loss of a single soldier in combat."[174] Many at Camp Douglas who had gained mining experience in California were now "eating the bread of idleness." Mining could change Utah while giving the men both action and the possibility of "enriching themselves and the country."[175]

Under Connor's auspices a company for mining silver had recently been organized about twenty miles west of Salt Lake City, and there were reports of gold near Deep Creek, some two hundred miles west.[176] Connor's trip north in October had the "double purpose of visiting the military post at Soda Springs and prospecting the country for the precious metals."[177] His estimate of the pace at which mining might change Utah was overoptimistic, for mining operations of size required extraction, processing large volumes of ore, and railway transportation. The *Times* agreed: "A few years hence, and the secluded cañons of the Rocky Mountains will be awakened by the snorting of the iron-horse. Already are the surveyors at work stretching their chains in the valley of the Timpanogos or on Provo River, and soon brawny arms will be hewing the rocks, grading the earth and bridging the torrents."[178]

Ireland's Sons and the Rights of Man

Until the recent work of Gerald McDonough, the importance of the Irish among those serving in the Utah Expedition in 1857–61, and of the 1862 California and Nevada volunteer units, has been little heralded within Utah history. Although the first group helped put down Utah's rebellion and the second assisted in federal control of the territory, the Irish among them were neither more nor less despised by the Mormons than others of the federal troops. McDonough emphasizes that individuals among the Irish have been recognized, but in their contributions as an ethnic group within Utah's non-Mormon population they have been forgotten pioneers.[179] The Irish were predominantly Catholic, a religion to which the Mormon theology openly affixed the disrespectful label of "the mother of abominations; and . . . the whore of all the earth."[180] Catholicism and Mormonism compete, both claiming to be the "one and only" true church.

The Irish formed Utah units of the Fenian Brotherhood, men who were implacably pressing for Irish independence from England

and sovereignty of their homeland. Mormons—like the Irish—were frustrated in their quest for independence and sovereignty as a state. Although many of the LDS leaders and their converts hailed from England, McDonough rejects the notion that harsh feelings long held by Irishmen against the Crown carried over to the commoners among the British people who were converts to Mormonism in Utah.

From 1845 to 1852, nearly a million Irish children, men, and women died in Ireland, while an equal number fled their homeland. The epidemic of a fungus that afflicted the staple of the diet for at least a third of Ireland's people resulted in widespread famine. Bitterness and resentment arose when "people starved while livestock and grain continued to be exported" to England, often under English military escort. The waves of emigration caused by the famine carried some of these feelings to every country where Irish emigrants gathered.[181]

As with other ethnic groups that flowed into Utah, the Irish were abused, not welcomed or integrated into American society. Many found refuge from unemployment and starvation in the ranks of the U.S. Army, often recruited as they stepped off the boat at New York's Castle Garden immigration station. David Emmons, historian of the Irish in the West, notes that Forts Sherman, Kearny, Gibbon, Casey, Cummings, Harney, McDermitt, McDowell, McGarry, McKinney, and Maginnis—all named for officers—read like the list of a gathering of Irish clans.[182] According to McDonough, Gen. Winfield Scott, general in chief of U.S. forces in the 1846 Mexican-American War, testified before Congress that of the 3,500 foreign-born troops then in service, more than 2,000 were from Ireland. When the troops of the Utah Expedition left Fort Leavenworth in July 1857, most of the enlisted men were foreign emigrants, and the majority of them were Irish. Of the officers, it is known that surgeon and Maj. John Moore, Capt. Albert Tracy of the Tenth Infantry, Lt. Henry B. Kelly (who accompanied Capt. Randolph B. Marcy on his 1857–58 midwinter trip to New Mexico), and another Lieutenant Kearny were all Irishmen.[183] It was at Camp Floyd, home to the Utah Expedition troops on the west side of Utah Lake, that in March 1859 the territory's first recorded St. Patrick's Day celebration took place, marked with a quiet tone and privacy distinctly different from the tenor of the festive, alcohol-fueled present day.[184]

Many of the Californians recruited by Connor in the spring of 1862 were of Irish birth, attracted initially to gold mines where their hopes went unfulfilled. Mining camps were listed by many recruits as their hometown, including Fiddletown, Poverty Bar, Chinese Camp, Chili Gulch, Jenny Lind, Angel Camp, Sonora, West Point, Mokelumne Hill, San Andreas, Don Pedro's Bar, and Campo Seco.[185] McDonough identifies Majors Patrick Gallagher, J. B. Moore, and Nicolas O'Brian; Captains McKean and Mathewson; and Lieutenants Clark, Quinn, Murray, and Egan—all of Irish descent.[186] "Gen. Conner [sic] was backed by an army principally made up of his own countrymen, so that the glory belongs to them as the sons of Erin and Saint Patrick," Dr. H. Quigley reported, adding, "The State Militia of California, comprising the National Guard of California, three regiments of infantry, and several battalions of cavalry shows that our race is also well represented."[187]

San Francisco's 1862 St. Patrick's Day celebration was notable for the prominent participation of Col. P. Edward Connor, together with "some 20 commissioned officers," his staff, and the regimental band of the Third California Infantry, from Benicia Barracks on Suisun Bay. The Irish-American Benevolent Society, Fenian Brotherhood, Sons of the Emerald Isle, Sons of Erin, and St. Patrick's Brotherhood were all represented.[188]

After their arrival in Utah, the Fenians among Connor's troops at Camp Douglas became, with the possible exception of San Francisco's, "the most ardent Fenians in the American west." Three circles of the Fenian Brotherhood existed at Camp Douglas: the Robert Emmet Brigade, the Wolf Tone Brigade, and the Patrick Sarsfield Brigade. Beginning in 1864 and continuing through 1867, notices for various Fenian meetings were prominent in the *Daily Union Vedette*. A regular feature of the *Vedette* was "Irish and Fenian news," and its editorials "frequently drummed for the cause of Irish Liberation."[189]

It is doubtful that Connor and his volunteers celebrated St. Patrick's Day in 1863. They were grieving from sixteen deaths, recovering from wounds and amputations, and healing frozen extremities sustained in the January foray at Bear River. The intensity of the criticisms leveled at Harding, Waite, and Drake was at its acme, and Indian depredations still a concern, all leaving neither time nor motivation for celebration.[190]

By 1864, conditions changed. The *Vedette* carried the item that stated, "Mr. P. Mooney [h]as the pleasure of announcing to the Soldiers of Camp Douglas, that he will give a St. Patrick's Ball on March 17th, 1864. Carriages will be in attendance, free of charge. Tickets, $5.00."[191] Follow-up coverage confirmed a gala evening: "The ball given on Saint Patrick's evening by the soldiers of this Camp, came off as announced, and was most thoroughly successful. The music was excellent, the company select and the supper a brilliant success. Great credit is due to the managers . . . [, for] no lack was discoverable." Not mentioned was the Fenian Brotherhood or pleas for the restoration of the Irish Republic.[192] By March 1865, conditions were even more suitable for the Irish, and Connor may have recalled the pomp of 1862 in San Francisco, because the Fenians became an integral part of the St. Patrick's Day program: "To-day, there will probably be one of the finest processions that has ever paraded in our Camp . . . and all the requisite arrangements have been made by the Fenian Brotherhood of Camp Douglas, to make this day . . . the scene of the grandest and most imposing that has ever been witnessed in our vicinity." The Fenians would meet in their hall; soldiers were instructed to wear full-dress uniform, and all would march to the camp theater to hear read "the dying speech of the Irish Patriot, R. [Robert] Emmet." Capt. Charles H. Hempstead would deliver the oration, and the evening would be capped with a "'grand Ball' on a scale of magnificence . . . never before arrived at in our Camp."[193] Nearly one hundred Fenians marched in the procession, carrying the Stars and Stripes and the Shamrock and Harp. Rev. Norman McLeod offered the prayer. So many tickets were sold that the dance floor was crowded, and the turnout better than anticipated. "On the whole," the *Vedette* declared, "the Fenians may feel justly proud of the day and the manner in which it was celebrated."[194] Hempstead's oration noted that "500,000 Fenians" gathered across the nation, including those "on the James, the Rappahannock, . . . on the banks of the Ohio and Mississippi, wherever that glorious flag waves triumphant, sustained by Ireland's exiled sons, shoulder to shoulder with the native born, advancing civilization, or fighting the battles of the Republic." The articulate editor proudly acclaimed, "Wherever the rights of man have needed the silver tongue of eloquence or the sweet strain of the poet, there has been found an Irishman to speak or sing."[195] On this celebration the influence of the Good Templars was felt: "One very credible and worthy feature connected with the ball . . . , given by the Fenians at this post, is the prohibition of the use of intoxicating liquors in the hall. This is an excellent clause in their programme."[196]

In 1866, Connor finally made a parade through Great Salt Lake's streets the featured celebration of the Irish holiday. At nine o'clock on March 17, the Fenian Brotherhood started from their hall on Camp Douglas and "passed down Temple street, headed by the Camp Douglas band." An "imposing appearance" was created by "three circles, numbering several hundred members, who were adorned with the regalia of the order." Three flags were carried: the Stars and Stripes, the new Irish flag, and, in the rear, the old Irish flag. "After parading the principal streets," the *Vedette* reported, "the procession repaired to Independence Hall, where an oration was delivered by Capt. Geo. P. Price."[197] The orator stressed "Ireland's love for liberty, . . . the bravery of her sons as displayed on the battlefields of the American nation—the records they had everywhere made as the friends of freedom, . . . [and] that men who were capable of winning freedom for others were worthy of freedom for themselves." Price concluded, "We will yet read of free Ireland and an Irish flag waving over an Irish Republic. Then will she celebrate each coming anniversary of St. Patrick with a great joy, quickened by the . . . impulses of a new and brighter destiny." The day's celebration was closed by a grand ball in the Social Hall, elegantly decorated. According to the *Vedette*, "The whole affair reflected credit upon the Fenian organization, which now numbers nearly 800 members in this Territory."[198]

Patrick Edward Connor had changed his surname from the obviously Irish "O'Connor" and signed mostly as P. Edward or P. Edw. Connor. The nicknames "Pat," "Paddy," and their variants at that time were not terms of familiar endearment but often ethnic slurs.[199] One example is George Q. Cannon's letter in 1866 to Brigham Young's son: "California troops are to be mustered out, . . . and there is every probability that *Pat's* presence here will not be needed . . . [and that] he will be as thoroughly despised and hated as tyrants and wicked men always are when they fall from power."[200]

Several of Irish descent have left their mark on Utah's history: Pony Express rider Howard Egan; Patrick Lannan, businessman and *Salt Lake Tribune* owner; supreme court justice Robert Newton Baskin; and many men of business and mining whose names are associated with buildings and other enterprises: the Keith O'Brien Building, the Gallivan Plaza, the Kearns and Judge buildings, and the Hogle Zoo and the brokerage firm of J. A. Hogle and Company. The surname for the Hogle family until October 1864 was Gilmore.[201] Jack Dempsey, Frank Layden, and John A. Moran, for whom the Moran Eye Center is named, are more recent. For more than thirty years Utah's Hibernian Society has sought recognition of the contributions of the Irish.

The *Vedette* Rides in Utah

The name "Union Vedette" appeared on the masthead of the news-paper, first published on November 20, 1863, by the officers and enlisted men of Camp Douglas's California Volunteers and funded with twenty thousand dollars personally provided by P. Edward Connor.[202] The military term for a sentry or outpost carrying information and warnings to its body of troops, especially when in a hostile environ-ment, "vedette" was appropriate in the name for an endeavor of non-Mormons amid a population hostile to their presence. "The great lever of human society, lifting it up to a higher point, and the mighty regulator of man's doings is a free, untrammeled, unwarped and inde-pendent press," wrote the editor, Capt. Charles H. Hempstead, Jr.[203] The lack of a free press had been "sorely felt since the troops arrived in these valleys," and so, Hempstead added, "we propose to supply the want." The gifted son of a Missouri trader, Hempstead arrived in Cali-fornia about 1852 and promptly secured a position as personal secre-tary to Governor John Bigler. Bigler appointed him in 1855 to the office of California's secretary of state, where he was also the third ex officio California state librarian.[204] President James Buchanan appointed him

The building on the Camp Douglas grounds that housed the printing offices of the *Daily Union Vedette*, a paper published from November 1863 by the officers and men of the California volunteers. Used by permission of the Utah State Historical Society.

as the superintendent of the U.S. Mint in San Francisco. Married in St. Louis in 1857, Hempstead returned to California, remaining in his position at the mint until the expiration of Buchanan's term. Enlisting into Union service in July 1862, he entered at the rank of captain.

At the *Vedette*'s startup, its first printer—Pvt. Van Buren De Lashmutt, Company G, Third California Infantry—explained: "We used a small printing press brought there by the Government to print army orders. Our success was phenomenal. Ordered a better outfit from Sacramento, at a cost of 40 cents per pound [for freight]."[205] Significant to the *Vedette*'s financial success was "sending several hundred copies" on the weekly stagecoach to the mines in Montana, which were "readily disposed of for one dollar per copy."[206] Solid evidence of the anger stirred up by the *Vedette*'s editorial contents within the local Mormon community came on April 8, 1866, when editor Isaac Mellen Weston received a letter written on a sheet of paper in symbolic red ink that contained one word: "Skedalee," meaning "get out."[207] On October 3 of that year, Weston was brutally beaten and told he had six hours to leave the city.[208]

From their arrival, the troops were faced with "the constant effort of some . . . to array the people against the Government and the soldiers, and inculcate the erroneous idea that the latter were sent hither to persecute and destroy," a *Vedette* article read. For those who were working "to mislead the multitude as to the intentions and wishes of the Government . . . we have little respect and far less care," but for most people who were "honest and sincere, though mistaken . . . , we have both." According to the article, "the bold denunciation and the covert sneer uttered against the Nation," and the "teachings which border on treason . . . [and seek] to wean them [the people] from their loyalty to the Nation," were issues faced by the editor-soldiers while engaged in their core mission of protecting the mail and the telegraph. The *Vedette* declared that for the nation, "struggling with a gigantic, unholy rebellion, . . . the duty of every good citizen to sustain by word and thought and deed our common country, is as plain as it is imperative."[209] Connor used the *Vedette*'s opening issue to tout prospecting, claiming that the mountains "abound in rich veins of gold, silver, copper, and other minerals." He assured any persons so engaged that they would have "the fullest protections from the military forces in this district."[210] In January 1864 the *Union Vedette* became Utah's first *daily* public newspaper; it continued to promote prospecting and the search for ore sites. The measured, Apollonian tone of its initial months eventually gave way to one more pugilistic and strident.

Near year's end, Mormons and volunteers suspiciously eyed each other; the Nauvoo Legion's officers were ordered to fly the national flag, an order superfluous outside of Utah: "A good and suitable stand of colors [will] be forthwith provided for the Regiment which you command. Said colors to be composed of Stars and Stripes. . . . The presence of a National flag with your command would be palpable evidence of its loyalty to the Constitution and laws of the U.S. while its absence might . . . seriously embarrass you."[211]

With regard to their capability for immediate action, the contenders were similarly constituted: the District of Utah at Camp Douglas totaled 1,307 men and nine field artillery pieces. Actually present for duty were 920 enlisted men and 42 officers.[212] Wilford Woodruff's November 2 record of the Nauvoo Legion stated that "about 950 men were reported ready for service on short Notice."[213]

The year ended as it began, adversaries immiscible, at tenuous stalemate: Mormon legislature versus non-Mormon federal officers; Nauvoo Legion versus California and Nevada Volunteers; Brigham Young versus Connor and Doty; theocracy versus republican government.

Chronology
1863

January 1	President Abraham Lincoln issues the Emancipation Proclamation, freeing some three to four million slaves in the ten states then in rebellion.
	Utah legislators are at an impasse with Governor Stephen S. Harding and Judges Charles B. Waite and Thomas J. Drake. Legislature refuses to print gubernatorial message.
	Mormons and Overland Mail businessmen work to remove California Volunteers away from Camp Douglas.
	Judge John Fitch Kinney issues an arrest warrant for three Shoshoni chiefs.
	Marshal Isaac L. Gibbs seeks aid from Col. P. Edward Connor.
January 22	Capt. Samuel Hoyt and sixty-nine infantrymen leave Camp Douglas for Bear River.
January 24	Connor and 225 cavalrymen leave, bound for Bear River.
	Brigham Young marries Amelia Folsom.
January 29	At the battle at Bear River—or "Boa Ogoi," as the Indians named the site—at least 225 Indian people are killed, with a loss of twenty-two California Volunteers.
February 20	Connor cites Brigham Young as preparing for war, requests increase of three thousand troops.
	Chaplain John A. Anderson publishes a full report of the Bear River events.
March 3	Mormons' mass meeting calls for Governor Harding and Judges Waite and Drake to resign and leave. They refuse.
March 8	Brigham Young reiterates his refusal to provide military forces to the Union.

March 9	Young attempts to provoke Connor into violence.
March 26	Lt. Anthony Ethier, with twenty-five troops, starts for Skull Valley; Mormons assist Indians with an ambush of the troops.
March 29	Connor is promoted to a brigadier general, commanding the District of Utah.
April 2–6	Capt. George F. Price's leads an expedition from Camp Douglas to Spanish Fork.
April 11–20	Lt. Francis Honeyman leads troops from Camp Douglas to Pleasant Grove and Spanish Fork. Mormons passively observe Indians attempting to kill trapped troops.
May 5–30	Connor expedition to Soda Springs escorts 160 Morrisite men and women for resettlement.
June 22–24	Connor writes to his superior officers requesting more troops to address Indian depredations incited by Mormons and describing Young's totalitarian state and disloyalty.
	Governor Harding resigns and takes a judicial post in Colorado Territory.
	James Duane Doty, superintendent of Indian Affairs, is named Utah's governor.
July 1–3	Battle of Gettysburg results in combined losses of more than fifty-one thousand men.
August 3	Judge Kinney is "elected" as Utah's first non-Mormon delegate to Congress.
August 29	John R. Murdock oversees the first LDS Church train company to arrive back in Utah.
September	Five or more church trains arrive back in Salt Lake City.
October 1–5	Six or more church trains return to Salt Lake City. Three trains—led by Daniel D. McArthur, Samuel D. White, and Horton D. Haight—carry contraband gunpowder.
November 19	Lincoln delivers his address at Gettysburg.

November 20   First issue of Camp Douglas newspaper, the *Union Vedette*, is published by men of the California Volunteers.

December 5   Utah delegate Kinney's request for a study of why California Volunteers are stationed in Utah, rather than fighting Confederates, is ignored.

CHAPTER 6

Colliding Worlds, 1864

The great busy Gentile world is coming to its doors . . . isolation, once its favorite and cherished creed, can no longer be either its policy or its destiny.

CAPT. CHARLES H. HEMPSTEAD, JR.

He presented himself as a non-Mormon, the first so honored to represent Utah, but John Fitch Kinney was openly Brigham Young's agent, working particularly for the removal of General P. Edward Connor and the California and Nevada Volunteers. "Mr. Kinney's position among the Mormons has never been more clearly defined," wrote the *Vedette*'s Charles Hempstead. "By some process . . . the good folks hereabout woke up one morning and found that Bro. Kinney had been unanimously nominated for Congress, by somebody; and on another bright morning it was further announced that he had been duly elected with like unanimity," the editor reflected.[1]

As Utah's nonvoting representative, Kinney expounded the worn themes for removing Connor. Kinney's claim in his January letter to Secretary of War Edwin Stanton and Gen. H. W. Halleck, that the camp was "located within the corporate limits of Great Salt Lake City," although specious, continued.[2] U.S. surveyor David H. Burr established in 1855 that claiming more than two thousand acres for Great Salt Lake City was illegal; federal law allowed only 320 acres. Burr accurately predicted that for the city to be as large as the Mormons claimed, would "require special legislation." It was not until 1871 that Congress awarded the desired acreage.[3]

Kinney contended that Utah was tranquil, at peace, with travel to and from mining areas safe and mail lines no longer endangered. He asked for the removal of Connor's command for the vacuous reason that it would "accommodate the people I . . . represent." Thoroughly justified was the Mormons' concern with stream water contamination for users downstream, and that orders had been given for nonfederal animals grazing on military grounds to be killed.[4] Presuming to speak for the commander, Kinney added that "Connor frequently . . . expressed an anxious desire to be transferred with his brave officers and men to the Potomac, where they could participate in the great struggle." Kinney also went to the fractious issue of Mormon loyalty: "I know that the people of Utah are loyal to the Constitution and Government of the United States." Contrary opinions were "only entertained by corrupt, weak, or mistaken, or ignorant minds," referring to Connor, Harding, Waite, Drake, and the officers and men at Camp Douglas.[5] The *Vedette* responded on the subject of troops living among the people: What loyal Californian "has been crazy enough to object to the presence of soldiers at the Presidio, Fort Point, or Alcatraz?" Or would "a Massachusetts Union man [be] complaining of the presence of Union troops in, around and all about Boston? . . . Loyal and peaceful men don't object to having loyal troops near them."[6]

Connor's reply insisted that tranquility did not exist in Utah. Of his location Connor wrote: "Douglas is on the public domain at least two miles distant from the nearest house in the city." As to acreage, Connor read the Mormons perfectly. On paper, they had extended their jurisdiction to include "the whole tract of country from the [Wasatch] mountains to the Jordan."[7] Utah's legislature lacked authority to lay claims to land that were antagonistic to the federal government's interests, Connor pointed out. Col. Robert Pollock's stern order that stray animals on government property were to be shot was rescinded before any were killed. Kinney's statement that Mormon leadership was unswervingly loyal received Connor's most severe response, for "pulpit harangues were but iterated and reiterated denunciations of the Union and outbursts of bold-faced treason." He told of Lt. John Quinn, who, while on official business south in the territory, was refused "forage for his animals at any price." Mormons had asserted that they would not sell any grain "to Uncle Sam's minions." Lieutenant Quinn was "absolutely prohibited from . . . seeking shelter from the winter storms in barns, sheds, and outhouses."[8] Connor cited a letter from twenty-six miners in the town of Franklin who wrote of "a constant stream of burlesque against . . . you and your soldiers—such as 'Thank God the buzzards are picking the bones of the U.S. Army.'" Some citizens of Cache valley were preaching for their men to "look well to their guns, and to lay in powder, and keep their horses fat . . . in readiness to be here in two hours." Mormons bragged "that we shan't prospect for gold."[9] Connor answered that it was "preposterous" that citizens seeking settlement and prospecting for ore "should be compelled to look for protection from the armed troops of the Union" against Mormons who were simultaneously professing loyalty and peacefulness. Flour, beef, and vegetables were the only subsistence items procured locally, all else brought from the East. For the local items, Young "or his chosen bishops derive the profits from the enormous and unreasonable prices demanded and necessarily paid."[10]

Connor addressed Kinney's speaking of troop transfer: "While an order transferring either myself or my command to the active scenes of the East would but be responsive to my own and the universal heartfelt desire of the troops under me, . . . neither they nor I have constituted Mr. Kinney our spokesman."[11] General Wright gave support to Connor's position at Camp Douglas, even adding that the camp should be reinforced, because he held "but little faith in the loyalty of the Mormons."[12]

The January 18 meeting of the State of Deseret legislature was immediately followed by that of Utah's territorial legislature. The *Vedette* reported that, apart from election of officers, "no business appeared to have been conducted."[13] George A. Smith's letter to Kinney supplied scant details: "'We sat down to draw up a memorial, asking admission into the Union, and then we did not know what kind of one we wanted and concluded to write you. What is the prospect of admission?'"[14] Somehow a request was formed, for Representative Henry Lunt of Iron County presented a "Memorial to Congress for the admission of Utah [not Deseret] as a State" during a late January session.[15] Presented to Congress in March, it was ignored.[16]

Charles Wesley Wandell, at the time a Beaver County Mormon in good standing, was the sole dissenter to the legislature's request that Connor and the federal troops be removed. Long a nonconformist, Wandell would later become a Josephite Mormon, and a mining engineer in Nevada.[17] After legislation to protect and strengthen Utah's mining was deemed urgent by Acting Governor Amos Reed in his opening legislative address, Wandell introduced a suitable bill. Had he forgotten Young's 1849 warning, "If any body comes here discovering gold and distracting my people, as the Lord liveth, I'll cut that man's throat!"?[18] By the time Mormon legislators carved up the bill, its provisions defeated all of its original intentions. Wandell voted against his own bill, but it sailed to passage. Acting Governor Reed promptly vetoed it, reasoning, "I can conceive of no more onerous and restrictive enactment" than creating a "'Superintendency of Mines.'" Such unrestricted powers in a few men "could hardly result in aught but evil." Furthermore, an annual tax of 20 percent on the value of the mines would prevent "the opening of a single mine in the Territory," just as Mormon lawmakers intended.[19]

Protecting Miners

"Thoughtless or reckless words" threatening miners and prospectors resulted in a "Circular" from General Connor on March 1. Alluding to LDS leaders, Connor expressed his hope that threats were not emanating from "any presumed or presumptuous authority"—and noted that land in Utah Territory was "the public property of the nation," to which citizens were "invited by public law and national policy . . . to enrich themselves and advance the general welfare from out the public store." Miners would "receive the amplest protection in life, property, and rights against aggression from whatever source, Indian or white," Connor promised. He warned that should "misguided men" obstruct citizens' rights or "throw obstacles in the way . . . of the public domain," they would be "tried as public enemies, and punished to the utmost extent of martial law." This did not exceed the responsibilities of his command, he insisted, for he was "here to preserve the public peace" and to "secure to all" their liberty and their rights. Connor's term "martial law" and the circular's final phrase were militant; such rights would be "enforced at every hazard and at any cost."[20] Governor James Duane Doty did not hold the authority for imposing martial law, nor did the degree of civil disloyalty yet give Connor sufficient cause to do so. In the *New York Times'* opinion, Connor "stuck up his martial threats as scarecrows," to warn ruffians.[21]

When Doty left for Washington the previous November, his purpose was to assure approval of the Shoshoni treaties, or to be enlightened on the administration's plans for Utah, or to seek his reappointment. At a Milwaukee stop, a surprise surfaced when the *Milwaukee Sentinel* published that Doty "has matured a plan for the settlement of the Mormon difficulty for all future time, and . . . will present it to the President for his sanction." However, the *Sentinel* remarked, "public policy" prevented "making this novel plan public at the present time." Doty's hotel room was then robbed—not of valuables or money but only "his papers and vouchers"—compelling him "to send back for duplicates."[22] Mormons come first to mind among those who would want knowledge of Doty's apparently secret and "novel" plan to end their long dispute with government. With his secret exposed, nothing developed—in Utah or Washington—of Doty's scheme to permanently solve the nation's problems with Mormons. At his Wisconsin home, his wife, Sarah, was preparing to come to Utah; the couple traveled together, arriving in mid-June.[23]

Doty's letter to Seward on April 16, written in New York, carried no reference to Connor's promises of protection to miners. It noted that funds allotted for the executive functions were "entirely inadequate" and that miners' settlements in Utah and Idaho had doubled prices for necessities.[24]

Failing to effect Connor's removal, Young moved to impugn his character, declaring, "If frauds, swindling, malfeasance in office, . . . which are bleeding the Treasury at a fearful rate, are fit subjects of inquiry, then surely a leak so large . . . should be exposed to the public."[25] It was Young's prices, not quartermaster malfeasance, that was bleeding the government. In March he accused Connor of "an extravagant expenditure of means, and a reckless waste of human life,"

Quarters of Gen. P. Edward Connor and his family on the grounds of Camp Douglas, 1864. Used by permission of the Utah State Historical Society.

possibly alluding to Bear River. Young claimed that "even the privates despise him," but Connor appraised it differently, for he moved his family from their city residence, formerly housing Harding, to recently completed quarters on Camp Douglas.[26]

Justice and Silence

January events silenced another perpetrator of John Dawson's beating. Jason R. Luce, while working for the Bannack and Salt Lake Express Company, chanced to meet one Samuel R. Bunting, a former Union lieutenant from Missouri. Ill will surfaced when Luce revealed he was a Mormon, whereupon Bunting beat him severely. After traveling independently to Salt Lake City, the two met at the Townsend Hotel, either by chance or by Luce's design. Luce asked the man his name. Bunting gave it, Luce drew his bowie knife, sending "a deadly blow in the neck, from behind, nearly severing the head from the body." Luce gave himself up, but not until "gloating over his triumph" for nearly a quarter of an hour. Brought before Mormon judge Aurelius Miner, Luce was charged with "wanton, brutal, and unjustified" murder, to appear—not in district court—but in the probate court. The *Vedette* questioned why the case was not correctly referred to the district court, scheduled to sit in March. With William Adams Hickman as his lawyer, Luce was tried and convicted in Judge Elias Smith's probate court after giving "a full confession . . . to the murder" and to "other eventful scenes in his most eventful life." The sentence: death by firing squad.[27]

Hickman held that his defense of Luce was proper and vigorous, claiming that the probate court had no jurisdiction, but he was denied this by Judge Smith and surprisingly by Acting Governor Reed. Moments before his execution in the courthouse yard on January 12, Luce "indulged in some severe remarks concerning those who had professed to be his friends, but who, he said, 'had betrayed him.'" Luce named his betrayer, but the *Vedette* declined to print it. Sheriff (and simultaneously militia colonel) Robert T. Burton positioned five executioners in the courthouse basement with one hundred Legion militiamen surrounding the building. Five guns fired, erasing any details Luce harbored of how Dawson came to his trail brutality, or its related secrets.[28] From arrest, to court, to execution, the process remained entirely under Mormon control. Numerous January articles regarding Luce appeared in the *Vedette*.[29] The *Times* wrote cryptically, "The recent trial and execution of Luce have troubled some. . . . But it is difficult to speak of them in other than dark sentences. It is . . . understood that the unhappy man, before death, made a confession or revelation, which touched the corns of certain persons not over tenderly. The confession has not come to the light, the receivers and holders evidently considering it not just the thing for the public eye; the contents, though, are hinted about in vague, ambiguous phrase."[30]

Omitted from the reports was that Luce was Hickman's son-in-law. Luce's anguish may have come from his father-in-law's failing to save him from execution. With what "dark sentences" Luce and Hickman might have bargained in exchange for a life imprisonment sentence in a district court manned by non-Mormons remains conjecture.

More Rumor against Harding

An April letter from Brigham Young to Charles Lee Armour, one of three justices of Colorado's supreme court, added to the accusations of impropriety by Stephen S. Harding that were made on his resignation as Utah's fourth governor. At Harding's leaving, the *News* published: "We have withheld from publication the authenticated document in our possession relative to the posthumous (?) child whose birth caused him so much anxiety, . . . [but] if he shall ever publish a history of his eleven month's sojourn in Utah . . . we will furnish him with copies of some of the most interesting papers on file, to embellish a work of that kind, and make it more saleable."[31]

Young was writing in answer to Armour's March 1864 request for "testimony" regarding misbehavior during Harding's time in Salt Lake City. The "authenticated document" material was not available as claimed. Young was unable to provide the information "relating to conduct of the kind you mention," but instead added a suggestive rumor: "I have been informed, that S. S. Harding, while in this City, was far from keeping house in a manner exemplary in regard to unlawful intercourse with women." Young admitted that the testimony sought by Armour "may continue to be unobtainable"; however, he added innuendo: "Men and women were seen at all hours to pass in and out of the house Harding occupied, but what they were doing while in the house can only be proved by themselves."[32]

Evidence weighs that accusations of Harding improprieties were invented. He was candid, transparently describing the many people living in his busy household. There was Attila L. Harding, his adult son, and Dr. and Mrs. Field from Quincy, Illinois, with their four-month-old infant, the family residing rent-free after interrupting their journey to California to live with Harding for a season. Mary, from Copenhagen, Denmark, served as their cook.[33] At irregular times, two younger women from Bristol, England, sisters Louisa and Anna Watkins, were employed as cooks and housekeepers.[34] Louisa "treats Till like a sister and to me is as kind as an own child," wrote Harding. A third housekeeper is documented, a young woman from Ireland whose name was not given, for she had come as a convert who had "seceded from the

Immediately upon the April 1864 surrender of Fort Pillow, on the Mississippi River, the Confederates under "born killer" Gen. Nathan Bedford Forrest commenced an indiscriminate butchery of the whites and blacks who had been previously wounded. Both white and black were bayoneted, shot or sabred; even dead bodies were horribly mutilated. Soldiers unable to speak from wounds were shot dead, and their bodies rolled down the banks into the river. The dead and wounded negroes were piled in heaps and burned. Out of the captured garrison of six hundred, only two hundred remained alive. "What they saw was not war but mass murder out of race hatred."

SOURCES: PARAPHRASED FROM "THE BLACK FLAG: HORRIBLE MASSACRE BY THE REBELS," NYT, APRIL 14, 1864; SANDBURG, STORM, 245–46, 247.

humbug" of the Saints.[35] When the Fields family moved out, Judge Thomas J. Drake, his wife, and three children moved in. Several Harding children visited the Salt Lake City household. Harding wrote, "I have much company almost every day. Many of the Mormon 'sisters' call on me and whilst I was writing this, my room was filled with the wives of the [Camp Douglas] officers, some of them beautiful and highly educated ladies." Of polygamy, Harding had "been told by a good Mormon sisters . . . that there was not a happy home in this city and Territory where the thing attracts subjects."[36]

Harding knew of Dawson's entrapment and emphasized that his own behavior was not such that he could be entrapped. Neither family letters, nor correspondence in the Harding Papers, nor the interpretive history of his several biographers suggests an out-of-wedlock child or improper behavior in the household. After Harding's move to Denver and then to Golden City, Attila lived intermittently with his father, who employed him as a court clerk in both cities.

An anonymous letter to the editor of the Rocky Mountain News charged Harding with having paid for a Salt Lake City woman to join him in Denver, where on arrival he "saluted her in the most affectionate manner possible." The letter asserted that since then, Harding had been "living and keeping house with this female."[37] Relevant to these unsubstantiated charges are the several political enemies Harding made after taking the supreme court position in Colorado. By his own authority, he had moved the spleenful Justice Armour from the prestigious court position in Denver to a less important seat. Harding made an enemy of Col. John Chivington by criticizing his barbaric killings at Sand Creek.[38] He angered many members of the bar over the jurisdiction of federal and district courts and for alleged preferential treatment of former Minnesota congressman James M. Cavanaugh. Harding's contention that Colorado was not ready for statehood also brought him even more enemies.

On a War Footing

Connor's militant words that miners would be protected by "martial law" and "at every hazard and at any cost" may explain Daniel H. Wells's spring move to *again* put the Nauvoo Legion on emergency alert. The *Vedette* received a letter from "A Friend to the People": "In the town of Springville—I heard a letter from Daniel H. Wells, read in public, which ordered the people to fill up their Companies, both infantry and cavalry, and to prepare their guns; and that fifty minute men from that town, with the best guns and a sack of cooked provisions each, should stand prepared at a moment's notice, for service. The same state of affairs exists at Spanish Fork, Provo, Payson, and other settlements south of Salt Lake City."[39] On April 5, Wells sent orders to Iron County Military District's Col. William Dame to be ready to move at "a moment's notice, whenever a hostile intention or demonstration should manifest itself." James G. Bleak of the southern settlements entered part of Wells's order into his historical record: "You will muster and [conduct] inspection of arms of forces in your District: it is also deemed wisdom for each settlement to keep a guard night and day," so that "houses, stables, corrals pastures, and ranges may not be robbed; nor men, women, nor children carried off."[40]

The *News* of April 27 published Wells's instructions, noting that "the officers and soldiers composing the Legion will realise the necessity of being as fully prepared as circumstances will admit to defend themselves against the reckless savage or *other lawless foe*," presumably meaning U.S. troops under Connor.[41] By April 28, Colonel Burton ordered Maj. Lot Smith of the First Battalion, First Cavalry, to prepare for muster and inspection by May 7, at the military site near the Jordan River bridge.[42] These actions did not, in any way, involve the only legal commander in chief of Utah's militia, Governor Doty, or his lawfully appointed stand-in, Acting Governor Reed.[43]

The purpose of placing the Mormons' militia "on a war footing," the *Vedette* observed, was "to keep the people in an eternal stew, looking for and expecting some attack by somebody, exactly whom nobody knew and nobody could tell." Even Doty "seemed as much at a loss as anybody else," according to the *Vedette*, cautioning that "all the bustle of mimic war . . . would be ridiculous were it not calculated to be serious." The Mormons' motivation was revealed in a letter from a reliable, intelligent Mormon of "the outer settlements": "'The service required, is to guard the hills, can[y]ons, etc., and if a party of men should appear, to inquire their business, order them to leave and *make them do so. The whole matter is simply and undeniably to try and prevent miners from prospecting the country.*'" Connor repeated his promise to protect the public domain: "While the rights of *bona fide* settlers . . . will be protected to the uttermost by the Government, neither Church nor State, nor Militia, Priests, Prophets, Generals or Captains, will be permitted to infringe one iota on the rights of those who desire to develop the mines."[44]

Neither Reed nor Doty challenged Wells's issuance of General Order No. 1 as null and void without gubernatorial sanction. Those at the *Vedette* knew which governor the Mormon people obeyed. However, a caution went out: "We warn militia Captains and tinselled Generalissimos not to trifle with so delicate a question. Men of less discretion than the Lieut.-General [Wells] . . . may take these secret orders . . . in earnest . . . [and] provoke difficulties, which all good men would desire to avoid."[45]

Hammering, Hammering the Message

Brigham Young spoke in an April conference: "'They are fighting in the East; let them fight and be d——d! They cannot get any assistance from Utah!'"[46] His disdain for the California Volunteers was clear: "'The boys can go up . . . some fine morning, and clean out the troops before breakfast. The troops are no better than the members of Congress.'"[47] Mormon elder John Taylor also spoke: "The United States is broken and never will be mended.'"[48] Young reiterated that the root cause of the immense war was "in the providence of God" and "was told us years and years ago by the Prophet Joseph." Could the country be saved? He answered: "Only by turning from their wickedness. . . . There will be war, famine, pestilence, and misery through the nations of the earth, and there will be no safety in any place but Zion."[49]

In the Tabernacle on June 5, Young hammered on: "Do you not think the Lord will chasten the nation which has killed his prophets, set at naught his message, and scourged and cast out his servants?"[50] On June 24 in Wellsville, Utah, he preached: "Did you not think brethren, you who were in Missouri and Illinois, that the inhabitants of those places did just as they pleased with regard to driving the Saints?' [Audience:] 'Yes.' And also in regard to killing Joseph? 'Yes.' . . . The war now raging in the nation is the consequence of their choosing to do evil instead of good."[51] The next day in Logan, it was the same insistent beat: "America has a right to reject the revelations given through Joseph [Smith], . . . and then the Lord has the right to . . . vex the nation. . . . They had a right to kill Joseph, and the Lord has the right to destroy the nation."[52] After the July 24 celebrations, Young addressed the Saints in the Bowery: "I have preached and prophesied for the last thirty years . . . that the Almighty would come out in his wrath . . . for persecuting the Priesthood of the Son of God."[53]

Reporting on the April conference, the *Vedette* commented that "during the entire session . . . we could detect no hearty or even simulated expression of regard for our country, or sympathy with the Government in its gigantic and holy struggle against rebellion." Speakers "indulge[d] in coarse ribaldry" against government and "chuckled malignantly over the horrors of the terrible civil war raging."[54] Their tone had been "apathetic . . . for the maintenance of human rights, liberty, and a free government," indicating "by words, looks, and tones, a grim satisfaction in . . . the defeats and mishaps of our armies."[55]

Making a clear distinction as to whom its criticisms were directed, the *Vedette* added, "The people . . . are . . . sound in their loyalty to Government . . . [and] at variance with those of their so called leaders."[56] Connor had a similar message: "Bad men have sought and still seek to educate the mass of their followers in . . . antagonism towards Government, and led them to the very verge of open-handed treason." He cautioned those of his command to rely "on the intelligence of the mass of the people" and not to retaliate against them for misdeeds of their leaders.[57]

Others confirmed Mormon leaders' disloyalty. William C. Phillips, retired editor of Austin, Nevada's *Reese River Reveille*, was passing through Salt Lake City and stopped to hear addresses in the Bowery. His observation: "The meanest, dirtiest part of each sermon was to iterate and reiterate the certainty that this Government must go down!" Those speaking were "unseemly anxious to impress this upon their ignorant hearers, to make semi traitors of them." The preachers were "most vulgar," Phillips said, adding that "their whole attempt appears to be to mislead their people and make them practical haters of our Government and nation."[58]

Entertainment While War Ravages On

Built at an estimated cost of at least one hundred thousand dollars, with a seating capacity of three thousand people, a parquet dress circle, and three balconies, the Salt Lake Theatre was a showcase success among Young's endeavors.[59] Samuel Bowles, the *Springfield (Mass.) Republican*'s editor, wrote after his 1865 visit: "The building itself is a rare triumph of art and enterprise. No eastern city of one hundred thousand inhabitants,—remember Salt Lake City has less than twenty thousand,—possesses so fine a theatrical structure. It ranks, alike in capacity and elegance of structure and finish, along with the opera-houses and academies of music of Boston, New York,

Philadelphia, Chicago and Cincinnati."[60] Bowles's fellow traveler A. D. Richardson remarked, "The receipts of Brigham's theater averaged eight hundred dollars per night," adding fifty thousand dollars a year to Young's income.[61]

Doors opened at quarter past six, with the curtain rising at seven. Neither Young nor other ranking priesthood men removed their hats, and ladies took no note. Some of the nation's best actors and actresses made visiting performances, including Mr. and Mrs. Selden M. Irwin and Thomas A. Lyne, but reliance was placed on local talent from David O. Calder, Hiram Clawson, John T. Caine, Philip Margetts, and others of the Deseret Dramatic Association.[62]

January's programs included performances of *The Hunchback* and *Green Bushes*, which played to a full house, followed by *Damon and Pythias*.[63] In midmonth, widely known humorist Artemus Ward arrived in the city but took ill, unable to appear until mid-February. Other attractions were *Jessie Brown, or The Relief of Lucknow*, and *The Spectre Bridegroom, or A Ghost in Spite of Himself*.[64] In March, *The Corsican Brothers*, with Selden Irwin as the brothers Franchi, drew immense audiences. In April, polygamists in the city for the LDS semiannual conference flocked to Irish playwright Dion Boucicault's *Colleen Bawn*, a melodrama of the murder of an unwanted wife. The *Times* gave praise— "The Irwins have made a good thing of it the past Winter"—adding that the "theatre is a big institution and a decidedly paying one too."[65] The *Times* explained why such entertainment appealed to the conservative society: "The proprietors and managers are the religious leaders of the people, so there are no conscientious scruples in opposition [to theater] as elsewhere." If leaders take "season tickets," followers will attend "infallibly."[66]

A "Snow" Storm of Stakes

Connor sent out several groups from Camp Douglas in the first part of May, each with a dual purpose. On May 9, Capt. Samuel P. Smith went northward to Idaho's Raft River to protect immigrants and search for minerals. On May 11, troops under Capt. Noyes Baldwin were ordered to protect Uintah Valley miners, while devoting most of their attention to "the discovery of placer mines."[67] By June, reports of the quality of southern mine claims of the previous fall and early spring were abundant in Salt Lake City. In February, Young uncharacteristically wrote a southern settlement bishop instructing Saints to occupy Meadow Valley and "claim, survey and stake off as soon as possible, those veins of ore that br. [William H. "Gunlock"] Hamblin is aware of . . . [and] likely to be easily found and profitably worked."[68] Thus Capt. David J. Berry's Second California Cavalry was ordered on May 13 to "proceed . . . by the most practical route to the Meadow Valley mining district, . . . [to] afford protection to miners from Mormons and Indians" while thoroughly exploring and prospecting. "If successful in finding placer diggings," Berry was to "at once report the fact."[69] Capt. Charles Hempstead headed a small detachment on May 22 to join Berry en route to Meadow Valley, located seventy-five miles northwest of the Mountain Meadows massacre site. "Our road was the main highway . . . to Cedar City, Iron County," wrote Hempstead, through settlements "at an average distance of six miles apart." Settlements were in a "prosperous condition as regards the approaching harvest," even Washington County's harvests would exceed their needs.[70]

Several weeks before Berry's departure, Connor had ordered Capt. George F. Price, with sixty-one men of the Second California Volunteer Cavalry, to find an all-weather route from Fort Mojave, Arizona Territory, to the Colorado River. Price stopped at the Mountain Meadows site, finding the monument to the emigrants placed in 1859 by Maj. James H. Carleton and the men of the First Dragoons, "torn down and strewed about far and near." Price and his men spent two days gathering up "the scattered bones for re-interment" and "erected a handsome and durable monument of cobble stones on the spot where the emigrants had been camped." On the eastern face of a new cross, they inscribed, "'Vengeance is Mine,' saith the Lord, 'and I will repay,'" and on the reverse, "'Erected by the officers and men of Co. M, 2d Cav. "C.V.," May 24th and 25th 1864.'"[71] Hempstead's party arrived after Price had departed, and stopped to pay respects to the victims. Leaving the grassy bowl to travel to Meadow Valley, the group "reined up to contemplate the scene" below them: "While we paused upon the

Charles H. Hempstead was California's secretary of state, state librarian, and director of the San Francisco Mint before coming to Utah with the California and Nevada Volunteers. He served as editor of the *Daily Union Vedette*. Color portrait by Lynn Faucett, used by permission of Fort Douglas Military Museum, Salt Lake City, Utah.

mountain height, bathed in the sunlight, a thundershower passed over the lower end of the valley, and a glorious rainbow mounted up to Heaven, one point apparently resting on the apex of the rude monument piously erected a few days before, above the gathered bones of the hapless victims, while the other was lost among the clouds. That silent yet gorgeous bow . . . seemed thus appealing to the angels above for vengeance, while the weeping cloud dropped gently down on the green graves the very tear-drops of heaven."[72]

On arriving at Meadow Valley, the Berry-Hempstead party measured it at fifteen miles long, finding a "splendid spring of lukewarm water." "Flocks of sheep and large herds of cattle and horses . . . were to be seen on every hand," for "the Saints had already pitched their tents, laid out a town site, surveyed the valley, and parcelled out the farm lots." Here Erastus Snow, the southern Utah mission president, with a large party of Dixieites returning from the mines, indicated to the troops that they were "elated" at having "gobbled up the prize, and left little for ungodly sinners, like us."[73] Earlier, Snow had told the Saints that "it was the intention of Genl[.] Connor and Gentiles to settle in there and not only claim the mines of silver in the vicinity, but also the farming lands, water privileges, etc."[74] On Hempstead's expressing "surprise that a *high* dignitary of the church was traveling the country leading a large prospecting party," since Young spoke powerfully against mining by the Saints, the reply came: "'Pshaw! . . . it's all nonsense. Why here is our President (Snow) and this whole party have taken up extensive claims on the Panacka lead, and we are going to work them too." Twenty to thirty men from St. George had taken up silver claims, while the Meadow Valley Company had "staked off 7,200 feet on one lead, 4,800 on another—and several thousand on yet another."[75] Erastus Snow, "heedless of the maledictions denounced against treasure-seekers, had gone in with a vim."[76] The mountain was "covered and spotted with stakes, . . . and so frequently did the St. George President's name appear stuck in the stakes, that it looked as though there had been a recent *snow* storm on that mountain."[77] The Dixie Saints were likely conflicted and confused when the same Apostle Snow, less than a year later, publicly said that he "wished any man that would go to the western mines as a miner to be cut off the Church."[78]

The *Vedette* explained the Panacka find was first noted by white men when Mormon elder "Gunlock" Hamblin was taken there by a "semi-civilized Indian, named Moroni." Reports claimed it to be "almost entirely pure metal—very little rock or earthy matter being mingled with the ore," meaning that silver, lead, and antimony "can all be separated . . . by cheaply constructed furnaces," not requiring expensive crushing mills. Hamblin, inexperienced in mining, joined with Stephen Sherwood and J. N. Vandermark, travelers with the Berry-Hempstead troops who had mining experience. In March 1864 the Meadow Valley Mining District was organized, its boundaries containing sixty square miles.[79] At least two other mining ventures established by Mormons preceded those of Meadow Valley. As early as 1849, Young secretly sent two companies to California for gold. The first, captained by James M. Flake in October, included Charles C. Rich and George Q. Cannon. The second, a month later, was commanded by Simpson D. Huffaker.[80]

In September 1863 when the Third California Infantry's men were sent to graze horses in Bingham Canyon, the officer's wives arranged a picnic party and accompanied them. At least one officer, Capt. A. Heintz, recognized signs of precious mineral within the canyon, which was only a short distance southwest of Salt Lake City.[81] "During the rambles of the party on the mountain-sides," a lady, Mrs. Robert K. Reid, wife of the Camp Douglas surgeon, "had a previous acquaintance with minerals in California, picked up a loose piece of ore." She and nineteen other shareholders, including Mrs. P. Edward Connor, staked a claim.[82] On September 17, 1863, George B. and Alex Ogilvie and several other Mormons, while dragging logs, uncovered an outcropping that contained silver.[83] "They stuck a stake in the ground, made their location," and readily informed Connor of their find. They organized in the name of the Jordan Silver Mining Company, with twenty-four people owning shares.[84] The Camp Douglas contingent joined in a coalition with Mormon bishop Archibald Gardner, whose West Jordan Ward members lived near Bingham Canyon.[85] Together the two groups—some fifty-two persons—formed the West Mountain Quartz Mining District: "[Its boundaries] covered all the Oquirrh range of mountains, from Black Rock at the southern end of Salt Lake, south of the 40th parallel of latitude. But little work

Miners' buildings in Alta City in Little Cottonwood Canyon, not far from Salt Lake City. General Connor encouraged mining in Utah, and he made the first silver claims in this Wasatch Range canyon. Used by permission of the Utah State Historical Society.

was done in the new discovery until the following spring."[86] "While the Mormon pioneers had previously located many veins and organized mining parties, the area encompassing Bingham Canyon was the first *recorded* mining claim in the Territory of Utah and also the first mining district to be formally organized and recorded," notes historian Leonard Arrington.[87] On the Oquirrh Mountains' east side were mines named Galena, Kingston, Empire, Silver Hill, and Julia Dean.[88] In March of 1864 a military post, Camp Relief, was established on the west, in Rush Valley; several companies of cavalry were posted there. By June the Rush Lake Valley Mining District was organized, with more than thirty ledges being worked. On its future promise, Connor founded the first non-Mormon settlement in Utah. Naming it Stockton, in honor of his hometown in California, the city was surveyed for more than eight hundred lots, anticipating ten thousand people. For Connor, who sunk eighty thousand dollars of his own money into the town's founding and the nearby mines and smelters, profits never materialized.[89]

The silver-bearing ore of the Wasatch Mountains on the valley's eastern side was first discovered by Connor himself, in Little Cottonwood in summer 1864. However, the district was not organized until 1868, when the first output of the notoriously productive Emma Mine, near present-day Alta, Utah, started.[90] The Wasatch Mountain Mining District would eventually extend over a seventy-mile expanse, from Weber Canyon north to Provo south.[91]

Young did not admit involvement of Saints in mining ventures in his March letter to his sons in New York City but disparaged the efforts by Connor's men. The "diggers on the bench," as he called them, had not induced "people to believe in their mining yarns," Young asserted, "and the miners who wintered here . . . have already nearly all left for the mines north and west," passing "quietly and chagrined out of our territory."[92] At odds with Young's opinion was K. W. Kearsing's new advertisement of assayer and refiner services in a Camp Douglas office; he was "now prepared to make Assays of Ores of every description."[93]

Change of Command Affects Utah

Rumors circulating at Camp Douglas said that Gen. George Wright, of the Department of the Pacific, would be replaced by "a prominent Maj. Gen." The *Vedette* gave Wright unqualified praise for having charted California's course without secessionists seriously threatening the state. Wright suffered with asthma and had unsuccessfully petitioned for the command's move to less humid Sacramento.[94] However, the true reason for Wright's release was to open a position where a surplus general could be warehoused. Although a West Point graduate, Maj. Gen. Irvin McDowell lacked ability to succeed on the battlefield, as had been twice proved at both battles of Bull Run; the Pacific coast appointment followed. In confirmation of his distinguished record, General Wright was made commander of the District of California.

On April 16, Young wrote to Hiram Clawson in New York City, and on April 23 to Kinney in Washington, that McDowell's appointment might also result in Connor's removal: "It is quite possible that the influence which pulled the wires for the appointment of McDowell . . . may also have the effect to remove the troops outside our borders, or at least away from proximity to our settlements."[95] The Mormon hopes proved an overreach, but McDowell checked Connor's independence far greater than had his predecessor. By midyear this was evidenced in two potentially catastrophic matters: Connor's attempt to regulate Utah's currency, and his festinate effort to establish a sizable provost guard—a military police unit—in downtown Salt Lake City, within a stone's throw of Brigham Young's front door.

Gold, Silver, and "Lincoln Skins"

In February the *Vedette* reprinted material from an earlier issue of the *New York Evening Post*, stating that "the first notes of the new National currency authorized by Congress . . . will be issued in a few days." Bills would be printed in $5, $10, $20, $50, $100, $500, and $1,000 denominations. Issued in the total amount of $300 million, the notes would be authorized for about 160 banks across the nation.[96]

California's legislature immediately reacted, asserting that Treasury notes would not be California's currency. Secretary of the Treasury Salmon Chase telegraphed that Californians were acting in contravention to the government's efforts to suppress the rebellion and urged immediate repeal. The *Vedette* was quick to voice concerns over its California men, who, "for nearly two years, . . . have received nothing but Treasury Notes" for wages of thirteen dollars per month. The value of the notes had ranged "from 75 cents down to the present price of 65 cents on the dollar." Rather than further deprive California's sons, the state should immediately pass legislation to compensate for the value lost to depreciation, the *Vedette* insisted.[97]

By July, elements in Utah were following California's path, for Connor notified Colonel Drum: "I have recently become cognizant of a persistent effort on the part of a few merchants and traders . . .

to institute a forced change in the currency of the Territory, viz, from national Treasury notes to gold coin." Connor's first impulse was action, "to arrest the originators . . . and crush out . . . so unpatriotic and suicidal a policy." After reflecting, however, he "deemed it proper to submit the facts to the department commander, and ask for specific instructions." Despite the gold flowing into the territory from the Bannack and northern mines, Connor claimed that "there is not sufficient gold and silver coin in the Territory to suffice for one day's need in commerce, trade, and barter." The national currency's depreciation, he wrote, would "disseminate among a suspicious people the opinion that the Government was fast going to pieces, and its pledged securities little better than blank paper." Connor blamed "a very few disloyal and greedy merchants" and asked Drum "for early instructions."[98] One week later, Connor wrote again, saying that the matter extended far deeper than the merchants and that the fault lay with Young. Also, one of the Mormon apostles supported gold currency "in contradiction to that provided by the nation." The apostle had announced "that $12 per hundred [pounds] would be charged for flour, and that a convention would be called early in August to establish prices."[99] Mormon price fixing was not news to Connor; he knew that each April and October, in conjunction with its semiannual conference, the "Price Convention" was held, where prices for goods and staples were set and to which the Saints pledged support. As Arrington wrote, "Young stated that he 'appeared as the representative of God in this convention as much as . . . [he had the previous day] at conference.'"[100] Connor was concerned that since the *Deseret News* had now been joined by another newspaper—the *Salt Lake Daily Telegraph*, published by Mormon journalist T. B. H. Stenhouse—the anti-greenbacks message that both sounded would be obeyed by all.[101] Their panic-inducing message was that people would retire "at night with pockets overflowing" with greenbacks, only to awaken in bankruptcy.[102] Connor did not know that worries over the paper currency were experienced elsewhere, for he again asked what should be done "to check this most villainous undertaking of rank and deeply dyed traitors."[103] After no response from San Francisco in three days, Connor moved—as he viewed it his responsibility—against issues he perceived having disloyalty as their cause and dire consequences their outcome. On July 9, Connor appointed Captain Hempstead—recently returned from Meadow Valley—as provost marshal and Capt. Albert Brown as provost guard.[104] On July 12 he again wrote to Drum, explaining his reasoning: Pushing gold currency "has its origin in the disloyalty of the church authorities and their determination to depreciate the national currency." It was Connor's plan that military presence in the town center would prevent disloyal acts and help quiet the currency debate. He added, "It has long been apparent that there was necessity for such guard to take care of soldiers visiting the city, and to prevent noisy demonstrations of disloyalty by emigrants passing through."[105] Connor's messages omitted several important facts: A store directly opposite the temple block's south gate was rented by a Camp Douglas officer by misrepresenting its use as a commissary. While Young was on a visit to Provo, one hundred cavalrymen occupied the space as a provost guard, setting off an immediate flare response from the Mormons. As Young returned from Provo, armed protectors accumulated until they numbered several thousand when he reached Salt Lake City.[106] In the Tabernacle on July 17 a non-Mormon observed that the "'Saints' who administered the sacrament, had arms buckled to their sides." Heber C. Kimball's speech was described as shockingly obscene, citing, "'I hate a Lincolnite. They don't like my calling their shinplasters Lincoln skins. . . . [T]hey can just kiss my——foot, (at the same time throwing himself into a vulgar obscene attitude).'"[107] Connor was seemingly oblivious that he had placed a contingent of armed men on Young's doorstep, for he continued bombarding San Francisco with letters of frustration and concern. Misreading the reasons for the large gathering of armed Mormons, Connor wrote on July 13: "Encouraged by the unfavorable news from the East [presumably referring to massive Union losses at Cold Harbor, the Wilderness, and Spotsylvania County], the Mormons are assuming a very hostile attitude. They have about 1,000 men under arms and are still assembling, and threaten to drive my provost guard from the city." Believing that his weakness of a reduced contingent of only three hundred men at Camp Douglas invited attack, Connor was overoptimistic that if conflict did occur, "I can hold my position until re-enforced from neighboring Territories."[108] Drum's reply to Connor urged him to be analytical, cautious, "to avoid a conflict with the Mormons": "Do so by all means. Is there not some other cause than the mere presence of the guard in the city? Examine closely. Remove the guards and troops sooner than their presence should cause a war."[109]

McDowell delegated to Drum the defusing of this patriotic, zealous, impulsive Irishman living among the contentious and exasperating Mormons. Drum wrote a response to Connor and read it to Maj. Edward McGarry, by whom he ordered it hand-carried—for reasons of security. This duplication also made Connor's staff officers directly aware of the critical importance of avoiding war with the Mormons' powerful militia.[110] Drum also sent an encoded telegram, noting that "means and men" sufficient to defeat the Mormons would leave California "in the hands of secessionists" and would "prove fatal to the Union cause in this department." For Connor, "true patriotism" would be "not to embark in any hostilities, nor suffer yourself to be drawn into any course which will lead to hostilities." Understanding that inaction would tax Connor's "forbearance and . . . prudence to the utmost," Drum wrote that "the general trusts it will not do so in vain.[111] Drum's eastbound messages of July 16 crossed with Connor's westbound telegram of the same day: "Any indication of weakness . . . on my part would precipitate trouble. . . . The removal of the provost guard under the circumstances would be disastrous in the extreme. . . . [A] firm front . . . to their armed demonstrations will alone secure peace and counteract the machinations of the traitor leaders of this fanatical and deluded people."[112]

July 19 and 20 instructions from San Francisco were the first serious, direct restriction placed on Connor by San Francisco superiors: "The necessity for posting a guard in the city is not apparent to the commanding general, while on the other hand much dissatisfaction may result."[113] "The major-general commanding directs me to say that he does not at this day deem it expedient to interfere by military force to regulate the currency in the District of Utah."[114]

On the eve of the normally boisterous Mormon celebration of July 24, Connor's response to Drum was terse: "McGarry has arrived; all quiet. The wishes of the commanding general will be strictly complied with."[115] However, in his letter the next morning Connor insisted that a show of military strength was more effective in prevention of hostilities with Mormon leaders than was any sign of weakness: "So long as my guns command the city . . . and the force under my command is not too much reduced, . . . Brigham Young will not commence hostilities . . . [and] I will not inaugurate them so long as peace is possible without dishonor."[116] Three days later Connor was allowed a guard of less than a company to be maintained in the city for police purposes only, without diverting their attention to the Mormon question.[117]

In this volatile atmosphere, two street encounters could have brought ignition. Several non-Mormon rowdies, drunk or feigning, harassed three Mormon women passing the temple block's south side. The *Salt Lake Daily Telegraph* thought that the death penalty of "mountain common law" should apply, since "the b'hoys ["Brigham's boys"] will not quietly see their sisters and their mothers insulted." The report expressed confidently, "There is not a jury in the Rocky Mountains who will ever convict the insulted who blows out the brains of the transgressor."[118] The second episode unfolded in mid-August when "two [Mormon] drunken ass-es wanting a row with some volunteers, insulted them by jeer and sneer . . . and finally hurrahed for Jeff Davis . . . on which it is reported three or four C.V.'s . . . drew their pistols and knocked down one of the offenders." The matter ended with the shooting and injury of a Mormon. The *Daily Telegraph* awarded responsibility equally to the troops and the instigators. At Young's order the "officials of the Theatre [were] to . . . permit no man to enter . . . without depositing his pistol or other arms."[119] By September, rules more severe were in force, as soldiers, with or without arms, were refused admission.[120]

Chief Pocatello's Near Execution

In midsummer the *Vedette* carried alarming news of sizable Indian groups gathering east of Salt Lake City: "We learn that 275 were at the crossing of Green River, well armed and mounted. They had surrounded several trains and were helping themselves promiscuously to everything they wanted. . . . The Indians had crossed Green River and robbed the Mail Station of provisions." A company of First Nevada

Cavalry, commanded by Capt. Noyes Baldwin, was sent with a mountain howitzer "to punish the marauders . . . and protect the road."[121] Connor left immediately and returned on August 1, erroneously confident that the plains eastward were safe. Huge numbers of Sioux, Arapahos, and Cheyennes were raiding along the Oregon Trail, resulting in five thousand men under Gen. Alfred Sully pursuing them near Fort Benton in Montana. Brig. Gen. Robert B. Mitchell, commanding the District of Nebraska, ordered that no emigrants would pass toward Fort Kearny without a hundred armed men in their company. In describing his service under General Mitchell, Capt. Eugene Ware repeatedly noted that Mormon travelers considered themselves in no danger from Indians. Ware told of stopping Apostle George Q. Cannon's "fine, four-mule light-running wagon with rubber cover," and Cannon's plea to be allowed to proceed because "he was going East . . . and if he were long delayed it would be very unfortunate." Ware continued, "He told me, as every other Mormon did, that he was not afraid of the Indians, and that no Indian ever killed a Mormon."[122]

The *Salt Lake Daily Telegraph*'s pages from July through October were replete with articles reporting eastern Indian troubles. In answer to Shoshoni raids on Ben Holladay's Overland Stage, Connor ordered Capt. J. W. Calder's Nevada Volunteers to find and arrest Chief Pocatello. Calder found Pocatello near Box Elder, made the arrest, and brought the chief to Camp Douglas.[123] On October 27, Connor, Governor Doty, Indian Superintendent O. H. Irish, and Holladay listened as interpreter Dimick Huntington queried Pocatello. The chief sat with "supreme indifference" and refused to answer "any question tending to incriminate himself," denying any involvement in recent raids. Connor informed Pocatello that if allegations of involvement proved true, he would "hang him between Heaven and earth—a warning to all bad Indians." To a suggestion that Pocatello be tried by civil authorities, Connor insistently replied that "more than twenty of his [Connor's] soldiers were buried within [Pocatello's] sight," and the military was the venue deserved.[124] Indian Commissioner William P. Dole, Interior Secretary John P. Usher, and Lincoln were soon involved, but the matter was rendered moot when Holladay dropped all charges, fearing even worse raids on his stage line should the chief be executed.[125]

McDowell Nettles Connor and Doty

Ten loyal "Union fellow-citizens" wrote to Connor in mid-September regarding dangers associated with Lincoln's November reelection. They pleaded for the "presence of Federal soldiers" in Austin, Nevada. As the "first place of consequence" for those traveling the Simpson Trail from Camp Crittenden to Carson City, Austin was besieged by Copperheadism and secessionist views among the emigrants stopping on their quest west. The citizens wrote, "We earnestly request . . . a sufficient force (military) until the November election as will protect Union interests, humble rebels, and defend the true interests of the Government."[126] The request from T. A. Watterson and nine other men was accompanied by an endorsement from First Nevada Infantry's Capt. George A. Thurston, who was then in Austin en route to Camp Ruby. For reasons not given, Connor did not assign Thurston, and his reply to Austin's citizens was copied to McDowell in San Francisco: "I have at present under my command no available troops for that purpose," presumably meaning from Camp Ruby. Connor suggested that "a detachment of cavalry from Fort Churchill" be sent, "if practicable," he added diplomatically.[127] Apparently McDowell considered Connor impertinent, for his reply, sent via Drum, was, "The general desires you to . . . raise these companies in Utah, as it may by difficult to send you forces from this part of the department."[128] McDowell's statement is disproved by the *Vedette's* report that a regiment was about to be raised "without difficulty," and in one instance forty-two California men signed up in the span of seven days.[129] McDowell was ignoring the proximity of California posts to Austin against the distance of four hundred miles from Camp Douglas, as well as that de facto Governor Young had repeatedly refused Mormons' service to the Union. McDowell wrote Doty, requesting "voluntary enlistment for the service of the United States four companies of infantry," sarcastically adding, "I have supposed the raising of these companies . . . would meet with no opposition from the community. Will you please write me fully on this question?"[130] Connor later explained his understanding of Doty's reply: "I have seen Governor Doty, and he informs me that he addressed to Major-General McDowell a letter in October last,

To Mrs. Lydia Bixby   November 21, 1864

Dear Madam,
I have been shown in the files . . . that you are the mother
of five sons who have died gloriously on the field of battle. I
feel how weak and fruitless must be any words of mine which
should attempt to beguile you from the grief of a loss so over-
whelming. But I cannot refrain from tendering to you the con-
solation that may be found in the thanks of the Republic they
tried to save.

   I pray that our Heavenly Father may assuage the anguish
of your bereavement, and leave you only the cherished memory of the loved and lost, and the solemn pride that must be
yours, to have laid so costly a sacrifice upon the alter of Freedom. Yours, very sincerely and respectfully.
                          Abraham Lincoln

SOURCE: FEHRENBACHER, LINCOLN: SPEECHES AND WRITINGS, 644.

*declining to raise volunteers in this Territory for reasons which commended
themselves to his judgment,* and which he would be pleased to give if
the departmental commander so desires."[131] Doty pointed out that if
Utah men wished to serve, they could choose to join Connor's existing
units, that military pay was inferior to mining or farm wages, that an
enlistment bonus was not offered for Utahans, and that using infantry
rather than cavalry was ineffective in the region.[132] Neither Doty nor
McDowell publicly admitted that only Young held the power to raise
troops from among the Mormons.

   On August 11, Colorado governor John Evans, unable to induce
Plains Indians to negotiate in exchange for subsistence and protection,
issued a proclamation authorizing "all citizens of Colorado . . . to kill
and destroy as enemies of the country . . . all such hostile Indians." He

promised arms and ammunition to citizens, but unless he could secure federal salaries as "regular soldiers," he could only authorize seized Indian property as payment.[133] Twenty days later, Colonel Chivington, one of the Colorado leaders in the 1862 victory at Glorieta Pass, imposed martial law in the Military District of Colorado "by request of the chief business men of Denver."[134]

Through summer and fall, Connor responded to Governor Evans's appeals, with further abrasive relations with McDowell, with jurisdictional authority disagreements, and with a request for leave petulantly delayed.[135] When Connor's leave was finally approved, McDowell criticized Connor's claim that peace in the territory resulted from his policies. Undoubtedly, the provost guard affair and the dispute over recognizing the federal currency were in mind when McDowell insisted that under Connor's policies "this department would have been involved in war with the Mormons."[136] Had he offered a retort, Connor would have insisted that peace—with Indians or Mormons—could be assured only from a show of strength. The *Vedette* spoke for Connor that troops would remain until loyalty and obedience to law existed, and while troops were present, "no overt act of treason can be attempted, and if attempted will be most efficiently treated."[137] The Connor and McDowell feuding was ended by change of command in February 1865, when "the Territory of Utah and that part of Nebraska west of the twenty-seventh degree of longitude . . . [were] added to the Department of Missouri," under Maj. Gen. Grenville M. Dodge."[138]

While troops were giving protection in Utah and elsewhere, Young continued giving the message that divine justice was at work. Recalling 1845 events, he said, "I addressed letters to all the Governors of States and Territories . . . asking them for an asylum . . . for the Latter-day Saints. We were refused . . . either by silent contempt or a flat denial. . . . Three members of Congress came to negotiate with us to leave the confines of the United States, and of the public domain."[139]

The Season's Returning Church Trains

In comparison with those of 1863, church trains of 1864 were composed of fewer wagons (170 versus 384) and fewer emigrants (2,697 versus 3,646).[140] Reduced agricultural output from drought and Indian attacks along the Overland trails had their impact. Many personal accounts leave graphic testimony of the dangers to which the 1864 emigrants were subjected.

Elizabeth Letitia Higginbotham Peery, gave an account of the attack on Pritchett's Company train: "Indians appeared and tried to stampede the horses. The Indians . . . wounded one of our party, a young Missourian, shooting him in the shoulder with an arrow; he could not pull the arrow from his shoulder as it was jagged. . . . The Indians would lie over on the sides of their horse to protect themselves, when they came near. . . . [W]e were in constant fear of another attack, we could see their signals in the night, indicated by fire."[141]

Frank M. Gilcrest's recollections were written years later: "On a portion of our trip up the North Platte, we were fortunate enough to have the protection of a troop of U.S. Cavalry, which was a source of great satisfaction to us, as this was a very dangerous part of the trip. . . . [But] we could hear their bugle calls. I used to think that the morning and evening bugle calls, echoing up and down the river was the sweetest music that I had ever heard."[142]

The Preston Company's Henry Ballard wrote that his captain could not get a telegraph transmitted "on account of the Indian disturbances": "The Indians had taken a small train of 15 wagons, killed the men and took two women and three children and run off a large amount of stock about the Cottonwood's station."[143]

A Saint of the Warren Company, Thomas Waters Cropper, left an extensive account of the group's trail experience near the Platte River. The travelers had joined trains, totaling 210 wagons, averaging ten people to a wagon. As they reached Plum Creek, "Indians were attacking and burning a train of about fifteen wagons." Cropper wrote, "The wagons were on fire, . . . horses were killed by being shot full of arrows. The soldiers buried the victims. . . . . There were fifteen graves." The company also encountered a burned-out ranch house: "A dead man lay where the house had stood. We stopped to bury the man. We camped that night in a bend of the Platt[e] River. . . . [I] counted in the moonlight fourteen indians crossing the river not far from our camp. . . . [T]he next day we saw . . . more than a thousand tepees . . . of Cheyenne and Sioux."[144]

Stephen Fairchild Wilson told of another Warren Company incident: "Our train passed by a small train of gentile freighters whose wagons were burning to ashes and all the provisions, bedding and clothing &c had been taken, also their animals, and 9 of the dead bodies of the freighters were lying stretched out side by side near the ruins, all of which was the work of the savage indians a few short hours before."[145]

John Smith's autobiography recorded that Indians "were very hostile," with "many people being killed, horses, mules and cattle stolen and wagons burned." He noted, "Many times, ranchers, traders, and also officers at government posts would use all argument possible to induce us to stop for safety. The answer I would give them was, 'We . . . have only provisions enough to take us home, if we keep moving, and we would rather run our risk fighting Indians than starve on the plains.'"[146]

Rev. H. N. Hansen left his account. As his company passed a burning house, "the owner of the place having being killed by the Indians that same day, perhaps not an hour before . . . it was difficult . . . to tell whether it was a white man or an Indian. . . . [The next day,] we came across a company of eleven teams, that had been shot down both men and beast. . . . A company of soldiers just left the spot . . . having buried the dead all in one tomb." Reverend Hansen also made observations on the Mormons' financial arrangements, where he perceived unfair exploitation, obscuring from the inexperienced emigrant the financial obligations of their transport: "These [wagons and] teams were sent freely for the purpose of bringing home the poor, and . . . each head of family . . . had to sign promisory [*sic*] notes agreeing to pay $60.00 for each person . . . drawing interest at the rate of ten per cent. . . . *[I]t looks like an expensive privilege.* . . . The masses coming from foreign lands of course could not speak nor read English, but they asked no questions but did as they were told, and not one [Mormon] explained what their signature meant."[147]

William McNiel corroborated Reverend Hansen's reservations: "After the wagons were loaded, we left for Utah, but they were loaded so heavy there was no room for men to ride and very little room for the women."[148] J. W. Pickett described his load: "We were loaded with freight for the merchants and church freight. The wagon I drove was a Newton wagon with no brakes. It was loaded clear to the Bows. I rode on the tongue of the wagon it was so loaded."[149]

George William Parratt indicated that financial accounts were settled at a stop on the Weber River, before reaching Salt Lake City. One day's entry read, "Stopted & Settled accounts with the Church bros R Neslen & J W Young Agents Charged 60 dollars each Adult with 50 pounds of Luggage this is the first & only rest we had."[150]

Charles Eugene Fletcher recorded: "When we got to fort Ke[a]rny we were Stoped. And not allowed to go on on account of the Indians[.] All trains Stoped here until Some four hundred wagons had been Stoped there[.] Then we were allowed to go on we travel two abrest making one drive a day making a corrall so large the cattle could be keep in the corrall during the night."[151]

The total number of emigrants killed in the 1864 season is unknown, but in October the *Vedette* republished a tally from the *Denver News:* "From the best information we can gather, near one hundred persons have been killed by the Indians along the Platte and Arkansas rivers, since the beginning of the outbreak about three months ago."[152]

Despite the risk of seizure and possible accusations of treason if discovered by Union soldiers, William Adams, a Parowan Saint of the Warren Company, wrote of carrying hidden gunpowder and admitted selling it to Utah Indians. A near catastrophe in 1863 involving his son Charles and hidden gunpowder was repeated with the father and another son, James: "[Lightning] killed three oxen . . . and ignited the straw in the wagon where there was five hundred pounds of powder. . . . By the assistance of the teamsters the fire was extinguished without any further damage." Although stunned, James was able to continue. Fearing that news of their gunpowder would come to the attention of the military, one of the travelers divided it among the wagons, and "when the officers came and searched the train they did not find as much as they expected and let the company proceed." Had the powder been confiscated, Adams admitted, "it would have been a great loss to me in my trade with the Indians," proving that Mormons did, as military officers charged, sell war matériel to natives.[153] The apparent demand in Utah makes it likely that other wagons and 1864 trains were also transporters of powder, guns, or both.

Other 1864 trail happenings give evidence that some Mormons plied these paths for more sinister reasons. Ohio cavalryman George W. McGillen wrote, "[O]ur regiment . . . was stationed at Fort Laramie . . . to protect the emigrants and stage lines against . . . the Sioux, Cheyennes, and Arapahoes." Utah residents "whom the Mormons did not want to leave, were murdered when they attempted to escape," the cavalryman asserted, adding, "Old Brigham Young would send his Danites . . . and murder them, then try to make it appear that the Indians did it." McGillen's troops were joined by "an old Danish gentleman and his daughter and another young lady" who were Mormons and "wanted to leave Salt Lake City to go East." McGillen continued:

> The daughter was a very fine singer, and was singing in the Salt Lake Theater. . . . Gen. Connor sent a squad with them down to South Pass, and then our men brought them down to us at Three Crossings. From there a detail went with them to Sweet Water post, a distance of 150 miles. The Indians were pretty ugly . . . but the most we feared were the Danites. We could at times . . . see the Danites following us on the foothills, and when we camped for the night we were careful to put out a good guard and picket. We finally got thru . . . without a fight with the Indians or the Destroying Angels, but it was only prevented by our vigilance. . . . I don't know if they got to the States safely, but they were unmolested as long as we were with them.[154]

As the church trains were returning in the fall months, the *Salt Lake Daily Telegraph* expressed apprehension stemming from the character of those in non-Mormon trains. Of fifteen thousand who were anticipated, "at least 6,000 are fresh from the ranks of the bands of guerrillas who have infested Missouri, Kentucky and Arkansas, for the three years last past." Whether "escape from the horrors of war" was their only drive was "not yet apparent. But to the *Daily Telegraph,* something was apparent: "Not a man [has] less than one revolver and a rifle, while the majority have Minie rifles and a pair of Colt's navy pistols. Their feelings are intensely bitter and savagely hostile to the Republic." It was troubling and "suspicious" to the *Daily Telegraph'*s editor "to see men who have been in the ranks of the rebellion, who have killed Union soldiers, and who still cherish rancorous feelings against all who stand by the old flag, cling to their weapons and refuse to part with them on any consideration."[155]

Only Soldiers May Vote

In all the territories, citizens were not permitted to vote in a presidential election. However, those in Utah for military service to the Union could vote for president, vice president, and congressmen "as though present in their respective States." The *Vedette* exhorted its California and Nevada Volunteers, emphasizing that "for many months you have carried the sabre or rifle . . . of a soldier of the Union army—for what? To help treason? No! To save your country? Yes!" Optimistic predictions said the eleven electoral votes of California, Oregon, and Nevada would go for the Union.[156] The *Vedette* trumpeted, well in advance of November's date, that all at Camp Douglas should "give President Lincoln their vote."[157] "A dishonorable peace and abandonment of the Union," the position represented by George B. McClellan, against "an honorable peace conquered at the point of the bayonet, and a Union cemented with the young blood of the nation," were the choices framed by Hempstead. The supporters of the first were "every traitor in the South, from Jeff[erson] Davis down to his humblest subaltern." The second position, represented by Abraham Lincoln, was supported by "every loyal man of the country" and had "the moral support and sympathy of every lover of Republican liberty throughout the world." It was to be "the Nation living and triumphant, or the Nation dead and dishonored."[158]

Young wrote Kinney his opinion, "that the army and the purse of Mr Lincoln will prove too powerful for the opposition, and that his re-election is almost, if not quite, sure." Young appraised the nation's politics: "[W]hat encouragement is there . . . to take part in politics under present circumstances . . . ?" The true patriot would give warning to his countrymen, but "is silenced by the clamor of contending factions." Kinney received praise for not having taken a position on the contemporary issues, while Young assured him that silence best served himself and those in Utah.[159]

Lincoln was strong at Camp Douglas, but elsewhere the more cosmopolitan judged, even in August, that reelection was impossible. Henry Raymond, the *New York Times* editor, wrote his friend Lincoln, "I am in active correspondence with all your staunchest friends in every state and from them all I have but one report. The tide is setting strongly against us." Their pessimism arose from two causes, "'the want of military success,' and the belief that the administration would insist, as the price of peace, on the abandonment of slavery."[160] Thurlow Weed, owner and editor of the pro-Republican *Albany (N.Y.) Evening Journal*, wrote that "nobody here doubts" the impossibility of reelection, for "the People are wild for Peace."[161] Historian Walter Stahr notes, "Peace Democrats declared 'after four years of failure to restore the Union by the experiment of war,' the time had come 'for the cessation of hostilities.'"[162] However, the news in early September told of Atlanta's fall, and only days later came Sheridan's victory over the fourteen thousand men of Confederate general Jubal Early in the Shenandoah Valley. State elections in October showed Union candidates winning in Indiana and Ohio, with the outcome in Pennsylvania very close.[163] Lincoln's tide was rising.

Seven days before the election, the *Vedette* addressed the circulating rumor that "the Supreme Court of California has decided that soldiers outside of the State are not entitled to vote." Seeing this as a frantic, specious effort to reduce the Lincoln vote, the *Vedette* laid out the facts that the California legislature had passed a law overriding an earlier court ruling, and without doubt servicemen's votes would be counted. Thus the *Vedette* declared, "We trust . . . that no soldier will refrain from casting his vote." The choice remained simple: "union or disunion— country or no country—triumph or submission to treason."[164]

On Election Day the *Vedette* waxed poetically, "To-day decides whether the Goddess of Liberty shall sit triumphantly on the throne of freedom or whether she shall be trampled in the dust, and America be stained and forever damned with slavery and the shackles of bondage." Unanimity was urged, without a single ballot cast for McClellan, for the volunteers should be for "Lincoln and Johnson, to a man—one and all."[165]

The national results caused the *Vedette* to exclaim, "Glorious! Glorious!" for the election of Lincoln and Johnson was "beyond a doubt." The *Vedette* pronounced, "Copperheadism is forever damned, and McClellan, Vallandigham, Wood & Co., have hung their harps on a prickly briar. Peals from the mouths of our thousands of cannon will rent the air . . . and millions of throats will be made hoarse with the huzzas of loyal men."[166] The *New York Times* announced that the latest figures "positively indicate that Mr. Lincoln has carried the State, and that the majority for him . . . will be from seven to eight thousand."[167] On November 12 the vote count of Grant's Army of the Potomac was published: "Pennsylvania soldiers give a majority of 3,780 for Lincoln. The Western regiments also give similar majorities for Lincoln. The total vote in the combined armies before Richmond and Petersburgh is put down at 18,000, the majority for Lincoln being 6,600."[168] When the news of Lincoln's reelection was received by the rebels at Fortress Monroe, more than eight hundred deserters crossed to Union lines in one body.[169]

In the 1864 presidential election, more than four million Americans voted, and unlike the 1861 vote, this vote tallied 55 percent for Lincoln. The *Vedette*'s editor judged this election—as did many others—"the most important National election of our history as a people."[170] As the remainder of the nation either celebrated or mourned, the *Deseret News*' opening page devoted only one small paragraph under the anemic title of "Eastern Items." Admitting that most newspapers were "full of flaming articles on State and Presidential elections," it printed only the obvious: "The votes cast . . . yesterday, doubtless decided who should occupy the White House in Washington for the next four years. We expect to print the result of the great campaign in our next issue."[171] However, this was *not* done. Nothing of any "great campaign" appeared in the next issue, dated November 16. The word "Lincoln" did not appear on any of its eight pages. Instead, it carried the sentence: "If we, in Utah, were permitted to enjoy the free exercise of the elective franchise we might feel a little more interested in these great National struggles for power, but as the utterance of our political sentiments can avail nothing, and having no power at the ballot box, we are obliged to cry *mum*."[172] The *News'* editorial and journalistic silence was a deafening message that Mormon leaders had neither loyalty to the Union nor interest in the freedom of four million enslaved people. Lincoln's reelection drove no celebration in the Tabernacle or the Bowery. Confirmed were the accusations made by Harding, Waite, Drake, Connor, Hempstead, Livingston, and the several officers of the California and Nevada Volunteers of the primacy of Mormon leadership's self-interest in the Kingdom of God.

The *News* reported on George A. Smith's address to the Utah military districts of Provo and Peteetneet, where Smith spoke to "impress on the minds of the citizen soldiers the necessity of being constantly prepared, armed and equipped as the law directs, minute-men indeed, for the protection of our homes and firesides." The threat that required the territory's military preparedness was unstated, leaving each Saint to speculate.[173]

Hempstead's exuberance in the *Vedette's* pages accentuated the contrast with the *News:* "With feelings of heartfelt gratitude to the God of Nations we write the words, 'The victory is won—a nation is saved.' Sing joyful hosannas all loyal men and loyal women of the land! Join in the glorious anthem of lovers of liberty throughout the world! Let the mighty shout of Freedom reach the footstool of the Eternal—'The victory is won—a nation saved!' . . . Freedom is crowned with fresh garlands, and sets [*sic*] enthroned in the hearts of the loyal men and loyal women of America."[174] Articulate language did not move Mormons into postelection celebration. The *News* remained bare to December's end, of even the simple fact that Lincoln had been reelected. Editor Albert Carrington followed Young's admonition of silence, for the word "Lincoln" was omitted from the publication, with only three minor, back-page exceptions.[175]

Without a Law

Connor and others often complained of extralegal justice administered in Utah. The murder of a California volunteer, accused of sexu-
ally molesting a child, supports these claims. The circumstances were
described by Young in a letter to Kinney, and in the *Vedette* by Hempstead. Young's account read:

> One of the Volunteers recently committed an abominable
> outrage upon a boy of about 12 years of age, whom he found
> alone in an out-of-the-way place, and threatened him with
> death if he would tell any person what he had done. The boy
> upon his return to the City described the crime. . . . [T]he
> offender . . . was arrested, and the offence was fully proved, but
> our legislators, never having contemplated the possibility of
> such a crime . . . , had made no provision for its punishment,
> and the criminal had to be discharged. In the evening . . . he
> was shot by some person unknown, while he was passing from
> the City up to Camp. The father of the boy was arrested; but
> he proved an alibi so clearly that he was discharged. Capt.
> Hempstead, the prosecuting counsel, fully exonerated him in
> his remarks.[176]

The *Vedette*'s report contained some particular differences. The young
victim was named Charles Monk.[177] Connor promptly ordered the
accused, Pvt. Frederick Jones of Company G, Third Californian Infantry, remanded from the provost guard's custody to the civil authorities. Judge Jeter Clinton concluded, on evidence not cited, that the
man was guilty, but because Utah lacked a statute against a specific sex
crime, he discharged the prisoner. After dark, Jones was returning to
Camp Douglas when four pistol shots were fired. Bishop Edwin Woolley, who alleged hearing the footsteps of a retreating assassin, was the
first to see Jones "dead and weltering in his blood." Hempstead and
Clinton arrested the boy's stepfather, one Charles Merrit, but witnesses
established an alibi for his whereabouts. Private Jones was convicted
in a court lacking authority. It lacked a jury, a court record, or a law

making his alleged action illegal. However, a verdict required Private Jones to be subjected to "mountain common law."[178]

Completing Promises to the Morrisites

Mid-October marked the departure of Capt. James W. Stillman with Company C, Third California Infantry, with a wagon containing quartermaster and commissary stores headed for Camp Connor at Soda Springs. Stillman was to relieve Capt. David Black and his company, garrisoned at the post since its establishment eighteen months earlier. Their charge was to protect both the trail to the Bannack and Virginia City mines, and the Morrisites brought by Connor from the shelter provided them on grounds at Camp Douglas.[179]

Shortly after Stillman's arrival, Capt. Samuel P. Smith, with men of the Second Cavalry and Third Infantry, left Camp Connor, destined for Nevada's Fort Churchill. About forty women were among the Morrisites delivered there on December 6. The Morrisites intended, "as soon as the roads will permit," to push over the Sierra to California, where they hoped to make permanent settlement.[180] Within a decade the Morrisite people had dispersed, some retaining their Morrisite affiliation. Some went to Omaha and Council Bluff, Nebraska, some to Malad City, Idaho, some to the upper Snake River valley towns of Firth, Blackfoot, and Idaho Falls; others migrated to Deer Lodge Valley, Montana, and a few returned to their country of origin in Europe. By 1940 fewer than a dozen remained.[181]

Mormonism's Enterprises

In November, Young wrote to Dwight Evelith, requesting that he purchase a pile driver and a thousand-pound hammer, like those used in the San Francisco harbor, together with all the related "machinery that is necessary that we cannot make here." Young wanted it "shipped up the Colorado River to the head of Navigation, where we are intending to erect a Warehouse."[182] That navigation up the Colorado was part of

Those who take exception to the severe military measures adopted in the Shenandoah Valley, will find occasion to reconsider their opinions, if they reason like the old campaigner with Sheridan, who thus stated the case: "It's hard when the women comes out on their knees, crying and praying, and their children clinging to them. But it's a good deal harder to go along the road, and find your own brother hanging to a tree, with his ears, his nose, his lips cut off, as I did mine last week!"

Union soldier, 1864

Source: Excerpted from "Why the Valley Was Cleaned Out," *DUV*, December 30, 1864, 1/4.

a larger plan for Mormon converts to reach Utah is outlined in a letter written shortly thereafter to his son Brigham Young, Jr., and Daniel H. Wells in Liverpool. The senior Young hoped "that the way will be open for our emigration to come by the Colorado River, and that Steam ship owners will be willing to charter their vessels to carry our people to Aspinwall on the Atlantic side and from Panama [City] on the Pacific side up the coast to the point that will suit us best."[183] Anson Call, appointed by the Deseret Mercantile Association to explore the river, reported to George A. Smith in December that the best site for a landing was less than a mile above the mouth of Black Canyon. "I am now engaged in St. George gathering laborers, mechanics, supplies, tools and every[thing] necessary," he wrote.[184] Young reported, "The news from the Colorado River is encouraging. Bro. Anson Call and a company of brethren have selected a suitable site for the erection of a warehouse . . . about 125 miles distant from St. George. . . . There is considerable interest . . . that the River would yet be an outlet and inlet for our traffic, and they are beginning to crowd in and occupy the land. We contemplate sending two or three hundred families down there . . . , as we no longer wish to see outside parties come in and take possession of the best places and reap the fruits of our toil."[185]

Having rid themselves of their charlatan friend, Walter Murray Gibson, Mormons moved to raise cotton in Hawaii. An early 1865 *San Francisco Bulletin* article documented that Mormons were "making preparations for the raising of cotton" and were starting a colony for that purpose. The article noted, "Young's agent . . . arrived . . . to obtain the necessary implements. Their avowed object is the raising of sufficient cotton for the wants of Utah."[186] A grand vision held that cotton and other Hawaiian products could also come close to Utah by Colorado River transport.

Change at the *Vedette*

Promoted to brevet major, Charles H. Hempstead assumed duties that made it "impracticable . . . to edit a daily paper at a distance of three miles from the place of publication." This news was made public on December 21. The *Vedette* editor had achieved his objective, "the establishment and maintenance of an exponent of the true interests of the people," and the previous year had seen "the dawn of a new era" in Utah, with industrial enterprise progressing. Hempstead observed, "The mines have attained importance, the people are prosperous; but above all, they have advanced in enlightenment."[187] After leaving the newspaper, Hempstead helped found a private school and entered into private law practice in Salt Lake City; he was welcomed into the Utah Bar with a dinner at the Globe Restaurant.[188] In 1866 he was a member of the inquest panel formed to investigate the brutal street murder of his friend and former fellow California volunteer John King Robinson. He was appointed U.S. attorney for Utah Territory in 1867 by President Andrew Johnson, a position he held until resigning in 1871. In that year he joined as co-counsel with Robert N. Baskin and George R. Maxwell, representing Paul Englebrecht over destruction of twenty thousand dollars' worth of liquor by city officers Jeter Clinton and John D. T. McAllister. Hempstead later became part of William

Samuel Godbe's Liberal Institute and supported Liberal Party goals, including Maxwell's candidacy for Congress.[189] Hempstead also participated with Connor in Utah mining ventures.[190]

Succeeding Hempstead at the *Vedette* was Fredrick Livingston, formerly a private of Companies G and H of the Third California Volunteer Infantry. He began his editorship with a salutatory to Hempstead, pointing out that "the *Vedette* was the offspring of his vigorous intellect, and was nourished into life and strength by his unremitting attentions." In addition to the innocuous, standard mission as a "chronicler of the times in which we live," Livingston emphasized that under his leadership the *Vedette*'s "true mission" would be "to combat heresies which oppress the people of Utah." Here was a warning that his words would be more aggressive and combative than those of his predecessor.[191] Within weeks Mormon leaders would wonder, Who *is* this new editor?

Manifesto for Statehood

As a parting shot into theocracy's camp, Hempstead commissioned a series of eighteen articles that began in early December. The author, identified only as "a gentleman of intelligence," was to examine laws enacted by Utah's territorial legislature, comparing them with the provisions of the Organic Act creating the territory and the parent laws of the U.S. government. Feigning optimism, Hempstead humorously offered that the gentleman's "suggestions shall meet the consideration of the Legislature about to assemble," and "much good will result."[192] Several among many important articles are paraphrased or summarized below.

The Laws of Utah, No. 1. This introduction to the series asserted that many of Utah's laws were "nothing more and nothing less" than "auxiliaries for the purpose of legalizing the practices and customs of the Mormon Church," and that "many of these objectionable laws have been thus far unnoticed by Congress." National neglect was especially puzzling, since attention had been directed to the Mormons by nearly every federal officer who had served in Utah.[193]

No. 2. Theocracy became official in Utah when the LDS Church was recognized as a corporation, first by its provisional government in February 1851, then by its territorial legislature in 1855. With Brigham Young as its trustee-in-trust, it was consequently able to acquire and sell property, regulate marriages, register births and deaths, and make all laws, rules, and adjunctions it deemed necessary. Although the 1862 Morrill Act limited church real estate ownership in *any* territory to fifty thousand dollars, "a different spirit of loyalty" existed in Utah, since federal law was ignored.[194]

No. 4. Mormon-run probate courts held original jurisdiction in civil and criminal actions, and as well in chancery as at common law. This would fester as an unsolved issue between Mormons and non-Mormons until the 1874 Poland Act returned such jurisdiction to district courts. An equally strong criticism was that the fundamentals descending from English common law were excluded in any court of the territory. For example, the existing law stated, "No report, decision, or doings of any Court, shall be read, argued, cited or adopted as precedent in any other trial."[195]

No. 6. A jury of six men were seated when the defendant demanded a jury trial, but before that demand was considered, the party accused had to deposit a fee to which the jury was entitled. Any man without money but accused of a public offense had little chance of justice, despite the U.S. Constitution and the Territory's Organizing Act, which guaranteed jury trial for criminal offenses. In Utah, not even a decision of a justice of the peace could be appealed.[196]

No. 10. "The Act concerning 'Justifiable killing and the prevention of public offenses' is among the most outrageous laws of the Territory," declared the *Vedette*. The operation of "mountain common law' was often the defense in murders in Utah, most notably in connection with allegations of sexual transgressions. "The idea of authorizing by law the killing of a man upon suspicion that he has committed, *or will commit*, certain acts—not punishable with death if committed—is as cruel and unjust as it is vile and barbarous." The recent killing of Private Jones was not highlighted.[197]

No. 11. Elections were held by ballot but were arranged such that the inspectors could tell how each man voted. Ballot voting's object of secrecy was "completely defeated" under Utah law. Thus, a voter's "freedom of choice" was a "farce."[198]

No. 12. Also objectionable was that "no person is considered a resident of the Territory unless he is a tax payer." A nonresident could not be a citizen and thus could not vote or hold office and was not equally treated by the law. All the more remarkable and inequitable was that "the law never has been applied to members of the Church." The *Vedette* noted, "It is folly to presume . . . that every man belonging to the Church and residing in Utah, pays taxes, aside from his tithing."[199]

No. 13. "The law concerning Common Schools is scarcely worth the paper upon which it is printed," not even providing for a county school tax. On the other hand, thousands of dollars had been appropriated to sustain "an immense and unwieldy militia law." Brigham Young directed and controlled the entire force, with nine [sixteen] military districts and a battalion of "Life Guards" in Salt Lake City to protect Young's premises and his tours through the territory.[200]

No. 17. This article in the *Vedette* series understated the harsh reception of federal officers to the territory: "They are regarded as strangers, intruders, and . . . annoyances are imposed . . . for the sole object of compelling them to resign." When an official, carrying out his duty, runs contrary to the theocracy, "other means are employed to get rid of him."[201]

No. 18. This final installment in the *Vedette* series emphasized the contradiction between the territory's request for federal funds to support a common school system and the lack of any local law or community effort to achieve it.[202]

These articles placed in one location the multiple issues that would block the granting of statehood for Utah until 1896. Their criticisms—particularly those of the first thirteen—would become the substance of an otherwise unwritten manifesto guiding successive waves of non-Mormon men and women who worked to see territorial government serve the needs of its people, beyond the mere canonization of the LDS Church's beliefs and practices into law.

The *Deseret News* did not engage against the *Vedette*'s analysis. At the year's turn Young dismissed its messages: "The Vedette has been unusually bitter of late, since the change of editor—two [*sic*] bitter to hold out very long; they will exhaust themselves for want of fuel, for it is very difficult to keep up a onesided warfare. . . . [C]ontemptuous indifference has more effect upon them than the most elaborate arguments and replies would have."[203]

As 1864 closed, the *Vedette*'s writings were instrumental in changing Utah's isolation from the non-Mormon world, and the world's isolation from what transpired in Utah. Isolation could no longer be Utah's destiny.

Chronology
1864

January 4	John Fitch Kinney asks Gen. H. W. Halleck to remove Gen. P. Edward Connor and troops from Utah Territory.
	Governor James Duane Doty is absent from the territory, returning about June 15.
January 12	Jason R. Luce is executed for the murder of an Idaho miner.
January 21	Memorials to Congress for statehood and for removal of Connor and troops are passed by the Utah legislature.
January 22	Acting Governor Amos Reed vetoes a bill strictly restricting mining.
February 5	Miners in Franklin, Utah, are threatened; disloyalty to the federal government is rampant among the area's Mormon citizens.
February 15	Connor answers Kinney's letter to Halleck, cites disloyalty of Mormons.
	Paper currency is issued by the U.S. government.
March 1	Connor issues a circular threatening "martial" law for the protection of miners.
	Colorado supreme court justice Charles Lee Armour asks Brigham Young to provide evidence of sexual impropriety by former governor Stephen S. Harding.
	Camp Relief is established in Rush Valley by Camp Douglas volunteers.
	Connor establishes the city of Stockton, Utah.
March 17	Kinney, in Washington, reads Utah's statehood request to Congress.

March 18	The Meadow Valley Mining District, at Panacka northwest of Mountain Meadows, is organized. Gen. Daniel Wells puts the Nauvoo Legion on war footing.
April	A "Price Convention," held by Mormons as part of their semiannual conference, sets the prices of goods and services to troops at Camp Douglas. Through spring and summer, Brigham Young speaks many times of LDS beliefs that the treatment Mormons received in Missouri and Illinois is the cause of the Civil War. Connor moves his family into Camp Douglas quarters.
April 15	Young answers Armour with aspersions of illegal conduct but no credible facts regarding Harding's personal life.
May 24	Capt. George F. Price and company, searching for an all-weather route from Arizona to the Colorado River, stop at Mountain Meadow, erect a stone monument, and place a new "Vengeance is Mine" sign at its top.
June 17	*Deseret News* accuses Harding of fathering an out-of-wedlock child. Capts. David J. Berry and Charles H. Hempstead and troops visit Mountain Meadow. Rush Valley Mining District is established.
July 5	Gen. George Wright is replaced by Maj. Gen. Irvin McDowell as commander of Department of the Pacific.
July 9	Connor orders Captain Hempstead, as provost marshal, and his company of cavalry to establish a provost guard opposite the south gate of the Salt Lake temple grounds. Several thousand Mormon men arm themselves to protect Brigham Young's return from Provo, Utah.

July 19	McDowell orders Connor to withdraw from the possibility of conflict.
July 24	Connor emphasizes that military strength, not weakness, is best at preventing hostilities.
	Young threatens to kill Connor.
	Westbound emigrant trains are beset by Indian attacks, with many deaths.
September	Young refuses admission of Camp Douglas troops to the Salt Lake Theatre.
	Silver-bearing ore is discovered in Bingham Canyon. The West Mountain Quartz Mining District is formed.
October 3	McDowell's request to Governor James Duane Doty for troops raised in Utah is denied for reasons Doty does not immediately explain.
	Mormon emigrant trains returning to Utah secretly carry gunpowder.
October 27	Connor and others interrogate Chief Pocatello at Camp Douglas. Connor considers a punishment of execution, but Ben Holladay of Overland Stage withdraws the charges against the chief.
October 31	California infantryman, accused of pedophilia, is murdered in the street on his way to Camp Douglas.
November 8	Lincoln is reelected by a wide margin.
	Deseret News omits printing any news of Lincoln or his reelection.
	Young purchases a thousand-pound pile driver for construction projects on the Colorado River.
December 5	Large number of Morrisite men and women are safely delivered to Fort Churchill from Camp Connor and Salt Lake City.

December 5   Eighteen articles reviewing the laws of Utah Territory are published in the *Daily Union Vedette,* noting the many disparities with the provisions of the Organic Act that created the territory.

December 21   Hempstead is replaced by Frederick Livingston as the *Vedette*'s editor.

CHAPTER 7

The Pen, the Sword,
Prophecy Unfulfilled, 1865

It is the kingdom of God or nothing.

BRIGHAM YOUNG

January's expression of empathy to the suffering of millions, spoken by the Mormons' behemoth, is the only one found from the Civil War years. Brigham Young said, "The Latter-day Saints, in all their drivings, and persecutions, and sufferings . . . , have not begun to suffer the distress, the heart wringing, the great woe and slaughter that now spread gloom over our once happy land. If we could behold at one glance the suffering that is endured in one day through the war which is now depopulating some of the fairest portions of the land, we should become sick at heart and cry to God to close the vision." His attention to the war victims' physical and psychological pain was fleeting, as he returned to the result Mormon leaders believed the war would bring: "It is the kingdom of God or nothing with us, and by the help of the Almighty we shall bear it off triumphantly to all nations, gather Israel, build up Zion, . . . and Jesus Christ will triumph, and we shall reign with him on the earth, and possess it and all its fulness with him."[1]

With the Pen, Not the Sword

At the *Vedette*'s helm, Pvt. Frederick Livingston was more than a horse soldier with a quill, more than a mere political hack able to turn a colorful phrase. He was a leader of the Garrison Lodge No. 65 of the International Order of Good Templars, a temperance fraternity whose creed—"Faith, Hope, and Charity"—served to unite, "in close companionship, the souls of men." The Templars were organized among the Third California infantrymen before they left California. After a charter was refused because such was not given "to roving bands of soldiers," Chaplain John Alexander Anderson intervened and the lodge was formed.[2] Templars emphasized not only temperance but brotherly love, honesty, obedience to law, and the idea that "all the unhallowed passions should dash their surges in vain about the foundation of our temples." Historian David Fahey notes that "Templars reflected the search for a new, universal, reformed world order based on human equality of race, gender, and class," for "a third of the rank and file were women."[3] Making no distinction by race in Northern states, Templars admitted blacks. Membership in northeastern and midwestern grand lodges peaked in the late 1860s and early 1870s. With more than 50 percent of its volunteers enrolled as active members, Camp Douglas claimed the largest number of Templars in any U.S. military unit.[4] Mormon leadership's depiction of these men as drunkards and lechers denotes a far lower judgment than their aspirations to live rectitudinous Templar principles would suggest was due them.

Supported by members of the Order of Good Templars, the Young Men's Literary Association, and Rev. Norman McLeod, Frederick Livingston embarked on a journalistic blitzkrieg of castigating, denouncing, and censuring theocracy far more severely than had Hempstead's "Laws of Utah" series. The following selected excerpts illustrate Livingston's intensity and penetration.

"Polygamy." The Saints "met with . . . unqualified, unrelenting hostility" wherever they lived because they "openly advocate, and persistently practice . . . a system of licensed prostitution, obnoxious to decency and virtue, and . . . offending the known laws of the land."[5]

"The Word of God." The billingsgate of a sermon by Bishop Edwin D. Woolley was dressed with this intentionally sarcastic title. "Yes, there is [*sic*] plenty gentlemen in this congregation," Woolley expounded, "and some white-livered gamblers—I know them by their eyes, yes, and hang-dog looks, and whores and whoremasters—they can't stay among us and bring up their bastards on us. . . . You can go to some houses in this ward and see some lone widow woman and a lot of strangers." Woolley would "kill them," he said, "but the filth will kill themselves." He named a woman of his ward, which the *Vedette* redacted: "I told Sister——— . . . if she persisted in going to camp . . . , what it would bring her to. Now . . . her daughter Lizzie is a whore, a *dirty, stinking, huzzy,* a *filthy bitch.* . . . Our streets are now filled with whores, thieves, gamblers, pimps, etc. The only way to purify it is to drive them out. Tear down their houses and send them where Gebow . . . went," Wooley said as he motioned toward the troops at Camp Douglas.[6]

"A Sensation" and "A Word to Loyal Men." "The Pasha of Deseret and his satraps are writhing" under the *Vedette's* criticisms, "like a coil of vipers handled with hot tongs." When a questioner asked, "'Why do you pitch indiscriminately into the Mormons," the *Vedette* answered that Mormon *leaders* were its target, for they—not the people—are "the sworn enemies of American citizens," inciting revolution and conflict. "When Heber Kimball proclaims, with jubilant thanksgiving, the downfall of the Republic, counsels enmity to the Union," and when Bishop Woolley "outrages decency and puts the fishwoman to blush with his insane abuse of Gentiles," and when Jeter Clinton "steps from his judicial bench into the Sabbath pulpit to counsel assassination . . . , *we* shall be found exposing the wrong-doers."[7]

"What Becomes of the Tithings?" "In a conversation with a . . . son of one of the Twelve [Mormon apostles], we once asked what salaries the Presidents of the Mormon Church and other officials receive. He answered, 'nothing.' 'But how is it,' we queried, 'that they always seem to be surrounded with more of the world's comforts than their neighbors?' 'O,' said he, 'they have better opportunities.' We guess that is true. Theirs is a labor of love, they don't get wages, poor fellows, nothing but 'opportunities.' . . . [Yet] the traveler in Utah cannot fail to be struck with the coincidence . . . that in every settlement the finest

house with its appropriate surroundings are certain to be President So-and-so's."[8]

"Alas for Our Modern Prophets." "We have all heard of that famous prophecy . . . foretelling calamity to the nation through civil war, with all its devastations and attendant horrors. . . . Have the words of Joseph the Prophet failed? Is it possible [that] the oracles of disaster, whom we have so often heard making hideous mirth of our national travail—. . . that these false prophets of evil are to be disappointed?"[9]

"A Sketch." "Human life was held at a cheap rate in Salt Lake, during the years 1857–8. The knife and revolver did a large business, and obnoxious persons were disposed of by the Woolley-Clinton process. . . . [A] Mormon assassin could kill . . . a Sergeant . . . of the United States, and escape punishment. . . . [T]hose who commit [such] crimes . . . would fain blot out the remembrance of the Mountain Meadow Massacre by destroying the two monuments erected there by army officers. . . . Who has forgotten . . . the Pike, McNeal, Parish, Potter and Forbes murders, and others *too numerous to mention?"*[10]

"Kinney on the Rebellion." In his speech before four thousand people in Provo, Utah's "surprise" congressional delegate John F. Kinney said: "[T]he murder of Joseph and Hiram [*sic*] Smith was the 'great first cause' of the war, and for which the nation will be broken up and destroyed and *ought to be."*[11]

"Is It a Prophecy?" "If the nation conquers this struggle and treason and secession are destroyed, then will Brigham stand convicted . . . as a false Prophet, having willfully and maliciously deceived the community. The rebellion must succeed to save him from defeat and disgrace—hence . . . he prays God that it may succeed—hence . . . his assistants cry 'amens' to the prayers."[12]

"Loyalty of Mormon Leaders." "The name of our honored, faithful, true and tried President is held in derision, scorn, and contempt. . . . The currency of the nation is styled by Brigham Young and his horde of polygamists, as *trash*, and. . . . [t]he troops stationed at Camp Douglas are cried down as a set of adulterers."[13]

Another Word of the Living God

Utah's non-Mormons desired the presence of a "Minister of the Gospel" who would preach the "Word of the Living God." Through the efforts of the Young Men's Literary Association, many of the Good Templars, and of Hempstead, Livingston, and Connor, the Rev. Norman McLeod arrived by stage on February 16. He had been in Denver, Colorado, where he "organized a church which is now prospering," and his supporters hoped for the same for Utah. Six days after arriving, Reverend McLeod organized a church and congregation at the hall of the Young Men's Literary Association.[14] With a qualified minister now present, the *Vedette*'s Frederick Livingston and Miss Ettie M. Hornsby were married on March 17 in the Good Templars Hall.[15] Ettie Hornsby is not identified as an apostate Mormon; however, Samuel Bowles, editor of the *Springfield (Mass.) Republican,* reported during his June visit to Salt Lake City that there were "fifty or more women in the camp, who have fled thither from town for protection, or been seduced away from unhappy homes and fractional husbands; and all or nearly all find new husbands among the soldiers."[16] Albert Deane Richardson, another journalist with Bowles, wrote, "Our military authorities receive all who go to them for protection." Richardson reported on a Mormon father who had recently told Col. Milo George at Camp Douglas "that the Bishop was urging marriage upon his three daughters who were opposed to Polygamy, and that he wished to move his family to the [Camp Douglas] fort."[17] Richardson added, "Many recanting Saints, chiefly wives dissatisfied with polygamy, have here sought the shelter of the national flag, and been sent from the Territory under military escort."[18]

The *Vedette* praised McLeod's sermon: "Rarely have we listened to a more argumentative or eloquent discourse. The purity of diction, the soundness of views, the breadth of argument, and the extent of christian [sic] charity exhibited, spoke alike for the head and heart. . . . It was a novel thing to hear the word of the living God proclaimed in Utah—to hear the preacher lift up his voice in behalf of country and teach Christ and Him crucified."[19]

McLeod's life in Utah proved stressful. Before year's end, he would survive an assassination attempt.[20] He would build a church and school

on Third South, west of Main Street, and befriend Dr. John King Robinson. When McLeod appeared before a House committee in 1866 "to
deliver a blistering assault on conditions in Utah," Connor warned him
not to return to Utah. McLeod was en route when he was notified of
Robinson's October 22 murder. Stopping in Denver, McLeod remained
there six years as a Congregational minister before he returning to
Utah. He then worked as a member of the non-Mormons' Liberal Party,
urging federal legislation against theocracy and polygamy.[21]

"Milking the Gentiles"

Under the name "Justitio," a Camp Douglas soldier wrote to the *Vedette*,
describing the overcharging and misweighing of goods purchased by
the volunteers: "We are as delighted to . . . feast upon their surplus
chickens, butter, and eggs, as they are to gloat over the prospect of
. . . inheritance of the riches of the entire nation, when the Gentiles . . . shall all be wiped out in true Kilkenny-cat style." Already paying prices 10 to 25 percent higher than local market prices, the soldiers had reweighed a purchase of carrots and potatoes, proving a 10
to 25 percent shorting of full weight. All knew of Heber C. Kimball's
admonishment, "'*Brethren, milk the Gentiles*,'" but the soldier replied,
"If the Mormon fraternity will deal honorably with the soldiers, the
soldiers will deal honorably with them."[22] Overcharging government
was not unique to Utah; however, here it was carried out through a
coordinated, organized effort of its theocratic leadership.

Other Battles

Wishing to appear indifferent to the *Vedette*'s castigations, the *Deseret
News* did not rebut Livingston's articles.[23] Instead Young wrote to James
Street, the Pacific Telegraph's man in San Francisco, that certain of
the telegraph employees were working to cause rupture of relations
between the "General Government" and the Mormon people. One
operator, he claimed, was "the right hand men of Gen. Connor" and

was undoubtedly using "his position to aid their schemes by reporting to them such items . . . as suits their purposes." Connor was "using means belonging to the company for his own purposes," said Young, and so "it would be well to look after the funds received here, and see what disposition is made of them."[24] Young's letter yielded little result, for soon a similar but more insistent letter went to Edward Creighton in Omaha: "The manager of the line here should not . . . make distinctions between citizens on account of their religious or political opinions" or "ask whether a person is a Catholic, Protestant, or a Mormon." Replacement of Connor with "a man of understanding, and of brain," was sought. Young's charge that no message could be sent or received "without passing through Gen. Connor's office," with all messages being "open to inspection," recalls the same accusations by non-Mormons against Young and his clerks.[25]

Young's letter to Charles C. Rich dismissed the *Vedette* as having any impact. "[E]verything moves on . . . as if such fellows did not have an existence," Young wrote, adding that although "nothing escape[s] them that they can use to malign and abuse us . . . nobody takes the least notice of them." Yet the *Vedette*'s editorials may have emboldened Governor James Duane Doty, for Young complained while at the legislative session that Doty had vetoed its "two most important Bills." Young admitted to his own "one-man power," contending that his affirmation-only voting actually amounted to "consent of the governed," whereas Doty's exercise of the veto was "a one-man power of the most odious and tyrannical kind."[26]

The Fourth Government

The General Assembly of the State of Deseret for 1865 convened on January 23 in the State House, the *News* announced. As customary, Young addressed them, beginning with thanks for bountiful harvests and for the mountains that "invited us to rest when we were . . . fleeing from . . . persecution which had sought to destroy us." He presented updates on the progress in coal mining, transcontinental railroad plans, cotton production, and establishing a new travel route via the Colorado River. Remarks on statehood were subdued: "There has been no change" in the State of Deseret's relationship to the federal government," Young reported, suggesting that the assembly "enact that the laws now in force in the Territory of Utah be in full force and virtue in law in the State of Deseret."[27]

As Utah's legal governor James Duane Doty wrote to Secretary of State William Seward on January 28, describing the unique, three distinct governments in the territory: the church, the military, and the civil. LDS Church leaders carried out all the appointments and held control "of all the civil and military officers not appointed by the President of the United States." That same group of men, in 1851, "formed an independent government, the 'State of Deseret.'"[28] Doty explained, "This form of government is preserved by annexing portions of all the State officers; the Legislature [of Deseret] being composed of the same men who are elected to the Territorial Legislature, and who by a resolution re-enact the same laws of the 'State' which have been enacted for the Territory of Utah." Doty included "a copy of . . . the proceedings of the Governor [Young] and Legislature of this embryo State [Deseret] at a session held in this city on the 23rd of this month, by which it will be perceived that this fourth government is now fully inaugurated." Two days later Doty secretly sent Amos Reed, the territorial secretary and Doty's long-standing Wisconsin friend, to Washington to personally report these peculiar conditions. To prevent Reed's mission from attracting notice from Mormon officials, Doty dispensed with designating a formal leave of absence to Reed.[29]

The "State of Deseret" charade gave the *Vedette* fresh ammunition for its nimble assaults. "[Brigham's talents take] to comedy naturally as a duck does to water. . . . His last appearance was as 'Governor' in that immensely funny affair, the farce entitled, 'The State of Deseret.' He took his role with that ridiculous gravity [of his] . . . and delivered his Message in a style superbly comic. . . . The audience, who were also actors, were very select and appreciative, consisting of Representatives of—Lord knows what, and Senators without salaries or sense. . . . [They all] went through the farce . . . , appearing to lose themselves completely in their parts and evidently forgetful that it was not reality."[30] The *Enterprise*, of Virginia City, Nevada, carried the Pacific's sentiments on the subject of Utah's multiple governments: "[The Territory has] two distinct Governments—two Legislatures, two Governors and two sets of administrative officers. . . . [T]he State [of Deseret] Legislature therefore convenes in solemn session, and the Governor [Young] promulgates his messages with the gravity of genuine authority." Though recognizing that these acts were "wholly illegal," the *Enterprise* had no profound "objection to this style of amusement . . . so long as Brigham is content to foot the bills . . . for the honor of being mentioned in the *News* as 'His Excellency, Governor Brigham Young;' still there is a smack of sedition about it."[31]

Continuing his "gubernatorial" address, Young descended to crudeness in insulting of Utah's federal officers: "Whether they quack like a duck . . . whether they ware [*sic*]——or tight breeches, they are as harmless as a rattlesnake in the Snow." They described themselves as "the top knots, the leaders, and rulers of the people," Young maintained, adding, "I then say Kiss my foot up along." Young queried his audience, "Are you satisfied?" At their answer, Young lashed out against the volunteers: "When Buchanan Army [*sic*] came to destroy us we met them in the mountains . . . and made them stay there and gnaw mules bones until we gave them liberty to come in and the Lord and the teams were pleased with us, but I don't think the Lord was pleased with us this last time." Young declared: "If we had taken Gen. Connor and cut [castrated] him and bound him out to a gimlet maker and sent the soldiers back to California I think the Lord would have been much better pleased." He then warned, "If Gen. Connor crosses my path, I will kill him so help me God. . . . He wishes to kill the Saints, take our grain and destroy our Daughters, and this I will not permit."[32]

Uncharitable Utah Stands Alone

"Of all the loyal states and territories of our cherished Union, Utah stands alone, inasmuch as her loyal (?) citizens have yet to contribute the first dollar to the U.S. Sanitary Commission," wrote "A Private Soldier" to the *Vedette*, adding, "Apathy in this respect is the best crucible in which to test the loyalty of any people." The soldier denied having

Number of Organizations Mustered by Governments for Service in the Union Army	
Missouri	447
New York	393
Pennsylvania	383
Ohio	315
Illinois	239
U.S. Colored Troops	186
Massachusetts	165
U.S. Indian Troops	4
Nevada	2
Oregon	2
Washington	1
Utah	0
SOURCE: DYER, COMPENDIUM OF THE WAR OF REBELLION, 39.	

"any expectation of waking up the loyal inhabitants. . . . to a sense of duty and patriotism," but he wished to stimulate his own comrades to contribute. No cause was "more worthy or deserving" than to "alleviate the sufferings of our fellow-soldiers, who are prostrated by disease, enduring intense agony from broken limbs, mutilated bodies, and wounds of every class." First sergeants, he recommended, might generate subscription lists, whereby soldiers could pledge an amount to be given on payday. The editor's endorsement asked every officer and soldier in camp to contribute to the relief of suffering comrades.[33]

The Union Army was the first army to include more than a million men under a single command. The U.S. Sanitary Commission was a private relief agency created by federal legislation on June 18, 1861. Its purpose was to meet the appalling inadequacy of medical care for what would become hundreds of thousand wounded Union men, by operating across the Union states, raising its own funds, and enlisting thousands of volunteers. Many women served as nurses and in a variety of roles, such as providing care on hospital ships, forming rest homes for the disabled, and improving camp conditions. Monies were raised from donations and from large-scale "Sanitary Fairs" in major cities. After the carnage at Shiloh, Ohio sent three steamboats as floating hospitals fitted with doctors, nurses, and medical supplies. Railroads carried commission supplies without charging. Telegraph messages sent by its volunteers were free. Major funding came from the continent's western segment, due in large part to the efforts of Thomas Starr King, minister of San Francisco's First Unitarian Church and a close friend of Camp Douglas chaplain John Alexander Anderson. After his time in Utah, Anderson served the Sanitary Commission. From September 1862 to August 1864, forty-two counties of California, together with support from Nevada and contributions from Oregon and Washington Territories, raised more than $484,000 in coin and more than $72,000 in currency. In one summer campaign in Virginia, the U.S. Sanitary Commission expended nearly $600,000 in caring for casualties.[34] Over the commission's existence, volunteers raised more than $25 million to aid the fallen.[35]

The *Vedette* singled out one ethnic group for particular praise, observing that Jews in the United States had "freely contributed their wealth to our Sanitary Commissions" and had "of their own labors erected five asylums for disabled soldiers," in New York, Philadelphia, Cincinnati, Chicago, and St. Louis. The *Vedette* claimed that forty thousand Jewish men had enlisted in Union armies and "made an honorable record during this war."[36] In San Francisco, where Jews had given "as earnest sympathizers with the suffering," others had also been generous: "Christians gave with loyal self-denial; . . . heretics, as citizens of a Republic to be saved." Even men of no religion gave, and resident aliens of every nationality; "English, German, French, Irish, Chinese, Italian, Hungarian, Russian, Spanish—gave with the fervor of native citizens."[37]

The trustee-in-trust of the incorporated LDS Church could not invoke penury as reason for contributing nothing. Historian Michael Quinn documents Young's wealth and that of the First Presidency in the war years, noting that "Young merged church accounts with his personal accounts in part to protect the church funds from federal

Major Henry Wirz, the Confederate officer commanding the Andersonville prison, was convicted of murdering Union prisoners, with his pistol, chaining them to one another, stomping them, and leaving them in a stockade. On the morning of November 10, 1865, he was executed by hanging. His neck was not broken in the fall as intended; about 250 spectators watched as he writhed for several minutes until he suffocated. During the prison's fourteen-month existence, thirteen thousand of forty-five thousand prisoners died.

SOURCE: *WIKIPEDIA*, S.V. "HENRY WIRZ,"
LAST MODIFIED MAY 3, 2015.

confiscation."[38] Large sums had been spent for purchases brought home by the out-and-back wagon trains. Recent expenditures also proved him wealthy: a thousand-pound hammer and pile driver ordered for the Colorado River project. In February, Young announced the acquisition by his agents of 6,500 acres of land on Oahu in the Hawaiian Islands. The purchase price of fourteen thousand dollars in gold included cattle, sheep, goats, horses, six houses, and five acres of cotton.[39] The location of these assets meant that "sugar and long-staple cotton can be brought by water to within 500 miles of this city," according to the *News*.[40]

Salt Lake City merchants were equally uncharitable, despite experiencing huge profits. "More than one merchant firm of this city boasts of having made from $100,000 to $300,000 the past season, clear profit," the *Times* observed.[41] Bowles recorded, "Several firms do a business of a million dollars or more each, a year, and keep on hand stocks of goods of the value of a quarter of a million. . . . One firm has just received a stock of goods, costing one hundred thousand dollars. . . . Another leading merchant paid one hundred and fifty thousand dollars for freights last year. . . . One concern made seventy-five percent profit."[42]

Falls the Lifeline of the Confederacy

At the tip of a triangular sandspit at the mouth of the Cape Fear River was built the most tremendous earthworks then existing on the North American continent. Technical advances in cannonading gave power sufficient to quickly level fortifications of brick and stone. But Fort Fisher was built with massive ramparts of sand—twenty to forty feet high. Shuddering with each Union shell's impact, sand absorbed much of the explosive's energy. Twenty-seven miles upstream was the port city of Wilmington, North Carolina's largest city in 1860 and by 1865 the Confederacy's most important seaport. With Wilmington a major railroad hub, the Cape Fear River navigable for one hundred miles above its mouth, this was now the major supply line for Lee's Army of Northern Virginia. Traffic safely passing Fort Fisher was considered by observers—North and South—as "the lifeline of the Confederacy." The fort was considered by some Union commanders, including Maj. Gen. Benjamin Butler, and by certain Confederates to be impregnable.

The 1861 naval blockade of all Southern seaports was difficult to enforce, and at Wilmington it remained relatively porous. More than 1,600 ships of all classes sought profit as blockade runners, bringing war materials and goods from Britain, Europe, Nova Scotia, and the Bahamas. By war's end, more than 1,450 ships had been captured or destroyed, but many others were skillful at evasion. Historian Chris Fonvielle cites seventy steamers had an 80 percent repeat passage despite the Union Navy's gunboats.[43]

On December 23 the first attempt to take Fort Fisher was made by General Butler. A ship packed with two hundred tons of powder was run aground and exploded near the fort's seawall, aiming to open a defensive line in the huge sandbanks. A ten-thousand-shell cannonade followed, then troops landed, but the efforts failed and Butler withdrew.[44] Two weeks later, Maj. Gen. Alfred Terry, leading nine thousand troops, and Rear Adm. David D. Porter, with about sixty vessels, renewed the attack. On January 15, gunboats and iron-clad monitors opened on the fort's sea face. With nearly twenty thousand shells fired, all but four of Fisher's thirty-one massive cannons were silenced by noon. Marines, sailors, and Union infantrymen, including one

Cartoons published across the nation were instrumental in forming and changing political and social positions. The Union's larger, longer purse from which to wage war is emphasized in this example. *Frank Leslie's Budget of Fun*, March 1, 1864, "Final Issue of the War—the Longest Purse Wins."

thousand men of Ohio's Twenty-seventh U.S. Colored Troops, made land attacks. After seven hours, the battle extending into darkness, with attacks from several directions, with most officers wounded, the fort surrendered. With Fort Fisher's fall, the nourishing artery to Lee's army was lost. Many judged this irredeemable, the doom of the Confederate war. Gen. Ulysses Grant ordered a celebration salute of one hundred guns to be fired by each army near Petersburg and Richmond. In Great Salt Lake City, the *Vedette* proclaimed: "Well may the rebels tremble . . . Lee has already removed his family from Richmond."[45]

Falls the Birthplace of Treason

Savannah surrendered on December 20. Sherman telegraphed Lincoln, "I beg to present to you as a Christmas gift the city of Savannah," complete with 150 heavy guns, "plenty of ammunition," and twenty-five thousand bales of cotton. Next, came Gen. P. G. T. Beauregard's abandonment of Columbia, South Carolina, burning large quantities of medical supplies. The city of sedition and "the birthplace of treason" fell when Beauregard ordered the evacuation of Confederate forces from Charleston, and three days later, on February 18, the city's mayor surrendered to Union general Alexander Schimmelfennig.[46]

Of Charleston the *Vedette*'s editor kvelled: "From that prolific source have come all the political heresies which have ever seriously threatened the peace, or endangered the existence of the Republic." There the "seeds of sedition" had grown "bitter fruits."[47] Charleston had long ceased to be militarily critical, yet it stood symbolic: "To hold it is a matter of honor; to lose it, signifies defeat and disgrace," according to the *Times*, which added: "Europe will now have no further doubt that the rebellion is near its end. . . . The lying press will no longer deceive . . . with stories of victories over the 'cowardly Yankees.' . . . The capture of Charleston is the knell to the Southern ear, foretelling the doom of the wicked Confederacy."[48]

In Salt Lake City this news was received with rejoicing "among those whose hearts beat responsive to the inspirations of patriotism," the *Vedette* reported. Before noon on February 21 "a procession of sleighs was formed on the main street of the city, several enthusiastic occupants bearing aloft the old banner, the teams being gaily decorated with the same glorious emblem." They drove the main avenues and streets "with exultant cheers." The two- and four-horse sleighs, loaded with Gentile merchants and citizens, proceeded to the street "where prophets most do congregate," but Young's Lion House, in which his family resided, was void of enthusiasm. At Camp Douglas a different reception awaited the procession. Honeyman's artillerymen fired a twenty-one-gun salute, "the Band played the National airs, and the air was filled with the booming of cannon, music and the cheers of our officers and men." The *Vedette* continued: "In the warm and ardent clasping of manly hands; in the impulse which made men as children, embracing like brothers met after long absence; in the unbidden manifestations of gladness . . . in all these things we saw evidences of that deep and abiding love of country which has borne the Nation so triumphantly through the great struggle nearly over." Returning to Main Street, Hempstead responded to requests with "one of his usual able and happy speeches," after which Judge Titus also supplied "a most excellent address."[49]

As celebrants tired and turned contemplative came questions: "But why was it that, with one exception, no Mormon took part in the demonstrations of joy[?] . . . Does the fall of Charleston . . . [mean that] a favorite Mormon prophecy had been indefinitely postponed? Is it for this they are silent?" Noting that "not a single National emblem was raised upon any of the flag-staffs of Salt Lake City under the jurisdiction of Brigham Young," the *Vedette* speculated that the truth of Young's "revelation scheme" must now have been put in doubt among his followers.[50]

From Death Threats to Conviviality

Young's letter to Liverpool on February 28 lays out a turnabout: "To celebrate the important victories achieved by the armies of the Union in the capture of Charleston and other prominent places in the South, and also the inauguration of Mr. Lincoln as President for the second term, a committee was appointed yesterday from among the folks on the Bench to erect a stand for an Orator, etc., and to take the necessary steps to make a grand demonstration in the City. The Chairman of the Committee, a Captain who has been Editor of the *Vedette* [Hempstead] applied to the City Marshal for the use of the Council House ground for the purpose."[51] Acting city marshal Andrew Burt noted that space at the Council House was "very limited," offering instead the City Hall grounds as "larger and better adapted." Burt clarified that "the Tabernacle . . . has been placed at my disposal"—by Brigham Young, Burt implied—and offered to call on Hempstead and accompany him in the site selection.[52] Mayor Abraham O. Smoot called the City Council together; he and chairman John Sharp determined to join the celebration, naming William H. Hooper as an orator for the event.[53]

The abrupt reversal from Young's threats of death to Connor on January 23 to plans for mutual celebration on February 28 seeks explanation. The deluge of nearly fifty fulminating articles in the *Vedette* in January and February were the antitheses of conviviality. The *Vedette*'s claims that its aggressive campaign had increased the paper's circulation and that conditions in Utah were gaining regional and national attention suggest that Young acquiesced, in part to end journalistic attacks. Mormon loyalty continued to be a national question, for the *Vedette*'s editorials documenting Utah's ennui at Charleston's fall circulated widely and likely had been included in letters that volunteers mailed to home and family. Anticipating that Connor might not remain in Utah, Mormons could hope to promote a more salubrious climate for his replacement.

It was not lost on Mormon leadership that Fort Fisher's fall, along with the cessation of resupply to the Army of Northern Virginia, the evacuation of Charleston, Sherman's campaign of destruction across the South, and the ongoing siege of Petersburg, could have only one ending. All gave undeniable evidence that the much-prophesied Kilkenny cat ending would not come about. Courting the winner— or appearing to do so—was in the Mormons' best interests. Was the Mormon leadership's outstretched hand a self-serving capitulation, or did the ordinary among the Saints not share the antifederal, antimilitary views broadcast from the pulpit?

Livingston was cautious, for the "cordial spirit . . . manifested by the city authorities . . . is certainly a somewhat unusual occurrence." He found it pleasing "that Mormons have an interest in the welfare of the nation, and not in its downfall; that they consider themselves a part of the Republic, and that their hopes and fears, like our own, are bound up in its destiny."[54] However, the *Vedette*'s tone soon returned to combative, with Livingston writing that treasonous Mormon "vultures are beginning to coo like very doves for friendship," wishing to "avoid future disgrace by, even at this late hour, assuming a loyal status."[55]

March 4 brought dreary rain in Washington; Lincoln signed the Freedmen's Bureau Bill, creating a one-year War Department agency to provide for former slaves. Senate chambers were crowded for the swearing in of the vice president and new senators. Lincoln and the entourage then moved to the east front of the Capitol, where forty thousand people, including soldiers and black citizens, stood in the

The LDS Tabernacle building, on the temple lot, under construction circa 1865.
Used by permission of the Utah State Historical Society.

mud, cheering approval.[56] Lincoln's speech was brief, but he left no
doubt of his position on slavery and total capitulation. He held the
combatants equally responsible; God had given "to both North and
South, this terrible war, as the woe due to those by whom the offence
came." He emphasized, "Fondly do we hope—fervently do we pray—
that this mighty scourge of war may speedily pass away. Yet, if God wills
that it continue, until all the wealth piled by the bondman's two hundred and fifty years of unrequited toil shall be sunk, and until every
drop of blood drawn with the lash shall be paid by another drawn with
the sword, . . . so still it must be said: 'The judgments of the Lord are
true, and righteous altogether.'" A negotiated peace allowing slavery
or disunion to continue was utterly unacceptable. Lincoln's closing
words, eloquently simple, were of endearing compassion: "With mal-
ice toward none; with charity for all; with firmness in the right, as God
gives us to see the right, let us strive on to finish the work we are in;
to bind up the nation's wounds; to care for him who shall have borne
the battle, and for his widow, and his orphan—to do all which may

achieve and cherish a just, and a lasting peace, among ourselves, and with all nations."[57]

March 4 also began in Salt Lake City as "stormy and disagreeable," but cleared by parade time as it had in Washington. From sunrise, the streets were alive with people eager for a place in the procession. One mile long, it moved at eleven o'clock west along Market Street to Third East Temple, then was joined by the cavalry and infantry from Camp Douglas under Colonel George, and Lieutenant Honeyman's two artillery pieces. The sidewalks, windows, and housetops were thronged by eager, enthusiastic onlookers. A profusion of national flags floated above buildings and ornamented sleighs and teams, with many hand-held by the occupants. Windows sported banners and mottoes. Bands marching in the street played a musical salute whenever passing the home of a prominent official. Sleighs of the Overland Mail Company had signs reading "faithful to the Government it serves." Miners from Bingham Canyon carried a sign: "Uncle Sam's right hand pocket—Bingham Canyon—Gold, Silver and Copper united." Several "prominent officials of the Mormon Church" participated in the procession. The sleigh of the Young Men's Literary Association held portraits of Washington and Lincoln, and a lithograph copy of the Emancipation Proclamation held aloft by an "American of African descent." At the parade stand were Doty, Connor and staff, Justice Titus, Reverend McLeod, Mayor Smoot, and Mormon dignitaries George A. Smith and William Hooper. After McLeod's prayer, Doty made brief, patriotic remarks. As the events concluded, the "vast concourse dispersed amid rousing cheers and salvos of artillery." Remarkable for its symbolic intent was Colonel Burton's Utah cavalry escorting the U.S. forces to their grounds at Camp Douglas.[58]

At 4 o'clock Col. Milo George and staff met on invitation at the city hall with the mayor and the city council for an "elegant repast." Mayor Smoot toasted Lincoln's health; other toasts—including one to Connor, who like Brigham Young, was notably absent. The group moved to the theater and finished the day with fireworks and "general rejoicings," the end of a "patriotic jubilee rarely, if ever before seen in Utah."[59]

Afterward, doubts regarding Mormon sincerity continued to appear in the *Vedette*. "Many are not prepared to believe in such miraculous conversions from former apathy," especially those "who have carefully watched the under currents of opinion among Mormons." Before the doubters indulged their hopes, Mormons would need to "conform their conduct to the easy requirements of loyalty . . . to render the deference due to National authority, and honor the liberal laws of the land."[60] The *San Francisco Bulletin* was equally skeptical: "One might well believe . . . that the day of miracles is not yet past."[61] It was not a spirit of reconciliation that prompted the *News* editor Albert Carrington to write: "It is easy . . . to fling filth at those who may differ from us in opinion; but . . . we are perfectly willing to let all who delight in feeding on such putrid and unwholsome [*sic*] matter find food that suits them elsewhere."[62]

Ten lengthy articles in the *Vedette*, totaling nearly six thousand words, described the preparation and details of the celebration, even praising the change in attitude of the Mormons of Utah. One, and only one, paragraph of the acknowledgment appeared in the back pages of the *News:* "The 4th of March was appropriately observed by flying national flags upon numerous public and private buildings, a military and civil procession a mile in length, speeches, artillery firing, etc., with fireworks and illuminations in the evening. Considering the snow and inclement weather, the turn-out was very enthusiastic and numerous; and, as very commendable and fortunate, the Police had no reports to make of the least disturbance."[63]

In a letter to Daniel Wells in the British mission, Young wrote, "The people from the Bench played a rather insignificant part in the procession, they not exceeding 250 men, probably, all told." He added, "They have scarcely a horse that can be used; money is so scarce that they cannot even pay for going to the Theatre, and the celebration of the anniversary of the Bear River battle had to be deferred for want of funds." This was disingenuous, for it was at his order that Mormons not sell forage, resulting in cavalry horses starving. And it was common knowledge that deep snows delayed the federal pay arrival.[64]

Ending the Effusion of Blood

It was heralded as "the Waterloo of the Confederacy" when nineteen thousand Confederate infantry and cavalry under Gen. George Pickett and Gen. Fitzhugh Lee were defeated on April 1 at Five Forks, only forty miles from Richmond.[65] Three days later, nearby Petersburg fell, ending its long trench-war siege. The *Vedette* of April 4 announced that "Richmond is in the possession of the United States forces" and shared its reaction: "Words come not . . . when the heart overflows with emotions too deep for utterance, we can only feel the gratitude, which finds no expression, . . . and, therefore, we say, *Gloria in Excelsis*."[66] However, news of Richmond's fall did not appear in the *Deseret News*.

Gen. Robert E. Lee retreated westward from Richmond, thinking that only a relatively small force of cavalry under Gen. Philip Henry Sheridan blocked his way from joining Gen. Joseph E. Johnston's Army of Tennessee. But Lee soon learned that two corps of Union infantry had moved to back up Sheridan. On April 7, Lt. Gen. Ulysses Grant opened an exchange of brief letters with Gen. Robert E. Lee: "The result of last week must convince you of the hopelessness of further resistance on the part of the army of Northern Virginia, and in this struggle I feel that it is so, and regard it as my duty to shift from myself the responsibility of any further effusion of blood, and by asking of you the surrender of . . . the Army of Northern Virginia."[67] Further exchanges followed, and two days after Grant's first note, Grant and Lee, each accompanied by military staff, met at Wilmer McLean's home in the Virginia village of Appomattox Court House for signing the surrender. The generous terms of Grant and Lincoln were gentlemanly presented. Grant arranged to feed Lee's hungry army. Lee and his officers and men would not be imprisoned or prosecuted for treason. Each man would be allowed his side arms, private animals, and baggage to return home.

Bullets would yet fly and death would yet call—at least until June 22, when Confederate brigadier general Stand Watie, the weather-beaten, bowlegged Cherokee commander of the Indian regiments fighting in Indian Territory was the last to lay down arms.[68] Yet the date April 9, 1865, and the word "Appomattox" both mark, in most minds, the end of the War of the Rebellion.[69]

The *Vedette* of April 11 devoted two pages of five columns each to pouring out details describing the ending of the most profoundly destructive events of the nation's existence. Included on its pages was Secretary of War Edwin Stanton's words to Grant on the afternoon of the surrender: "Thanks be to Almighty God for the great victory with which he has this day crowned you and the gallant army under your command." Stanton ordered a two-hundred-gun salute fired at every military post to commemorate the Army of Northern Virginia's surrender.[70]

No words of celebration were printed by the Mormons' official voice. The *Deseret News* was journalistically, editorially silent.[71] Nothing of the war's end could be found in the LDS priesthood speeches given in the conference of April 7–9. Stripped of fatidic authenticity were the words by Brigham Young and others of the war's outcome; of Europe's violent involvement; of earth's rebirth in its Kingdom of God perfection; of reformed political and social order. Silence shouted that the millennialistic fervor of Utah's theocracy was stunned.

The Death Angel Broods

The events of Good Friday, April 14, in Washington, D.C., profoundly changed the course of history in the Western world. John Wilkes Booth altered his plan to kidnap Lincoln to force resumption of prisoner exchange, and instead plotted the same-day assassination of the U.S. president, vice president, and secretary of state and the commander of the Union armies. Lincoln sat in the box at Ford's Theatre beside his wife; Vice President Andrew Johnson remained at his residence, the Kirkwood Hotel; Secretary of State William Seward lay abed with a broken arm and jaw sustained nine days earlier in a carriage team runaway, and Lt. Gen. Ulysses Grant traveled to Philadelphia by private railroad car.

The ball from Booth's pistol entered Lincoln's head but did not exit, producing irrecoverable damage to the brain whose workings had successfully navigated the labyrinthine obstacles that four years of ghastly war had placed before him. Lewis Powell entered the Seward home, slashed the bed-bound man's face, severing the facial nerve and facial muscles but failing to kill. Michael O'Laughlen could not enter Grant's locked and guarded Pullman car. A change of heart led George Atzerodt to leave the city without approaching Andrew Johnson at his hotel.[72]

Lincoln died at 7:22 A.M. on April 15, 1865. Livingston's words reached lyrical: "The wing of the Death Angel broods over the Capitol and his shadow has fallen upon all the land. There is consternation in the public places, and the hearts of the people are appalled with a sadness that is something more than sorrow. Our banners droop low and the cities are clothed in the habiliments of woe. Nature herself is hushed to silence as though in sympathy with the National bereavement." The *Vedette*'s pages were trimmed in black; its editorial noted that eighteen hundred years after the Crucifixion of the Messiah, the anniversary of that day had seen "the assassination of the great Liberator, whom martyrdom has . . . made immortal." The editorial concluded, "'As Christ died to make men holy, he has died to make them free.'"[73] The *Vedette* published extensive reports of the attacks on Lincoln and Seward, what was discovered of Booth's plot, actions taken to restore administrative government, the communications from other nations, and the bitter hostility arising against secession sympathizers.[74]

On April 19 the *Deseret News*, also trimmed in black, published much of the same information from wire reports that had appeared in the *Vedette*.[75] The *News* was flatly factual, noting that in Salt Lake City, "business was generally suspended, flags were draped in mourning at halfmast, stores and other public buildings were closed and craped [*sic*], . . . the [play]bill for Saturday evening was postponed to Monday, and deep gloom palpably rested upon the minds of the citizens." Many in the Tabernacle were clad in black, as "Elders W. Woodruff, F. D. Richards and George Q. Cannon delivered feeling and appropriate addresses upon the solemn occasion." The April 17 theater performances had not been cancelled, but the theater was notable for the black draping of the proscenium, the proscenium boxes, and two large national flags that arched from the center over the drop curtain. Double meaning was evident in the *News:* "Alas for the times when our Chief Magistrate can be thus dastardly stricken down by the hands of an assassin."[76]

Utah's various officials planned a eulogy. Chaired by Doty, with Hempstead and Stenhouse as secretaries, resolutions were adopted and committees made plans for the following day. Judge Titus, Superintendent O. H. Irish, Captain Hempstead, Col. Robert T. Burton, and Col. J. C. Little formed the Committee of Arrangements; Mayor Smoot and aldermen Sheets, Raleigh, Thomas McKeon, and H. H. Felt represented the city and the city council. Amasa M. Lyman, "the most openly patriotic of the Mormon General Authorities at the time," was named to represent the Mormons, and Rev. Norman McLeod for the non-Mormons.[77] The *News* announced that "all classes of our citizens" were invited to participate at noon on April 19 in the Tabernacle "to testify their respect for the memory of President Abraham Lincoln."[78] Brigham Young did not attend.[79]

A crowd of three thousand assembled, "religious differences for the time . . . ignored, and soldiers and civilians all uniting as fellow citizens in common observance of the solemn occasion." Lyman spoke for forty-five minutes, holding "the vast audience in unbroken silence and wrapped [*sic*] attention" with an "earnest and eloquent outburst of feeling, . . . appropriate for the occasion." Concluding, Lyman said, "Let us pray that the demons of war . . . shall be chased from the earth by the searchlight of gentle peace . . . [that] out of the wreck and ruin . . . there will spring into existence a government that will extend the principles of our great Constitution."[80] Reverend McLeod "spoke with a deep feeling which, coming from his own, appealed direct to the hearts of his hearers."[81] In the *News* report, only the Mormon men—Smoot, Little, Richards, Lyman, and Woodruff—were praised, with a brief note that McLeod gave "an eulogy."[82]

"Repressing the Savages" Takes Connor for Eight Months

To Secretary of War Stanton went this message on January 14: "It is the universal wish of loyal men in Utah that a department of the plains, including Nebraska, Colorado, Utah, and Montana, be created, under General Connor. Without it we feel it to be hopeless to maintain our communication with the East." Signing the plea were six prominent men concerned with Utah matters: H. S. Rumfield, general agent, Overland Mail; James Duane Doty, governor; Amos Reed, secretary; William Reynolds, general superintendent of Overland Stage Line; G. W. Carleton, manager, Western Union Telegraph; and Utah's supreme court justice John Titus.[83] Absent from this distress call was any acknowledgment of why an Indian campaign had formed in winter's cold and hardship. Unmentioned was the preceding November's action of the seven hundred men of the First and Third Colorado Cavalry who had opened fire on the quiet camp of several hundred peace-seeking Cheyennes and Arapahos at Sand Creek. Ignored by Col. John Chivington were the Stars and Stripes flown by Black Kettle as a promise of peace, and the white flag of surrender quickly raised after the troops began firing. Upwards of two hundred, many of them women and children, were mercilessly killed and mutilated.

Even with January's cold and winter's minimal forage for animals, one thousand warriors attacked the stage station at Camp Rankin, near Julesburg, Colorado. The *Times* had only one solution. Because Indians had "undisputed possession of about 800 miles of the road," the mail and travel had already been "entirely suspended" and must remain so until the War Department intervenes to repress the savages."[84]

Connor's 1865 plan for protection of the Overland routes, submitted to Gen. H. W. Halleck and relayed to Maj. Gen. John Pope, resulted in "all hands" having confidence in General Connor, and a very strong "general wish that he should be placed in charge . . . for the whole region." By February's end, Connor was ordered to Denver; at the end of March, Maj. Gen. Grenville Dodge merged the districts of Utah, Colorado, and Nebraska into the District of the Plains, commanded by Connor, with headquarters in Denver.[85] Policy from Washington vacillated from killing Indians on sight to benevolently giving them money, food, and reparations. Inadequate supplies, unsuitable animals, and mutiny among some troop elements also hampered Connor, now overoccupied and detached from Utah affairs.[86]

With Connor gone, non-Mormons were without protection they had enjoyed since October 1862, when he and the Volunteers arrived. Shortly after his departure, an apostate wrote to Connor of escalating intimidation. R. H. Atwood, a former Brighamite Mormon now among the apostate Josephite Mormons renouncing polygamy, was already planning to leave the territory on May 1. Atwood wrote, "The fear that was gradually leaving the people has since your departure returned, and they are afraid of being placed in greater bondage than ever. Heavy threats are made by Brigham and his colleagues against those who dare to differ . . . [while] dark deeds are contemplated and enacted." Young had ordered that "none of his people [were] to be allowed in the street after 10 P.M." and had "organized a strong police force in every ward . . . to patrol night and day." There was "greater surveillance than ever," and an attempt had been made "to assassinate Mr. Maloney," who is otherwise not identified.[87] Connor endorsed Atwood as "a missionary of a branch of the Mormon Church . . . [who] are anti-polygamists and loyal."[88] Atwood's observations were confirmed by Camp Douglas's Lt. Col. Milo George. In a letter to Captain Price, now of the District of the Plains in Denver, George wrote, "A system of espionage and insolent interference with the affairs of individuals not belonging to the Mormon Church has been organized in Great Salt Lake City . . . by dictation of Brigham Young. . . . The footsteps of Gentiles, even the most respectable, are persistently dogged about the streets after night-fall by parties evidently set to watch them, . . . and there has been shown such a disposition to violence . . . that citizens, considering their lives in danger, have called upon me for protection."[89] Price telegraphed Connor, now in St. Louis with General Dodge, "Mormons very insolent; Brigham preaching violence."[90] Troubled by these reports, Connor responded to Dodge, "I regret that Utah is taken out of my command. I pity those poor fellows who, relying upon my promise of protection, have declared their independence of Brigham."[91] In August, Captain Price, now acting adjutant general at Fort Laramie, wrote Dodge that in Connor's absence Mormons "indulged in all manner of threats, and warned gentiles to leave; [saying] that they could not hunt for gold and silver any longer." If Indians attacked, "no assistance would be rendered . . . by that archtraitor and violator of Congressional laws, Brigham Young." Price implored, "One thousand infantry and one regiment of cavalry should be sent to Utah."[92] Six days later, another message to Dodge reinforced the urgency: "Mormons tried to murder Rev. Norman McLeod, . . . but failed. . . . Indians in Southern and Western Utah are also committing depredations, instigated . . . by Mormon leaders . . . attempting the same policy which they tried there three years ago, . . . to force every man, woman, and child, not a Mormon, to leave the Territory. The commanding officer . . . earnestly asks for more troops."[93] One day later, Pope abolished the District of the Plains, creating separate districts for Wisconsin, Minnesota, Iowa, Missouri, Kansas, Nebraska, Colorado, Dakota, and Utah. Brig. Gen. P. Edward Connor was named to command the District of Utah, headquartered at Salt Lake City.[94]

Connor's report of his earlier accomplishments in Utah was not lenient toward the Saints. The community was "bitter and unrelenting," its leaders preaching sermons intended to "instill . . . hatred toward our Government." At every opportunity they called the war "a 'Kilkenny cat' affair, . . . [saying] they did not care which side whipped," for at war's end, Mormons "would return to Jackson County, Mo., and control the destinies of the United States." Connor summarized his control of the Shoshonis achieved by the Bear River action; his founding of Utah's first independent, daily newspaper; his troops' successful search for rich ore bodies; and the influx of non-Mormons into Utah to found new industries. He was confident these would end Utah's isolation, and this gave him optimism for Utah's future. His report was formally indorsed by both Maj. Gen. G. M. Dodge and Maj. Gen. John Pope, then forwarded to the secretary of war.[95]

A Visit Breeds New Critics

Interest in the transcontinental railroad led House Speaker Schuyler Colfax to devote the summer between the Thirty-eighth and Thirty-ninth Congresses to an extensive tour west of the Mississippi. With him were William Bross, editor of the *Chicago Tribune* and lieutenant governor of Illinois; Albert Deane Richardson, formerly a journalist for Horace Greeley's *New York Tribune* and recently escaped from Confederate imprisonment; and George K. Otis, agent for Ben Holladay's Overland Stage. The prominent editor of the *Springfield Republican* in

Massachusetts, Samuel Bowles, made five visitors. An incisive analysis of Mormon society, polygamy, and theocracy constituted a significant portion of Bowles's account of their travels, which was published the following spring.[96]

From Atchison, Kansas, to his post at Julesburg, Colorado, these five dignitaries shared the stagecoach with Gen. P. Edward Connor. Bowles wrote admiringly of the improvements under Connor's command:, "The soldiers have ceased to be thieves and bullies; a new and better social tone is visible in all the mining region; the laws are better respected; soldiers guard the whole central line of travel, and cavalrymen escort every stage." Connor had been a mere private when first at Fort Leavenworth; presently he arrived as the commanding general of the District of the Plains, "comprising a larger territory, and embracing more delicate and important responsibilities than any other single military district in the country." Upon Connor's departure at Julesburg, Bowles expressed "real regret and a large respect" for him as "a genuine gentleman and a valuable commandant."[97]

Bowles also judged that "Colfax's reception in Utah was excessive if not oppressive," stemming from obvious "rivalry between Mormon and Gentile."[98] Feted by Mormons with a "hot sulphur bath," a fine dinner, and a visit to the Tabernacle, they settled in the Salt Lake House Hotel. Evening street speeches praised Mormons' "industry and prosperity and taste," while noting benefits the "iron horse" would bring.[99] Secure mail, safe travel, telegraph services, and more rapid transportation should be government's responsibility, said Colfax, while stressing the people's converse obligation of "*allegiance to the Constitution, obedience to the laws, and devotion to the Union.*"[100] Of mineral wealth he warned, "If you don't develop it," emigration will.[101]

At the Congregational church services, Reverend McLeod's sermon was "most excellent." Richardson's poor health, resulting from his 1863 imprisonment and several failed escape attempts until successful in December 1864, was apparent.[102]

Bowles described Mormons as eager to "prove their loyalty to the government, their sympathy with its bereavement, their joy in its final triumph," all of which their earlier silence and sneers had put in some doubt. Mormons wished to be known as "men of intelligence, virtue, good manners and fine tastes," and Bowles found "a great deal of true and good human nature and social culture," as well as "business intelligence and activity" and "generous hospitality."[103]

A picnic followed floating in the Great Salt Lake's hypersalinity. The group visited the cotton factory, Young's flour mill, Brother Jennings's new tannery, and the silkworm project of Brother Watt.[104] Colfax insisted on protocol; like Harding, he would be "the visited," not the "supplicant visitor." A two-hour call was made by Young and eight "high dignitaries of the church."[105]

Young had returned to the city only a day earlier from Spanish Fork, where he, Indian Superintendent Orsemus H. Irish, and several ranking officials had pushed through a treaty in which all Indian land was relinquished and all Indians in the territory were to be moved to the Uintah Reservation. Young wrote to Liverpool Saints that Colfax and party had been paid "every attention" and had "expressed great satisfaction at the kindness . . . and delight at the beauty of our City and the fruits of our industry."[106] Recording Young's responses to questions about the war, Bowles wrote: "Had he been President when Mason and Slidell were captured, he would have speedily put them 'where they never would peep'" before they could negotiate with England.[107]

Bowles found Young's sermon to some five thousand Saints as a "very unsatisfactory, disappointing performance": "His address lacked logic, lacked effect, lacked wholly magnetism or impressiveness. It was a curious medley of scriptural exposition and exhortation, bold and bare statement, coarse denunciation and vulgar allusion, cheap rant and poor cant. . . . It was a very material interpretation . . . of scripture, very illogically and roughly rendered; and calculated only to influence a cheap and vulgar audience." Heber C. Kimball's "vulgar and coarse speech" also got special mention.[108]

In Richardson's independently published account of the two-hour meeting with Young, polygamy was the subject:

A Mormon Elder: That infamous law [Morrill, 1862] against "polygamy" strikes at our religious liberty and is unconstitutional.

Colfax: It certainly violates no section of the Constitution, and accords with the practice of all civilized nations.

Elder: What right had Congress to enact it?

Our [Colfax] *Party:* The same it would have to interfere with a sect, which, like the South Sea Islanders, should consider human sacrifice a religious duty, or like our New England ancestors, should interpret the scriptural injunction, "Thou shalt not suffer a witch to live," as requiring them to drown old women on the charge of witchcraft.

Brigham: The cases are not parallel. As I read His word, God nowhere requires the taking of human life, except in the single case of His Son, who was given as a sacrifice and atonement for all our sins. Besides, our system is entirely voluntary.

Our Party: True; but the comparison holds good, insomuch as your system conflicts with civilization and public morality. If you had a revelation requiring you, like Abraham, to sacrifice and slay your son, would you do it?

Elder: Yes, if convinced that it was a revelation from God."[109]

Vedette editors remained unconvinced of any true change in Mormon attitudes. They predicted, before Colfax arrived, "exactly the kind of farce which would be enacted" to impress these influential visitors. No Utah resident "possessed of ordinary intelligence . . . has one particle of faith in the demonstrations of loyalty." These were merely a "stroke of policy."[110]

However, Bowles found several matters in Utah praiseworthy. There were not many poor, there existed "an abundance of the substantial necessaries of life," and "the general scale of living is generous."[111] Appreciation was due "for the wealth they have created and the order, frugality, morality and industry." The power the church system, its sweep of influence, had increased the Speaker's "respect for the personal sincerity and character of many of the leaders."[112]

In a day at Camp Douglas, the group "heard the black, sad side of Mormonism, as told to them by its victims," then "made a long excursion over to Rush Valley, where the discharged California soldiers were . . . developing silver mines."[113] Non-Mormons entertained the Colfax group with "a large and most brilliant social party," where they were "not reluctant to show . . . their ladies, as the Mormons generally seem to be, and their ladies are such, in beauty and culture, as no circle need be ashamed of." Bowles observed non-Mormons becoming numerous and influential, with "many families of culture and influence." They came to Utah as government officers, representatives of telegraph and stage lines, members of business firms having branches there, and merchants. Bowles noted, "They have organized a literary association, established a large and growing Sunday School, largely made up of children of Mormon parents, have weekly religious services led by the chaplain at Camp Douglas, conduct an able and prosperous daily paper . . . and in every way are developing an organized and effective opposition to the dominant power."[114]

The evening's entertainment with the non-Mormons was broken by the announcement of the unexpected death of Governor Doty. The acute onset of severe "internal" pain on June 6 had confined him at home until his death on June 13. Praise by the *Vedette* appeared on June 15, for "publicly discharging duty with honesty to his government, honor to himself, and satisfaction to all of his constituents." His funeral was conducted at home, and in fulfillment of an alleged deathbed request, he was buried at Camp Douglas, where Reverend McLeod officiated. Flags hung at half-mast under a two-day general cessation of business. Colfax and Governor Bross served as pallbearers, as did Judges John Titus and Thomas J. Drake, Superintend Irish, and Marshal Gibbs.[115] Doty's only surviving son, Lt. Col. Charles Doty, was not able to arrive until July 14.[116] Not until June 21 did Doty's obituary appear in the *News*, where it carried faint praise: "In his intercourse with the citizens, . . . he manifested that openness and affability of approach so characteristic of men accustomed to western life and manners."[117] Young's letter to Liverpool lacked any accolades for Doty, as might be expected from Doty's repeated criticism of Young; his veto of legislative bills; his critical analysis of four simultaneous Utah governments mailed to Seward; his sending Amos Reed to secretly report to Washington; and his having teamed—not with Brigham Young—but with Young's hated rival, General Connor, in controlling the Indians. On the other hand, Judge Drake traveled from Idaho a second time to deliver a special tribute to Doty before the Young Men's Literary Association. He spoke tenderly of their friendship, dating back to school days in Cayuga County, New York, that was rekindled at Drake's 1862 arrival in Salt Lake City.[118]

Young's letter to England also noted, "A petition has been signed by all of our civil officers that live in the city and neighborhood, and another has also been signed by the Gentile business men here, asking President Johnson to appoint Col. [O. H.] Irish[,] Superintendent of Indian Affairs[,] as Governor."[119]

Biographer Alice Elizabeth Smith's evaluation of Doty in Utah balanced praise and criticism: exercising compromise "was a new role for him," but "for the most part Doty's handling of affairs in Utah won him respect and esteem of the Gentiles." His friend Amos Reed wrote of Doty: "A man of great talent, of great experience with both white and red men, of great goodness of heart and urbanity of manners, he is held in high esteem by the people of this Territory, and exercises a remarkable influence over all the Indians who look up to him as their Alpha and Omega. . . . He has . . . brought about peace and good will with most of the Indians in the Territory."[120]

A panoply of advertisements from Atchison, Boston, Chicago, Denver, New York City, Philadelphia, Portland, St. Louis, San Francisco, and Virginia City now crowded the *Vedette*'s pages. The *Vedette* proudly touted its financial and editorial success across seven states: "Every mail is bringing us big lists of new subscribers, job work and advertisements, from the three or four surrounding territories, together with subscriptions and advertisements from the Atlantic and Pacific slopes. . . . [All] are benefited by having a big paper published at these headquarters." The *Vedette* counted its staunch subscribers at three thousand.[121]

Disguise Loyalty and Prepare for War

On the major factions in Utah, Bowles observed, "There is no more love lost between the soldiers and the Mormons than between the soldiers and the Indians. The 'boys in blue' regard both as their natural enemies, and the enemies of order and the government; and the feeling is cordially reciprocated. General Conner [*sic*] . . . has never even seen Brigham Young; and the latter . . . has no desire ever to see him."[122] This was written during Bowles's June visit, but in "Supplementary Papers," written later, he confirmed reports of Captain Price and Colonel George: "Since our visit . . . Mormons have repudiated their professions of loyalty to the government, denied any disposition to yield the issue of Polygamy, and begun to preach . . . more vigorously than ever, disrespect and defiance to the authority of the national government. . . . New means are taken to drill the militia of the Territory, and to provide them with arms, . . . and an open conflict . . . is apparently braved, even threatened."[123] Bowles cited George A. Smith's words, calling alarm: "The northern army burned and destroyed everything in the South, and abused, by force, all their women, and said they would be here some day to treat the *fair women* of Utah in like manner, and that all [men] . . . should have plenty of arms, and when they [federals] approached, God would fight the battles and the Saints would be victorious!" According to Smith, no government "could ever stand on North American soil that was opposed to Mormonism and polygamy."[124] The diary of a southern Utah Saint confirmed the message given by Mormon leaders on their tour of the Saints in the territory's south counties: "Br. G. A. Smith, Amasa Lyman, and others gave us some very good . . . doctrine pertaining to self government, domestic happenings, self preservation, etc. Exhorted us to prepare for War. Keep our powder dry, and rifles in shooting order, and be ready at a moments notice."[125] Bowles also recorded what Young had proclaimed: "He said . . . [t]hat he had his soldiers and rifles and pistols and ammunition and plenty of it, and cannon too, and would use them. He was on it! The governor of this Territory [by this time, Charles Durkee] was useless and could do nothing. He [Brigham] was the real governor of this people, and by powers of the Most High he would be governor of this Territory forever and ever, and if the Gentiles did not like this, they could leave and go to hell!" The old report was repeated by Young: "Nine-tenths of the people of the Territory were southern sympathizers."[126]

Irascible Heber C. Kimball's message was also clear: "And you, brethren, grease your old firelocks. And you, sisters, grease your old firelocks, too. . . . The abolitionists of the North stole the niggers and caused it all. The nigger was well off and happy. . . . I used to live in the South, and I know! Now they have set the nigger free; and a beautiful thing they have done for him, haven't they? . . . They threaten to come here and destroy us. Let them come. I . . . will resist them."[127]

A Divided Fourth of July Celebration

At Camp Douglas, these words introduced the July 4 holiday: "No more secession. No more slavery. The Union has triumphed and the Nation lives! The self-sacrifice of hundred thousands has sealed it; the spirit of a martyred President has sanctified it. . . . It is fitting . . . that we renew our vows of fidelity to . . . Liberty and Union, now and forever." Exceeding a traditional July Fourth commemoration, the *Vedette*'s words were a poetic paean to the Civil War's end.[128]

Nauvoo Legion colonel Robert T. Burton led a mile-long parade through the city's streets that was "a pageant of immensity in numbers and appearance," and followed by "a great, a grand, a joyous gala day in Salt Lake City and Camp Douglas." As the parade ended, it bifurcated, with non-Mormons gathering at Camp Douglas for Reverend McLeod's oration, whose poetic quality and emphasis rang reminiscent of a *Vedette* editor's words: "Where is the patriot whose heart does not beat high with hope . . . for the triumph of principles for which we have made so many, and such costly sacrifices." He paid tribute "to the fallen brave, the martyrs of liberty . . . that at Donnelson [*sic*], at Shiloh, at Chancellor[s]ville, at Petersburg, . . . slumber beneath the soil redeemed by their blood." He hoped that "under the sanction and the smile of God . . . the once torn and divided nation" would be uplifted, "investing . . . American citizenship with a . . . divine sacredness."[129]

Ten thousand Mormons flocked to the Bowery, where Kinney read the Declaration of Independence and George Q. Cannon spoke.[130] Cannon's focus was customary, using quotations from Washington, John Adams, James Madison. Nowhere in his lengthy speech was the Civil War's end cited as reason for rejoicing. Moreover, the war received no comment, and the word "Lincoln" was not heard. No better an instrument than the Constitution had ever been devised by human intellect, but according to Cannon, the liberty it granted led to abuse—an allusion to limits on Saints' religious marriage practices. Cannon explained that another abuse of constitutional rights was evident in President Martin Van Buren's response to Mormons suffering from mob violence: "Gentlemen, your cause is just, but we can do nothing for you." Concluding, Cannon affirmed the Saints' view of government and religion entwined: "We doubly rejoice, for not only do we see in it the birth-day of civil and religious freedom, but . . . redemption for all mankind, till a regenerated world . . . should bask in the [Mormonism's] eternal sunshine of salvation, exaltation and glory."[131]

Ohio congressman James M. Ashley was on the podium despite a stressful arrival from Fort Bridger at half past one o'clock that morning. His brief address was complimentary to the Mormons with sympathy for past mistreatment: "Driven forth from Illinois and Missouri you sought a shelter and home in a foreign land. After you had established the foundation of what now bids fair to be a mighty power, you became . . . attached again to the United States . . . , keeping as best you may the laws under which you live." Ashley also expressed a desire to become acquainted with the "leading and distinguished citizens" of Utah, in order to understand their wants.[132]

In the differing celebrations of those at Camp Douglas and those gathered in the Bowery is proof that two societies occupied the same space but lived in alien, parallel worlds.

Ashley's Visit and Spies at the *Vedette*

James Ashley was an influential man in Washington. A lifelong opponent of slavery, a friend of the temperance movement, a radical Republican from northwestern Ohio, he led Lincoln's January 1865 fight in the House of Representatives for approval of the Thirteenth Constitutional Amendment, outlawing slavery in all states. To reach the requirement of approval by two-thirds *of those present*, Ashley needed for some representatives to be absent and for fifteen Democrats to vote with the Republicans. It has been widely admitted that the amendment's passage was largely due to his extraordinary efforts.

It was in Ashley's desk that Utah Territory's requests for statehood were ignored for six years. During that period, Ashley had supported enabling acts for statehood for three other territories—Nevada, Colorado, and Nebraska.[133]

On July 6, Ashley and Bvt. Col. John B. Frothingham paid a visit to the *Vedette* offices and were interested and "pleased with the pioneer

Ohio's James M. Ashley figured prominently in Lincoln's push for the Thirteenth Amendment. He held up Utah's (or Deseret's) appeals for enabling acts leading to statehood because of LDS polygamy and theocracy, with its repudiation of federal law. Brady-Handy Photograph Collection, Library of Congress, LC-BH824–5303[P+P].

Newspaper of Utah." Ashley spoke humorously of his own printing experience, "having served in the several grades of the art, from 'devil' to 'typo.'" Later, the two visitors witnessed the dress parade at the camp.[134] A visit to Rush Valley with Capt. D. B. Stover occupied Ashley on Friday, July 7. Ashley was "highly pleased with that settlement and its rich silver mines close by."[135] He spoke on July 11 to a large group of members and guests of the Young Men's Literary Association. Sharing the commitment to temperance with the many Good Templars and Dashaways members in this audience, he noted "the advantages of lyceum improvements, literature, humanity, and the principles of pure patriotism and social progress, complimenting the Association on its efforts, spirit and success." Moving to sensitive issues, he spoke, "in terms emphatic, plain and unmistakable, to . . . the future policy to be pursued towards those that heretofore held themselves in defiance of its laws and interests." Demonstrating "comprehensive knowledge" of Utah, Ashley "boldly stated" that citizens must show "*real* loyalty to the laws" before the territory's admission as a Union State could be achieved. Emphatically he continued: "This people *must* and *shall respect, obey and recognize* the Government and its official representative . . . at the peril of their highest interest—though that be life and property. That fanaticism or folly, religion or rascality, in the leaders of this ecclesiastically enslaved people, would be hereafter no excuse for injustice . . . to any and all . . . who shall settle in this Territory." Justice Titus expressed pleasure that Ashley's Committee on Territories was "sound" on the true interests of Utah and "hoped the time was coming . . . when this one-man power, father of crime, massacre, assassination, robbery and reproach, would be showed up in its true history."[136]

Young repeatedly asserted that he ignored the *Vedette's* articles, but a letter from David Calder to Young contained information from the paper's pending issue, indicating the presence of spies in the *Vedette's* offices and proving that Young's concern with the newspaper's messages was significant. The *Vedette's* article reporting on the speeches of Ashley and Titus were written late on July 11 and published on July 12, yet Calder wrote on July 11, "I am informed that he [Ashley] said that the [Mormon] people of this territory had been charged with having hard feelings and saying hard things of the government, but great allowance should be made . . . [because] they were driven from their homes by a mob . . . and the government . . . did not address the wrongs inflicted upon them." Calder's letter continues: "Judge Titus was called upon, . . . and its [Titus's] foul mouth and forked tongue gave utterance [?] to 'Mountain Meadows' [illegible]!—he made the dose so strong that it is doubtful that it can remain on the stomach. *The 'Vedette' has a different version of the affair—which you will see.*"[137]

Further evidence of infiltration and spying comes also from the history recounted by James Campbell Livingston, Sr., an 1853 Scottish emigrant. "Young called a secret meeting" whose purpose "was to pick out a man to be a spy against the government of the United States," Livingston wrote. A man was wanted "who could get into Fort Douglas and get the secrets of the Army and give Pres. Young word of everything." Young told his candidates, "'If you are caught, it will mean the firing squad.'" Placing his hand on Livingston's shoulder, Young said, "'This is the man the Lord wants.'" Following his assignment, Livingston arranged for a keg of whiskey to fall from his wagon, to be found by a group of soldiers. When one of the troops became "'fuzzy,'" Livingston took his clothes and his name and number and "went into Fort Douglas and replaced the man." The "fuzzy" trooper was given money and wisely disappeared. Each night, Livingston got word to Young, but "was always back in place to answer roll call." Soldiers at times would accompany Livingston to the city. Because the soldiers were seen near the Livingstons' Twentieth Ward house, his wife was threatened with excommunication, but the "'highest officers of the church told [the accusers] to 'lay off.'"[138]

Before departing Salt Lake City on July 14, Ashley met with Young and others of the LDS Church. Ashley sought to know whether Mormons "were likely to yield obedience to the laws of the United States without further legislation." Young asked Ashley whether he should obey God or man, claiming that Mormons were obeying a revelation from heaven in their practice of polygamy. Ashley insisted that the sovereignty of one's country is supreme in temporal affairs and that the laws of the United States must be obeyed.[139] His firsthand experience with Mormons' unyielding defense of polygamy was influential in Ashley's 1869 bill to balkanize Utah Territory, reducing its size and influence by ceding land to adjacent states and territories. Dividing its population among other civil entities was seen as "the best disposition of the Mormon question."[140]

The Puzzling James Duane Doty

Beginning with his reasons for coming to the territory, the career of James Duane Doty in Utah presents a series of puzzles. Alice Elizabeth Smith opens this initial issue, admitting uncertainty about what had induced him to leave his family, a pleasant home, and a magnificent library acquired over a lifetime. Missed were the luxuries of his "Grand Loggery" home on the Fox River near Lake Winnebago, filled with Indian artifacts and memorabilia dating back to his first wilderness expedition with military officer and politician Lewis Cass. Lost was time with grandchildren and for submitting to the Smithsonian his research, accumulated in years of studying the area's Indian languages, for he took great interest in the Menominees, Winnebagos, Sioux, and Chippewas. To what end did he relinquish "the prospects of a comfortable old age"?[141]

Born in Hudson Valley and raised in upper New York State, Doty was twenty when he became the secretary of the expedition led by Governor Lewis Cass, who sought firsthand information about Michigan Territory, where he was to serve. For nine years Doty was a federal judge, riding the rural court circuits of the former Northwest Territory, until his slander of President Andrew Jackson's deceased wife brought disfavor.

Alice Smith emphasizes that opinions about Doty were never middling. Lauded for his humane verdicts on Indian rights, he made some rulings that brought only critical and "angry protests." He served in the Michigan legislature in 1834–35 and as a representative to Congress for four years. He was implicated in—but not charged with—the 1835 failures of the Bank of Wisconsin and the bank at Mineral Point.[142] Prolonged investigations in the legislature concerning bank funds and titles issued in his "Madison-for-the-state-capital" projects brought him to the brink of financial ruin, ending "for all time" his "vision of wealth and power." With President Harrison's election in

James Duane Doty was the Utah superintendent of Indian
Affairs and then served as the appointed territorial governor.
His record in the same offices in Wisconsin and his failed
business schemes earned him an evaluation as a controversial maverick. His conflicts in Utah with LDS leadership were
subdued, less obvious than those of other federal appointees.
Used by permission of the Utah State Historical Society.

1840 his fortunes brightened. Appointed as Wisconsin's governor
and superintendent of Indian Affairs, he served until 1844. However,
hate and vilifications resurfaced, intensified. In land speculation and
boom he was "cool, crafty, calculating," and "a consummate political
manipulator . . . of unusual charm." A century later, Wisconsin residents would continue to "regale visitors with tales of the founding of
their capital city in graft and corruption."[143] Doty, who "seemed always

to be regarded as Wisconsin's Suspect Number One in shady deals," was implicated and investigated in the 1856–58 Wisconsin railroad scandal, "'the blackest episode in the history of the state.'" Biographer Smith used the derogatory terms "Mephistopheles" and Wisconsin's "evil genius" in her descriptions. Through his pre-Utah life he was a promoter, a speculator in canals, roads, and railroads, not "the affable, mild-mannered, non-combative gentleman" that many in Utah found him. He had a Janus face: "an aggressive, self-willed, opinionated person, full of intrigue, dishonesty and corruption."[144]

At Lincoln's 1860 election, Doty was sixty-one, a recent Republican convert whose financial escapades left him no better off "in wealth and power" than he "had been ten years before."[145] Finances were seemingly Doty's motivation in August 1861 to seek an appointment from the new administration, but he returned from Washington empty-handed. In September he "promptly accepted" the position as Utah's superintendent of Indian Affairs, despite the post's troubled public record and years of negative national press focused on Mormons. Whatever his Utah aspirations, Doty "gave no outward indication of them."[146]

Financial stress, not relief, followed his arrival in Utah, for territorial monies for Indian subsidies for 1861 were shared with Colorado and Nevada, and he received no salary for the first six months of 1862, and no funds for goods or food for Indians.[147] Money for 1862 was "cut to the bone" at $10,500, and one-third of this went to pay interpreters; $20,000 due in December was not sent. Henry Martin, still in Utah as a "Special Agent to the Indians," unsuccessfully "bombarded Washington with demands of expense money and annuity goods" so that Doty and agent Luther Mann could continue to work on treaties.[148] When Doty was appointed governor, his salary was $2,500 per year, plus $1,500 for official expenses. In 1864 the Dotys purchased a home near Salt Lake's City Hall.[149]

Smith cites examples of Doty's early judicial decisions as giving "convincing evidence that civil law and justice were to predominate" in his decisions and that his judicial career was characterized by accuracy, caution, and fairness—a characterization that makes all the more puzzling one of his last Utah gubernatorial acts.[150] Amid the tumult of

Lincoln's second inaugural, the visit of Colfax and friends, and preparations for a highly important meeting with Utah's Indian groups, Doty made time to act on an appeal from southern Utah Mormons. He granted "a full and complete Pardon" to one George Wood, a Mormon of Parowan, Utah, sentenced to life at hard labor in the territorial prison as a confessed, convicted murderer. Controversy marks the crime's history, as well as Doty's enigmatic ruling.

Established fact is that on July 27, 1862, Wood, an early Mormon colonizer to southern Utah's Iron Mission, went to the house of forty-four-year-old Olive Olivia Curtis Coombs Higbee in Cedar City, where he fired several revolver shots into her and into her thirteen-year-old daughter. When his gun fouled, he bashed in the mother's head with the pistol butt. He rushed outside, found the wounded child, and also pistol-bludgeoned her head. Thinking he had killed both victims, he reported his acts to local Mormon leaders. The mother died; however, her daughter, Emily, survived—albeit with lifelong, severe neurologic disability. At the trial in the probate court at Parowan, Judge Silas S. Smith heard Wood plead guilty and ask for the court's mercy. Finding "the facts being fully established," Judge Smith sentenced Wood to life imprisonment at hard labor.[151] Two weeks later, however, Wood was placed in protective custody to shield him from violence, and the arrival of Hosea Stout, Mormon attorney and former U.S. attorney for Utah, was pending. Southern Utah's most prominent Mormon, George A. Smith, became involved, and certain influential people of Iron County now inexplicably considered the sentence "rather punitive" and "rather like a farce."[152]

Olive Curtis Coombs, along with her husband, Abraham, and her stepdaughter, Katherine, were among the 258 Mormons on the ship *Brooklyn* when it sailed into San Francisco harbor at the end of the Mexican War in 1846.[153] In California, they farmed, had three children, and were called to Utah because of the pending Utah War. Beyond this, fact becomes difficult to identify in contradictory histories of their journey, their life in southern Utah, and the reasons for Olive's murder. Historian Melanie Sturgeon details differing accounts, one contending that Olive was an abuser of alcohol, was divorced, and married Ezra Higbee and that both she and her daughter Emily were falsely accused of prostitution. Emily, thirteen years old, may have been seduced by Wood's twenty-year-old son, Joseph, but George Wood claimed that Emily was the initiator. Sturgeon explains the position held by Olive Coombs's descendants, that she was a virtuous, talented, and educated widow, whom fate—and Mormons—treated badly, and was murdered for the contents of a ledger because it contained details of the Mountain Meadows massacre, or because it contained facts regarding the stolen property of her allegedly dead husband.[154] Wood's killing of Olive Coombs, and the reaction of LDS governance to the murder, are important within the fabric of Utah history but are here relevant to the question of why Doty gave clemency.

At sentencing, Judge Smith was stern: "May the example thus made be a warning to prevent others from the unlawful shedding of blood."[155] Far from a deterrent, Wood's case proved that punishment for murder in Utah Territory could be a charade. Transferred to Warden Albert P. Rockwood's prison in Salt Lake City, Wood found that his ties to influential Mormon leaders resulted in very little time spent within prison walls. From January 1, 1863, Wood was "hired out" to work at the Salt Lake City ironworks owned by Daniel H. Wells until December 24, 1864. On that date the court clerk wrote to Doty, requesting clemency for Wood.[156] Conflicting with the alleged dates of Wood's term of service with Daniel Wells is the May 8, 1863, action by Mormon attorney John Varah Long, who wished "to hire the services of George Wood" for twelve months at ten dollars a month. This was approved by the three penitentiary directors, all Mormons. On February 27, 1864, Warden Rockwood penned a letter to Isaac Haight, stating that Wood "has absconded" and was thought to be in Iron County. Rockwood wrote to Brother (Henry) Lunt, authorizing him to assist in the capture and return of Wood. Ignored, Rockwood wrote a third letter, this to Iron County sheriff D. F. Clark: "Whereas George Wood [is] a convict of the penitentiary from your county . . . [and] *whereas he has taken innumerable liberties beyond the limits[,] therefore I must lock him up.* You are authorized and required to return him." Clark ignored Rockwood's order but wrote that Wood would soon return to Salt Lake City.[157]

Apparently Wood did return to the penitentiary, for on February 24, 1865, a writ of habeas corpus was sought by attorneys Long and

Lynch, "that cause may be shown . . . why said George Wood should not be returned to the full enjoyment of his liberty." The writ was allowed consideration in Judge Elias Smith's probate court in Salt Lake City.[158] In his journal for March 1, 1865, Elias Smith notes he ruled the "prisoner was legally held."[159]

A clemency petition was sent on March 6, 1865, by Warden Rockwood, who untruthfully certified that Wood had been industrious, obedient, and attentive and had not attempted to evade his punishment.[160] On March 8 a petition was signed by 209 Mormon men. Wood had "no professional advisor," swore the eighteen signers, who were also the very grand jurors who had voted for his indictment, with Silas S. Smith as the presiding judge, and Edward Dalton the prosecuting attorney.[161] Petitioners were men from the upper levels of the LDS Church, beginning with Wood's longtime, influential friend George A. Smith. Wilford Woodruff, William H. Hooper, Franklin D. Richards, Feramorz Little, Thomas S. Eldredge, A. Milton Musser, Joseph L. Heywood, and even Orrin Porter Rockwell signed. They justified Olive's murder: she "kept a house of ill fame in the town of Beaver, and . . . established a similar place to decoy away youth, in the town of Cedar." Her daughter was "engaged in the same disreputable business."[162] The petition dwelled on Wood's family responsibilities and alleged good standing. On March 8—the same date the appeal was signed—Doty wrote: "And whereas it is made satisfactory . . . by petition and representation of numerous citizen of said Territory, that the said George Wood now is a fit subject for the Executive clemency. Now therefore . . . having carefully considered the case, and the representations made in behalf of the said Wood, I . . . hereby grant unto the said George Wood, a full and complete Pardon of said crime."[163]

Doty did not give further explanation. There is no evidence of questioning the jurisdiction of two separate probate courts in a capital criminal case. Mormons might have argued the defense of the "mountain common law," which allowed immediate killing of the perpetrator on disclosure of a sexual crime, but they did not. Non-Mormon judges would not accept an unproven allegation of an immoral sexual act as justification for murder. Doty knew the law required a judge "never to interfere with the finding of a Jury or the judgment of the law, except

in cases of manifest injustice, or where circumstances or proofs alter-
ing the phase of the affair were discovered after the sentence was
imposed."[164] Doty held no trust in the word of Utah's "fourth government," which included many of the 209 men of the State of Deseret
who signed the petition. In giving total forgiveness, Doty overlooked
that Wood offered no remorse and that Rockwood's own documented
record of "numerous improprieties" in allowing long, continuing
absences from prison could not be construed as fulfilling Wood's debt
to society. Wood was neither elderly nor ill. Pardon was out of keeping
with the punishment in other blatant murders of the time, notably the
prompt execution of Jason Luce. Clemency in this case was not consistent with the judicial wisdom of either Reed or Doty.

The timing and circumstances of Doty's death constitute another
puzzle. For years Doty had experienced brief bouts of "rheumatism"
but in Utah he pursued a vigorous, demanding life, traveling thousands of miles about the territory on horseback or wagon without significant health issues, according to his biographer and to both the
Vedette and the *Deseret News*. Thus, the sudden onset of "violent internal pain" on June 6, with death in the late evening hours of June 13,
is curious.[165] Doty may have anticipated his own death, for he gave
his official papers to Superintendent O. H. Irish, because Secretary of
State Amos Reed, Doty's trusted friend, was absent, busy with mining
colleagues in New York City and Washington.[166]

An alternate explanation is suggested for Doty's transformation
from a lifelong contrarian politician who would "not abandon his maverick qualities" and was an "evil genius" in stirring controversy, into a
mild, moderate, adaptive administrator: Doty came to Utah hoping
for financial gain and a senatorial appointment from the state that
would emerge from the territory. Kinney, a non-Mormon, had secured
from Young the appointment as Utah's representative to Congress.
When it became clear that neither Utah—nor Deseret—would be
granted statehood, and that any hope for election to the U.S. Senate
would never come to him in the convoluted systems that existed in
Utah, Doty appears to have settled on bettering himself financially for
retirement. He complained to Seward in the spring of 1864 of inadequate funds and the doubling of the cost of living with the influx of

mining venturers. Historian David Mollenhoff suggests that Lincoln had planned or promised Doty a prestigious appointment in southern California, but Lincoln's untimely death ended such hopes.[167] With the appeals by Mormons to release George Wood, money may have come to "grease the wheel" of a Doty pardon. That Doty was provided a pretentious "Judge Shaver funeral," one far out of proportion with his regard by Mormon leaders, adds to the circumstantial evidence.[168] Businesses were closed, the city was draped in black. Rev. Norman McLeod conducted services at the Doty residence, and an entourage of thirty to forty carriages followed the body to the burial site at the Camp Douglas cemetery.[169]

Even with Bowles, Colfax, and several eastern visitors present in the audience, no mention of Doty was included in Young's lengthy address in the Bowery on June 18. The *News* had little praise for the man and nothing of his accomplishments in Utah: "He made many friends . . . and his sudden death called forth many and sincere expressions . . . of mourning and regret."[170] Doty never returned to the secret plan he had for Lincoln to permanently solve the government's conflict on the Mormon question. The theft of his papers in 1864 from his Washington hotel room, apparently revealing his intentions, ended whatever he planned to propose.

Sarah Collins Doty made no public statement regarding her husband's unexpected death or his alleged deathbed request for burial in Utah rather than at his beloved island in Wisconsin. She soon returned to Oshkosh, to live with her widowed daughter, Mary, and her granddaughter, Nellie. Widow Doty sold Grand Loggery in 1868 for $4,500, an amount that does not explain her personal worth of $20,000, an $18,000 increase over that reported before going to Utah.[171] She died in Oshkosh in 1871.

Who Benefits from Doty's Death?

Whether Doty's death was by natural or unnatural cause, it served Mormon interests in several ways. First, Doty could never speak of a bribe, if one had "lubricated" Wood's pardon. Next, he was not present, as the senior federal official, to participate in or object to the provisions of the June 1865 Spanish Fork Indian treaty. He was absent from what historian Andrew Love Neff insistently describes as "the greatest peace pow-pow in the annals of Utah history."[172]

Orsemus H. Irish, a New York native, was made Indian agent at the Omaha, Nebraska Reservation in 1861 and was appointed Utah's superintendent of Indian Affairs on February 2, 1864, to replace Doty.[173] Congress provided for extinguishing Indian land titles by treaty on February 23, and a bill followed in May requiring that all Indian lands in Utah, except those of the Uintah Valley reservation, be surveyed, divided into tracts not to exceed eighty acres, and sold to the highest public bidder.[174] All of the Utah's tribes were to be settled in the Uintah Valley, the reservation Lincoln set aside in October 1861 at the request of Superintendents Benjamin Davis and Henry Martin.[175] Irish did not arrive in Salt Lake City until August 25, 1864, and on September 26 he wrote Commissioner Dole, recommending that treaties be made with the "Utahs, Par Vants, and Pie-Edes, as soon as they can be congregated in the spring."[176] In early 1865, Irish published warnings that "'all white settlers must forthwith remove from the Uintah Reservation" and that by spring "all persons found therein unlawfully," without a license to trade or permission of proper Indian authorities, would be removed.[177] In February 1865, Congress approved "A Bill to Extinguish the Indian Title to Lands in the Territory of Utah Suitable for Agriculture and Mineral Purposes."[178] Dole instructed Irish on March 28 to proceed with treaty making. Superintendent Irish invited Brigham Young—who held no territorial or Indian Affairs position—to accompany him, because, as Irish justified to Dole, he had been advised to make use of Young's influence.[179] When it became known that Young was to be involved in the Indian negotiations, all non-Mormon territorial officials and military leaders at Camp Douglas refused to be associated with the palavering.

Through April and May 1865, thirteen Mormons were the first whites killed in what became Utah's Black Hawk War. On April 18, Doty, Irish, and the commander at Camp Douglas, Lt. Col. William M. Johns, received requests from Mormons in Sanpete County for U.S. troops to answer these brutal attacks. Connor denied permission, since it did not threaten Overland travel. Doty's plea to Washington to allow him to activate the local militia was reportedly "filed without action."[180] On May 29, Orson Hyde wrote Young, "This war is on a scale that cannot well be kept within ourselves tho I shall take no measures to disclose it outside the priesthood of God."[181]

Under the urgency of renewed Indian violence, Irish and Young drew up plans for Spanish Fork and left Salt Lake City together on June 5, 1865. Irish claimed that Doty had approved a draft of the treaty, but because he had suddenly taken ill, was not traveling with them. This is another puzzling element, since Doty did not fall ill until June 6. Young, Irish, and others were at the Spanish Fork Indian Farm on June 6, 7, and 8 with "at least five of the church's twelve apostles" and two Nauvoo Legion colonels, Warren Snow and Robert T. Burton. According to historian John A. Peterson, deploying the military officers was a provocative extralegal act.[182] Fifteen chiefs, without Black Hawk, agreed to relinquish all claims, excepting the Uintah Reservation, to which they pledged themselves to move "'within one year after ratification of the treaty.'" Granted in return were "the privileges of fishing, gathering roots and berries on the unappropriated public domain." The treaty provisions called for funding of twenty-five thousand dollars, but payments were to be made "in agricultural implements, stock and other useful articles rather than money." It was a hard sell for Irish, when it surfaced that several tribes in addition to Utes would be settled on the Uintah site. Chief Sanpitch was humiliated and refused to come out of his tepee, saying, "I do not want to give up my title to the land I occupy." Irish was the only federal authority to sign the petition. Young's signature misrepresented to observing Indians that he held legal authority, when he was officially no more than a witness to their "X" marks.[183] The causes of the Black Hawk War were multiple and complex, but several historians of Utah's tribes hold that the deprivations and demands of the June 1865 Spanish Fork Treaty to be the major instigator of the war.[184]

Irish distributed a large quantity of blankets, leggings, and clothing, which was received by many "with childlike eagerness."[185] In Payson, Utah, on the morning of June 8, Young admonished the Indians "to remember the good advice given them." He said Colonel Irish had done all he possibly could for them, that he was their friend. Young blessed them, told them to recall his advice and counsel to them in the past, assured them he was still their friend, and "advised them to sign the treaty and accept its provisions for their benefit.[186] Doty's death, combined with Irish's subservience to Brigham Young, resulted in the return of de facto control of Indian matters to Young, where it remained throughout the Black Hawk War and until his death in 1877.[187]

Doty's status with Brigham Young had an inauspicious beginning when Doty wrote to Dole in 1862 that Young's report on Indian action was "without foundation in truth" and that delegation of authority to Young rather than to U.S. officers only increased Young's power and weakened that of the United States."[188] Death ended not only Doty's behind-the-scenes criticism but also the liaisons Doty had built with Gen. P. Edward Connor—Brigham Young's most hated rival for power—when the two labored cooperatively, without Young, to reach treaties with Utah's northern tribes.

Finally, Doty's death opened the way for Young to propose a new governor for the territory, one of his choice. Highly unusual and extraordinarily warm was Young's invitation to "have the pleasure" of both Colonel and Mrs. Irish in accompanying his party of priesthood dignitaries on a trip to visit Cache Valley and the northern settlements.[189] Young circulated the idea that "civil officers of the city" and "Gentile businessmen" had favored President Johnson with a request to appoint O. H. Irish as Utah's governor. It soon became clear that non-Mormons did not approve of Young's new ally. Connor asked for "federal officials who can resist either the threats or flatteries of Brigham Young."[190] "We are opposed to the appointment of the gentleman named for several reasons," was the blunt, non-Mormon position on Irish. For the *Vedette* the most serious reason was that Irish openly socialized with Mormon leaders who were "at variance with the laws of the land." Irish sought non-Mormon's support "while coquetting in our very faces with the shameless advocates of a system wholly subversive of everything we hold sacred in morality."[191] In 1866, as the Black Hawk War seared hot in Sanpete, Sevier, and Piute counties, Irish returned to Nebraska as a revenue collector, subsequently active in business, politics, law, and the Bureau of Engraving.

On July 18 another officer from Babylon, Wisconsin's Charles Durkee, was appointed by President Andrew Johnson to Utah's governorship. Durkee had served in the House alongside his friend James Doty and later served in the Senate. He was "a plain, dignified, practical man, . . . of wide integrity and spotless purity of character," the *Vedette* allowed.[192]

The *Vedette's* Case for Blacks Voting

Who in the vanquished rebel states would be given voting privileges? According to the *Vedette*, the success of "'reconstruction,' as securing the benefits of national triumph and of future peace, depends in great measure on the disposition made of the delicate question." In the *Vedette's* analysis, there were three classes of southern men: "the masters and the slaves forming the extremes, united by an intermediate class, the 'poor whites.'" Slaves were the only exception to the "prevailing disloyalty of the South," since "from them has come all the local assistance our armies have received in their marches and campaigns." The position held at Camp Douglas was that slave masters and "intermediate" whites, by their rebellion and secession, had forfeited their voting rights, while the slaves' willingness to take up arms earned them privileges lost by their masters.[193]

While ownership of property was used as voter qualification in much of the South, education and intelligence were better measures, claimed the *Vedette*. "True the negro is no less a negro because he is free"—that is, although he is free, he is yet uneducated—"but it is equally true, that none of God's children are so humble [lacking intelligence] as not to have a just claim to protection of life and those inalienable rights co-existent therewith," including "the simple yet inestimable privilege of depositing a ballot." Progressive and forward-thinking for its time, the *Vedette* admitted paternalism: "We have the negro and cannot get rid of him—he seems destined as a heritage of the Republic. We have enslaved him and the consequences are still fresh. . . . Let us not, by casting them off, create . . . a race of paupers, but rather, by encouragement, strive to make them men, with the feelings and aspirations of men." The *Vedette* summed, "It is not our creed, that traitors have any right . . . superior to those possessed by men, who found their freedom in fighting to subdue their rebel masters."[194]

Connor Returns

Colorado's civil authorities and a host of military dignitaries met on October 14 in Denver to honor General Connor, back from his Powder River Indian campaign. The report of the *Denver News* described the celebration as "the *ne plus ultra* of feasts," with "viands and choice wines," and a distinguished program of toasts and honoring speeches by Colorado governor William Gilpin, Maj. Gen. Emory Upton, Gen. Blair M. Hughes, and other military officers who served with Connor. The evening's fitting tribute: "Wheresoever General Connor's lot in life may be cast, he will carry with him the best wishes and highest esteem of every true citizen of this Territory."[195] The next day, Ovando James Hollister, editor of the *Black Hawk (Colo.) Mining Journal*, gave a lengthy review of Connor's frustrated attempts to bring the Indians under control: "The Indians escaped subjugation through circumstances over which Connor had no control. He did all that one could do, more than . . . five men of a million would have done. . . . I am sorry he was not better supported during the season. He has an extraordinary prestige with the Indians, and is, without doubt, . . . the best man in the West to deal with them, whether with the sword or pen."[196]

A similar banquet and ovation followed at Camp Douglas on October 26, attended by Charles H. Hempstead; Idaho's delegate-elect to Congress, J. McDonald; E. D. Holbrook and J. J. Tracy of the Overland Mail Company; and a number of the city's non-Mormons. Many toasts were proffered, even one by the Utah Bar Association, with a response by Mormon stalwart William Ivins Appleby.[197] The line of carriages escorting Connor back to camp received no acknowledgment from Young as they passed by his house. After eight months' absence, Connor took command of the District of Utah from Lt. Col. W. Willard Smith on October 29.[198]

The Season's Emigration

No church teams were sent to bring in Saints on the Perpetual Emi-grating Fund system in 1865.[199] However, at least nine freight teams arrived in Salt Lake City in the autumn months, carrying an estimated 645 paying passengers and at least 130 nonpaying travelers.[200] Those at Camp Douglas estimated a larger number: "Over one thousand souls . . . have left their homes and fatherland from the British Mission, this year, for 'Zion.'" Many of them, the *Vedette* noted with evident con-cern, would "be prevailed upon to enter into the accursed system of polygamy [and] take the damning oaths of the endowment house."[201]

The specter of the 1856 season's snow disasters lingered in mem-ory, for substantial concern was expressed in private Mormon corre-spondence for the safe arrival of the wagons before winter weather ensnared them. Young wrote to his son on December 15, "The last of the teams belonging to this season's emigration arrived in the City on the 30th [of last month]." Snow began falling the next day, but "the Saints here have breathed freely since the safety of the emigrat-ing Saints has been assured."[202] At the October conference, plans were begun to send five hundred teams in 1866, "to help up the poor."[203]

Paper and Ink Matters

The *Vedette* notified subscribers that September and October delays in receipt of paper from eastern manufacturers necessitated restricting delivery to only Utah readers.[204] The *Vedette* did not directly accuse the *Deseret News* or the *Salt Lake Daily Telegraph* of robbing its paper supply, but made the case on circumstantial evidence. A *Vedette*-bound wagon was found upended at Bitter Creek. Four mules, the teamster, two dis-charged soldiers guarding the wagon, and over eight hundred dollars' worth of newsprint and ink were missing. It was "more than possible" that a telegraph about the team had reached "others." A "Mormon ox freight train" was noticed passing the Point of Rocks station about the same time as did the *Vedette*'s wagon. The paper and the ink had not been destroyed or cached. Not an Indian prize, the heavy paper and ink could not have been taken away by placing it on the backs of four mules. A reward of two hundred dollars was offered, but the editor was not optimistic, explaining with an editorial wink that in Utah "all things are the Lord's, [and] that as the saints are the rightful inheritors of the Lord's property, it is no harm for them to take it, and use it in his service."[205]

Near this time the *Vedette* offices and printing operation moved from Camp Douglas to the storage building of a former teamster's office, with an alley entry behind the Salt Lake House hotel. The newspaper claimed that the expense of increasing its sheet size, from fourteen inches to twenty-two and a half inches, required an increase in subscription rates.[206] It was soon evident that the downtown location was irritating Mormon dignitaries, for the non-Mormon landlord was threatened with lawsuits seeking damages—charges that would be heard by all-Mormon juries—for having rented to the newspaper.[207] The *Vedette* did not soften its editorial position because of being situated in "the business heart" of the city. In his history of Fort Douglas and the *Vedette*, Charles Hibbard considered the change in location as marking a shift from representing officers and men at Camp Douglas to representing the city's general non-Mormon population.[208]

Within a month, Frederick Livingston made a surprise announcement: "To-morrow dissolves my connection and association with the *Daily Union Vedette* . . . [for I am] taking leave of my employers." He would remain in the "immediate vicinity," but no more information was offered.[209] His duties or activities in the city thereafter are uncertain, for military records show he was not mustered out until July 27, 1866, at Camp Douglas. Without formal announcement of the change in the *Vedette*, Capt. George F. Price, Second California Cavalry and district inspector, moved into the editor's role.

Preparing for the Battle of Armageddon?

The *Vedette* was distressed on learning of the sale of arms by individuals mustered out of service. When the government gave its "honorably discharged soldiers the priviledge [*sic*] of *retaining* his arms and accoutrements" at a price less than half their original value, it was noble and generous. However, the *Vedette* stated, "it is with feelings of shame that we are compelled to chronicle the fact that a large number of our recently discharged soldiers have, for mere gain, disposed of their arms," not only to Mormons, "whose loyalty is questionable," but also to "the enemies of our country, our constitution and our laws," namely, Confederates or sympathizers.[210]

In early November the interest of Camp Douglas men and officers was caught by the encampment of "the 'Mormon Army' . . . [of] militia men . . . on the 'other side of Jordan,'" three miles outside the city. "Ostensibly it is a militia outfit, but Brigham's policy and pugnacity is at the head of it," ventured the *Vedette*.[211] The following day, the number in the review was estimated at "between a thousand and fifteen hundred," with the event "witnessed by a very large number of spectators from the city and from Camp Douglas." Non-Mormons and "our military officers were received and treated with the utmost respect."[212] Young wrote to his son that "considerable interest has been felt of late, both on the part of the officers and men, throughout the Territory in military matters, and a very commendable diligence has been shown in attending drill and in *purchasing arms* and uniforms."[213]

In late November the *Vedette* reprinted from the *San Francisco Chronicle:* "Young has mustered and equipped a considerable Mormon army, and is subjecting it to an industrious drill in sight of General Connor's troops. The Mormon newspaper says our [U.S.] troops did not like Indian fighting . . . , and hints that they had better try the polygamists. . . . It would be a most lively idea to take the paper at its word, and teach that foreign camp to be a little more respectful."[214] Cleveland's *Daily Leader* made an aggressive call for military reaction: "The Republican party began its political history by denouncing slavery and polygamy [and is] now ready to give a quietus to polygamy, even if it does not adopt the same suicidal policy which . . . killed its twin sister." The *Leader* continued: "In Utah there exists a one-man power superior to and in direct contravention of the authority of our national government. . . . The sooner this power is crushed, and the national authority re-established, even though it be done by force of arms, the better."[215]

A mystery troubled Camp Douglas editors in the fall months. The "Great Arch-Apostle" was travelling about, but the content of his discourses is not published in the *Deseret News*. The *Vedette* editors had "read that 'Brigham spoke half an hour' or 'Brigham addressed the congregation nearly an hour.' . . . We read of his speaking some seven times, and though the purport of all other's discourses is given, nothing whatsoever is said of the nature of his. Why is it?" The answer, according to the *Vedette:* "In some entirely Mormon settlements, certain warlike preparations are openly progressing, but in others, where Gentiles, Josephites, and Mormons of doubtful loyalty to Brigham are interspersed with 'the faithful,' no signs . . . are seen." Keeping their preparations for war hidden explained the silence, claimed the *Vedette*.[216]

The *New York Sunday Times*, on November 10, also assigned serious intent to Mormon preparations: "It looks as if we were about to have another war with the Mormons. Brigham Young defies the United States government, and is arming his people for the contest."[217] Young and Heber C. Kimball, with their military staff, had returned from a four-week tour, and from their "speeches, and military drills and reviews," the message was that "war, open or concealed, their voices alike do not dissuade."[218] Young and his priesthood hierarchy were "treasonably disposed . . . and preparing for resistance." According to the *Times*, "The burden of the Mormon sermons to the people is to arm, and 'arming they are.' . . . There is actually an individual [David James Ross] designated as 'Drill-Master-General,' who has been for a long time actively engaged in the business of arming and drilling the forces of the Church of Latter Day [*sic*] Saints for the great battle of Armageddon." The *Times*, sympathetic to the Mormons' treatment in Missouri and Illinois, touched softly, urging moderation, preferring that the "power of the Prophet will be nullified" through "natural agencies," without open warfare.[219]

Rather than ranting against the Mormon militia units review, the *Vedette*'s view was reasoned and balanced, albeit strongly phrased: "[Territorial law] relating to the militia makes it incumbent on all white male residents to enrole [*sic*] themselves and conform to the orders of the proper authorities respecting military drill." Because the territory was situated in Indian country, where any day the settlements could be jeopardized, "it is the duty as it is the right of the settlers to arm and drill themselves . . . to repel the invasions of the uncouth savage."[220]

Yet, little sympathy came for the *Salt Lake Daily Telegraph*'s recent complaint—repeatedly voiced by Young—that Utah had not been furnished with its quota of arms. The *Vedette* framed its questions: "In what particulars have 'this people' [the Mormons] shown their loyalty to the Government from which they claim munitions of war? . . . How did Utah show her loyalty when she arrayed her citizens against the forces of the parent Government in 1857 and 1858[?] What use did she make of her arms in 1857 at the Mountain Meadows? How did she employ them . . . in 1862 [against the Morrisites?] . . . How many of her loyalists stepped forward during the late gigantic rebellion to assist the Government in the greatest struggle it has ever had?" Evidence of Utah loyalty was lacking, insisted the *Vedette;* rather, "she sneers at and jeers Congress, and yet asks it to make concessions to her."[221]

While territorial law invested the governor with singular authority as commander in chief of the Territorial Militia, Governor Durkee was placed, in actual function, behind Lot Smith, the burner of government trains; behind Col. Robert Burton, of the Morrisite camp siege; and far back from Daniel Wells, militia commander in the Utah War—all "traitor chieftains who are the secretly sworn and proved enemies of the Government he represents."[222] Durkee's irrelevance was proved at the recent muster, when Burton was "elected" to the rank of a major general, "to fill the vacancy occasioned by the resignation of George D. Grant." "Wells was on the ground every day and was in command of the troops," according to Young's report to his son in Liverpool.[223] Young did not mention Governor Durkee, who, by territorial law, supervised the militia, called it to service, and commissioned its officers.[224] Possibly because of the attention given the subject in the *Vedette*'s pages, Young told Hooper in Washington "not to say anything about the public arms."[225]

The *Vedette*'s final reason for denying arms to Utah focused on theocracy's claim of a maintaining a republican government, despite establishing "a monarchy on its ruins." Mormon leaders were determined "to make an aggressive warfare upon the Government whenever it may be deemed practicable to do so." Any supply of arms to Utah would "increase her power for consummating the nefarious designs of her disloyal leaders against the best Government the world ever saw—the Government to the support of which our life—our all is pledged."[226]

"A Show of Collision"

Most of the volunteers had been mustered out by this time, but not to let the Mormon military review pass unanswered, Connor ordered the remaining troops to parade on the same grounds near the Jordan River bridge where Wells and Burton had marched their troops. Some 850 weary men of the Sixth Infantry Volunteers, under Col. Carroll H. Potter, had marched down Parley's Canyon in early October.[227] Formerly Confederate prisoners, having sworn allegiance to the United States, they were sent west to the Indian wars labeled as "galvanized Yankees."[228] This unit was reviewed, together with the battle-tested First Veteran Michigan Volunteer Cavalry, commanded by Lt. Col. George Briggs; Lt. Col. William Johns's Third California Volunteer Infantry, recently returned from road building at Denver; Lt. Col. Milo George's First Nevada Cavalry Volunteer Battalion; the Second California Volunteer Cavalry with Capt. Albert Browne's company of provost guards; and finally Lieutenant Honeyman's detachment of artillery.[229] Numbers were reduced, owing to fatigue of the horses, sick lists, guard duty, or the absence of those away on detached service.[230] Although a comparison of Utah's rested, unstressed troops against Union men weary from real marches and dangerous campaigns was inappropriate, Young wrote Hooper, "Our Militia compared very favorably with them in their marching and evolutions."[231]

Mormon loyalty and patriotism were found wanting when the district commander and staff spent weeks "hunting, high and low, through Seer and subjects, for a building to rent and occupy as Head Quarters." However, they found that "from father to son, from boy to Bishop, all have acted as if *under obligation* to refuse to rent their vacant buildings as soon as *they learned it was to be used or occupied for Government use!*" Furthermore, Mormon owners prevented the "*sub*-leasing of any building to Uncle Sam or his Army officers."[232]

Treatment of troops sent by Connor to Fort Ephraim and the communities in Sanpete County proved to be another experience of disloyalty. Two companies of the First Nevada Cavalry under Capt. John H. Dalton and Lt. Daniel R. Firman, were sent for reconnaissances after several raids and murders by Chief Black Hawk. When they arrived at the Mormon settlement at Moroni, the "Captain's lady being along with him, and the night being extremely cold," lodgings were sought, "for which the Captain offered willingly any price," but Mormons "stubbornly refused because the military uniform was visible." This happened even though "there were scores of capacious dwelling houses, [and] vacant rooms . . . that might be rented under the urgency of the occasion." The Mormon leaders declared, "'No, there is not a single place in our town that can get her in, nor yourself neither.'" It was also "impossible to buy produce or forage." At Ephraim, the situation was the same: "The Bishop [warned] his Saints that the troops would rob and steal, seduce and carry of everything they could get their hands on. Doors were to be closed and locked and no forage or provisions were to be sold."[233] Young was fully aware that troops sought forage in outlying areas. His report to Hooper in Washington was matter-of-fact: "The troops that are here are being distributed in the various settlements . . . to get forage for their horses. Three Companies of Cavalry, under the command of Major Baldwin left here about a week ago; two of the companies will stay at Provo . . . and the other . . . will go on to San Pete valley."[234]

Albert Deane Richardson, the journalist with Colfax and Bowles at their summer visit, analyzed Young's goals for the saber rattling and verbal attacks: "Brigham is quite too sagacious to desire actual war." Something less, "a show of collision—a little bloodshed," would serve better: "If some hot-headed officer . . . could be irritated into the use of force, and kill half a dozen Mormons it would strengthen Brigham immeasurably, and do more to enthuse his present followers, and procure new converts all over the world than years of patient labor." Mormons could "thrive for half a century on a little martyrdom."[235] As it had since 1857, threatening to provoke the federal government carried significant risk but, if successful, might favor the survival of the Utah's theocracy without its giving up its peculiar religious practices.

Fires—Accidental and Not So

Faust's Livery Stable in the city was consumed by flames on November 23, despite the heroic work of locals and by Captain Browne's provost guards. The cavalrymen saved the adjacent buildings, which were pulled down to prevent spreading.

In the morning hours of December 19, the Camp Douglas guard saw a light in the usually dark commissary warehouse. Investigating, he found a fire burning near a stack of whiskey barrels. One caught fire and exploded "scattering flame and destruction." Immediately the building was a "sheet of flame." The camp aroused, and near superhuman efforts by Colonel Potter and his officers and men saved the adjoining quartermaster's building. The losses were severe, since the commissary had recently been restocked "from cellar to dome," and stores were "lost at a season when it will be difficult to replace them."[236]

There were those "saintly individuals who . . . rubbed their Godly hands over the catastrophe and the prospect of enormous profits to be extorted from Government." Some stores—bacon and sugar—were saved, and Fort Bridger, though miles away, had "considerable of a surplus on hand." Loyal merchants were also ready to assist "without seeking to exhort famine prices."[237] Young himself wrote, "It will afford me great pleasure to assist you all in my power to procure everything that you may need[,] . . . furnished to you at the usual rates."[238] His letter the following day detailed prices, and contrary to dark predictions of price gouging, Young's prices were in line with the current "Wholesale Market Report."[239] A Saint was heard to say, "'This is a dispensation of Providence for the manifold iniquities of Camp Douglas,'" prompting "Bro. Faust" to whisper in his ear, "'Friend—how about my stable the other day, are Brigham and the Lord after me, too?'" The *Vedette* led the reader to a conclusion: "That the fire was not accidental is highly probable, as no fire was on the premises and everything was secure when the building was locked up for the night at sundown. No person had proper ingress after night, and the catastrophe may be set down to some imp of Satan, rather than to any special Divine agency."[240]

Six of Twenty-Five

The Civil War ended without the millennial creation of the Kingdom of God on earth. Stalemate continued, with Brigham Young preparing for and threatening violence against a parent government that would not compromise on the principles of obedience to federal law and the establishment of true republican function in Utah.

On December 21 the cry went up from the non-Mormons at Camp Douglas: "BULLY FOR CONGRESS! Glory Halleluiah!!" Occasioning the celebration was the introduction by New York representative Hamilton Ward, Sr., of a resolution in the Committee on Territories, to sweep polygamy from the territories just as slavery had been swept from the rebellious states, even "if it takes the whole power of the Government to do so."[241] However, Ward's bill received no support and died. Notably, Benjamin Wade's bill, introduced in 1866, was the sixth attempt by Congress since 1860 to limit the religious sacrament for which many Saints were ready to give up all, including their lives. In 1860, there had been two attempts, the Logan Bill and the Nelson Bill. In 1863, three bills were introduced, by Browning, Richardson, and Julian. In 1866, Wade's Bill was thrown on the growing bone pile of legislation against Mormon Utah's dictatorship, theocracy, and polygamy. The list of proposed but unapproved legislation would grow to include at least twenty-five bills.[242] Although the financial strength of the Church of Jesus Christ of Latter-day Saints was deeply damaged in 1887 by the passage of the Edmunds-Tucker Act, it was not until the even more punitive Cullom and Struble bills of 1889 were teetering on the edge of passage that the Saints—however dishonestly—consented to give up plural marriages and the theocracy that their Kingdom of God required.

Chronology
1865

January	Large numbers of Indians rise up on the Plains, and many deaths result. Gen. P. Edward Connor is assigned the task of controlling Indians.
	Daily Union Vedette editor Frederick Livingston elevates the paper's level and frequency of criticism of Brigham Young and polygamy, publishing many such articles through January, February, and March.
	Young complains of irregularities and violation of the privacy of telegrams by the Camp Douglas telegraph office.
January 15	The Fort Fisher and the port city of Wilmington, North Carolina, fall, severing the last lifeline of the Confederacy.
January 21	Men and officers at Camp Douglas initiate donations to the United States Sanitary Commission and publicize that Utah has contributed nothing to this Civil War relief organization.
January 23	The legislature of the State of Deseret meets, and Young gives his gubernatorial address.
	Sermons by Young and other Mormon leaders are filled with antigovernment sentiment. Young states that Connor ought to have been castrated, and again threatens to kill Connor if their paths cross.
January 25	Governor James Duane Doty writes to Secretary of State William Seward describing the competing divisions of government within Utah Territory.
February 16	Rev. Norman McLeod arrives in Utah to start non-Mormon church services.

Troops at Camp Douglas complain of Mormons' "milking the Gentiles," by overpricing goods sold to men at the camp.

Plans progress for use of the Colorado River as shipping route. Mormons purchase land in the Hawaiian Islands and prepare for increased settlements there.

February 18   Charleston, South Carolina, "the birthplace of treason," surrenders.

February 21   Volunteers parade through Salt Lake City streets and celebrate at Camp Douglas. Mormons do not participate in the celebration.

February 25   *Deseret News* increases its daily publication volume by 50 percent and adopts new technology.

March 4   Lincoln's second inauguration is celebrated jointly by Mormons and non-Mormons. The troops are suspicious of Mormons' participation and purpose. Mormons refuse to sell forage to volunteers, even though government animals are dying.

March 28   Connor takes command of the District of the Plains.

April   Massive profits of Utah businesses are revealed. With Connor absent from Utah, violence against non-Mormons rises.

April 9   Gen. Robert E. Lee meets with Lt. Gen. Ulysses S. Grant at Appomattox for the surrender of the Army of Northern Virginia.

Profuse outpouring of joy appears on the pages of the *Vedette*. The *Deseret News* is silent and devoid of celebration.

April 14   President Abraham Lincoln is shot while sitting in Ford's Theatre; Seward, at home, sustains severe knife injuries as another target of the assassination plot.

April 15	Lincoln dies in the early morning.
	Lincoln's death, Seward's injury, and events in Washington are covered in the *Vedette* and the *Deseret News*.
April 19	Eulogy service for Lincoln is held in the Tabernacle and attended by at least three thousand people. Reverend McLeod and Mormon elder Amasa M. Lyman speak, honoring the fallen president.
June	Weeklong visit to Utah by House Speaker Schuyler Colfax, Albert Deane Richardson, George K. Otis, Samuel Bowles, and William Bross. The visitors are seemingly impressed but later are highly critically of Utah in books, journals, and lectures.
	Growing numbers of subscribers and advertising clients throughout the western states and territories swell the success of the *Vedette*.
June 6–8	Governor Doty pardons convicted killer George Wood. Unexpectedly ill, Doty is unable to participate or object to the treaty signed by Brigham Young and O. H. Irish, extinguishing all Indian title to lands in Utah Territory that are suitable for agriculture and mining.
June 13	Governor Doty dies.
June 18	Young condemns Orson Pratt for publishing Lucy Smith's book, *Biographical Sketches of Joseph Smith, the Prophet, and His Progenitors.*
July 4	Mormons and non-Mormons jointly organize and participate in a Salt Lake City celebration, including a parade. Congressman James Ashley addresses the parade crowd. Mormons then move to the Bowery to hear John Fitch Kinney and George Q. Cannon, while the non-Mormons go to Camp Douglas to hear Reverend McLeod.
July 11	Ashley speaks, with strong criticism of Mormons.

	Contents of Ashley's speech, to be published in the *Vedette*, are leaked to Mormons before publication.
July 14	Ashley meets with Brigham Young, urging against polygamy.
	Scores of women take refuge at Camp Douglas, fleeing from the demands of polygamous marriages.
July 18	Charles Durkee of Wisconsin, a longtime friend of Doty's, is named as Utah governor.
July 22	Brigham Young invites U.S. marshal Orsemus H. Irish to accompany Mormon leaders on a trip north, during which Young touts Irish to replace Doty as territorial governor.
July 31	*Vedette* favors voting privileges for blacks.
August 1	Walker Brothers advertises that the public should examine its "fine gunpowder" for sale.
	Brigham Young orders the destruction of Lucy Mack Smith's book.
August 23	First Presidency signs church-wide proclamation "Hearken O Ye Latter-day Saints," repeating the message to turn in or destroy all copies of the Smith book and condemning Pratt to hell.
September 4	Young and company leave to tour southern settlements and go directly to St. George, while sending Franklin D. Richards and A. M. Musser to visit seven settlements off the main route.
September 29	Young and his entourage return to Salt Lake City from their southern Utah visit.
September 30	Durkee arrives by Overland Stage to assume the Utah Territory governorship.
October 10	Lt. Col. W. Willard Smith replaces Lt. Col. Milo George as commander of the District of Utah.

October 16   Reverend McLeod returns to Salt Lake City after
                  an extended trip to California and Nevada to raise
                  money for building a church in Salt Lake City.

October 26–29   Connor assumes command of the District of Utah,
                  headquartered at Great Salt Lake City.

November 4   Review of Utah's Nauvoo Legion on grounds near
                  the Jordan River; Robert T. Burton is advanced to
                  the rank of major general.

November 15   *Vedette* offers a two-hundred-dollar reward for sto-
                  len newsprint and printing ink.

November 23   Fire destroys Faust's Livery Stable in Salt Lake City,
                  which has no firefighting equipment.

                  Vedette moves its offices and print operation to
                  downtown Salt Lake City.

                  Of the military units then assigned to Camp Doug-
                  las, 850 men march in review on the same grounds
                  as had the Mormons.

                  The Nauvoo Legion is put on alert, but the cause is
                  uncertain.

December   Camp Douglas troops traveling south against
                  Indian depredations are refused food and animal
                  forage by Mormons.

December 19   A "not accidental" fire destroys nearly the entire
                  contents of the commissary warehouse at Camp
                  Douglas.

December 20   Capt. George F. Price succeeds Frederick Livings-
                  ton as editor of the *Vedette*.

December 21   Congressional representative Hamilton Wade of
                  New York enters a resolution to sweep polygamy
                  from the territories.

Epilogue

If you look for truth, you may find comfort in the end; if you look
for comfort, you will not get either comfort or truth.

C. S. LEWIS

Revisiting the decade of 1856 to 1866 in Utah requires substantive
reconsideration of earlier views, a new paradigm. A fanatic and
radicalized fundamentalist group, the Mormons advocated violent
progression of the only true Kingdom of God on earth to full world
dominance, for they believed it millennially destined to be. Buchanan's 1857–58 Utah Expedition profoundly influenced the Mormon
people, deepening their preexisting distrust in state governments and
hatred of the federal government and contributing to the antagonism
held by Mormons leaders through—and beyond—the Civil War years.

Religionists had staked claim to a massive reach of the "Great Interior Basin." The LDS Reformation of 1856 sought to force-cleanse the
Saints of wrongdoing, to prepare and qualify them for God's blessings. It also resulted in federal officers fleeing from the territory and
warning newly elected president James Buchanan of Mormon purges
and revolt in Utah. In December 1857, Utah's forty-one thousand people—with few exceptions members of the LDS Church—were declared
by Buchanan to be guilty of the "first rebellion" of a territory against
the parent government.[1] Shortly after his March 1857 inauguration,
Buchanan sent what began as a 2,500-man U.S. Army force to replace
Brigham Young with a new territorial governor and restore federal law

in the territory.[2] Although Buchanan found polygamy "deplorable . . . and revolting to the moral and religious sentiments of all Christendom," it was Utah's theocracy—"a strange system of terrorism"—that prompted his action.[3] In 1857 the Mormons' army held seven thousand white men, not counting an unknown number of allies, mostly imaginary, from western Indian tribes joining with them—their so-called "battle-ax of the Lord," ready to punish Mormons' persecutors and to aid in avenging the blood of the prophets.[4] Mormons were ready to fight an all-out war because their punishing experience with government in Missouri and Illinois had led them to believe that U.S. forces intended to annihilate them.[5] The Rubicon would be crossed should federal troops attempt to enter the Salt Lake valley. Guerrilla warfare—which LDS forces had already begun—would accelerate attrition and desolation. Blood spilling was no empty bluff to Bvt. Brig. Gen. Albert S. Johnston and to President Brigham Young through the winter and spring standoff.

Buchanan's peace commissioners Lazarus Powell and Ben McCulloch persuaded Young to accept the president's demand for capitulation, and a catastrophic bloodbath was narrowly avoided.[6] Buchanan's firm demands saved countless lives, almost certainly including those of Brigham Young, Daniel Wells, Lot Smith, and many of the Standing Army of the Kingdom of God. Had these men survived a war of rebellion, they and other Mormon military leaders would likely have been tried and punished for treason. Buchanan's generous pardon for all followed Young's capitulation. The Utah Expedition seriously diminished the federal treasury, occupied a significant portion of sixteen thousand regular officers and men of the U.S. Army, and identified a core of capable leaders who would soon serve either North or South in the Civil War.[7]

From 1845 until 1927 the endowment ceremony performed by men of the Mormon priesthood required all attendees—including women—to swear an oath. Since the oath was memorized and not codified in written form, it was administered with slight variations in phrasing by various officiators, but it called for faithful Saints "to avenge the blood of Joseph Smith *upon this nation,* and so teach your children; and you will from this day henceforth and forever begin and carry out hostility *against this nation,* and keep the same a profound secret." In February 1927 the LDS Church First Presidency acted to remove this secret oath of vengeance and retribution against the national government.[8]

Eight days before Confederates opened their bombardment of April 12, 1861, on Fort Sumter, Young wrote to Charles C. Rich, leader of the LDS Church mission in Liverpool: "[There exists] much uncertainty as to what course the Administration would pursue. But whatever course they [Union leaders] take, the debt [with God] they have contracted . . . will result in their overthrow." Any other outcome "would rob justice of its claim."[9] Whatever the actions of North or South, Young was confident that "the results will be controlled for the advancement of truth on the earth," meaning the Kingdom of God under his leadership.[10]

From 1860 the Mormons stood resolute, isolated from the tragic, fraternal conflagration that consumed the nation, continuing to work for statehood—or any form of independent sovereignty. Unity of the people was also maintained through repeated philippics from the pulpit that evil federal forces would be sent to destroy God's innocent people, their living prophet, and the apostles of his church.

Young's refusal to send men against slavery and secession remained steadfast, for he saw the war in a very different dimension, of its accelerating the rise of the Kingdom of God on earth. Neither Stephen S. Harding nor James Duane Doty, each appointed by Lincoln and confirmed by the Senate as *the* governor of Utah Territory, challenged Young on his lack of legal authority to make this denial or to act as the civil ruler of the territory. Lincoln held no trust in the same people who had been ready to pitch in against Buchanan's U.S. Army. It proved wise that these two governors and Lincoln repeated Buchanan's decision to seek Young's obedience to federal law and to keep travel and communication open across the continent without resorting to open war.

Young permitted Representative John Bernhisel to pledge "a home guard for the protection of the telegraph and mail lines and overland travel within our boundaries," provided they would receive the same pay and benefits given to other volunteer groups.[11] Such a unit served the Union for ninety days. Capt. Lot Smith's ninety-five cavalrymen, commanded in the field by Gen. James Craig, were in reality controlled by Utah's Lt. Gen. Daniel H. Wells and Brigham Young. Little remembered amid the pride placed on Utah's brief contribution of one cavalry company is that in August 1862 Young *refused* an urgent request from General Craig to reenlist the Lot Smith company—or a different hundred men—for a second ninety-day tour. Utah's payment of Civil War tax of more than twenty-six thousand dollars came from taxation of whisky and property, but Utah gave nothing additional toward the war debt. The war's direct costs were about $6.7 billion, measured by the share of gross domestic product, or $24.7 trillion in 2012 dollars.[12] Neither the LDS Church nor Utah citizens, including the territory's über-wealthy Mormon and non-Mormon merchants, contributed cash or goods to the United States Sanitary Commission, which served the war's immense number of casualties. Utah was the *only* state or territory not to do so, and the only state or territory not to send a single organized unit of volunteers into the Civil War.

Troops entering Utah in 1857 and 1862 and mining flourishing in Idaho and Montana brought about prosperity never before experienced by Utah's people. The quantity of cash and "greenbacks" led to an influx of goods and luxuries not available earlier. Merchants became wealthy beyond expectation. Mormons' out-and-back wagon trains carried freight and human cargo that accelerated Utah's economic growth. Gunpowder and war munitions arrived secretly in unknown quantities to answer the demands of Utah's large private army.

Lincoln sent infantry and cavalry from California and Nevada to Utah in part to protect the transcontinental emigration. The volunteers also gave Lincoln protection from a repeat blockade of travel and the telegraph by Young's own army, which could have isolated the Pacific states and territories once again. Mormon allegations of immorality among Connor's men must be weighed against the fact that a majority of these troops were Good Templars, actively committed to temperance and to principles of high moral living, and that an untabulated number of Mormon women chose to marry Camp Douglas soldiers. Many of the California and Nevada men were well-behaved Irishmen, advocating sovereignty for their homeland as fervently as

Mormons did for theirs. Surprisingly, Utah's first celebration of St. Patrick's Day was quiet, held on the western shore of Utah Lake in 1859. St. Patrick's Days at Camp Douglas in 1862, 1864, and 1865 were also respectful and temperate.

On Mormon allegiance to the Southern rebellion, Young noted in his August 1861 office journal: "The Brethren are gratified by hearing of the continued success which attends the Southern Confederacy."[13] In February 1862, Mormon George Sims wrote to a Saint in England: "The South at this time is being worsted. The sympathies of our brethren is [sic] divided . . . but the South gets the greatest share. The wise among us read the programme of the wars in the revelations of Joseph and [even] the successes or reverses of our common foes never leads us to the conclusion that peace will again be restored among the enemies of truth."[14] The early settlers of the colonies in southern counties of Utah Territory were reported by George Armstrong Hicks as "all southerners and southern sympathizers." He added, "There were but two Union men . . . myself and an old friend from Nauvoo by the name of John P. Chidester."[15] James D. McCullough wrote to George A. Smith regarding 1861 election results in southern Utah settlements, "The Secessionists have taken the liberty to run me for Representative in opposition to Bishop Crosby without my consent and against my wishes." Reporting the results, McCullough said, "[Some] precincts voted the Union Ticket, but polled a light vote. . . . No general news, but Huza for the cesessionist [sic]. You remember . . . that I was raised in the South."[16] Despite his own prophecy of the combatants' mutual destruction, Young instructed Utah's congressman, William Hooper, in a May 1862 letter to ask his longtime friend Col. Thomas Kane "wheather [sic] he thinks it possible for the union to be broken, and . . . what he thinks about it."[17] Judge Elias Smith was removed from the *Deseret News* editorship because of an 1863 editorial that too openly sounded "the tone of the Southern cause."[18] From his summer 1865 visit to Great Salt Lake City, Samuel Bowles quoted Young as having said "that nine-tenths of the people of the Territory were southern sympathizers; that the North was wrong, and [that] this people [the Mormon people] sympathized with the South."[19] The legacy of identification with the South has persisted in southern Utah to the present era. A school founded in 1911 by the LDS Church in St. George in Washington County had by 1970 taken the name "Dixie College," nicknamed its students "the Rebels," and titled its yearbook as *The Confederate*. Students donned blackface for events, and the Confederate flag flew on the campus as recently as the 1990s. In 2011 the school reached university status and was granted the controversial name "Dixie State University" by the Utah legislature. In 2013 a statue, *The Rebel*, which depicted a mounted Confederate cavalryman saving his companion and had been on campus for some thirty years, was removed.[20]

When Morrisite Mormons, whose millennialism was far more urgent than that of the Brighamite Mormons, were attacked at Fort Kington because their organized body of apostates had grown to several hundred and threatened Brigham Young's preeminence, the incident proved that Utah remained a theocratic dictatorship. The event evinces a chilling déjà vu of the murders at Mountain Meadows. Both attacks took place in the functional—or virtual—absence from the Utah Territory of any U.S. military force. In both, an ecclesiastical militia committed multiple murders after captives raised a white flag of surrender. In both, the property of those killed was stolen by the perpetrators. The commanding officers in both were Brigham Young and Lieutenant General Wells. Neither event was investigated in a military court. No executive investigation was brought by Governor Alfred Cumming in 1858 or Acting Governor Frank Fuller in 1862; both were tools of Brigham Young. No Mormon bishop's court was called. No church or militia leader publicly decried the immorality of attacking, maiming, and killing helpless people under a white flag. For Mountain Meadows, just one man, John D. Lee, among several score who were known as perpetrators, was found guilty and received capital punishment. For the Morrisite killings, not a single militia leader—or any of several hundred militiamen—was found guilty of any crime, in trials that were delayed many years.

What ruler of a loyal territory would absent himself on the day a contingent of seven hundred U.S. Army volunteers arrived to guard his people? If Great Salt Lake City had been home to loyalists, Col. P. Edward Connor's men would not have entered it under arms, threatened with an attack by the people in the territory they had been called to protect. For years Mormon efforts in and outside Washington, D.C., were aimed at Connor's removal and a distant relocation of Camp Douglas. In no other urban area of the Union did the inhabitants have reason—carried for years—to object to the presence of U.S. troops protecting them.

Connor was outspoken on Utah's disloyalty, repeatedly writing that the Mormon leaders continually taught hatred of the federal government. Mormon regard for the Confederacy was in part because it was capable of destroying that government. Connor's judgments of Mormon disloyalty were not generated out of a personal vendetta of an irresponsible, irrational anti-Mormon. Nor was it emanating from deeply held religious convictions, for Connor was a casual Catholic. Rather, he repeatedly cited objective evidence from official military records. After-action military reports of field officers were published, as in the case of Lt. Anthony Ethier, in which Mormon observers intentionally gave Ethier misinformation about Indian attackers that nearly resulted in his twenty-five cavalrymen being killed. Mormons in Spanish Fork, Utah, lied to Capt. George Price about the presence of Indians in the vicinity; military spies sent by Price told of the "perfect understanding" that existed between the Mormons and the Indians thereabouts. When Lt. Francis Honeyman and five artillerymen found refuge in an adobe building against an attack of more than one hundred Indians, local Mormons watched—unmoved as Indians fired hundreds of rounds into the hut—without giving aid or firing a shot in defense of the troops.

Against threat of death and forced removal from the territory, Governor Harding and supreme court justices Thomas Drake and Charles Waite also held evidence-based judgments that Mormons were disloyal. With the vicious beating of Governor John Dawson still fresh in his memory, Drake was emphatic: "I have not entered a Mormon house since I came here; your wives and daughters have not been disturbed by me, and I have not even looked upon your concubines or lewd women."[21] Harding was explicit: "That I have done you wrong in representing you to the Government as disloyal is simply preposterous. Your people, public teachers, and bishops have time and time again admitted the fact."[22] Two weeks before Gettysburg, the speeches of Young and his apostles were filled with "flippant expressions of disloyalty and vulgar threats against the Union," and "each reverse to our arms" was met with "mock tears and sneering lamentations," alleging it as evidence of "the sure destruction of the Constitution and Union."[23]

Repeatedly the *Vedette* pointed out that the speeches of Young and other elders were not printed verbatim or accurately in the *Deseret News* but were cleansed of disloyal statements and of foul, crass language. The level of allegiance to Southern causes and the Confederacy by Young and Mormon leadership undoubtedly vacillated over the course of the war. Perhaps it was only gasconade, but Young was—at the least—keeping all options open, to move to open Southern support if that became more propitious, or to remain with the Union if that offered the highest likelihood of sovereign independence. No statement equaling the bravado, rhetoric, and exaggeration made in LDS sermons or public comments critical of the Union was ever directed toward the South.

If Lincoln's suspension of habeas corpus had applied in Utah, many arrests and imprisonments would have taken place for treasonous and denigrating words from the Saints. Abundant evidence proves the violation of the military mails and telegraph. Mormon spies infiltrated the ranks at Camp Douglas; plans for troop movement were known in advance; and the *Vedette*'s contents could be circulated before publication.

Either duped or by intent, the highest ranks of Mormon leadership were chummy with the mountebank and Confederate spy Walter Murray Gibson. His role in carrying or facilitating communications between Mormons and Confederate leaders in the South, members of the secret Knights of the Golden Circle, and known Confederate sympathizer and Indian superintendent Benjamin Davis remains a matter for ongoing research. The details of the relationship of Gibson's daughter, Talulah, to Brigham Young suggest she made a cat's-paw of Young, and their true relationship remains an enigma.

A revisit to the bizarre account of governor-elect John W. Dawson reveals evidence that he was innocent of the charge of soliciting sex. A story was concocted out of anger against Washington's selection of non-Mormon federal officials, whom the Mormons judged to have evil motives. This summed with the humiliation and frustration generated by Dawson's denial of the petition the Mormons wished approved for the cherished state called Deseret. Henry Martin and Dr. Robert Arthur Chambers joined with John F. Kinney, Frank Fuller, widow Albina Williams, and possibly others in the plot. They participated with several Mormon leaders to weave the specious story. When a group of sociopathic young Mormon men, believing their leaders' accusations, castrated Dawson, most of the perpetrators were punished— and silenced in death—by Mormon apparatchiks.

When Young and several select leaders took the unusual if not unprecedented step of visiting Governor Stephen Harding at his quarters rather than awaiting his supplication at their door, they almost certainly misread the impact of Harding's 1828 visit with Joseph Smith and other principals of the early church in Palmyra. From his exposure to the prophet and his believers, and his ownership of the first printed page of the *Book of Mormon,* which he gifted to the LDS Church, they expected a positive relationship. However, Harding's encounters with Calvin Stoddard, Martin Harris, Lucy Mack Smith, and both the senior and junior Joseph Smiths were not faith building but farcical, planting seeds of disbelief in Harding's mind that were nourished out of dormancy when he came to Utah. Harding's criticism of polygamy and Mormon-controlled government is better understood within the context of his first encounters with early Mormonism's originators. Rumors of sexual impropriety were used against Harding as they had been with Colonel Steptoe, Dawson, and other officials when their writing, their actions, or both made their further presence in Utah unacceptable.

James Duane Doty's inexplicable clemency for southern Utah Mormon George Wood after his brutal murder of Olive Olivia Curtis Coombs raises the disturbing question of bribery. Her murder and the near murder of her thirteen-year-old daughter were either another instance of mountain law for suspected sexual misbehavior or an attempt to prevent exposure of Iron County men in the Mountain Meadows massacre. Doty's untimely death, by whatever cause, resulted in his absence from the pivotal ultimatum and Indian treaty signed at Spanish Fork in June 1865. His record of fairness and wisdom in dealing with Indian tribes predicts that he would have sought more moderate terms than excluding all Utah land of any value from ownership by Native peoples, and that he would have understood that forcing various tribes that held irreconcilable and long-standing differences to share the same reservation land would not be accepted by tribal leaders.

From Doty's arrival as superintendent of Indian Affairs, not only did his energy and accomplishments displace Young from his accustomed position as the Indians' notable benefactor, but Doty had also worked closely with Young's detested opponent for power in the territory, P. Edward Connor. When Doty died, he was not sincerely mourned by Mormon leadership, nor were his accomplishments praised. Orsemus H. Irish danced briefly at the end of Young's strings, and Young remained the premier figure in relations with the Indians throughout the Black Hawk War and for the final twelve years of his life.

In the last weeks of 1864 and early in 1865 Charles Hempstead, the *Vedette*'s editor, commisioned a series of articles analyzing territorial laws that could have served as a manifesto for others to accomplish statehood. All of the criticisms and needed changes taken up by the Liberal Party from 1870 to its disbanding in 1893 were already catalogued and readily available from the *Vedette* publications.

By autumn of 1864, editorial and public silence was the Mormon mode. Lincoln's reelection in November received not even recognition of the simple fact that he was victorious over the failed Union general and peace-at-any-cost Democrat George B. McClellan. The fall of Fort Fisher at the mouth of the Cape Fear River in January 1865, severing the supply route to Lee's Army of Northern Virginia, was met with Mormon silence. It became undeniable that the Kilkenny-cat ending would not be. If this mistake of prophecy was the subject of serious discussion among the topmost fifteen men of LDS Church leadership, no such admission appeared publicly. Silence in the press and in public speeches followed the occupation of Charleston—the birthplace of the rebellion—and the ominous Confederate defeats at Five Forks, Petersburg, and Richmond. No celebration in editorial commentary was to be found at Lee's somber surrender to Grant at the village of

Appomattox Court House in April 1865. There was no comment on the magnanimous terms Grant and Lincoln gave to Lee, no exulting at the end of slavery, at the affirmation that "all men are created equal." Theocracy's leaders did not speak the obvious, that the lands of Europe escaped their prophesied violence, that required millennial events did not take place.

The historian searches the pages of the *Deseret News* in vain for the positive expressions of praise, hope, and optimism that are found in the stirring words of the *Daily Union Vedette:*

"When this storm of battle is past and the sun of Peace shines through the clouds of war, our foes are again our brother; and, although the history of the past four years, written as it is in the best blood of our nation, records scenes of darkest cruelty and deepest hate, yet the guardian spirit of Liberty, who watches over the destinies of the Republic, will write across each damning record the gentle word 'forgiven.'" And of slavery, the *Vedette* added: "With slavery abolished there is little cause for sectional jealousy left, and we may all felicitate ourselves that soon, and very soon, the sun of our Liberty will shine upon us brighter and more glorious that ever it shone before. For the nation will have been purified by the fiery ordeal of war."[24]

Research during the sesquicentennial has added information that expands on the position of the Latter-day Saints during the Civil War and builds on the purported heroism and implied generosity of the Saints for having supported a national government that did not support them. Historian Kenneth Alford contends that almost four hundred Mormons patriotically served the United States in the Civil War. Awarding them the honor due to all war veterans is highly appropriate, but honoring them with the designation of "Civil War Saints," as his book's title grants, is an extension permitted only by Alford's unusual definition of the term. The totals aim to strengthen the case for loyalty and allegiance of the Mormon people to the United States, and to indirectly lessen the disloyalty cited abundantly by contemporary, in-residence military officers and federal officials.[25] A total of 104 individuals—103 men and one woman—are identified as "Saints" outside of Utah at the onset of the Civil War who acted on their loyalty to the federal government by joining Union units in their own locale.[26]

A group of unidentified Utah veterans of the Civil War, undated. Courtesy of Special Collections Department of the J. Willard Marriott Library, University of Utah, Salt Lake City.

Adding to the number of loyal Saints is praiseworthy. However, this pales in comparison with the nearly four million who served and the 752,000 casualties—still an underestimated total—experienced by the societies of the North and the South.[27]

The end of the War of the Rebellion and the O. H. Irish treaty of June 1865 witnessed by Brigham Young did not result in territorial peace. Utah's own Black Hawk War, which pitted Mormon settlers against portions of the Northern Utes and their allies, began in 1865 and brought raids netting thousands of horses and cattle taken from the Mormons and the deaths of at least seventy white settlers. Young assiduously avoided asking U.S. troops at Camp Douglas for help in the Black Hawk War, leaving federal and military officials little informed about its severity. Historian John A. Peterson estimates that Utah's Indian population declined from twenty-three thousand in 1865 to ten thousand in 1872 because of this war, its associated starvation, and the effects of diseases on a weakened people.[28]

The completion of the transcontinental railroad in May 1869 brought fresh emigration, including many non-Mormons who continued the disdain for "the Mormon problem." In 1871, Governor J. Wilson Shaffer outlawed the Nauvoo Legion, prohibiting musters, drills, and any movement of armed men unless at his order. When the Legion prepared to march in the Fourth of July parade in defiance of the order, Acting Governor George A. Black ordered three companies of soldiers and a section of artillery from Camp Douglas, under the command of Col. P. Regis de Trobriand. "If your militia, under arms, parades tomorrow, I will pitch in," de Trobriand told Legion general Daniel Wells. Wells backed down, and once again bloodshed was avoided. The *New York Times* observed, "The supremacy of the United States laws over the decrees of the Mormon Church was for the first time fully vindicated."[29]

Like many Mormon historians, Grant Underwood emphasizes that LDS millennialism and world empire did not end in 1865 or even with Young's death. Orson Pratt stated in 1879 that the millennium would bring "one government, one kingdom, . . . everlasting in its nature" with "dominion over the whole of our globe." John Taylor, about to go underground for his polygamy, declared in 1885, "'You will see trouble, trouble, trouble, enough in these United States," adding, "I tell you in the name of God, Woe! to them that fight against Zion, for God will fight against them."[30]

The commentary in the *Salt Lake Tribune* on the July Fourth celebration in 1885 had a familiar ring to readers of comments that had appeared in the *Daily Union Vedette* in 1864–65: "The Mormon polygamists celebrated the Fourth of July by insulting the United States Government. Upon all their public buildings they placed the National flags at half-mast and refused to raise them to full mast or take them down altogether at the request of some indignant citizens."[31] Following the Pioneer Day celebration on July 24 one year later, the *Tribune* judged matters as before: "The manifestations of disloyalty indulged in by the Mormon chiefs, in the Tabernacle on Pioneer Day, . . . rang out from even the invocations; altogether made up a programme which in any other land except ours would have caused the arrest of every false priest engaged in the treasonable exercises."[32]

Dates of Statehood for Western Territories	
California	1850
Oregon	1859
Kansas	1861
Nevada	1864
Nebraska	1867
Colorado	1876
Idaho	1890
Wyoming	1890
Utah	1896

Some five hundred Mormons served as enlisted men and officers in the Mexican War in the U.S. Army's Mormon Battalion of 1846, marching from Council Bluffs to the Pacific Ocean, to occupy and hold California for acquisition by the United States under the terms ending that war. Mormons served with honor and distinction in the Spanish-American War and in all subsequent U.S. conflicts. Only in the Civil War did Utah's Mormon men not serve their country in combat roles.

Forty years of conflict between Mormons and non-Mormons, from 1850 to 1890, were punctuated by the failure of a government effort to completely "buy out" all Mormon property on the North American continent, attempts to repeal the Organic Act creating Utah Territory, and at least twenty-five unsuccessful attempts by Congress to bring Mormons under federal law. From 1870 a cadre of non-Mormons, including Connor, Hempstead, and Robert Newton Baskin, worked within the Liberal Party to battle the Mormon-organized People's Party, until 1890, when the LDS leaders in Utah Territory finally yielded to soften their theocracy and promised—untruthfully—to end polygamy. Statehood was granted in 1896. Polygamy sanctioned at the highest levels secretly continued to at least 1910. The elements and functions of Utah's powerful theocratic empire, made evident by its unique status among all other states and territories in the Civil War era, continued

Three ensigns above Salt Lake City, north of the Utah State Capitol. Beside the Stars and Stripes and the State of Utah flag flies that of the State of Deseret, the Flag of the Kingdom of God. Courtesy of David Jolley.

well into the first quarter of the twentieth century. Some would charge that theocracy exists in Utah today.

On July 26, 1847, two days after their arrival in the Great Salt Lake valley, Brigham Young and nine of his inner circle climbed to a small peak overlooking their developing settlement. He declared that an ensign would there be raised, symbolic of their governing of the Kingdom of God and denoting Mormon sovereignty over the area.[33] Joseph Smith, Jr., had suggested a Mormon flag in 1844. Sam Brannan, a controversial early Mormon, had his version of the Mormon ensign raised on the ship *Brooklyn* when he arrived in San Francisco Bay in 1846 with more than two hundred other Saints.[34] According to Michael Quinn, other versions of the Flag of the Kingdom of God of the State of Deseret were depicted in the ensuing years, including those by Brigham Young, John Taylor, and Wilford Woodruff. In the margin of his journal, Woodruff drew a diagram of a flag with distinctively characteristic Mormon emblems of the sun, moon, and stars to serve in his suggested ensign.[35] Most present-day Mormon faithful think only vaguely of the Kingdom of God as a part of their unique theology. Present-day Mormon apostles speak less of an imminent millennial end of times, with men of the Mormon priesthood, under divine revelation, governing the world in preparation for Christ's return. However, almost 150 years after Brigham Young called for placement of a symbolic ensign, LDS Church president Gordon B. Hinckley stood on the same ground north of Salt Lake City to dedicate the Ensign Peak Nature Park. Three flags were then raised; the Stars and Stripes of the United States of America was at the center, with the State of Utah flag at one side. With its canton of twelve blue stars symbolically surrounding a single larger, central star, and with twelve stripes alternating blue and white, the Flag of the Kingdom of God of the State of Deseret was the third placed in the winds over Salt Lake City. The three flags continue to fly there to this day.

Revisiting the events of the Civil War years is intended to repair, where discomfort may allow, the damage inflicted by *the silent artillery of time* upon Utah's history.

Notes

Abbreviations Used in the Notes

ASP1   William P. MacKinnon, *At Sword's Point, Part 1*

ATC   Samuel Bowles, *Across the Continent*

BOP   Will Bagley, *Blood of the Prophets*

BYLC   Brigham Young Letterpress Copybooks, 1844–77, CR 1234 1, box 3, vol. 3; box 4, vol. 4; box 5, vol. 5; box 6, vol. 6; box 6, vol. 7

CDBY   Richard S. Van Wagoner, ed., *The Complete Discourses of Brigham Young*, 5 vols.

CR   LDS Church Records (Enter online at http://churchhistorycatalog.lds.org/ and search for one of the call numbers below.)

CR 100 1   Historical Department office journal, 1844–2012

CR 100 102   Historian's Office history of the Church, 1839–circa 1882

CR 100 137   Historical Department journal history of the Church, 1896–2001

CR 1234 1   Brigham Young office files, 1832–78 (bulk 1844–77)

DIU   Horace G. Whitney, *The Drama in Utah*

DN   *Deseret News*, published at Salt Lake City

DUV   *Daily Union Vedette*, a newspaper published initially at Camp Douglas, then at Great Salt Lake City, Utah Terr., by U.S. volunteers

EMD	Dan Vogel, *Early Mormon Documents*, 5 vols.
FK	David L. Bigler, *Forgotten Kingdom*
GBK	Leonard J. Arrington, *Great Basin Kingdom*
GGSL	John Gary Maxwell, *Gettysburg to Great Salt Lake*
GHU	Brigham D. Madsen, *Glory Hunter*
Harding-Lilly	Stephen Selwyn Harding Papers, 1808–91, Harding MSS, Lilly Library, Indiana University, Bloomington
JDD	Alice Elizabeth Smith, *James Duane Doty*
JOMO	C. LeRoy Anderson, *Joseph Morris and the Saga of the Morrisites (Revisited)*
LDS_CHL	Church History Library, Church of Jesus Christ of Latter-day Saints, Salt Lake City
Mill. Star	*Millennial Star*, an LDS newspaper published in Manchester and Liverpool, England
MPOT	Mormon Pioneer Overland Travel, 1847–68, database, https://history.lds.org/overlandtravels/
MR	David L. Bigler and Will Bagley, *The Mormon Rebellion*
NAB	National Archives and Records housed in Washington, D.C.
NACP	National Archives and Records housed in College Park, Md.
NYT	*New York Times*
RG	Record Group
RMSA	T. B. H. Stenhouse, *Rocky Mountain Saints*
RNB	John Gary Maxwell, *Robert Newton Baskin and the Making of Modern Utah*
SDU	*Sacramento Daily Union*
SF	Brigham D. Madsen, *The Shoshoni Frontier and the Bear River Massacre*
SFB	*San Francisco Bulletin*
SHIU	Gerald M. McDonough, *A Short History of the Irish in Utah*
SLDTel	*Salt Lake Daily Telegraph*
SOO	Fred B. Rogers, *Soldiers of the Overland*
SPV	Joseph Morris, *The "Spirit Prevails"*
TSTU	E. B. Long, *The Saints and the Union*
USHS	Utah State Historical Society, Salt Lake City
UV	*Union Vedette*, published briefly as a weekly from November 20, 1863, to January 4, 1864, before its name change to *Daily Union Vedette*

VT   *Valley Tan*, a newspaper published at Salt Lake City, Utah
                  Terr., by U.S. troops
WOR   Robert Nicholson Scott and Henry Martyn Lazelle, *The War
                  of the Rebellion*

Preface

1. Mormonism is classed an "indigenous millennial movement." Kelly J. Baker, "Millennialism," in J. I. Ross, *Religion and Violence*, 2:466.

2. *UV*, July 8, 1864, 4/1.

3. *CDBY*, 3:1710. "Killkenney" is an alternate spelling.

4. "A Plague o' Both Your Houses," *DUV*, January 18, 1865, 2/2 (italics in the original).

5. "An Item for Camp Pedlars," *DUV*, February 6, 1865, 2/4.

6. "Canting Hypocrites," *DUV*, June 14, 1865, 2/1.

7. Orson Pratt, cited in Hardy, *Doing the Works of Abraham*, 83.

8. "Little Johnny Jump Up," W. W. Phelps to Young, undated, CR 1234 1, General Correspondence, Letters from Church Leaders, 1840–77, reel 54, box 40, folder 29, image 11.

9. *Mormoniad* (1858), cited in Deverell, "Thoughts from the Farther West," 8.

10. Pratt to Queen Victoria, 1841, cited in Hansen, *Quest*, 3, 6–11.

11. "Remarkable Vision," *Mill. Star*, August 4, 1842, 3:69.

12. Brigham Young reorganized the Council of Fifty in 1845. *BOP*, 15, 20.

13. O. Pratt, "Kingdom of God—Part I," 1.

14. August 24, 1856, *CDBY*, 2:1162.

15. Young, August 2, 1857, CR 100 137, cited in Hansen, *Quest*, 164–65.

Introduction

1. Of 10,500 armed conflicts occurring in twenty-six states, 384 were "principal battles" with significant impact on the war's course. Civil War Sites Advisory Commission, *Civil War Battlefields*.

2. Historian Robert Freeman cites one Mormon combat fatality. Henry Wells Jackson, an 1846 Mormon Battalion veteran, was captured by Confederates as he traveled to recover mail carrier wages. Imprisoned three months, he joined the Union as a cavalry lieutenant. He died in May 1864 after a gunshot wound of the chest. Freeman, "Latter-day Saints in the Civil War," in Alford, *Civil War Saints*, 286–87. Others claim that the death of teamster Mark Murphy occurred four months after uneventful service in Lot Smith's cavalry. Fisher et al., *Utah and the Civil War*, 96.

3. Hundley, *Prison Echoes*, 44.

4. Rable, *God's Almost Chosen Peoples*, 1.

5. Richards, review of Rable, *God's Almost Chosen People*, 283.

6. Bitton, *Ritualization of Mormon History*, 116.

7. Woodruff, *Journal*, December 11 and 31, 1861, 5:606, 617.

8. Roberts, *Comprehensive History*, 3:520. Prodigious efforts at statehood by skipping territorial status were made. Placing blame on Taylor oversimplified the complexities and competing issues. See Saunders, *Printing in Deseret*, 56–60.

9. Even in March 1836 at the dedication of the temple in Kirtland, Ohio, Joseph Smith said, "If any more of our brethren are slain or driven from their lands . . . we will give ourselves no rest until we are avenged . . . to the uttermost." *History of the Church*, 2:410–33, cited in Homer, *Joseph's Temples*, 109.

10. Bancroft, *History of Utah*, 451n28 (italics added).

11. Remy, *Journal to Great Salt Lake*, 2:72.

12. Cited in Homer, *Joseph's Temples*, 238, 270, 274, 287–88, 302. See also Henry G. McMillan, *The Inside of Mormonism*.

13. U.S. Senate Committee on Privileges and Elections, *Proceedings*, 1:78–79; 3:71; 4:7, 68–69, 76–77, 108, 111.

14. George F. Richards to Edward H. Snow, February 15, 1927, LDS_CHL, CR 100–14, #2, cited in Buerger, "Endowment Ceremony," 104–105, 105n118 (italics added).

15. Langworthy, *Scenery of the Plains*, 93.

16. Bigler, *Winter with the Mormons*, 49–50 (italics added). "Duck hunting" was one of many Mormon euphemisms for sanctioned murder.

17. *ASP1*, 45.

18. Possibly Colt's revolving carbine. CR 1234 1, reel 87, box 74, folder 1.

19. Bagley, *Golden Visions*, iii.

20. *RNB*, 80–104.

21. "President's Message," VT, December 28, 1858, 1/1.

22. Young to Alexander, October 16, 1857, cited in O. F. Whitney, *History of Utah*, 1:645.

23. "Proclamation by the Governor," in Buchanan, *Utah Expedition*, 34–35.

24. To Utah legislators, Young admitted: "No one . . . wishes to deny the right of the Government to send its troops when, where and as it pleases" if "done clearly within the authorities and limitations of the Constitution." *ASP1*, 489.

25. "The thread is cut that has hitherto connected us; and now we have to act for ourselves and build up the kingdom of God on the earth." September 20, 1857, *CDBY*, 1:1343.

26. "Washington Correspondence," *Missouri Republican*, May 18, 1859, reprinted in *VT*, June 22, 1859, 2/5.

27. *ASP1*, 264–67.

28. Wells to William Dame, August 1, 1857, cited in *ASP1*, 232–33.

29. Typescript of letter, Young and Wells to Dame, September 14, 1857, in Gibbs, *Mountain Meadows Massacre*, 9–10.

30. Young to Eldredge, June 30, 1857, CR 1234 1, April–August 1857, box 18, folder 6, images 25–26.

31. "The Mormons," *NYT*, February 6, 1858 (italics in the original).

32. Martineau Record Typescript, William R. Palmer Collection, 21–25, James A. Martineau Journal, Entries for 5–23 August 1857, LDS Archives, cited in *ASP1*, 235–36, 236n23.

33. "T[racy]" to "N.," February 3, 1858, cited in *ASP1*, 456. Satisfaction may have varied by rank; one historian claims that teamster Alexander Toponce reported a "miserable winter . . . short of grub and short of rations." McDonough, *Short History of the Irish*, 8.

34. Powell, an able statesman, "had no faith in the sincerity of the Mormon apostles" but credited Utah's masses with integrity. *Biographical Sketch*, 53. McCulloch, formerly a Texas Ranger, lost the Second U.S. Cavalry appointment to Albert S. Johnston; he later became an officer in the secret Knights of the Golden Circle, a pro-slavery group. In 1861, when McCulloch marched on the San Antonio arsenal with 550 cavalrymen, including 150 Knights, the Unionists surrendered. He became a Confederate general but was killed in 1862 in Arkansas. Keehn, *Knights*, 185.

35. Powell and McCulloch were compatriots of Houston and Blair in the Battle of San Jacinto.

36. "I offer now a full and free pardon to all who will submit themselves to the authority of the federal government. . . . who shall submit to the laws, a free pardon for the seditions and treason heretofore by them committed." Proclamation by President James Buchanan, April 6, 1858.

37. Young to Bernhisel, December 30, 1861, BYLC, CR 1234 1, box 6, vol. 7, p. 78, image 109.

38. Lincoln's administrations did not implement the draft in any of the states and territories west of the Rocky Mountains.

39. McMurtrie, *Beginnings of Printing in Utah*, 14–17. Saunders describes money printing efforts by John Kay, Thomas Bullock, Robert Campbell, and Truman O. Angell. Saunders, *Printing in Deseret*, 41–44.

40. The Pony Express, organized by the firm of Russell, Majors and Waddell in the winter months of 1860, operated for nineteen months, from April 1860 to October 1861, when the Pacific Telegraph line was completed.

41. "Local Matters," *DUV*, November 11, 1864, 3/1.

42. "A Sign of the Times," *DUV*, February 23, 1865, 2/1.

43. Bell, "Visit to Brigham Young," 209.

44. "Gloria in Excelsis," *DUV*, April 4, 1865, 2/1.

45. "Gen. R. E. Lee Surrenders His Army to Lt. Gen. U.S. Grant and the Gallant Forces under His Command," *DUV*, April 11, 1865, 2/1, 2/3.

46. Sandburg, *Storm*, 353.

47. The phrase is from Lincoln's 1838 address in Springfield, Illinois.

1. Transition from a Utah War to a Civil War, 1859–1860

1. "Affairs in Utah," *NYT*, February 8, 1859.

2. "From Utah, Mormon Sentiment," written at Camp Floyd, January 18, published in *NYT*, February 15, 1860.

3. "The Results of Our Utah Policy," *SFB*, February 14, 1860, 2/1.

4. A May 17, 1859, decision by Attorney General Jeremiah S. Black left the governor as the supreme authority in the territory.

5. Johnston to Cumming, *VT*, May 17, 1859, 2/3.

6. "Attention, Emigrants!" *VT*, May 17, 1859, 2/3. A Camp Floyd force escorted emigrants to California by the northern route in early June.

7. "Affairs in This Territory," *VT*, May 10, 1859, 2/1.

8. "Prospective Troubles with the Mormons," correspondence, *Missouri Republican*, reprinted in *VT*, May 24, 1859, 1/5.

9. "Civil War Impending in Utah," *St. Louis Democrat*, reprinted in *VT*, May 24, 1859, 3/1.

10. *FK*, 131–32.

11. "Affairs in Utah," *NYT*, May 11, 1860. The 1859 period is treated in detail in *MR*, 330–54.

12. "News Items," *Weekly Arizonian* (Tubac), May 19, 1859, 1/4.

13. *MR*, 336.

14. Carleton, *Mountain Meadows Massacre* (1902); Campbell to Porter, July 6, 1859, S. Exec. Doc. 42, 14–16, cited in *FK*, 177; Carleton, *Mountain Meadows Massacre* (1995).

15. "Details of the Mountain Meadows Massacre in Utah," *Holmes County (Ohio) Republican*, July 14, 1859, 2/5.

16. Du Bois, *Campaigns in the West*, 117–18.

17. "Army Matters," reprinted in *VT*, May 24, 1859, 3/4.

18. Untitled, *VT*, May 24, 1859, 2/2.

19. Ferguson to Cumming, May 11, 1859, reprinted in *VT*, May 24, 1859, 2/3. Ferguson did not list this cannon in his January 1858 report of munitions for the defense of Echo Canyon. *MR*, 267. The *San Francisco Bulletin* reported that Hartnett and Indian Superintendent Jacob Forney had upheld Cumming "in every step," reprinted in *VT*, May 24, 1859, 2/4.

20. "Affairs in This Territory," *VT*, May 10, 1859, 2/1.

21. Others at Fort Bridger's winter stay included Governor Cumming and his wife, Elizabeth; Secretary John Hartnett; U.S. attorney John M. Hockaday; Marshal Dotson; Indian agents Forney and Garland Hunt; and Salt Lake City postmaster Hiram F. Morrell.

22. Eckels to Cass, September 27, 1859, in Buchanan, *Utah Territory: Message of the President* (1860), 33–39.

23. Ibid., 38.

24. "Resignation of Utah Judges," *New York Daily Tribune*, March 16, 1860, 4/4.

25. "Past and Present," *VT*, December 28, 1859, 2/2.

26. MacKinnon, "Hammering Utah," 133–34.

27. Forsyth was unsuccessful.

28. MacKinnon, "Hammering Utah," 142–43.

29. Ibid., 149.

30. Historian Matthew Grow notes that Kane and Young planned Mormon settlements in Mexico; however, those were after 1865. Grow, *"Liberty to the Downtrodden,"* 272–74.

31. Young to Hooper, December 1, 1859, BYLC, CR 1234 1, box 5, vol. 5, p. 317, image 390. Importation of slaves had been illegal in any port within the U.S. jurisdiction from January 1808, under a law signed the previous year by President Thomas Jefferson.

32. Bernhisel to Young, July 31, 1862, CR 1234 1, Utah Delegate Files, reel 71, box 61, folder 6, image 81.

33. Zanjani, *Devils Will Reign*, 122–23.

34. "Congress," *Springfield (Mass.) Republican*, March 29, 1860, 4/2. Logan would later be instrumental in the formation of the Grand Army of the Republic.

35. "The Mormons: Challenge from Judge Cradlebaugh to Mr. Hooper for a Public Discussion," *Washington (D.C.) Star*, republished in *NYT*, January 21, 1860.

36. Young to Hooper, February 20, 1860, BYLC, CR 1234 1, box 5, vol. 5, p. 386, image 451s (underlining in the original).

37. "The Utah Ulcer," *Mobile (Ala.) Register*, February 10, 1860, 2/2.

38. "How President Buchanan Suppressed the Rebellion in Utah," *Ohio State Journal* (Worthington), April 3, 1860, 1/1.

39. "Accompanying Documents," *Mountaineer* (Salt Lake City), February 4, 1860, 2/3. The *Mountaineer* was a Mormon joint venture by Ferguson, Seth Blair, and Hosea Stout, using *Deseret News* presses. Published weekly from August 27, 1859, to July 20, 1861, it countered the non-Mormon *Valley Tan*.

40. "Affairs in Utah," *NYT*, May 3, 1860.

41. "Discourse," John Taylor, delivered June 17, 1860, published in *DN*, January 9, 1861, 1/5.

42. "From Washington," *NYT*, April 5, 1860.

43. *RNB*, 189–90.

44. "Polygamy in Congress," *Perrysburg (Ohio) Journal*, April 12, 1860, 2/3.

45. "Personal and Political," *Springfield (Mass.) Republican*, May 3, 1860.

46. "Report of the Secretary of War," *DN*, January 25, 1860, 5/4.

47. Utah Territorial Papers, U.S. Department of State, RG 59, NACP, cited in *TSTU*, 53, 57n67.

48. Col. C. F. Smith immediately succeeded Johnston as Camp Floyd commander, and he was followed by Col. Philip St. George Cooke.

49. Maj. Henry Heth's troops figured prominently in the first Confederate shots fired at Gettysburg.

50. Johnston, *Gen. Albert Sidney Johnston*, 243.

51. "From Utah," *NYT*, April 4, 1860.

52. Ibid.

53. "The Anti-Polygamy Bill," *DN*, May 16, 1860, 3/3 (italics added).

54. "Affairs in Utah: Sermon by Orson Pratt," *NYT*, June 7, 1860.

55. Forney to Anderson, May 5, 1859, *VT*, May 10, 1859, 2/3.

56. Young to Hooper, April 12, 1860, BYLC, CR 1234 1, box 5, vol. 5, p. 453, image 520s.

57. Young to Hooper, April 19, 1860, BYLC, CR 1234 1, box 5, vol. 5, p. 470, image 537.

58. Young to Hooper, May 17, 1860, BYLC, CR 1234 1, box 5, vol. 5, p. 516, image 588 (underlining in the original).

59. Young to Hooper, May 24, 1860, BYLC, CR 1234 1, box 5, vol. 5, p. 522, image 593s.

60. "Affairs in Utah: Investigation of Dr. Forney's Affairs," *NYT*, June 7, 1860.

61. "Affairs in Utah: The New Judges, the Mountain Meadows Massacre," *NYT*, August 7, 1860.

62. "Letter from Great Salt Lake," *SFB*, April 27, 1859, 1/1. Kinney opened a hotel in Salt Lake City, and Chandless claims that Kinney bilked the government by requiring jurors to board there for the entire term of court. Chandless, *Visit to Salt Lake*, 185–86.

63. Woodruff, *Journal*, November 26 and December 4, 1849, 3:513–16.

64. *Mill. Star*, November 10, 1860, cited in *TSTU*, 15–16.

65. Rocky Mountain Lodge No. 205 was formed at Camp Floyd. Homer, *Joseph's Temples*, 272–73, 273n55–58.

66. "Affairs in Utah: The Chief Apostle Hyde on the United States Government and People," *NYT*, November 5, 1860.

67. "Will the South Resist?" *DN*, November 21, 1860, 1/2. The 1856 Republican Party had labeled slavery and polygamy as "twin barbarisms."

68. Young to Hooper, November 29, 1860, BYLC, CR 1234 1, box 5, vol. 5, p. 641, image 717s. "Their property" presumably referenced the small number of Utah slave owners.

69. The resolution named South Carolina's James L. Orr, Missouri's Gen. Alexander W. Doniphan, and Governor John Wood of Illinois. "Letter from Washington: Utah Matters," *SFB*, May 28, 1860, 1/1.

70. "From Utah," written May 25, published in *NYT*, June 19, 1860.

71. *CDBY*, 3:1696.

72. Young to Hooper, December 27, 1860, BYLC, CR 1234 1, box 5, vol. 5, p. 660, image 738 (underlining in the original).

73. M1091, Subject File of the Confederate States Navy, 1861–65, RG 45, roll 0045, NAB (underlining in the original). A "Letter of Marque" authorizes what would otherwise be acts of piracy. The notice is in error regarding the timing of Gibson's travel: he left San Francisco in June 1861, not July, and arrived in Hawaii on July 4, 1861.

74. See Bailey, *Hawaii's Royal Prime Minister;* McGhie, "Life and Intrigue"; and Taylor, "Walter Murray Gibson."

75. Adler and Kamins, *Fantastic Life,* 1–8.

76. Michener and Day, "Gibson," 118.

77. U.S. House Committee on Foreign Affairs, "Report of Mr. Stanton."

78. Musser, "Oceanic Adventurer," 1718.

79. Gibson to Young, May 30, 1859, Gibson Name File, LDS_CHL, cited in Adler and Kamins, *Fantastic Life,* 45.

80. CR 100 1, vol. 23, pp. 296–97, images 300–301.

81. Typescript, Brigham Young Papers, 1857–77, MS B 93, box 1, folder 1, USHS.

82. CR 100 102, vol. 30, p. 3, image 19.

83. CR 1234 1, reel 86, box 74, folder 37, image 2. Bailey claims there is no known record of the LDS baptism of Walter Gibson's sons, John Lewis Gibson and Henry H. Gibson. Bailey, *Hawaii's Royal Prime Minister,* 105.

84. CR 1234 1, Journal D, September 30, 1858–June 18, 1863, reel 84, box 72, folder 5, p. 43, image 40; CR 100 1, vol. 24, p. 70, image 74.

85. "Lectures on the Malaysian Islands: Lecture III," *Mountaineer,* April 7, 1860.

86. CR 100 1, vol. 24, p. 295, image 103.

87. Adler and Kamins, *Fantastic Life,* 46–47.

88. Henry H. French to Young, March 27, 1860, CR 1234 1, General Correspondence, Incoming, reel 37, box 27, folder 13, images 20–30.

89. Young to H. H. French, March 30, 1869, CR 1234 1, General Correspondence, Outgoing, reel 27, box 19, folder 5, image 63.

90. CR 1234 1, reel 86, box 74, folder 37, image 5. Near this time, Young presented Gibson with a gift of an engraved gold watch, which he treasured and carried with him to the Hawaiian Islands.

91. Walter Gibson's daughter's name in the census is misspelled as "Toledah," and her birthplace is listed as "Ga.," as she sometimes claimed birth in Elberton. John Gibson is listed with the eastbound Mormon missionary train "of Messrs. Rich and Lyman," according to the *Mountaineer,* June 16, 1860. John Gibson had returned to Salt Lake and was listed in the October census, living with the Daniel Wells family in the Eighteenth Ward.

92. CR 1234 1, President's Office Journals, 1852–63, reel 84, box 72, folder 5, p. 173, image 170.

93. *CDBY,* 3:1532, 1537, 1546, 1557, 1715.

94. CR 100 1, vol. 24, reel 4, box 3, p. 374, image 387. Gibson used the law firm of Willard and Howe, 98 Broadway, New York City. CR 1234 1, Journal D, September 30, 1858–June 18, 1863, reel 84, box 72, folder 5, image 2.

95. CR 1234 1, Journal D, September 30, 1858–June 18, 1863, reel 84, box 72, folder 5, p. 177, image 175.

96. P. H. Young to B. Young, November 20, 2860, CR 1234 1, General Correspondence, Incoming, from Family Members, reel 57, box 44, folder 7, image 1.

97. November 18, 1860, *CDBY*, 3:1715.

98. CR 100 137, vol. 53, reel 18, p. 1, image 123.

99. CR 100 1, vol. 24, reel 4, box 3, p. 377, image 390.

100. CR 1234 1, reel 86, box 74, folder 37, images 6–7.

101. Gibson to Young, January 9, 1861, CR 1234 1, reel 38, box 28, folder 6, images 3–9; CR 1234 1, reel 38, box 28, folder 61. "Go together" alludes to block voting.

102. Ibid.

103. Gibson to Young, April 12, 1861, CR 1234 1, reel 38, box 28, folder 6, images 24–42.

104. "Jefferson's Inaugural Address," *DN*, March 6, 1861, 2/1.

105. "What May Be Expected," *DN*, March 6, 1861, 4/1.

106. Woodruff, *Journal*, March 7, 1860, 5:440.

107. LDS Church officials' response to questions was that no sealing in marriage to Young "or anyone else within the Mormon congregation" took place. Adler and Kamins, *Fantastic Life*, 221n5.

108. Young to Gibson, March 5, 1861, CR 1234 1, reel 27, box 19, folder 12, images 2–7. Charlotte Talula Young was born March 4, 1861, allegedly to Clarissa Clara Decker. Photographer-historian Brent Herridge contends that Talula was born to Brigham Young and his alleged Bannock Indian wife, Sally, then raised by Decker. Herridge, pers. comm., March 2014.

109. Adler and Kamins, *Fantastic Life*, 47.

110. Young to Gibson in San Francisco, April 2, 1861, BYLC, CR 1234 1, box 5, vol. 5, p. 736, image 809s.

111. Gibson to Young, May 13, 1861, CR 1234 1, reel 38, box 28, folder 6, images 45–56.

112. Young advised Gibson to "call on the Sandwich Islands *if you can make it convenient* for there are many native brethren on those islands." Young to Gibson, March 5, 1861, CR 1234 1, reel 27, box 19, folder 12, images 2–7 (italics added).

113. Young to Gibson, in care of Evelith, July 2, 1861, BYLC, CR 1234 1, box 5, vol. 5, p. 818, image 895. Henry was likely attracted by the Pikes Peak gold rush. No definitive Confederate records list John Lewis Gibson as having served. William H. Gibson is listed for First (Orr's) Rifles, Company E. Hewett, *Roster of Confederate Forces;* Evans, *Confederate Military History;* Hewett and Lawrence, *South Carolina Soldiers.*

114. Gibson to Young, CR 1234 1, reel 38, box 28, folder 6, images 57–69.

115. Young to Gibson, Honolulu, September 18, 1861, BYLC, CR 1234 1, box 5, vol. 5, p. 882, image 961s.

116. Personal Diary of Walter Murray Gibson, typescript, MS 4075, LDS_ CHL, March 24, 1862, p. 7, image 13.

117. Young to Gibson, Lanai, Hawaiian Islands, May 16, 1862, BYLC, CR 1234 1, box 6, vol. 6, p. 255, image 292s.

118. Young to Gibson, Lanai, Hawaiian Islands, July 18, 1862, BYLC, CR 1234 1, box 6, vol. 6, p. 339, image 376.

119. CR 1234 1, Letterbook, reel 6, vol. 5, pp. 911–12, images 1018–19.

120. Adler and Kamins, *Fantastic Life*, 58.

121. From Gibson Diary, September 1861, cited in Adler and Kamins, *Fantastic Life*, 223n41. Of Toombs, the *Vedette* stated that he was "hand in glove, heart and soul with treason" and was "lately Jeff Davis' Secretary of State." *DUV*, January 9, 1864, 4/2.

122. Michener and Day, "Gibson," 121–22.

123. Ibid., 112.

124. The USS *Saginaw* had visited "various Japanese and Chinese ports." Schenck to Welles, November 27, 1861, U.S. Naval War Records Office, *Union and Confederate Navies*, ser. 1, vol. 1, 218.

125. LDS missionaries entered Sandwich Islands in 1850, but the Utah War brought their recall.

126. Gibson to G. A. Smith, March 13, 1864, MS 3691, Captain Walter M. Gibson, circa 1870, LDS Historian's Office, extracts, reel 1, folder 1.

127. Gibson to Young, April 7, 1864, CR 1234 1, reel 40, box 29, folder 19.

128. John L. Gibson to Young, July 15, 1864, CR 1234 1, reel 49, box 29, folder 19, images 76–78.

129. Gibson was buried in Hawaii. Talulah remained there, married Frederick Harrison Hayselden in 1875, had three children, and died in 1903. Henry Gibson raised stock on Lanai, married, and had four children. John Lewis Gibson died there at age thirty-six from a fall from a horse.

2. A War for the Advancement of Truth on the Earth, 1861

1. The renaming of the fort honored Sen. John J. Crittenden of Kentucky, who sought compromise to avoid war.

2. CR 100 102, vol. 31, reel 14, box 14, p. 20, images 34–35.

3. "Correspondence," Clayton to Cannon, *Mill. Star*, January 26, 1861, 23:59.

4. February 10, 1861, CR 100 102, vol. 31, reel 14, box 14, p. 57, image 71.

5. "Remarks by President Brigham Young," delivered April 6, published in *DN*, May 1, 1861, 1/2.

6. "Civil War in America: Its Importance as a Warning to the Saints," May 11, 1861, CR 100 102, vol. 31, reel 14, box 14, p. 190, image 203.

7. Quinn, *Mormon Hierarchy: Extensions*, 271.

8. *CDBY*, 3:1789.

9. Young to Hooper, April 25, 1861, BYLC, CR 1234 1, box 5, vol. 5, p. 773, image 846.

10. The Pony Express promised ten-day delivery from St. Joseph, Mo., to Sacramento, Calif. "The Pony" was never profitable.

11. "The Pony Express," St. Joseph Convention and Visitors Bureau, www. stjomo.com/see-do/experience-history/the-pony-express/. Quotation from "To Our Readers," *DN*, January 30, 1861, 4/1.

12. Woodruff, *Journal,* April 25, 1861, 5:569 (capitalization and errors as in the original). When the Pony Express Club numbers increased, the members were careful "to keep the news among themselves" lest *Extra* sales would decline. September 18, 1861, CR 100 102, vol. 31, reel 14, box 14, p. 398, image 412.

13. Young to Evelith, January 1, 1861, BYLC, CR 1234 1, box 5, vol. 5, p. 664, image 740s.

14. "Clippings," *DN*, January 2, 1861, 3/3.

15. From the *NYT* correspondent, reprinted as "Latest by Telegraph and Pony Express," *DN*, March 6, 1861, 4/2.

16. Lamon, *Life of Abraham Lincoln,* 505–26.

17. Stashower, "Lincoln Must Die," excerpted from Stashower, *Hour of Peril.*

18. "Eastern News by Telegraph and Pony," *DN*, March 13, 1861, 2/4.

19. Young to Hooper, March 7, 1861, BYLC, CR 1234 1, box 5, vol. 5, p. 714, image 791s.

20. "Latest by Telegraph and Pony Express," *DN*, March 13, 1861, 4/2.

21. Young to Hooper, March 28, 1861, BYLC, CR 1234 1, box 5, vol. 5, p. 729, image 800f.

22. Young to Hooper, February 7, 1861, BYLC, CR 1234 1, box 5, vol. 5, p. 689, image 767s (underlining in the original).

23. Young to Kane, Philadelphia, September 21, 1861, BYLC, CR 1234 1, box 5, vol. 5, p. 887, image 966.

24. Grow, *"Liberty to the Downtrodden, "*212–35.

25. Young to Kane, Philadelphia, September 21, 1861, BYLC, CR 1234 1, box 5, vol. 5, p. 887, image 966.

26. Records of the Utah Superintendency of Indian Affairs, 1853–70, RG 75.15.13, microfilm M834, roll 1, NAB.

27. Caleb B. Smith, Accounts of Brigham Young, cited in *BOP*, 253, 472. Forney was appointed on August 27, 1857, only two weeks before the massacre at Mountain Meadows.

28. "Superintendent Davis and the Indians," written December 16, published in *DN*, December 26, 1860, 8/4.

29. Davis to Dole, June 30, 1861, U.S. Office of Indian Affairs, *Report, 1861,* 129–30, 132–33.

30. "Return of the Superintendent," *DN*, January 2, 1861, 8/3. That funds for his Indians were extremely inadequate in the Civil War years was also the complaint of Superintendent Doty.

31. Young to Hamblin, January 8, 1861, BYLC, CR 1234 1, box 5, vol. 5, p. 668, image 746.

32. Compton, *Frontier Life*, 178–88.

33. "Further Secession Movements," *Mountaineer*, January 26, 1861, 2/1 (italics in the original). The reference to the Everglades implies that Davis served in the Seminole Wars. However, he is not listed in Sprague, *Florida War*.

34. *BOP*, 178, 253–54, 428n28.

35. "Affairs in Utah," written May 31, published in *NYT*, June 25, 1861.

36. Smith to John L. Smith, June 13, 1861, CR 100 012, vol. 31, reel 14, box 14, p. 245, image 259.

37. This would be $509,000 in 2012 dollars, by CPI (www.measuringworth.com/uscompare/). Juanita Brooks and Bagley contend that Young billed for property stolen from the Mountain Meadows victims. *BOP*, 253–54, 428n23.

38. C. M. Orton, "'Dixie,'" 3. According to Confederate records, Benjamin F. Davis was in the Fifth Regiment, Florida Infantry. Organized in 1862, the regiment lost 35 percent of its men at Chancellorsville; it also fought at Gettysburg, the Wilderness, Spotsylvania, Cold Harbor, and Petersburg. Only Maj. Benjamin Davis, five officers, and forty-seven men remained at Appomattox Court House. RG 109, War Department Collection of Confederate Records, Compiled Service Records, Florida, microfilm M225, roll 2, NAB.

39. On May 14, "four heavy wagons, freighted with the products of the South for the General Tithing office," arrived in Salt Lake City, likely influencing Young's mood as he started south. "Tithing Produce from the South," *DN*, May 15, 1861, 4/3.

40. "Excursion through the Southern Counties," *DN*, May 22, 1861, 8/2.

41. May 25, 1861, CR 100 102, vol. 31, reel 14, box 14, p. 213, image 227 (italics added).

42. Brooks, *Mountain Meadows Massacre*, 182–83, 183n.

43. May 25, 1861, CR 100 102, vol. 31, reel 14, box 14, p. 213, image 227.

44. Woodruff, *Journal*, May 25, 1861, 5:577 (italics added).

45. May 25, 1861, CR 100 102, vol. 31, reel 14, box 14, p. 213, image 227.

46. Carleton, *Mountain Meadows Massacre* (1995), May 25, 1859, 9–16.

47. May 25, 1861, CR 100 102, vol. 31, reel 14, box 14, pp. 213–14, images 227–28.

48. Cleland and Brooks, *Mormon Chronicle*, 2:314. No connection between the Mountain Meadows victims and the killers of the Smith brothers has ever been established.

49. Calder to Young, June 4, 1861, BYLC, CR 1234 1, box 5, vol. 5, pp. 798–99, images 873–74. Stephen DeWolfe was the prosecuting attorney in the unsuccessful 1859 attempt by Judge Cradlebaugh to bring the Mountain Meadows murderers to justice. DeWolfe served briefly as territorial secretary, edited the non-Mormon newspaper the *Valley Tan*, and later was Robert Newton Baskin's law partner.

50. Young to Hooper, June 9, 1861, BYLC, CR 1234 1, box 5, vol. 5, p. 799, image 874.

51. "President Young's Visit South," *DN*, June 12, 1861, 4/1.

52. Young to Lyman and Rich, June 13, 1861, BYLC, CR 1234 1, box 5, vol. 5, p. 800, image 875.

53. Cited as JH in C. M. Orton, "'Dixie,'" 8, 14n25.

54. J. W. White, *Lincoln and Treason*, 1.

55. Taney authored the fateful 1857 *Dred Scott* decision.

56. Jonathan White emphasizes that Lincoln's April call-up of seventy-five thousand men declared the rebellion "too powerful to be suppressed by the ordinary course of judicial proceedings, or by the powers vested in the Marshal by law." J. W. White, *Lincoln and Treason*, 125n7.

57. Neely, "Constitution and Civil Liberties," 37. Note that this Pennsylvania State University historian is not the author of the same name who wrote of Governor Dawson.

58. Neither a Supreme Court decision nor a circuit court case, *Ex parte Merryman* remains "the first case listed on the federal judiciary's 'Landmark Cases Related to Understanding Terrorism Cases" website." J. W. White, *Lincoln and Treason*, 3, 6.

59. August 24, 1861, *CDBY*, 3:1906.

60. J. W. White, *Lincoln and Treason*, 77–78.

61. Neely, "Constitution and Civil Liberties," 233–34. Neely indicates that most arrests were made for purposes beyond stifling dissent.

62. Ficklin had a versatile role in the Utah War as an army scout and an interim U.S. marshal and in helping resupply horses to Johnston in the winter of 1857–58. *ASP1*, 36, 390, 447, 450, 457. A Virginian, Ficklin was a suspect in the Lincoln assassination, was a blockade runner, and ran mail contracts in Texas after the war.

63. Young to Hooper, Washington, D.C., December 20, 1860, BYLC, CR 1234 1, box 5, vol. 5, p. 652, image 730.

64. Young to Hooper, February 7, 1861, BYLC, CR 1234 1, box 5, vol. 5, p. 689, image 767. Paid at $250 per mile, construction through Nebraska was immensely profitable, for costs were only $67 per mile. Dick, *Story of the Frontier*, 306.

65. One-half the salary was paid in advance, the remainder on reaching Utah. MPOT, Narrative of the Edward Creighton Company, 1861.

66. "Affairs in Utah," *NYT*, July 8, 1861.

67. Young to Maughan, July 12, 1861, BYLC, CR 1234 1, box 5, vol. 5, p. 829, image 907.

68. "Affairs in Utah," *NYT*, July 26, 1861.

69. "Pony Express, Letter from Salt Lake," *Sacramento Daily Union*, August 29, 1861, 3/6.

70. Young to Wade, October 18, 1861, BYLC, CR 1234 1, box 5, vol. 5, p. 903, image 983.

71. CR 100 102, vol. 31, reel 14, box 14, p. 460, image 474. Lincoln returned a reciprocal congratulation.

72. Quinn, *Mormon Hierarchy: Extensions*, 272.

73. Young to McAllister, October 19, 1861, BYLC, CR 1234 1, box 5, vol. 5, p. 906, image 987.

74. Browne, *Resources of the Pacific Slope*, 434.

75. Young to Carpentier, October 24, 1861, BYLC, CR 1234 1, box 5, vol. 5, p. 909, image 991.

76. Browne, *Resources of the Pacific Slope*, 439–40.

77. Young to Hooper, January 24, 1861, BYLC, CR 1234 1, box 5, vol. 5, p. 677, image 755.

78. Sandburg, *Storm*, 35.

79. CR 100 102, vol. 31, reel 14, box 14, p. 106, image 120.

80. Canning and Beeton, *Genteel Gentile*, 92, 99 (underlining in the original).

81. MS 1322, LDS_CHL, George A. Smith Papers, Outgoing, March 11, 1861, image 9.

82. Young to Lyman, Rich, and Cannon, April 18, 1861, BYLC, CR 1234 1, box 5, vol. 5, p. 764, image 837s.

83. Wells to Joseph W. Young, April 22, 1861, BYLC, CR 1234 1, box 5, vol. 5, p. 787, image 861s.

84. Jenson, *Church Chronology*, 65.

85. "Departure of the Governor," *DN*, May 22, 1861, 8/2.

86. "Departure of the Governor," CR 100 102, vol. 31, reel 14, box 14, pp. 205–206, images 219–20.

87. Cumming is sometimes confused with his nephew of the identical name (1829–1910), who served with the Augusta Volunteer Battalion, the First and Tenth Georgia Regiments. *Antietam on the Web*, http://antietam.aotw.org/officers .php?officer_id=26.

88. Young, the Bowery, July 7, 1861, *CDBY*, 3:1882.

89. Young to Hooper, April 25, 1861, BYLC, CR 1234 1, box 5, vol. 5, p. 773, image 846s (italics added).

90. Young, January 14, 1861, *CDBY*, 3:1728.

91. Young, February 10, 1861, *CDBY*, 3:1775. In his fourth annual message, Buchanan said: "I reiterate the recommendation contained in my annual message of December 1858 and repeated in that of December 1859, in favor of acquisition of Cuba from Spain *by fair purchase*." Buchanan, *Works*, 11:29.

92. Davis and Wilson, *Lincoln-Douglas Debates*, 98.

93. Young to Kane, September 21, 1861, BYLC, CR 1234 1, box 5, vol. 5, p. 887, image 966.

94. CR 1234 1, Journal D, September 30, 1858–June 18, 1863, reel 84, box 72, folder 5, p. 294, image 292.

95. "Affairs in Utah," *NYT*, July 22, 1861.

96. "Affairs in Utah," *NYT*, July 16, 1861.

97. "Affairs in Utah," *NYT*, August 2, 1861.

98. MPOT, Trail Excerpt: John Frantzen, The Journal of John Frantzen 1837–1905, 21–24.

99. Utley, review of *Indians and Emigrants*, 228.

100. Bagley and Grunder, "Phebe Ann Woolley Davis."

101. Dick, *Story of the Frontier*, 347.

102. Young to Hooper, December 20, 1860, BYLC, CR 1234 1, box 5, vol. 5, p. 652, image 730s. Young reported a total of twenty-nine wagons in the 1860 season. Circular to Bishops, BYLC, box 5, vol. 5, p. 695, image 772s.

103. Young to Benson, February 4, 1861, BYLC, CR 1234 1, box 5, vol. 5, p. 687, image 765.

104. Hartley, "Latter-day Saint Emigration," 245.

105. Utah teamsters favored Chicago wagons built by Peter Schuttler because they were "of the best thoroughly seasoned material and workmanship." Young to Hooper, January 31, 1861, BYLC, box 5, vol. 5, p. 683, image 761s.

106. Young to Elders Nathaniel V. Jones and Jacob Gates, December 20, 1860, BYLC, box 5, vol. 5, p. 650, image 728. Gates and Jones were supervising emigration for the summer of 1861, working with Cannon and others in Liverpool.

107. Of the Perpetual Emigrating Fund, one Saint recorded, "When you came with the Church Trains you had to pay a certain amount for food and transportation, or pay what you could when you started and the rest as soon after you got there, with interest, until paid." MPOT, Joseph Horne Company, Trail Excerpt: Sarah Bethula Palmer Sharp, Autobiographical Sketch, 1931, 5. Another emigrant noted: "At the foot of the Little Mountain, Elder A. Milton Musser and others as agents of the Church met us and took promissory notes of those indebted for amounts due for their emigration." At Florence, additional charges were levied for excess baggage. MPOT, Joseph Horne Company, Trail Excerpt: Journal History of the Church, September 13, 1861, 1b–1h.

108. Young to Cannon, May 9, 1861, BYLC, box 5, vol. 5, p. 785, image 859s.

109. First Presidency's "Instructions," April 15, 1861, BYLC, box 5, vol. 5, p. 759, image 832s.

110. Young and Wells to Joseph W. Young, April 29, 1861, BYLC, CR 1234 1, box 5, vol. 5, p. 774, image 847. Copies also went to the other captains. Candidates for message carrier would include Orrin P. Rockwell, William A, Hickman, and Howard Egan.

111. Ibid. (underlining in the original).

112. MPOT, Thomas, Edward P., Autobiography, Trail Excerpt: Job Pingree Company, 1861.

113. MPOT, Homer Duncan Company, David John, Journal, 1856–1908, reel 1, 1:253–64; MPOT, Joseph Horne Company, Eliza Seamons England, Trail Excerpt: "Pioneer Sketch, in Daughters of Utah Pioneers, Salt Lake City, Utah, Scrapbooks.

114. MPOT, Joseph Horne Company, Trail Excerpt: Mary Hebden Holroyd Thomas, Sketch of the Life of Dinah Williams Holroyd, 1921, 4–5.

115. MPOT, Sixtus E. Johnson Company, Trail Excerpt: Seth E. [Guernsey] Johnson, Autobiographical Sketch [ca. 1922], [13]–16. Another sibling, Nephi Johnson, participated in the massacre at Mountain Meadows.

116. "News from Home," *Mill. Star*, October 12, 1861, 23:662–63.

117. "Arrival of Immigrant Companies," *DN*, September 18, 1861, 4/3.

118. "Arrived from the Plains," *DN*, September 25, 1861, 4/3.

119. Young to Bishop Andrew Moffitt, Manti, Utah Terr., July 18, 1861, BYLC, CR 1234 1, box 5, vol. 5, pp. 834–35, images 912s–13; "Last Emigrant Company," *DN*, October 2, 1861, 4/2.

120. Calculations made from MPOT, Chronological Company List, https://history.lds.org/overlandtravels/companydatelist.

121. The Department of the Pacific, formed by the merging of the Departments of California and Oregon, was placed under Johnston's command on January 15, 1861. Command passed to Brig. Gen. Edwin V. Sumner on April 23, 1861. "A New Nomen for Camp Floyd," *DN*, February 13, 1861, 4/2. Following his resignation, Johnston wended his way south and became the ranking officer of the Confederacy at the Battle of Shiloh.

122. In August 1860 the total complement was 320 men—18 officers and 302 enlisted men. Mathis, "Camp Floyd in Retrospect," cited in T. G. Alexander and Arrington, "Camp in the Sagebrush," 19.

123. "The Army and the Crisis," *DN*, February 20, 1861, 4/1. The abbreviation "inst." stands for *instante mense*, meaning "this month."

124. Woodruff to G. A. Smith, February 20, 1861, CR 100 102, vol. 31, reel 14, box 14, p. 89, image 102.

125. "The Army and the Crisis," *DN*, February 20, 1861, 4/1 (italics added).

126. T. G. Alexander and Arrington, "Camp in the Sagebrush," 16. Alexander notes that eight hundred of the mules were sold to Young's friend Ben Holladay.

127. "The Sale at Fort Crittenden," *DN*, March 27, 1861, 4/2. Nixon, a thirty-two-year-old polygamist, advertised in the *Mountaineer* as also doing business in Salt Lake City and Fairfield. "Latest Importations," *Mountaineer*, April 27, 1861, 4/5.

128. Advertisement, *DN*, April 3, 1861, 8/3.

129. Young to Pratt, New York City, July 13, 1861, BYLC, CR 1234 1, box 5, vol. 5, p. 827, image 905s.

130. Young to Clawson, Calder, and Caine, July 18, 1861, BYLC, CR 1234 1, box 5, vol. 5, p. 833, image 911.

131. Young to Andrew Moffitt, July 16, 1861, BYLC, CR 1234 1, box 5, vol. 5, p. 834, image 912.

132. Wells to Lewis Robison, July 16, 1861. BYLC, CR 1234 1, box 5, vol. 5, p. 835, image 913.

133. T. G. Alexander and Arrington, "Camp in the Sagebrush," 18.

134. William Laud, *Diary*, 6, Manuscript Section, Church Historian's Office, cited in Moorman and Sessions, *Camp Floyd*, 260.

135. Young to Evelith, July 23, 1861, BYLC, CR 1234 1, box 5, vol. 5, p. 840, image 918.

136. Affidavit, George Goddard, August 30, 1861, CR 100 102, vol. 31, reel 14, box 14, pp. 379–80, images 393–94.

137. Young to Clawson, July 26, 1861, BYLC, CR 1234 1, box 5, vol. 5, p. 845, image 923.

138. Young to Evelith, July 23, 1861, BYLC, CR 1234 1, box 5, vol. 5, p. 840, image 918.

139. U.S. Senate, "Volunteer Troops," 7. Colonel E. D. Waite was named as commander of the department at Salt Lake City but declined the post for reasons of health.

140. Young to Hooper, Washington, D.C., January 3, 1861, BYLC, CR 1234 1, box 5, vol. 5, p. 666, image 744.

141. As early as August, eastbound troops were met by the Mormon emigrant trains coming west. MPOT, David H. Cannon Company, Trail Excerpt: Bartlett Tripp Journal, 1861 May–Aug., 1–25.

142. Wells to West, August 2, 1861, BYLC, CR 1234 1, box 5, vol. 5, pp. 857–59, images 935s–37 (italics added).

143. Dickson, "Protecting the Home Front," 155.

144. Ibid., 143–59; Ephraim D. Dickson III, pers. comm., August 2012. Aaron Johnson of Springville, Utah, is the polygamist, bishop, and Legion general implicated in the Parrish-Potter murders and other bloodletting in the 1857 period.

145. Johnson in Springville, Utah, to Col. Wm. B. Pace, in Provo, Special Order No. 1, dated September 2, 1861, USHS, Ser. No. 1622, Third District Court files, Case No. 44825.

146. Burton to Smith, MSA 384A, 685, Utah Territorial Records, USHS.

147. The other military districts were Peteetneet, Davis, Tooele, San Pete, Iron, Pauvan, Juab, Box Elder, Richland, Wasatch, Summit, and Piute. Ephraim D. Dickson III, pers. comm., August 2012.

148. Dickson, "Protecting the Home Front," 144.

149. "Remarks by Pres. Daniel H. Wells," September 10, 1861, published in *DN*, December 18, 1861, 1/1.

150. "Passing Events," *DN*, January 2, 1861, 4/1.

151. "Remarks of President Brigham Young," April 6, 1861, published in *DN*, May 1, 1861, 1/2–2/1.

152. "Remarks of President Heber C. Kimball," April 6, 1861, published in *DN*, May 1, 1861, 1/1 (italics added).

153. "Pony Express from St. Louis," *Alta California* (San Francisco), June 11, 1861, 1/3 (italics added).

154. "Effect of Secession in England," *London Times*, February 22, 1861, reprinted in *DN*, March 6, 1861, 3/2.

155. In 1847, Rockwood was among the first body of Saints to enter the Salt Lake Valley; he served in the territorial legislature, as warden of the territorial penitentiary, and wrote an account of its history. Dickson, "Protecting the Home Front," 146.

156. February 26, 1861, CR 100 102, vol. 31, reel 14, box 14, pp. 89–91, images 103–105.

157. "Eastern News by Telegraph and Pony," *DN*, May 1, 1861, 2/2.

158. "Remarks of Hon. Stephen A. Douglas," *Plain Dealer* (Cleveland), June 26, 1857, 2/2.

159. "Squatter Sovereignty Abandoned by Its Father," *National Era*, July 16, 1857,

http://segonku.unl.edu/~brogers/utahexpedition/sources/national-era16071857.html.

160. "Utah" to Douglas, May 2, 1861, BYLC, CR 1234 1, box 5, vol. 5, p. 783, image 857.

161. "History of Joseph Smith," *DN*, September 24, 1856, 1/1.

162. Brigham Young Office Journal, June 12, 1861, cited in *TSTU*, 16.

163. Brigham Young Office Journal, August 5, 1861, cited in *TSTU*, 17. "Abel" is not a spelling error.

164. "Affairs in Utah," *NYT*, July 8,1861.

165. Brigham Young Office Journal, August 27, 1861, cited in *TSTU*, 37.

166. "Peace! Peace!" *Mill. Star*, August 10, 1861, 23:504. A simoom is a cyclonic dust storm, of low humidity and high temperature.

167. Detzer, *Donnybrook*, 488.

168. Rawley, *Turning Points*, 56–57.

169. U.S. Senate, "Volunteer Troops," 9–10.

3. Lies When Truth Is Precious, 1861–1862

1. Bagley, "Terror to Evil-Doers," 322.

2. The 1860 Salt Lake County census reports a total of thirty slaves. Hooper's household held two black males; Major Smoot's household also lists two black males. Albina held one black female, as did "Percilla" Williams.

3. Also spelled as "Haun's," but "Hawn's" is correct and preferred. Michael Marquardt, pers. comm., August 2013.

4. "Murders on the Mohave," *SDU*, April 2, 1860, 2/5. Williams was warned in May 1852 by Mormon trail-tough Return Jackson Redden to paint the horns of his cattle in order to protect them from *white* "Indians" raiding near Carson Valley. Redden identified the raiders as Mormons. *MR*, 56–57, 57n12.

5. O'Donovan, "Orphan Child," 94. Mogridge had previously been married to William Smith, brother of Joseph the prophet, and to Samuel Lowry. The wives of William's two 1851 marriages, Lydia Phelps and Lucy Ann Thomas, were no longer in the house. Phelps had remarried, and Thomas, as O'Donovan notes, disappeared from history.

6. "Murders on the Mohave," *SDU*, April 2, 1860, 2/5.

7. Astill to Farr, April 3, 1860, MS 14660, LDS_CHL; O'Donovan, "Orphan Child," 95–97.

8. At this hearing, Thomas's brother denied belief of Mormon involvement. William Williams, May 31, 1890, Statement to J. H. Hill. Thomas S. Williams Mexican War Pension, Affidavit, Albina M. Williams, July 30, 1889, Deposition A to Special Examiner E. W. Hart, Case of Albina M. Williams, No. 2674, microfilm 480149, LDS_CHL.

9. Hooper to Smith, May 21, 1860, CR 100 102, vol. 30, p. 138, image 156.

10. Hooper's 1860 household also included Eliza Humphrey, age seventeen, domestic, born in Africa; her race is apparently white. 1860 federal census.

11. Flenniken, previously appointed by Buchanan to replace Cradlebaugh, was reappointed; Crosby was also a reappointment. John Fitch Kinney had been named chief justice for the second time in June 1860.

12. Young to Bernhisel, December 30, 1861, BYLC, CR 1234 1, box 6, vol. 6, pp. 78–79, images 109–10.

13. Bernhisel to Young, January 24, 1862, CR 1234 1, reel 71, box 61, folder 5. Two years later, when John Dawson spoke against William Mitchell's 1862 Indiana reelection, one editor asked sarcastically, "Didn't Billy [Mitchell] get Johnny [Dawson] the office of Governor of Utah to stop his mouth?" *Elkhart Review*, April 5, 1862.

14. No evidence has been found that any official contacted by Bernhisel attempted to verify the allegations.

15. Caleb Blood Smith became acquainted with Lincoln while in Congress in the 1840s. Smith's appointment as Interior secretary was part of a bargain for Indiana's support of Lincoln. Emma Lou Thornbrough claims that Lincoln "had little enthusiasm for Smith, who soon resigned for a federal judgeship." Thornbrough, *Indiana in the Civil War Era*, 109–10, 109n42.

16. "On Whigs and Americanism of Indiana," *Cleveland Morning Leader*, May 29, 1860, 2/2; Neely, "President Lincoln," 2.

17. Potterf, "John W. Dawson," 1, 3, 4–7. No charge of indecency has been found; in July 1857, Dawson was charged in the Court of Common Pleas with assault and battery, apparently in a dispute with Turner. Allen County, Ind., Court of Common Pleas, v. C, 123, 127.

18. Dawson, *Charcoal Sketches*, foreword.

19. Potterf, "John W. Dawson," 11–13.

20. Tullidge, *History of Salt Lake City*, 249.

21. Bancroft, *History of Utah*, 604.

22. Linn, *Story of the Mormons*, 919.

23. O. F. Whitney, *History of Utah*, 2:37–38.

24. Cowley, *Wilford Woodruff*, 649.

25. Neff, *History of Utah*, 648–49.

26. Carman and Luthin, *Lincoln and the Patronage*, 108.

27. Morgan, *Great Salt Lake*, 272.

28. Colton, *Civil War in the Western Territories*, 183.

29. Furniss, *Mormon Conflict*, 232.

30. Neely, "President Lincoln," 1644:2.

31. Mary Jane Woodger, "Abraham Lincoln and the Mormons," in Alford, *Civil War Saints*, 53.

32. One example: "Governor Dawson of Utah in Trouble, a Woman Involved," *Cincinnati Daily Press*, January 29, 1862, was a front-page reprint from the *Deseret News*. Potterf, "John W. Dawson," 6.

33. Neely, "President Lincoln," 2; "Letter from Salt Lake: Our New Governor," *SDU*, November 12, 1861, 1/6.

34. "Federal Officials for Utah," *Rocky Mountain News* (Denver, Colo.), December 21, 1861.

35. Letters Received, U.S. Department of the Interior, Office of Indian Affairs, RG 75, NAB, cited in *TSTU*, 54. Dawson also included his view that the Indians were "substantially under the influence of the Mormons."

36. Potter pushed for congressional bills extending the railroad westward, for he knew of Doty's financial interest in railroad construction. *JDD*, 364–65.

37. "Federal Officials," *DN*, October 23, 1861, 5/1 (italics added).

38. From Milwaukee, Martin may have written to Wisconsin representative John Fox Potter or to James R. Doolittle, also from Wisconsin, who was chair of the Senate Committee on Indian Affairs.

39. Martin's information was reprinted elsewhere, as "The Mormons Contemplate Independence," *SFB*, October 10, 1861, 1/3. Young sent a "called" group of two hundred men to the Uinta Valley for settlement, but they reported it to be "misrepresented and . . . not adapted to sustain large settlements." CR 100 137, vol. 55, reels 18–19, image 200. The *Deseret News* described Uinta Valley as "one vast 'contiguity of waste,' . . . valueless, excepting for nomadic purposes, hunting grounds for Indians." "Uinta Not What Was Represented," *DN*, September 25, 1861, 4/3.

40. U.S. Office of Indian Affairs, *Report, 1861*, cited in G. O. Larson, "Uintah Dream," 361–62. On October 3, Lincoln made more than two million acres an Indian reservation, as Martin and Davis had suggested.

41. "Affairs in Utah: . . . The Superintendent of Indian Affairs in Trouble," written October 17, published in *NYT*, November 3, 1861.

42. "Interesting Communications," *DN*, October 23, 1861, 8/1.

43. Handwritten item, Henry Martin, October 14, 1861, CR 1234 1, reel 62, box 49, folder 4.

44. "Letter from Salt Lake: Our New Governor," *SDU*, November 12, 1861, 1/6. Doty wired Washington that his predecessor was a secessionist, referring not to Martin but to Benjamin Davis, who was present in Utah when Confederate spy Walter M. Gibson was socializing with Mormon leadership.

45. Anonymous, *Minutes of the Apostles*, 318. It was only six months earlier that the Bear River area had been made safe by Connor's battle with the Northern Shoshonis.

46. "Affairs in Utah," written December 7, published in *NYT*, December 28, 1861. Born in Virginia, Anderson was thirty-six, unmarried, and living in the Thirteenth Ward. He married in 1862, had at least five children, and became prosperous in Salt Lake City.

47. *Winona (Minn.) Argus*, April 25, 1855, 2, 3. The 1860 census lists Chambers, his wife, Marie, and his daughter, Florence, in Winona, Winona County, Minn. O. F. Whitney, *History of Utah*, 2:660; "Surgeons and Physicians," *DN*, October 2, 1861, 8/4.

48. "Governor's Message," *DN*, written December 10, published December 18, 1861, 5/1–6/1. Approximately 210,000 Indiana men served in the Civil War, and millions of dollars in equipment and supplies were contributed to the Union by Indiana's citizens.

49. "The Governor's Message, *DN*, December 18, 1861, 4/3. Bernhisel's pleas for appointees from Utah residents resulted in Jesse C. Little's appointment as Assessor, and Robert T. Burton as Collector of Internal Revenue. Neff, *History of Utah*, 652.

50. Young's report to Woodruff, December 10, 1861, CR 100 102, vol. 31, reel 14, box 14, p. 530, image 544. This is another instance of violation of the telegraph.

51. CR 100 102, vol. 31, reel 14, box 14, p. 534, image 548.

52. His letter appeared January 8, 1862, in the *Weekly Times and Union*. Neely, "President Lincoln," 4.

53. CR 100 102, vol. 31, reel 14, box 14, p. 536, image 549 (italics added).

54. Turner, *Brigham Young*, 320.

55. *DN*, October 14, 1861, reprinted as "The 'Amende Honourable,'" *Mill. Star*, December 21, 1861, 23:814–16.

56. Young argued Utah's territorial laws could remain "in force until so disapproved by Congress." "The Voice of the People," *DN*, January 8, 1862, 4/2. In 1866, Chief Justice John Titus documented that Utah's territorial laws had never been submitted to Congress at any time prior to 1861. "Legal Ruling," *DN*, October 24, 1866, 5/1.

57. December 23, 1861, BYLC, CR 1234 1, box 6, vol. 6, pp. 70–75, images 101s–106s.

58. December 21, 1861, CR 100 102, vol. 31, reel 14, box 14, p. 545, image 559. Unsuccessful attempts to memorialize a constitutional convention were made in 1852, 1853, 1854, and 1856. Morgan, *State of Deseret*, 92–93.

59. *MR*, 89.

60. "Remarks of Brigham Young," written January 19, published in *DN*, February 19, 1862, 1/1.

61. Young to G. A. Smith, Bernhisel and Taylor, August 30, 1856, cited in *MR*, 89n40.

62. "Meeting at Santaquin," *DN*, January 15, 1862, 2/3.

63. CR 1234 1, Federal and Local Government Files, 1844–76, reel 62, box 49, folder 5, image 2.

64. Ibid., images 3–5. Two different draft versions are found in images 8–11.

65. John T. Caine, a well-known faithful Mormon and Young's frequent scribe, would later represent Utah in Congress for more than nine years.

66. Potterf, "John W. Dawson," 8.

67. In the 1860 census the children were Ephraim, Phebe, Manassah, Mary, Thomas, and Francis (Frank), ages fifteen, thirteen, nine, six, five, and one. Priscilla is listed only in the slave section, and Norma was yet unborn.

68. Daughter Norma was born on November 15, 1860, and died on November 18, 1868.

69. December 22, 1861, CR 100 102, vol. 31, reel 14, box 14, p. 563, image 577.

70. December 24, 1861, CR 100 102, vol. 31, reel 14, box 14, p. 567, image 581.

71. December 30, 1861, BYLC, CR 1234 1, box 6, vol. 6, p. 79, image 110.

72. "The Last Sensation," *DN*, December 25, 1861, 4/4.

73. Dawson to C. B. Smith, December 26, 1861, Robert Todd Lincoln Collection, MS A 32, USHS.

74. "Departure of the Governor," December 31, 1861, CR 100 102, vol. 31, pp. 582–85, images 596–99. Judge Crosby was accused of delaying his departure for want of funds for the passage of a female companion, Mrs. Leo Hawkins.

75. "Reports," December 30, 1861, CR 100 102, vol. 31, reel 14, box 14, p. 576, image 590. The 1860 census lists Lydia Katz as age seventeen and the daughter of Mormon parents, carpenter Michael Katz and his wife. Catherine, with six other children, all living in the Nineteenth Ward.

76. "Governor Dawson's Statement," written at Bear River Station, January 7, published in *DN*, January 22, 1862, 2/4.

77. "Departure of the Governor," *DN*, January 1, 1862, 4/2.

78. Firmage and Mangrum, *Zion in the Courts*, 217; *MR*, 41; Cannon, "'Mountain Common Law,'" 308–27.

79. December 31, 1861, CR 100 102, vol. 31, reel 14, box 14, p. 582, image 596.

80. "Governor Dawson's Statement," *DN*, January 22, 1862, 2/4. Dawson was certainly unaware that Hanks had "recently helped an LDS policeman slit a young thief's throat, 'from ear to ear.'" Richard K. Hanks, "Eph Hanks: Pioneer Scout," MA thesis, Brigham Young University, 100, cited in Quinn, *Mormon Hierarchy: Extensions*, 549.

81. Ephraim Knowlton Hanks served three years at sea on the U.S. man-of-war *Columbus*, was a hunter for Company B of the Mormon Battalion, a legendary

figure of the plains, an Indian fighter, and a tavern owner at the Mountain Dell Station. Bigler and Bagley, *Army of Israel*, 152n25.

82. "Disgraceful Outrage," *DN*, January 8, 1862, 5/4; "Governor Dawson's Statement," *DN*, January 22, 1862, 2/4. Reynolds allegedly was in a relationship with Albina's daughter. Historian Harold Schindler blames Lot Huntington for stealing eight hundred dollars in a metal box at the stage station. Schindler, *Orrin Porter Rockwell*, 316.

83. CR 100 1, vol. 26, box 3, p. 36, image 42.

84. "Governor Dawson's Statement," *DN*, January 22, 1862, 2/4. Several of the attackers met violent ends. O. P. Rockwell's eight shots to the stomach ended Lot Huntington's alleged escape west of Camp Crittenden on January 16. The next day, the alleged escape of Moroni Clawson and J. P. Smith was foiled when officers "put their revolvers to the back of their heads and 'stopped them.'" Stenhouse, *Rocky Mountain Saints*, 592n. William Hickman corroborated: "They were both powder-burnt." When Hickman paid Jason Luce's bail, Luce said that "he was called on by Bob Golden who was captain of police, to give the Governor a good beating" and that "Golden said he had his instructions what to be done." Hickman, *Brigham's Destroying Angel*, 149. Unanswered is whether the killings of Clawson, J. P. Smith, and Huntington were carried out to achieve extralegal justice, to erase all witnesses who knew whether orders for the criminal attack had come from the LDS priesthood, or to avoid embarrassment to the cause of Utah's statehood, or some combination of these.

85. Handwritten letters, Dawson to Lincoln, Robert Todd Lincoln Collection, Papers of Abraham Lincoln, MS 8190 8, LDS_CHL.

86. Record of the Bureau of Indian Affairs, Utah Supremacy, RG 75.15.13, M834, NAB.

87. Bernhisel to Smith, January 31, 1862, images 3–4, George A. Smith Papers, MS 1322, LDS_CHL.

88. Beating, castration, and lynching continuing well into the twentieth century, with the largest numbers occurring in Mississippi and Georgia.

89. Historian Michael Quinn states that, for at least a decade after 1847, murder, castration, and beheading were punishments imposed on Mormon men and women for sexual misconduct. Quinn, *Mormon Hierarchy: Extensions*, 241–61; Quinn, "Culture of Violence," 16–28.

90. Dawson to Dole, February 27, 1862, Record of the Bureau of Indian Affairs, Utah Supremacy, RG 75.15.13, M834, NAB.

91. Cannon to Young, January 29, 1874, CR 1234 1, reel 52, box 38, folder 18.

92. Griswold, *Pictorial History of Fort Wayne*, 1:341 (italics added).

93. Dawson, *Charcoal Sketches*, 9 (italics added).

94. Potterf, "John W. Dawson," 9–10 (italics added).

95. "Dust to Dust: Brief Biographical Sketch of the Late Hon. John W. Dawson," *Fort Wayne (Ind.) Morning Gazette*, September 11, 1877, in Obituaries

for John W. Dawson, MSS A 5701, Manuscript Collections, Utah State Historical Library. Late in life, Dawson wrote essays on Johnny (Chapman) Appleseed, considered by several historians as the most important source of information about that important and eccentric character.

96. Potterf, "John W. Dawson," 11; "Dust to Dust."

97. Knecht and Crawley, *History of Brigham Young,* 325 (italics added).

98. Report in Dawson's *Weekly Times and Union,* January 29, 1862, cited in Neely, "President Lincoln," 2.

99. Joseph Silver's wife, Emma Temple Silver, was run over by a wagon on August 4, 1861, as they traveled in the Milo Andrus Company. Joseph remained at Cold Springs, hoping for her recovery from arm, leg, and chest injuries. "Accident to and Detention of an Emigrant," *DN,* January 1, 1862, 8/2. A machinist, he later helped build a paper manufacturing plant.

100. Silver to Young, January 27, 1862, CR 1234 1, reel 40, box 29, folder 5.

101. Chambers to Lincoln, February 19, 1862, OCLS No. 17870, Lincoln Financial Foundation Collection, Allen County Public Library, Fort Wayne, Ind. (underlining in the original).

102. *Winona (Minn.) Daily Republican,* July 20, 1867, 3; *Winona Republican Herald,* October 15, 1932, 3.

103. Bernhisel to Young, January 24, 1862, CR 1234 1, Utah Delegate Files, reel 71, box 61, folder 5, image 21.

104. Bernhisel to Young, January 3, 1862, CR 1234 1, Utah Delegate Files, reel 71, box 61, folder 5, image 2.

105. "Utah Applying," *NYT,* January 9, 1862. As attorney general for Utah Territory, Stout never defended the United States in court. Court substitutes sometimes appeared but often did not. Brooks, *On the Mormon Frontier,* 713–14.

106. Bernhisel to Young, January 10, 1862, CR 1234 1, Utah Delegate Files, reel 71, box 61, folder 5, images 11–12.

107. Bernhisel to Young, January 24, 1862, CR 1234 1, Utah Delegate Files, reel 71, box 61, folder 5, image 20.

108. Stenhouse, *Rocky Mountain Saints,* 592.

109. "Letters from Old Albums, Frank Fuller, Secy. of Utah in the 60s," *Deseret Evening News,* July 29, 1916, 3/4.

110. Waite, *Mormon Prophet,* 123–24. Charles B. Waite and Catherine Van Valkenburg were married on April 26, 1854, in Lee County, Iowa.

111. "Local and Other Matters," *DN,* March 20, 1872, 8/1.

112. Fuller to Young, December 5, 1871, CR 1234 1, reel 46, box 34, folder 4; Fuller to Young, March 30, May 1, and May 16, 1872, CR 1234 1, reel 47, box 34, folder 12.

113. "Life among the Mormons," *SFB,* October 8, 1861, 1/1.

114. Rémy, *A Journey to Great-Salt-Lake City,* cited in Homer, *On the Way to Somewhere Else,* 74.

115. *FK*, 91.

116. O. F Whitney, *History of Utah*, 4:668–71.

117. CR 1234 1, President's Office Journals 1852–63, Journals August 8, 1858–June 18, 1863, reel 84, box 72, folder 5, p. 220, image 218.

118. Waite, *Mormon Prophet*, 40, 89.

119. Waite describes Steptoe's entrapment by Brigham Young, using the wives of two Mormon men absent on missions. Waite, *Mormon Prophet*, 36, 86.

120. Handwritten, Dawson to Lincoln, January 13, 1862, Robert Todd Lincoln Collection, MS A 32, USHS.

121. Bernhisel to Young, January 17, 1862, CR 1234 1, reel 71, box 61, folder 5, image 13.

4. Disloyalty amid Peace and Prosperity, 1862

Epigraph. "The New Mormon Complication," *New York Post*, April 30, 1862, republished in *Richmond (Va.) Daily Dispatch*, May 28, 1862, 4/1; in *Charleston (S.C.) Mercury*, May 31, 1862, 1/4; and in others.

1. Young to Bernhisel, January 14, 1862, BYLC, CR 1234 1, box 6, vol. 6, pp. 107–108, images 137s–38.

2. Young to Bernhisel, January 14, 1862, BYLC, CR 1234 1, box 6, vol. 6, p. 105, image 136. Golding, a militia sergeant, had been with Burton's unit guarding Hooper and Chauncey West on their April 1862 journey east.

3. Bernhisel to Young, February 7, 1862, CR 1234 1, reel 71, box 61, folder 5. At Cumming's request, Bernhisel sent him a copy of an affidavit regarding Albina Williams and several *Deseret News* articles relating to its contents.

4. "Affairs in Utah: The Judgeship, Etc.," written February 27, published in *NYT*, March 22, 1862.

5. "Remarks," by Young, January 19, 1862, published in *DN*, February 19, 1862, 1/1. "Cleanse the inside of the platter" that meant Mormon transgressors should suffer death before those outside the faith.

6. Saunders, *Dale Morgan*, 1:78.

7. "Affairs in Utah," written March 5, published in *NYT*, April 6, 1862.

8. "State of Deseret: First General Election," *DN*, February 26, 1862, 4/1. The Mormon concept of "unity" finds expression in the tactic of offering only single candidates. In 1840 John Taylor said "the church of Christ" was not "divided into sections." He continued: "The Holy Spirit did not inspire one party with one opinion and another party with another opinion; God was not the author of confusion; there was one God, one faith, and one baptism." *Mill. Star*, November 1840, 1:179.

9. *CDBY*, 4:1935.

10. "Speech of Hon. John F. Kinney," delivered January 22, published in *DN*, February 5, 1862, 2/1.

11. Doty to Wells, January 20, published in *Mill. Star*, April 19, 1862, 24:244.

12. "The Utah Indian Superintendency," *DN*, December 18, 1861, 4/3.

13. "Affairs in Utah: State vs. Territory," written March 19, published *NYT*, May 4, 1862.

14. "The New Mormon Complication," *New York Post*, April 30, 1862, republished in *Richmond (Va.) Daily Dispatch*, May 28, 1862, 4/1; in *Charleston (S.C.) Mercury*, May 31, 1862, 1/4; and in others.

15. "Remarks, by President Brigham Young," delivered in the Bowery, July 6, published in *DN*, August 6, 1862, 1/1.

16. CR 1234 1, Journals 1832–77, President's Office Journals 1852–63, Journal August 8, 1858–June 18, 1863, reel 84, box 72, folder 5, p. 331, image 329.

17. *CDBY*, 4:1935, 1937–38. Steptoe was sent to investigate the death of Capt. John Gunnison, allegedly killed by Indians. President Franklin Pierce appointed Steptoe as Utah's governor in February 1855, but the colonel declined.

18. Ferguson Letters, 1855–56, MS 5183, LDS_CHL, cited in Bagley, "'Bright, Rising Star,'" 16. A basilisk is a legendary reptile, reputedly the king of serpents and able to kill with a single glance.

19. Young, January 19, 1862, *Journal of Discourses*, 9:157.

20. "Constitutional Convention," *DN*, January 29, 1862, 4/1 (italics added).

21. "Affairs in Utah," written January 30, published in *NYT*, February 27, 1862.

22. Pendleton to Smith, February 26, 1862, George A. Smith Papers, MS 1322, LDS_CHL.

23. *CDBY*, 4:1935.

24. *CDBY*, 4:1944.

25. "Injudicious Examples and Practices," *Mill. Star*, February 29, 1862, 24:136.

26. "The Great Mormon Movement," *Daily Oregonian* (Portland), March 10, 1862, 2/1.

27. Young to Bernhisel, January 4, 1862, BYLC, CR 1234 1, box 6, vol. 6, p. 87, image 118. Not until 1869 were these three requirements met for Utah Territory's land ownership. *GGSL*, 117–40.

28. "Affairs in Utah," *NYT*, January 11, 1862.

29. Smith to Cannon, February 17, published in *Mill. Star*, April 12, 1862, 24:236. Sims to Staines, February 24, 1862, CR 1234 1, reel 28, box 19, folder 20.

30. G. O. Larson, "Utah and the Civil War," 60n7; "Affairs in Utah," written January 23, published in *NYT*, February 16, 1862; "Affairs in Utah," written July 22, published in *NYT*, August 9, 1863.

31. "The Voice of the People," *DN*, January 8, 1862, 4/2. The five authors: Daniel Wells, William Hooper, John Taylor, George A. Smith, and Abraham O. Smoot.

32. French, "Stephen S. Harding" (thesis), 9.

33. Undated MS, cited in French, "Stephen S. Harding" (thesis), 10.

34. "Did Hoosier's Fake Dream Found Mormonism?" *Indianapolis Sunday Star*, April 23, 1911.

35. Harding to Pomeroy Tucker, February 1882, *EMD*, 3:155.

36. This title sheet was printed on June 26, 1829. Harding later gave the sheet to Mormon elder Robert Campbell, who placed it with the LDS Church records. Harding to Tucker, June 1, 1867, *EMD*, 3:83–84, 84n8, 164. Robert Lang Campbell was the Salt Lake City recorder and Brigham Young history office scribe when Harding arrived in Utah as governor.

37. Harding to Thomas Gregg, 1882, *EMD*, 3:160.

38. Harding to Pomeroy Tucker, February 1882, *EMD*, 3:160; "Did Hoosier's Fake Dream Found Mormonism?" *Indianapolis Sunday Star*, April 23, 1911. Slight differences in wording appear in the *Star*'s article—"I knew the Greek alphabet and the system of shorthand then in vogue and with these adjuncts I nearly filled up the page"—and the plates are described as golden.

39. *EMD*, 3:369–70, 369n19.

40. Harding to Pomeroy Tucker, February, 1882, *EMD*, 3:163. See also *A Biographical History of Eminent and Self-made Men*, 1:77–81.

41. Gregg, *Prophet of Palmyra*, 52.

42. French, "Stephen S. Harding" (thesis), 95–96, 107.

43. *Biographical History of Eminent and Self-made Men*, 77–81; French, "Stephen S. Harding" (thesis), 14–15.

44. Bernhisel to Young, March 14, 1862, CR 1234 1, reel 71, box 61, folder 5.

45. Senator Henry Smith Lane and soon-to-be Secretary of the Treasury Salmon P. Chase were probably also Harding supporters. Harding's appointment was approved by the Senate the same day that Dawson's was officially rejected. Bernhisel to Young, March 25, 1862, CR 1234 1, reel 71, box 61, folder 5.

46. Transcript, Harding to Julian, May 26, 1862, MS A 3182, USHS.

47. Typescript, S. S. Harding to his children, in care of Mr. and Mrs. Abe Yater, Osgood, Iowa, June 13, 1862, Harding-Lilly. Twenty-six years old at the time, Attila Leonidas Harding, or "Till," lived with his father and served as his personal clerk in Utah and subsequently in Colorado.

48. Harding may have been incorrect, for Bigler and Bagley note that Young paid Alfred Cumming "a visit of ceremony" shortly after his arrival. *MR*, 361, 361n62.

49. Typescript, Harding to "My Dear Wife and Children," July 9, 1862, Harding-Lilly (underlining and strikeout in the original).

50. Harding to Young, July 16, 1862, CR 1234 1, reel 39, box 28, folder 21.

51. G. A. Smith to Stout, July 30, 1862, cited in Tegeder, "Lincoln and the Territorial Patronage," 88.

52. Typescript, Harding to "My Dear Wife and Children," July 25, 1862, Harding-Lilly (underlining in the original). Harding refers to Lucy Ann Decker, age thirty-two, and Clarissa Caroline Decker, age thirty-four.

53. "Dear Son," August 6, 1865, MS A 3182, USHS.

54. Handwritten letter, Harding to Anastasia Harding, October 28, 1862, Stephen S. Harding Papers, MS B 29, box 1, folder 4, USHS.

55. "Remarks of President Brigham Young," *DN*, August 27, 1862, 1/1.

56. "Synopsis of a Discourse Delivered by President George Q. Cannon," September 10, published in *Mill. Star*, October 4, 1862, 24:626.

57. "A Discourse Delivered by President George Q. Cannon," delivered January 5, published *Mill. Star*, November 15, 1862, 24:725–26.

58. Orson Hyde, *Mill. Star*, May 18, 1862, 24:273.

59. Young to Cannon, January 7, 1862, BYLC, CR 1234 1, box 6, vol. 6, p. 91, image 122.

60. "The News," *DN*, February 12, 1862, 4/1.

61. Wright to Stanford, January 11, 1862, U.S. Senate, "Volunteer Troops," 44.

62. *TSTU*, 70–71. The bill ruled that persons in polygamy be found guilty of bigamy, with fines up to $500 and prison terms up to five years; all acts of the Utah legislature regarding polygamy were annulled, and the LDS Church could hold no more than $50,000 in real estate.

63. "Necessity of Protecting the Overland Route," *SFB*, June 25, 1861, 2/1.

64. "The Polygamy Question," *SFB*, June 4, 1862.

65. "Polygamy and a New Rebellion," *NYT*, June 19, 1862.

66. "Are We to Have Another Mormon War?" *SFB*, July 15, 1862, 2/3.

67. Bernhisel Papers, July 11, 1862, cited in *TSTU*, 74, 81n66.

68. "Affairs in Utah," *NYT*, written June 21, published July 16, 1861.

69. "Affairs in Utah," *NYT*, written December 19, 1861, published January 11, 1862.

70. "The New Theatre," *DN*, March 12, 1862, 2/1.

71. *DIU*, 7–8; Young to Cannon, Liverpool, March 11, 1862, BYLC, box 6, vol. 6, p. 161, image 193.

72. "Affairs in Utah," written March 27, published in *NYT*, April 29, 1862.

73. *DIU*, 29.

74. "Affairs in Utah," *NYT*, written October 16, published November 8, 1862.

75. *DIU*, 3–4, 10.

76. Young to Lyne, November 22, 1862, BYLC, CR 1234 1, box 6, vol. 6, p. 433, image 470.

77. "Affairs in Utah," written December 3, published in *NYT*, December 26, 1862.

78. *DIU*, 30.

79. *CDBY*, 4:1995.

80. "Progress of the War," *DN*, April 23, 1862, 5/1.

81. Bierce, "What I Saw of Shiloh," 10.

82. Young to G. Q. Cannon, Liverpool, April 12, 1862, BYLC, CR 1234 1, box 6, vol. 6, p. 201, image 237s.

83. "Remarks," *DN*, July 30, 1862, 1/2.

84. Monson, "The Priesthood in Action," *Ensign* 22, no. 11 (1992): 48.

85. Stack, "Mormons Warned against Baptizing Holocaust Victims," *USA Today*, March 5, 2012. LDS Church president Monson announced safeguards for access to online genealogical data and instructed members to proxy-baptize only their own direct ancestors.

86. Young to Bernhisel, Washington, April 14, 1862, BYLC, CR 1234 1, box 6, vol. 6, p. 205, image 241s (italics added).

87. Brooks, *Mountain Meadows Massacre*, 63; *MR*, 173–74.

88. Young to Bernhisel, Washington, April 15, 1862, BYLC, CR 1234 1, box 6, vol. 6, p. 206, image 242.

89. Doty to Dole, August 13, 1862, cited in Morgan, *Shoshonean Peoples*, 281.

90. Tullidge, *History of Salt Lake City*, 254.

91. Wells to Terry, April 24, 1862, BYLC, CR 1234 1, box 6, vol. 6, p. 219, image 255.

92. CR 1234 1, Journals 1832–77, President's Office Journals 1852–63, Journal August 8, 1858–June 18, 1863, reel 84, box 72, folder 5, p. 364, image 361.

93. Illegible (probably Wells) to Burton, April 24, 1862, BYLC, CR 1234 1, box 6, vol. 6, p. 220, image 256s; requisition of Wells, April 25, 1862, documenting Fuller's authorization, cited in Tullidge, *History of Salt Lake City*, 254.

94. Wells to Robinson, April 25, 1862, BYLC, CR 1234 1, box 6, vol. 6, p. 223, image 259.

95. Thomas, Adj. Gen., "Report on [Twelve] Measures Taken to Secure the Overland Mail Route to California," April 24, 1862, *WOR*, ser. 1, vol. 50, part 1, 1022–24.

96. Thomas to Young, April 28, 1862, *WOR*, ser. 3, vol. 2, 27 (italics added).

97. Young to Lot Smith, April 30, 1862, BYLC, CR 1234 1, box 6, vol. 6, p. 241, image 277.

98. "Requisition for Troops," *DN*, April 30, 1862, 3/1. Significant financial gain resulted from the Mormon Battalion's service during the Mexican War. Federal salary money, guns, munitions, and equipment were vital in the trek of the Mormon body to Utah. *FK*, 25n10.

99. Doty to Dole, August 13, 1862, cited in Morgan, *Shoshonean Peoples*, 280–81.

100. Hewett, *Roster of Union Soldiers*, "Utah Territory." Thirteen names are misspelled.

101. "Departure of the Company for the Protection of the Mail and Telegraph Lines," *DN*, May 7, 1862, 5/2.

102. "Affairs in Utah," written April 25, published in *NYT*, July 4, 1862. Don Quixote's decrepit mount was named Rosinantes; "Yeager" is a generic term for European hunting rifles, and Mississippis were probably Kentucky long-barreled, rifled guns.

103. "Captain Smith's Command," *DN*, May 14, 1862, 4/4.

104. "Latest from the Plains," telegram, Burton to Fuller, *DN*, May 21, 1862, 4/1.

105. "The Celebration of the Fourth of July," *DN*, July 23, 1862, 8/3.

106. Of the sixty-two names published in the *Deseret News*, only fifty-three were listed in Hewett's *Roster of Union Soldiers*. E. M. Weeler of the Hewett list is likely Mahlon Weiler, from the *News* list, and Elijah Malin Weiler by Alford's list. Alford, *Civil War Saints*, 527–28. Teamsters L. Barnard, Henry Bird, James Carrigan, R. Hereford, Mark Murphy, and A. Randall are not in Hewett's listing. R. P. Atwood's telegram of July 26 lists "50 men and pack animals," while Joseph S. Rawlings's telegram of July 30 lists forty-four men.

107. "The Expedition after the Indians," *DN*, August 13, 1862, 4/1.

108. Young to Cannon, Liverpool, August 6, 1862, BYLC, CR 1234 1, box 6, vol. 6, p. 345, image 382s.

109. "Return from the Road," *DN*, June 4, 1862, 8/1; Young to Young, Jr., Washington, D.C., June 5, 1862, BYLC, CR 1234 1, box 6, vol. 6, p. 267, image 304s. Acting Governor Fuller requested federal payment for the services of Burton et al., claiming they were called at his directive as acting governor. Young to Bernhisel, August 29, 1862, BYLC, CR 1234 1, box 6, vol. 6, p. 376, image 412s.

110. "The Expedition after Indians," *DN*, August 13, 1862, 4/1.

111. Stanton to Craig, August 24, 1862, *WOR*, ser. 1, vol. 13, 592. Craig had praised Lot Smith and his men as "the most efficient troops he had for the present service, and thought . . . of recommending President Lincoln to engage our services for three months longer." Lot Smith to Young, June 15, 1862, Tullidge, *History of Salt Lake City*, 257.

112. Craig to Halleck, August 25, 1862, *WOR*, ser. 1, vol. 13, 596.

113. Typescript, Harding to Seward, August 29, 1862, Harding-Lilly (underlining and strikeout in the original). The allusion here is to military officers acting on Lincoln's habeas corpus suspension.

114. Ibid.

115. Young to Thomas, August 25, 1862, CR 1234 1, Telegrams 1861–77, S–Y, 1862, reel 59, box 45, folder 25.

116. MacKinnon, "Utah's Civil War(s)," 304–305.

117. "Interview Extraordinary between the Governor of Utah and Brigham Young," *New York Tribune*, September 3, 1862, reprinted in *SFB*, October 21, 1862, 1/5.

118. Cannon to Young, April 4, 1862, CR 1234 1, reel 51, box 38, folder 9.

119. "To Presidents and Emigrating Saints," *Mill. Star*, February 22, 1862, 24:122–23.

120. Young to Eldredge, New York City, April 11, 1862, BYLC, CR 1234 1, box 6, vol. 6, p. 197, image 230s.

121. Clawson to Creighton, May 1862, BYLC, CR 1234 1, box 6, vol. 6, p. 246, image 282s.

122. Young to Cannon, June 5,1862, BYLC, CR 1234 1, box 6, vol. 6, p. 265, image 302s; Young to Eldredge, June 5, 1862, BYLC, CR 1234 1, box 6, vol. 6, p. 283, image 320s.

123. "Affairs in Utah," written May 15, published in *NYT*, July 3, 1862.

124. Young to Evelith, San Francisco, July 17, 1862, BYLC, CR 1234 1, box 6, vol. 6, p. 336, image 373. Trail excerpts do not reveal guns, gunpowder, or munitions in 1862; however, Young's telegram instructing John Ray Young to purchase twenty-two more wagons and teams and Hooper an additional three, to empty the church warehouse at Florence, raises that question. MPOT, Trail Excerpt: John R. Young Reminiscences, August 17, 1862, 1–2, and Letter, October 29, 1862. The departure point was not moved to Wyoming, Neb., until 1864.

125. Kirby, *Mormonism Exposed*, 292–93.

126. "Fatal Resistance to the Laws," *DN*, June 18, 1862, 4/1.

127. The American Psychiatric Association's *Diagnostic and Statistical Manual* provides terms and criteria for the classification of mental disorders.

128. *FK*, 210.

129. *SPV*, 5.

130. *JOMO*, 31–34.

131. *JOMO*, 2.

132. *JOMO*, 29.

133. Howard, "Men, Motives and Misunderstandings," 115.

134. *JOMO*, 30–42. Anderson thinks Young dismissed Morris's letters because of their disorganization, poor spelling, and bad grammar.

135. "The Re-organization of the Holy Priesthood," Revelation No. 5, September 6, 1860, in *SPV*, 17.

136. *SPV*, 669. Published in San Francisco in 1886 by George S. Dove, a disciple who survived Morris, this book records more than three hundred revelations and a number of prophecies Morris revealed during the period 1857 to June 1862.

137. In one account, Morris escaped death at the hands of a group led by Chauncey West in November 1860 only because their hunt was been interrupted by a severe storm that threatened the roof of the tithing house. Holley, "Slouching," 252; "Morrisite War," *UV*, July 14, 1867, 2/4.

138. Hickman, *Brigham's Destroying Angel*, 212 (italics in the original).

139. Holley notes that Morris had been twice excommunicated for adultery and had lived for a year with the wife of Thomas Virgo, a "crazy man." Holley, "Slouching," 253.

140. R. W. Young, "Morrisite War," 471. At the later Morrisite arraignment, Judge Kinney allegedly remarked, "I have been misinformed. . . . You were represented to me as a banditti of low, degraded men—robbers and thieves; but I see . . . a class of intelligent men." George S. Dove in *SPV*, 8.

141. February 11, 1861, CR 100 137, reel 18, vol. 54, p. 4, image 76.

142. *RMSA*, 594.

143. CR 100 102, vol. 31, reel 14, box 14, p. 67, image 80. Young did not officially become LDS president and prophet until 1847.

144. George S. Dove in *SPV*, 4.

145. Eardley, *Gems of Inspiration*, 17, cited in *JOMO*, 64, 64n22. This is possibly Benjamin Watts, a devout Saint from Iron County, who came to Utah with Woodruff and emigrated south with the George A. Smith Company.

146. Ibid.

147. CR 100 102, vol. 31, pp. 71–72, images 84–85.

148. April 6 is also the date of founding of the LDS Church.

149. Ten acres of bowery, church, school and cabins were established in 1853 by Thomas Kington, a Weber County bishop. Abandoned during the 1857 Utah War, it remained so until occupied by Morris and his followers. Launius and Thatcher, *Differing Visions*, 214–15n11.

150. CR 1234 1, Journals 1832–77, President's Office Journals 1852–63, Journal August 8, 1858–June 18, 1863, reel 84, box 72, folder 5, p. 279, image 277.

151. Ibid., p. 290, image 288.

152. Ibid., p. 295, image 293.

153. Ibid., p. 301, image 299.

154. Ibid., p. 307, image 305.

155. Ibid., p. 332, image 330.

156. Ibid., p. 334, image 332.

157. Ibid., p. 340, image 338.

158. Banks had physically assaulted Young after not receiving a church position he had been promised. Excommunicated, he was readmitted, but Young likely had not forgotten the episode. Howard, "Men, Motives, and Misunderstandings," 120.

159. Ibid., 119.

160. *RMSA*, 595.

161. Lawrence believed that "use of force would provoke armed resistance and . . . the innocent would suffer." *JOMO*, 107. Lawrence left the LDS church, joined William S. Godbe's LDS faction, was critical of Young, and worked against theocracy as a Liberal Party member. *GGSL*, 148, 150, 171; *RNB*, 101,163, 199, 199n109, 207–10, 223, 228, 233, 259, 267, 307.

162. Burton, a three-wife polygamist with twenty-seven children, held many important positions. A Council of Fifty member, he soon became a militia major general. *FK*, 212.

163. Historian Janet Seegmiller cites a smaller number of men and two cannons in the force. Seegmiller, *"Be Kind to the Poor,"* 218.

164. *RMSA*, 599.

165. Eardley, *Gems of Inspiration*, 28, cited in *JOMO*, 133; George S. Dove in *SPV*, 7.

166. George S. Dove in *SPV*, 7.

167. *FK*, 213. "Morris had been shot [three times] 'with one ball through the Head & two in the breast & shoulders," Woodruff, *Journal*, June 16, 17, 1862, 6:56, 57.

168. The 1877 Poland Act had changed court jurisdiction and jury selection, so U.S. attorney Sumner Howard tried Burton for the murder of Morris, and Jeter Clinton for that of Banks. The *New York Herald* reported: "Banks was delivered over to Surgeon Jeter Clinton, who, taking a knife from . . . [another doctor's] case, escorted the wounded counselor over a hill . . . with the ostensible purpose of dressing his wound. He dressed it thus: locating the knife in the original wound back of the neck, he gave it a vicious thrust, . . . killing his man instantaneously." "Murder Territory," *New York Herald*, republished in *Salt Lake Tribune*, August 17, 1877, 3/2. Neither man was convicted.

169. Other sources give the name as Mrs. Swanigg or Swanee.

170. *FK*, 213.

171. Woodruff, *Journal*, June 18, 1862, cited in Seegmiller, *"Be Kind to the Poor,"* 222.

172. *RMSA*, 599–600.

173. *FK*, 216; "Burton Arrested," *Salt Lake Tribune*, July 27, 1877, 4/2. Daniel Wells appeared in court, complaining that "our best citizens" were being harassed, and he threatened to bring court officers "more trouble than they wanted." A verdict of "not guilty" was found in March 1879. "President Wells' Cool Impudence," *Salt Lake Tribune*, July 28, 1877, 2/1. See also *RNB*, 167n72.

174. "Murder Territory," *New York Herald*, republished in *Salt Lake Tribune*, August 17, 1877, 3/2.

175. Young to Bernhisel, June 26, 1862, BYLC, CR 1234 1, box 6, vol. 6, p. 304, image 341s (italics added). Livingston and Holladay were long acquainted with business and political matters in Utah. With John H. Kinkead of St. Louis, Livingston opened Utah's first non-Mormon mercantile and freighting operation in the city in the fall of 1849.

176. "Mr. Ben Holladay can render you important assistance in procuring an early payment of those a/c's, for it was chiefly through his instrumentality and much for his benefit that the service was rendered." Young to Bernhisel, October 16, 1892, BYLC, CR 1234 1, box 6, vol. 6, p. 414, image 450s.

177. In 1851, Livingston helped territorial secretary Broughton Harris remove twenty-four thousand dollars in gold from Salt Lake City when Harris deemed that elections were illegal and refused to distribute the federal funds. S. H. Harris, *Unwritten Chapter*, 57–61. Livingston wrote of Capt. John Gunnison's murder in 1853. Fielding, *Unsolicited Chronicler*, 176n5.

178. O. F. Whitney, cited in Seegmiller, *"Be Kind to the Poor,"* 217.

179. Bernhisel to Young, July 31, 1862, CR 1234 1, reel 71, box 61, folder 6. On March 17, 1864, Joseph A. Young, on meeting Livingston in New York City, wrote, "We were not extremely cordial, [and] I could not ascertain what he was

doing." Joseph A. Young, "Journal of a Mission to the Eastern States [1864]," MS 233, Special Collections, Manuscripts Division, J. Willard Marriott Library, University of Utah.

180. *CDBY*, 4:2023.

181. Bancroft, *History of Utah*, 618.

182. "The Davis County Bandits," *DN*, June 25, 1862, 10/2.

183. Harding to J. H. Beadle, December 23, 1871, cited in Hickman, *Brigham's Destroying Angel*, 216.

184. Harding tells of the lone Mormon who signed the petition: "I had sunk to sleep, when a voice was heard outside, calling for the Governor. My son, . . . a six-shooter always in reach, inquired, 'Who is there ?' The reply came back, 'Bill Hickman. . . . I have business with the Governor.' . . . He then stated that he had lain awake that night, thinking about the petitions, and added, 'I . . . got up, and rode fourteen miles to sign them. Has any Mormon signed?' I answered that they had not. He . . . took up a pen, and wrote . . . in letters as large as John Hancock signed to the Declaration, his name—'BILL HICKMAN.' Then . . . he said in a confident tone of satisfaction, ' . . . There's one Mormon who does as he pleases.'" Ibid.

185. "Interview Extraordinary between the Governor of Utah and Brigham Young," *New York Tribune*, September 3, 1862, reprinted in *SFB*, October 21, 1862, 1/5.

186. "How They Waste Away," *DN*, July 9, 1862, 8/2.

187. "The Horrors of the Battle Field," *DN*, July 16, 1862, 3/4. Baker wrote his letters on June 2 and June 5, 1862.

188. W. Q. Maxwell, *Lincoln's Fifth Wheel*, 155, vii.

189. Ibid., vii.

190. "Importance of Continued Revelation," *Mill. Star*, July 12, 1862, 24:441.

191. Young to Gibson, July 18, 1862, BYLC, CR 1234 1, box 6, vol. 6, p. 339, image 376 (italics added).

192. *SOO*, 257.

193. General Orders, No. 17, by Gen. George Wright, Department of the Pacific, San Francisco, April 23, 1862; U.S. Senate, "Volunteer Troops," 62–63.

194. *SOO*, 13, 21.

195. Bvt. Maj. James H. Carleton was originally ordered to Utah and might have caused more trouble than Connor, since he was one of the first officers to inspect the site and write of the killings of Mountain Meadows. Carleton to Mackall, June 24, 1859, RG 393, NAB, cited in *BOP*, 230, 424n25. Confederate action in New Mexico caused his reassignment.

196. "California News," *DN*, April 30, 1862, 3/3; Wright to Thomas, Washington, D.C., May 13, 1862, in U.S. Senate, "Volunteer Troops," 63–64.

197. "A Needless War in Prospect," *NYT*, May 26, 1862.

198. "California Volunteers for Salt Lake," *DN*, June 18, 1862, 8/3.

199. Wright to Thomas, Washington, D.C., June 28, 1862, U.S. Senate, "Volunteer Troops," 79.

200. Thomas Starr King was a Unitarian preacher, a stalwart in California's support of the Union, and a close friend of Henry W. Bellows, minister of New York City's First Unitarian Church and the organizing head of the 1862 U.S. Sanitary Commission. King raised large amounts of money from California to support the commission. It was through the common denominators of church ministry and strong Union allegiance that Anderson was later recruited to work for the Sanitary Commission.

201. George W. Martin, "John A. Anderson—A Character Sketch," Kansas Historical Collections, 7:320, Kansas Historical Society, Topeka. Stockton was Anderson's first post. "Appointment of a Regimental Chaplain," *SFB*, June 17, 1862, 3/5.

202. Martin, "John A. Anderson," 7:320.

203. "Proposed Regimental Library," *SFB*, June 25, 1862, 2/5.

204. "Presentation of a Canvas Chapel Tent," *SFB*, September 23, 1862, 1/2.

205. "Rev. John A. Anderson," in Connelley, *Standard History of Kansas*, accessed April 2014, www.ksgenweb.com/archives/1918ks/bioa/andersja.html.

206. "Rev. Docr. [*sic*] Anderson," *DUV*, October 22, 1864, 2/2.

207. Martin, "John A. Anderson," 7:321.

208. Ibid., 7:320, 512, 514–515n. Kansas State Agricultural College was "one of the first free schools of college level in the United States where systematic daily manual work became an obligatory branch of instruction for all male students."

209. Kansas Historical Society, "Anderson Family Papers," www.kshs.org/p/anderson-family-papers/13973. The Anderson family were also close friends of Andrew Carnegie, and Anderson's Junction City church housed an organ gifted by Carnegie.

210. "Col. Connor's Command," *DN*, June 25, 1862, 11/4.

211. Richard C. Drum, July 5, 1862, *WOR*, ser. 1, vol. 50, part 2, 5–6.

212. Diary of Van B. De Lashmutt, cited in *SOO*, 258. De Lashmutt was the first printer of the *Union Vedette* at Camp Douglas.

213. Order No. 1, *WOR*, ser. 1, vol. 2, 50, 55.

214. "Arrival in the City," *DN*, September 10, 1862, 5/4. Connor almost certainly carried or had studied maps of the Salt Lake City area created by Captain Simpson.

215. Anderson to his parents, September 18, 1862, John Alexander Anderson Papers, MSS 445, 2.03–2.06, Anderson Family Papers, Kansas Historical Society, Topeka.

216. *San Joaquin Republican*, May 22, June 11, and August 23, 1857, cited in *GHU*, 37, 37n46. The U.S. Constitution, Article IV, Section 4, states: "The United States shall guarantee to every State in the Union a Republican Form of Government."

217. W. M. Wall statement, December 12, 1857, in *ASP1*, 491.

218. *San Joaquin Republican*, October 18, 1857, April 16, 17, 1858, cited in *GHU*, 37, 37n47.

219. Connor to Drum, September 14, 1862, *WOR*, ser. 1, vol. 50, part 2, 119.

220. "The California Troops on the Plains," *SFB*, October 31, 1862, 2/3; *GHU*, 65. During Connor's 1846 service with the Texas Mounted Riflemen, his company was under the command of Col. Albert Sidney Johnston.

221. Connor to Drum, September 14, 1862, ser. 1, vol. 50, part 2, 119–20.

222. Sears, *Landscape Turned Red*, xi. Five days after the battle Lincoln issued his preliminary Emancipation Proclamation.

223. W. Q. Maxwell, *Lincoln's Fifth Wheel*, vii (italics added).

224. "The Field of Retribution," *SDU*, September 1, 1862, 1/3; "The Contest on the Old Field," *Alta California* (San Francisco), September 7, 1862, 1/3.

225. Connor to Halleck, September 21 and 24, 1862, *WOR*, ser. 1, vol. 50, part 2, 133.

226. Connor to *San Francisco Bulletin*, cited in Tullidge, *History of Salt Lake City*, 275.

227. "California Volunteers," *DN*, October 15, 1862, 8/2.

228. "Affairs in Utah," written September 17, published in *NYT*, October 12, 1862.

229. "Secession Movements in Nevada Territory," *DN*, September 10, 1862, 5/2.

230. Connor to Drum, September 16, 1862, *WOR*, ser. 1, vol. 50, part 2, 125.

231. Connor to McGarry, September 29, 1862, *WOR*, ser. 1, vol. 50, part 2, 144.

232. Brown to Drum, October 3, 1862, *WOR*, ser. 1, vol. 50, part 2, 148–49.

233. *CDBY*, 4:2056.

234. *MR*, 327–28.

235. *SOO*, 41.

236. Wright to Thomas, Washington, D.C., October 20, 1862, in U.S. Senate, "Volunteer Troops," 108.

237. *SOO*, 42.

238. "Affairs in Utah," written October 22, published in *NYT*, November 15, 1862.

239. *SOO*, 44.

240. *SOO*, 44–46; "The California Troops on the Plains," *SFB*, October 31, 1862, 2/3.

241. "Arrival of Col. Connor's Command," *DN*, October 22, 1862, 5/2.

242. *SOO*, 48, 49.

243. Hibbard, *Fort Douglas*, 17. Firing a nine-pound shell, the gun had a range of nine hundred yards, or about a half mile.

244. "Arrival of Col. Connor's Command," *DN*, October 22, 1862, 5/2.

245. Some accounts hold that the troops entered the city with fixed bayonets, but this is not specified in military records or in Anderson's reporting.

246. *SOO*, 51.

247. Young did not return to the city until October 25. "President Young's Trip North," *DN*, October 22, 1862, 5/3; "Affairs in Utah: Brigham Young Returns from a Preaching Tour," written October 29, published in *NYT*, November 23, 1862.

248. *SOO*, 44–46.

249. *SOO*, 52–53.

250. Connor, a Democrat, worked for attain a monument in Stockton to honor Stephen A. Douglas; naming installations for recently deceased prominent men was a military custom. Douglas had become Young's hated enemy, and Connor may also have intended the name to irritate.

251. Order No. 14, Connor to Drum, October 20, 1862, *WOR*, ser. 1, vol. 50, part 2, 195.

252. Cole, *Civil War Artillery*, 298.

253. Connor to Adjutant General, November 9, 1862, *WOR*, ser. 1, vol. 50, part 2, 218.

254. Anonymous, *Minutes of the Apostles*, October 26, 1862, 1:315–16.

255. October 30, 1862, *CDBY*, 4:2076.

256. "Notice," *DN*, November 5, 1862, 6/4. Arrington notes that Mormons did not realize that loyalty oaths were generally required at military posts. *GBK*, 472n29.

257. "Letter from Salt Lake," signed by "Liberal," written November 27, published in *SDU*, December 5, 1862, 1/5.

258. Typescript, Harding to Judge [unnamed], November 11, 1862, Harding-Lilly.

259. "That Cat," *DN*, November 12, 1862, 4/3.

260. *SFB*, November 17, 1862, cited in *SOO*, 56.

261. *SOO*, 57, 61.

262. "Letter from Salt Lake," signed by "Liberal," written November 27, published in *SDU*, December 5, 1862, 1/5.

263. "Affairs in Utah," written November 27, published in *NYT*, December 21, 1862.

264. "Mormonism in Utah," *NYT*, December 26, 1862.

265. "Something New in Deseret," *DN*, November 12, 1862, 4/4.

266. "Discovery of Gold in Utah Territory," written November 21, published in *SFB*, December 2, 1862, 1/1. Mormons prevented federal land surveys, a prerequisite to sale.

267. "Letter from Salt Lake," signed by "Liberal," written October 21, published in *SDU*, October 29, 1862, 3/3; "For the Cotton Country," *DN*, October 22, 1862, 8/2.

268. Aird, Nichols, and Bagley, *Playing with Shadows*, 174.

269. Ibid., 172–74, 172n8, 173n10, 174n12. Washington was a small Mormon settlement near St. George. It was also in Washington County.

270. James G. Bleak, *Annals of the Southern Utah Mission*, James G. Bleak Papers, Accn 194, Special Collections, J. Willard Marriott Library, University of Utah, 71, 84–87.

271. Snow to Young, March 10, 1862, cited in C. M. Orton, "'Dixie,'" 10, 14n35.

272. Connor to Drum, December 20, 1862, *WOR*, ser. 1, vol. 50, part 2, 256–57.

273. A. Wilson Green, "Battle of Fredericksburg," National Park Service, www.nps.gov/frsp/fredhist.htm.

274. "The Battle of Fredericksburg," *DN*, December 24, 1862, 4/1.

275. "Proclamation of the Governor of Utah Territory," *DN*, December 3, 1862, 8/1.

276. *RMSA*, 603.

277. Harding, "Message to the Territorial Legislature of Utah," 1–5 (italics in the original).

278. *TSTU*, 123.

279. "Letter from Salt Lake," signed by "Liberal," *SDU*, July 19, 1862, 1/3. Stenhouse also thought Harding's welcome by Young and Wells was unprecedented.

5. Who Will Blink First? 1863

1. Morgan, *State of Deseret*, 95, 99.

2. "Affairs in Utah," *NYT*, written December 17, 1862, published January 11, 1863.

3. U.S. Senate, *Report of the Committee on Territories*, 1.

4. French, "Letter from Stephen S. Harding," 160–61.

5. "Affairs in Utah," written December 17, 1862, published *NYT*, January 11, 1863.

6. French, "Letter from Stephen S. Harding," 160.

7. Wells to Harding, January 26, 1863, Utah Territorial Militia Records, A383A, part 1, image 717, USHS.

8. "Emancipation and Its Effects," *DN*, January 7, 1863, 1/2.

9. "The Emancipation Proclamation," *DN*, January 7, 1863, 1/4.

10. "Message of the Governor of the State of Deseret," *DN*, January 21, 1863, 1/1.

11. James Madison, "Republicanism, Nationalism, and Federalism," No. 39, in Wright, *Federalist*, 280–81.

12. Wright, *Federalist*, 27.

13. Jefferson's Letter to the Danbury [Conn.] Baptists: The Final Letter, as Sent, January 1, 1802, *Library of Congress Information Bulletin*, June 1998 (italics added).

14. "The Admission of Utah," *NYT*, January 22, 1863.

15. Young to Bernhisel, January 24, 1863, BYLC, CR 1234 1, box 6, vol. 6, p. 456, image 492s.

16. Young to George Q. Cannon, November 13, 1862, BYLC, CR 1234 1, box 6, vol. 6, p. 424, image 461s.

17. "Affairs in Utah: The Troops Amusements," written January 8, published in *NYT*, February 8, 1863; "Camp Douglas," *DN*, January 7, 1863, 8/2.

18. Young to Bernhisel, January 24, 1863, BYLC, CR 1234 1, box 6, vol. 6, p. 456, image 493s.

19. Harding to Seward, March 11, 1863, Lincoln Papers, Library of Congress. Ben Holladay, the Overland Stage owner, maintained ties with Young for the same reason. Twice daily, Concord Coaches traveled through Utah on the St. Joseph, Mo., to Sacramento, Calif. run. The full fare was $150. "Utah," *SFB*, January 1, 1863, 2/2.

20. Hulbert, in Rumfield, "Letters," 231.

21. Cook to Center, March 2, 1863, in Rumfield, "Letters," 288–91, 288n1.

22. Rumfield to "My dear Frank," March 8, 1863, Rumfield, "Letters," 292–93.

23. Harding to Seward, April 11, 1863, Utah Territorial Papers, U.S. Department of State, 575, RG 59, NACP.

24. Briefly: two settlers killed in Cache County, July 23, 1860; attack on Hagerty emigrant train near City of Rocks at Raft River, September 7–9, 1860; Otter Massacre on Oregon Trail near Salmon Falls, September 9, 1860; attack on emigrant parties at American Falls on Snake River, August 9–10, 1862; attack on McBride-Andrews party on Snake River, September 12, 1862; John Henry Smith killed at Bear River near Richmond, Cache Valley, January 6, 1863; George Clayton and Henry Bean killed at Marsh Valley, January 14, 1863.

25. *JDD*, 369–72.

26. Dwyer, *The Gentile Comes to Utah*, 8–9, 18–22, cited in *JDD*, 369, 438n26. As Young had been appointed superintendent of Indian Affairs in 1850, the failures were in part his.

27. *SF*, 178; Connor to Drum, February 6, 1863, *WOR*, ser. 1, vol. 50, part 1, 187.

28. *JDD*, 373.

29. *SF*, 179; Connor to Maj. Edward McGarry, September 29, 1862, *WOR*, ser. 1, vol. 50, part 2, 144. Mark Twain would defend Connor's policy: "Humanitarians want somebody to fight the Indians that J. Fenimore Cooper made. . . . The Cooper Indians are dead. . . . That kind that are left are of altogether a different breed, and cannot be successfully fought with poetry, and sentiment, and soft soap, and magnanimity." "The Indian Row," *Alta California* (San Francisco), August 11, 1867.

30. Neither Gibbs nor Rockwell was known to be a combatant in the fray.

31. According to Madsen, it was Rockwell who reported to Connor that the Indians had "thrown up intrenchments." *SF*, 182, 182n30. Sagwitch's

granddaughter Mae T. Perry claims that Bear Hunter thought Connor would not open fire but would—by custom—demand the guilty to be delivered, with nothing further taking place. *SF*, appendix B, 233.

32. "Expedition for the Arrest of Indian Chiefs," *DN*, January 28, 1863, 4/2.

33. Madsen estimates that the four companies carried sixteen thousand rounds. *SF*, 180–81.

34. "Letter from the Plains," written February 7 and 9, published in *SFB*, February 20, 1863, 1/1.

35. *SF*, 181.

36. "Anniversary Oration," *DUV*, January 30, 1864, 1/1. Hempstead was the *Union Vedette*'s first editor.

37. Connor to Stanton, February 6, 1863, *WOR*, ser. 1, vol. 50, part 1, 186.

38. Ibid.

39. Fighting dismounted was especially effective with troops equipped with repeating rifles. Four men dismounted, three fired, while one attempted to control the horses, reducing firepower by one-fourth.

40. "Anniversary Oration," *DUV*, January 30, 1864, 1/1.

41. *FK*, 230.

42. Connor to Drum, February 6, 1863, *WOR*, ser. 1, vol. 50, part 1, 185–87.

43. Doty to Dole, February 16, 1863, cited in Heaton, "Shoshone Adaptation to Mormon Settlers," 159.

44. "Massacre at Boa Ogoi," *SF*, appendix B, 231–38.

45. "Letter from the Plains," *SFB*, February 20, 1863, 1/1.

46. Crookston, *Henry Ballard*, 63. Official minutes of the Logan Ward recorded "the movement of Col. Connor as an intervention of the Almighty." Edward William Tullidge, "The Cities of Cache Valley and Their Founders," *Tullidge's Quarterly Magazine* 1, no. 4 (July 1881): 536, cited in *SF*, 194, 239n88.

47. Connor to Drum, February 6, 1863, *WOR*, ser. 1, vol. 50, part 1, 185–87.

48. *SF*, 186, 258n45.

49. Madsen's report states, "From seven to fourteen troopers were killed and perhaps twenty wounded in this first half-hour exchange." *SF*, 187.

50. "Letters from the Plains," written February 7, published in *SFB*, February 20, 1863, 1/1.

51. "Anniversary Oration," *DUV*, January 30, 1864, 1/1. Counts of women and children killed vary widely from 5 to 265, and an accurate total number is not possible. *SF*, 189–91.

52. "Anniversary Oration," *DUV*, January 30, 1864, 4/1.

53. None of the totals are precise, but the count from Chivington's Sand Creek massacre totaled as high as 163; at Custer's Washita River, up to 150; and at Col. James W. Forsyth's Wounded Knee, 300 or more.

54. Madsen questions if the place of Catholicism in Mormon theology as "the most abominable above all other churches" and "the mother of harlots" was

an element of friction between the non-Mormons and Mormons. *SF*, 66. See *Book of Mormon*, 1 Nephi 13:5, 14:16.

55. R. H. Orton, *Records*, 179. Quinn identifies Chase as a former Danite; his dying request for a blessing was denied by the Mormon leaders. Quinn, *Mormon Hierarchy: Extensions*, 276, 552n118.

56. *SF*, 196. Cold injuries appear far more severe at the time of injury than after several days of recovery. The level of amputation is almost always less than initially estimated.

57. *SF*, 200. Martineau's diary says simply, "The next morning . . . a dead squaw was found with a little baby trying to suck her icy breast. It was killed for pity, by the soldiers." Godfrey and Martineau-McCarty, *Uncommon Pioneer*, 132.

58. Fleisher, *Bear River Massacre*, xi.

59. Maughan to Young, February 4, 1863, CR 1234 1, reel 40, box 29, folder 10. This complex message, related thirdhand from Indian women whose English was rudimentary, merits suspicion.

60. Fahey, *Temperance and Racism*, 151.

61. "Massacre at Boa Ogoi," *SF*, appendix B, 231–38. Notably, Martineau's record does not mention torture.

62. Fleisher, *Bear River Massacre*, 206.

63. Hart, *Bear River Massacre*, 165–67, 172.

64. Harding to Wright, February 16, 1863, *WOR*, ser. 1, vol. 50, part 1, 314–15.

65. Connor to Drum, February 6, 1863, *WOR*, ser. 1, vol. 50, part 2, 185–87.

66. "Matters at Salt Lake," *SFB*, April 27, 1863, 1/1.

67. *SDU*, February 12, 1863.

68. Kelly and Birney, *Holy Murder*, 50–51, 221–22. Rockwell remained loyal to Young, but after Bear River they drifted apart.

69. Halleck to Connor, March 29, 1863, *WOR*, ser. 1, vol. 50, part 2, 369.

70. "Promotion," *DN*, April 1, 1863, 1/3.

71. "Matters at Salt Lake," *SFB*, April 27, 1863, 1/1.

72. "Names of Dead Ring Out at Ceremony," *Salt Lake Tribune*, January 30, 2013, 1/2.

73. Utah Territorial Papers, U.S. Department of State, RG 59, NACP, cited in *TSTU*, 147.

74. Harding to Wright, February 16, 1863, *WOR*, ser. 1, vol. 50, part 2, 314–15.

75. Connor to Drum, February 19, 1863, *WOR*, ser. 1, vol. 50, part 2, 318–20.

76. Drum to McAllister, February 20, 1863, *WOR*, ser. 1, vol. 50, part 2, 320.

77. Draft of an unsent letter to Lincoln dated March 1863, Great Salt Lake City, CR 1234 1, reel 62, box 49, folder 12, images 2–16.

78. "Mass Meeting in the Tabernacle," *DN*, March 4, 1863, 4/1.

79. Remarks of Brigham Young, Inclosure 2, Connor to Drum, March 15, 1863, *WOR*, ser. 1, vol. 50, part 2, 372–73.

80. Reply of His Excellency Governor Harding to the Mormon Committee, Inclosure 2, Connor to Drum, March 15, 1863, *WOR*, ser. 1, vol. 50, part 2, 373.

81. Reply of His Honor Judge Drake, Inclosure 2, Connor to Drum, *WOR*, ser. 1, vol. 50, part 2, 373–74. Judge Drake may also spoken courageously, given that his wife and their three children were living in Salt Lake City.

82. Connor to Drum, March 15, 1863, *WOR*, ser. 1, vol. 50, part 2, 370–72.

83. Young to Rossé, March 7, 1863, BYLC, CR 1234 1, box 6, vol. 6, pp. 515–16, images 551–52.

84. Connor to Drum, March 10, 1863, *WOR*, ser. 1, vol. 50, part 2, 344.

85. *WOR*, ser. 1, vol. 50, part 2, 371.

86. Connor to Drum, March 15, 1863, *WOR*, ser. 1, vol. 50, part 2, 370–71. Apostates fearing for their lives while leaving had been commonplace for years. Historian Polly Aird documents more than 160 apostates in forty families, including her ancestor Peter McAuslan, who left Utah in June 1859 only after securing U.S. military protection. Aird, *Mormon Convert, Mormon Defector*, 254–55.

87. Connor to Drum, March 10, 1863, *WOR*, ser. 1, vol. 50, part 2, 344.

88. Wright to Connor, March 11, 1863, *WOR*, ser. 1, vol. 50, part 2, 347.

89. Wright to Thomas, March 14 and March 30, 1863, *WOR*, ser. 1, vol. 50, part 2, 350, 369–70.

90. U.S. Senate, "Volunteer Troops," 155–56.

91. The *WOR* records cite "Old Soldier," but Madsen clarifies that it was "Little Soldier," a Northern Shoshoni. *GHU*, 94.

92. Report of Lt. Anthony Ethier, April 6, 1863, *WOR*, ser. 1, vol. 50, part 1, 200–201.

93. Report of Capt. George F. Price, April 6, 1863, *WOR*, ser. 1, vol. 50, part 1, 201–203.

94. One of the officers went among the Mormons at Spanish Fork, pretending to be a recent emigrant. He saw the Indians and Mormons in "perfect understanding" with one another. Mormons cursed his brothers-in-arms, wishing that the savages might overcome them. "Matters at Salt Lake," *SFB*, April 27, 1863, 1/1.

95. Report of Capt. George F. Price, April 6, 1863, *WOR*, ser. 1, vol. 50, part 1, 201–203.

96. Report of Col. Evans, April 17, 1863, *WOR*, ser. 1, vol. 50, part 1, 205–208. Lt. F. A. Peel was killed and two sergeants were wounded in the engagement.

97. Wright to Thomas, May 4, 1863, *WOR*, ser. 1, vol. 50, part 1, 204.

98. March 3, 1863, *CDBY*, 4:2094.

99. Ibid., 2092.

100. Ibid., 2092, 2095–98. Historian O'Donovan reports an 1847 meeting wherein Young would have had killed Enoch Lovejoy Lewis, the son of the black elder Q. Walker Lewis and his legal white wife, Matilda, had they been "far

away from the Gentiles" rather than in Massachusetts. O'Donovan, "Mormon Priesthood Ban," 84. Some interpret "mixing seed" as either cross-racial offspring or sexual intercourse.

101. Harding to Seward, March 11, 1863, Abraham Lincoln Papers, Library of Congress (italics in the original).

102. Connor to Lincoln, March 8, 1863 (italics added), quoted in Waite, *Mormon Prophet*, 105–107.

103. "Matters at Salt Lake and on the Plains," written April 24, published in *SFB*, May 4, 1863, 1/3. Descendants of John V. Long say that Connor commandeered the Long home during his first winter. Hance and Warr, *Johnston, Connor, and the Mormons*, 29. It is highly improbable that Connor violated Amendment III of the Bill of Rights: "No Soldier shall, in time of peace be quartered in any house, without the consent of the Owner, nor in time of war, but in a manner to be prescribed by law."

104. *GHU*, 115n46.

105. Turner, *Brigham Young*, 325, 327, 475n64–65.

106. "Utah Affairs," *New York Herald*, March 19, 1863, 1/4; "Dispatches to the Associated Press," written March 18, published in *NYT*, March 19, 1863.

107. "Arrest of Brigham Young for Polygamy," *DN*, March 11, 1863, 4/3. Other views hold that Young wished to be arrested by civil authorities, not by military officers.

108. "The Muss in Mormondom," *Springfield (Mass.) Republican*, March 12, 1863, 4/1.

109. "Affairs in Utah," written April 1, published in *NYT*, April 26, 1863. Scandinavian surnames were most common in the *Times* list of those pardoned.

110. R. W. Young, "The Morrisite War," 468, cited in *JOMO*, 146.

111. Eardley, *Gems of Inspiration*, 32, cited in *JOMO*, 145.

112. "Matters at Salt Lake," written April 15, published in *SFB*, April 27, 1863, 1/3; "Matters at Salt Lake City," written April 24, published in *SFB*, May 4, 1863, 1/1.

113. Stenhouse to Greeley, June 4, 7, 13, and 19 and July 1, 1863, CR 1234 1, reel 40, box 29, folder 13.

114. Waite, *Mormon Prophet*, 119.

115. *Biographical History of Eminent and Self-made Men*, 77–81.

116. Bowles's comment on Harding in Colorado was the opposite of the appraisals by Connor and others in Utah: "He brought . . . scandalous, Mormon ways of living, as to shock . . . public opinion, which is now uniting to drive him out." *ATC*, 61. Of all that is known of Harding, he did not live a Mormon way of life.

117. "Affairs in Utah," written June 24, published in *NYT*, July 12, 1863; Waite, *Mormon Prophet*, 115. Waite later returned to Utah.

118. "Matters at Salt Lake," written April 24, published in *SFB*, May 4, 1863, 1/3; McDonough, *Hogles*, 31. Connor wrote that four-fifths were "loudly and notoriously disloyal." *WOR*, ser. 1, vol. 50, part 2, 530.

119. Waite, *Mormon Prophet*, 140. Connor and the Second Cavalry left May 6.

120. Connor to Drum, April 22, 1863, *WOR*, ser. 1, vol. 50, part 2, 411.

121. *SOO*, 100.

122. Barnard, Bybee, and Walker, *Tosoiba*, 57–58, cited in *JOMO*, 161.

123. *Contributions to the Historical Society of Montana* 1 (1876): 199, cited in *SOO*, 105.

124. Connor to Drum, June 2, 1863, *WOR*, ser. 1, vol. 50, part 1, 226–29.

125. Barnard, Bybee, and Walker, *Tosoiba*, 62, cited in *JOMO*, 162.

126. *SOO*, 108–109.

127. "Matters in Salt Lake and on the Plains," *SFB*, May 4, 1863, 1/3.

128. "Conference at Provo," *DN*, July 1, 1863, 9/4.

129. "Affairs in Utah," written July 30, published in *NYT*, August 18, 1863.

130. "The Election," *DN*, August 8, 1863, 4/1.

131. *ASPI*, 108. MacKinnon notes that also overlooked were "Kinney's 1855 indictment in probate court for gambling charges, [and] ownership of a disreputable hotel," and his bold maneuvering "for appointment as Utah's governor while Colonel Steptoe dithered over President Pierce's offer." Ibid.

132. Historian Michael Homer details the complex relationships between Kinney and Mormon leadership prior to 1860. Homer, "Federal Bench and Priesthood Authority," 89–110.

133. Both Heth and Reynolds had served in Utah as part of the army forces of the Utah Expedition, as had many others of Union and Confederate forces.

134. *GGSL*, 58–65.

135. Stewart, *Pickett's Charge*, x.

136. R. Alexander, *Five Forks*, 50.

137. Quoted in Guelzo, *Gettysburg*, 404.

138. The *Deseret News* reported very briefly on July 15 on what was then known of Gettysburg. "Progress of the War," *DN*, July 15, 1863, 4/1.

139. Clark and Editors, *Voices of the Civil War*, 142.

140. Faust, *This Republic of Suffering*, 69.

141. Camp Douglas also provided a smaller theater and in November 1863 had shows on Monday, Thursday, and Saturday. Hibbard, "Fort Douglas," 99.

142. "Affairs in Utah," written July 8, published in *NYT*, July 26, 1863.

143. "Battalion and Pioneer Festival," *DN*, July 22, 1863, 5/1.

144. Connor to Drum, June 11, 1863, *WOR*, ser. 1, vol. 50, part 2, 481. The next day, Connor wrote to Halleck, asking if reinforcements could be sent from Denver rather than from California.

145. Connor to Drum, June 22, 1863, *WOR*, ser. 1, vol. 50, part 1, 229.

146. Connor to Drum, June 24, 1863, *WOR*, ser. 1, vol. 50, part 2, 492–94.

147. Phebe Westwood to Dave [Westwood], June 19, 1863, "Sub-inclosure" in Gallagher to Hempstead, *WOR*, ser. 1, vol. 50, part 2, 500. Dave Westwood worked as a blacksmith with the Overland Mail.

148. "Affairs in Utah," written June 11, published in *NYT*, July 12, 1863.

149. Bradley to Young, June 23, 1863, CR 1234 1, General Correspondence Incoming, General Letters, reel 40, box 29, folder 8, images 148–49 (underlining in the original).

150. Connor to Drum, June 24, 1863, *WOR*, ser. 1, vol. 50, part 2, 492–95.

151. Connor to Halleck, February 15, 1864, *WOR*, ser. 1, vol. 50, part 2, 749.

152. Connor to Drum, June 24, 1863, *WOR*, ser. 1, vol. 50, part 2, 493.

153. Ibid., 493, 495.

154. Wright to Thomas, July 10, 1863, *WOR*, ser. 1, vol. 50, part 2, 516.

155. Thomas A. Marshall was appointed to Indian Affairs but did not serve; Orsemus H. Irish was not on-site until August 1864.

156. *GHU*, 93, 98.

157. *JDD*, 373.

158. Connor to Drum, October 27, 1863, *WOR*, ser. 1, vol. 50, part 2, 658–59.

159. Doty to Wright, August 9, 1863, *WOR*, ser. 1, vol. 50, part 2, 583–84.

160. Doty, "Report," October 24, 1863, in U.S. Office of Indian Affairs, *Report, 1863*, 539–40.

161. "Affairs in Utah," written October 14, published in *NYT*, November 8, 1863.

162. *JDD*, 375.

163. U.S. Supreme Court, *Miller v. U.S.*, 78 U.S. 268 (1870), which upheld the government's "right to confiscate the property of public enemies wherever found."

164. MPOT, Daniel D McArthur Company (1863), Trail Excerpt: E. L. [Edward Lennox] Sloan, Letter, in CR 100 137, September 25, 1863, 2–3.

165. MPOT, Daniel D. McArthur Company (1863), Trail Excerpt: Ebenezer Farnes, Reminiscences [ca. 1910], 10–14.

166. MPOT, Samuel D. White Company (1863), Trail Excerpt: David Dunn Bulloch, Recollections of David D. Bulloch, 42, transcribed from "Pioneer History Collection," Pioneer Memorial Museum [Daughters of Utah Pioneers Museum], Salt Lake City.

167. William Richardson, Autobiography, 18–20, LDS_CHL, cited in Bagley, "Terror to Evil-Doers," 316, 316n7.

168. McLachlan, William, Journal, CR 100 137, October 1863, 13–19.

169. "Affairs in Utah," written September 10, published in *NYT*, October 3, 1863 (italics added).

170. "Brigham Young on the War," written October 9, published in *NYT*, November 8, 1863.

171. Young, October 3, 1863, *CDBY*, 4:2162.

172. HOH, 33:966.

173. "Affairs in Utah," written October 30, published in *NYT*, November 28, 1863; "Affairs in Utah," written October 14, published in *NYT*, November 8, 1863.

174. Connor to Drum, October 26, 1863, *WOR*, ser. 1, vol. 50, part 2, 655–57.

175. *RMSA*, 713.

176. Twenty-two participants, including Judge and Mrs. Charles B. Waite, Mr. and Mrs. George B. Ogilvie, and Dr. and Mrs. Robert Reid, formed the Vedette and Copper Mining Company at Great Salt Lake City on November 17, 1863. "Notice," *UV*, November 27, 1863, 2/4.

177. "Affairs in Utah," written October 9, published in *NYT*, November 1, 1963.

178. "Affairs in Utah," written October 20, published in *NYT*, November 28, 1863.

179. McDonough, *Short History*, explores the forgotten role of the Irish in Utah. Journals and gravestones indicate that many members of the Utah Expedition were Irish; of seventy-four burial reports at Camp Floyd, thirty of the deceased had Irish surnames. Gerald M. McDonough, e-mail message to author, March 2014. Some 144,000 Irish served in the Civil War's Union ranks. *SHIU*, 1–25.

180. *Book of Mormon*, 1 Nephi 14:10.

181. *Wikipedia*, s.v. "Fenian Brotherhood," last modified November 24, 2014, http://en.wikipedia.org/wiki/Fenian_Brotherhood.

182. Emmons, *Beyond the American Pale*, 154.

183. *SHIU*, 5, 8–9.

184. The *Valley Tan*, March 15, 1859, 3/3, carried a small, short notice: "This is St. Patrick's day, and the few Hibernians in this Territory will celebrate, not in a public, but a private manner."

185. *GHU*, 50.

186. *SHIU*, 9.

187. Quigley, *Irish Race in California*, 246, 248.

188. "Celebration of Saint Patrick's Day" and "More of St. Patrick's Day," *SFB*, March 18, 1862, 3/6, 3/4; "St. Patrick's Day," *California Farmer and Journal of Useful Sciences*, March 14, 1862, 180.

189. *SHIU*, 12.

190. The *Deseret News* carried no recognition of an 1863 St. Patrick's Day celebration, and the *Vedette* had not begun publication.

191. *DUV*, March 17, 1864, 2/4.

192. "St. Patrick's Ball," *DUV*, March 19, 1864, 2/2.

193. "Local Matters," *DUV*, March 17, 1865, 3/2. Emmet was a student who participated in the failed 1798 Irish Rebellion. On threat of arrest he fled to Europe, but he returned to Ireland in 1803, where he was convicted of treason and executed.

194. "Local Matters," *DUV*, March 20, 1865, 3/1.

195. "Capt. Hempstead's Oration," *DUV*, March 21, 1865, 2/1.

196. "The Fenian Brotherhood Ball," *DUV*, March 15, 1865, 3/1.

197. "Local and Miscellaneous," *DUV*, March 19, 1866, 3/1. Price was at this time the editor of the *Vedette*.

198. Ibid.

199. "Paddy" alluded to a wagon often carrying arrested Irishmen. The term also alluded to rice paddies, linking them with Chinese in racial insult. "Mick" was a racial slur, and political cartoons frequently depicted an Irishman as an inebriated monkey. Email messages to the author from Robert Voyles, director, Fort Douglas Military Museum, August 2013, and Gerald M. McDonough, February 2014.

200. Cannon to Brigham Young, Jr., "Correspondence," *Mill. Star*, March 24, 1866, 28:317 (italics added).

201. McDonough, *Hogles*, 30, 44.

202. Connor to Barnes, April 6, 1865, *WOR*, ser. 1, vol. 48, part 2, 1185; "The Union Vedette," *Black Hawk (Colo.) Journal*, December 19, 1865, 2/3.

203. "Salutatory," *UV*, November 20, 1863, 2/1. Subsequent editors were Frederick Livingston, George F. Price, Stephen E. Jocelyn, O. J. Goldrick, and Norman McLeod. The *Vedette* passed to the private ownership and editorship of Philip L. Shoaff and Company in October 1866. McMurtrie, *Notes on Early Printing*, 5. Subsequent editors were Isaac Mellen Weston, Judge Daniel McLaughlin, and Adam Aulbach. The *Vedette* ceased publication in November 1867, and most of its equipment was sold to Godbe, Harrison, and Tullidge, who published *Utah Magazine* and fully supported mining as critical to Utah's financial progress. *SOO*, 131–33; *GBK*, 243.

204. Governor Bigler's appointment of Hempstead came after Bigler's dispute with Secretary of State James W. Denver over possession of the state seal. Hendricks, *Government Roster*, 193.

205. Following his muster out of the volunteers, De Lashmutt moved to Nevada, where he published the *Washoe Times*. He later became the mayor of Portland, Oregon. *SOO*, 132, 266n1.

206. De Lashmutt, Narrative, MS, cited in *SOO*, 266n1.

207. G. Owens, *Salt Lake City Directory* (1867), 29.

208. Weston did not leave. He and Capt. Stephen E. Jocelyn were the first to reach the mortally wounded Dr. John King Robinson. "News from Salt Lake City," *New York Herald*, October 19, 1866, 1/4.

209. "Salutatory," *UV*, November 20, 1863, 2/1.

210. "Important Circular from General Connor," *UV*, November 20, 1863, 3/3.

211. Order No. [blank] Headquarters, 2nd Brigade, 14th Ward, Salt Lake City, to Col. A. L. Fulmer, 1st Regt., 2nd Brigade, December 12, 1863, MS A 1165, Utah Territorial Militia Records, USHS.

212. At Camp Douglas was Col. Robert Pollock, with twelve companies; Fort Bridger, Maj. Patrick Gallagher, with two companies; Fort Ruby, Lt. Col. Jeremiah

B. Moore, with two companies; and Camp Connor, Capt. David Black, with one company. Correspondence—Union and Confederate, Organization of Troops in the Department of the Pacific, *WOR*, ser. 1, vol. 50, part 2, 711–13.

213. Woodruff, *Journal*, November 2, 1863, 6:135; *CDBY*, 4:2171.

6. Colliding Worlds, 1864

Epigraph. "Gen. Connor and the Mormons," *DUV*, February 19, 1864, 2/1.

1. *UV*, January 14, 1864, cited in *TSTU*, 214.

2. Kinney to Halleck, January 4, 1864, *WOR*, ser. 1, vol. 50, part 2, 715–17. Of Lincoln shaking hands with "the 'yaller' and the black," Kinney wrote that government is "transforming a large number of Negroes daily into white men. A wonderful invention!" Kinney to Young, January 1, 1864, CR 1234 1, reel 72, box 63, folder 2 (underlining in the original).

3. Burr to Whiting, September 30, 1855, in Buchanan, *Utah Expedition*, 123; *GGSL*, 137–38.

4. A thousand troops, horses for three hundred cavalry, and other animals were upstream of several thousand people who relied on the water for drinking and household use. *FK*, 233.

5. Kinney to Halleck, January 4, 1864, *WOR*, ser. 1, vol. 50, part 2, 715–17.

6. "Brother Kinney Once More!" *DUV*, February 3, 1864, 2/1.

7. Connor to Halleck, February 15, 1864, *WOR*, ser. 1, vol. 50, part 2, 748–51. Surveys by Mormons began in 1847, but the required U.S. surveys were not yet done.

8. Ibid.

9. M. Monchard, M. Lebeau, Pete Luffing, and twenty-three others, to Connor, February 5, 1864, *WOR*, ser. 1, vol. 50, part 2, 751–52.

10. Connor to Halleck, February 15, 1864, *WOR*, ser. 1, vol. 50, part 2, 748–51.

11. Ibid.

12. Wright to Halleck, March 5, 1864, *WOR*, ser. 1, vol. 50, part 2, 778.

13. "The State of Deseret," *DUV*, January 20, 1864, 3/1.

14. Smith to Kinney, January 8, 1864, CR 100 137, cited in Morgan, *State of Deseret*, 100n169.

15. Untitled, *DUV*, January 26, 1864, 3/1.

16. *TSTU*, 223. Kinney maintained a law practice in Washington, to which William Clayton forwarded paperwork. *DN*, April 6, 1864, 7/3.

17. Soon disfellowshipped for his support of mining, Wandell lived a complicated life. Returning from California in 1857 with George Q. Cannon, they saw the Fancher party's remains at Mountain Meadows and were among the first to learn that Utah militiamen did much of the killing. In 1870–71, using the name "Argus," Wandell wrote letters to Young, published in the *Utah Reporter*, asking "hard questions about the massacre." *BOP*, 268–69. He died in Australia in 1875 while a Reorganized LDS Church missionary. Any hard evidence he may have had

of Young's involvement in the massacre perished in a 1907 fire. Reeve, *Making Space*, 120, 200n29.

18. Untitled, *UV*, January 1, 1864, 1/4.

19. "Gov. Reed Vetoes the Mining Bill," *DUV*, January 22, 1864, 2/1. Despite vetoing the mining bill and others ill conceived, Reed was honored and thanked by the Mormons for "respectful conduct." "Utah Legislature," *DUV*, January 27, 1864, 2/4.

20. Connor, "Circular," March 1, 1864, *WOR*, ser. 1, vol. 50, part 2, 774–75.

21. "Affairs in Utah," *NYT*, March 27, 1864. In February 1857 the attorney general ruled that "the power to suspend the laws, and to substitute the military in the place of the civil authority is not . . . within the legal attributes of a governor of one of the territories." Then-governor Young ignored this and, backed by his militia, declared martial law in September. *ASP1*, 289–92, 291n24.

22. "Governor Doty at Washington," *Milwaukee Sentinel*, January 11, 1864.

23. *JDD*, 378–79; "Affairs in Utah," written June 15, published in *NYT*, July 3, 1864.

24. Doty to Seward, April 16, 1864, Utah Territorial Papers, NACP. RG 59, 607. An estimated one hundred thousand treasure seekers crossed the midcontinent that season. *JDD*, 379–80.

25. Young to Kinney, February 3, 1864, BYLC, CR 1234 1, box 6, vol. 6, p. 748, image 797.

26. Young to Kinney, March 7, 1864, BYLC, CR 1234 1, box 6, vol. 6, p. 814, image 853; *GHU*, 115n46. Connor wrote Harding in 1863, that Young wanted Harding's former living quarters, but Bishop Woolley allowed it to Connor. Connor to Harding, July 5, 1863, Harding-Lilly.

27. "Murder," *UV*, December 11, 1863, 3/1; "The Confession of Jason Luce," *DUV*, January 13, 1864, 2/1.

28. According to Hickman's autobiography, Luce was ordered to participate in Dawson's attack by city police captain Bob Golden, who by 1870 was the wealthy territorial assessor. Hickman, *Brigham's Destroying Angel*, 149.

29. "Murder," *UV*, December 11, 1863, 3/1; "The Execution of Luce," *DUV*, January 13, 1864, 2/1; "The Confession of Jason Luce" and "The Counsel for Jason Luce," *DUV*, January 14, 1864, 4/1; "The Execution of Luce," *DUV*, January 14, 1864, 5/2.

30. "Affairs in Utah," written January 21, published in *NYT*, February 14, 1864.

31. "Gone at Last," *DN*, June 17, 1863, 8/1.

32. Young to Armour, April 15, 1864, BYLC, CR 1234 1, box 6, vol. 7, p. 129, image 161s.

33. Harding to "Sell," February 24, 1863, Harding-Lilly.

34. Harding to "My Dear wife and children," February 8, 1863, MS A 3182, USHS.

35. Harding to "Sister," November 1, 1863, MS B 29, box 1, folder 2, Harding Papers, USHS.

36. Harding to "My Dear wife and children," February 8, 1863, MS A 3182, USHS.

37. "Judge Harding and the Bar of Colorado," *Rocky Mountain News* (Denver, Colo.), February 6, 1865, 4/1.

38. "Third District Meeting," *Rocky Mountain News* (Denver, Colo.), February 1, 1865, 3/3.

39. Untitled, *DUV*, April 8, 1864, 2/1.

40. Wells to Dame, April 5, 1864, cited in Bleak, *Annals of the Southern Utah Mission*, 158.

41. "Military," *DN*, April 27, 1864, 5/2 (italics added).

42. Burton to L. Smith, April 28, 1864, Utah Territorial Militia Records, MSS A 1101–1104.

43. *FK*, 243.

44. "The Nauvoo Legion—General Order No. 1—Wars and Rumors of Wars," *DUV*, May 20, 1864, 2/1 (italics in the original).

45. Ibid.

46. "One of Bro. Kinney's Loyal Inhabitants," *DUV*, April 11, 1864, 2/2.

47. "A Familiar Epistle to Bro. Brigham," *DUV*, April 12, 1864, 2/2.

48. "Another Sermon at the Tabernacle," *DUV*, April 15, 1864, 2/1.

49. *CDBY*, 4:2183.

50. *CDBY*, 4:2192.

51. *CDBY*, 4:2201.

52. *CDBY*, 4:2202.

53. *CDBY*, 4:2215.

54. "An Hour at the Tabernacle," *DUV*, April 11, 1864, 2/1.

55. "The Teachings of the Tabernacle," *DUV*, April 18, 1864, 2/1.

56. Ibid.

57. "Circular," *DUV*, April 23, 1864, 2/3.

58. "Preaching," *DUV*, July 2, 1864, 1/4.

59. *GBK*, 211, 211n67.

60. *ATC*, 103.

61. A. D. Richardson, *Beyond the Mississippi*, 358–59.

62. Lindsay, *Mormons and the Theatre*, 26.

63. Advertisement, *DUV*, January 22, 1864, 3/3, and January 28, 1864, 3/3.

64. Advertisement, *DUV*, February 27, 1864, 3/3, and February 29, 1864, 3/1.

65. "Affairs in Utah," written March 31, published in *NYT*, April, 30, 1864.

66. "Affairs in Utah," written April 22, published in *NYT*, May 15, 1864.

67. M. G. Lewis to Baldwin, May 11, 1864, *WOR*, ser. 1, vol. 50, part 2, 846.

68. Young to Bunker, February 6, 1864, BYLC, CR 1234 1, box 6, vol. 6, p. 757, image 807s.

69. M. G. Lewis to Berry, May 13, 1864, *WOR*, ser. 1, vol. 50, part 2, 845. On May 11, 1864, Rev. John B. Raverdy, a Catholic priest from Denver, blessed the Camp Douglas cemetery. W. R. Harris, *Catholic Church in Utah*, cited in Pedersen, "History of Fort Douglas," 92, 92n104.

70. "Editorial Notes of a Trip Southward to the New Dorado," *DUV*, June 29, 1864, 2/1. Portions of the "main road" became U.S. Highway 89, and much of it is present day I-15.

71. "Our Notes of Travel Continued—A Visit to the Mountain Meadows," *DUV*, June 30, 1864, 2/1.

72. Ibid.

73. "Our Notes Continued—Snow Storms and Birch Stakes—The Mines," *DUV*, July 1, 1864, 2/1.

74. High Council Meeting, "Minutes," June 11, 1864, cited in *GHU*, 111, 111n 24.

75. "Our Notes Continued—Snow Storms and Birch Stakes—The Mines," *DUV*, July 1, 1864, 2/1.

76. One of Young's maledictions: "Can you not see that gold and silver rank among the things that we are the least in want of? . . . The colossal wealth of the world is founded upon and sustained by the common staples of life." Sermon, October 25, 1863, cited in *GBK*, 473n41.

77. "Our Notes Continued—Snow Storms and Birch Stakes—The Mines," *DUV*, July 1, 1864, 2/1.

78. CR 100 137, August 31, 1865, cited in *GBK*, 474n42.

79. "Editorial Notes—Discovery, Location, etc, of the Panacka Lead," *DUV*, July 2, 1864, 2/1; "By-Laws of the Meadow Valley Mining District," *DUV*, August 11, 1864, 4/1.

80. *GBK*, 74.

81. *RMSA*, 714. Stenhouse credits Col. E. D. Buel, from his manuscript "Mining Districts in Utah."

82. *GHU*, 106.

83. Arrington, "Abundance from the Earth," 196.

84. *TSTU*, 203; *RMSA*, 713–14. George Ogilvie was soon denounced by LDS officials as an apostate. *GHU*, 105–106, 106n4.

85. *FK*, 244.

86. *RMSA*, 714. The first profitable mining of lead-silver ores in the district occurred in 1865. Lund, *Engineering Geology*, 50.

87. Arrington, "Abundance from the Earth," 200 (italics in the original).

88. *FK*, 245.

89. *GHU*, 113.

90. *RMSA*, 716.

91. *FK*, 245.

92. Young to Joseph A. and John W., March 28, 1864, BYLC, CR 1234 1, box 6, vol. 6, p. 850, image 888s.

93. Advertisement, *DUV*, July 2, 1864, 4/1.

94. "Brig. Gen. Wright," *DUV*, January 9, 1864, 2/1; "General Wright's Farewell," *DUV*, July 5, 1864, 2/1.

95. Young to Clawson, April 16, 1864, BYLC, CR 1234 1, box 6, vol. 7, p. 134, image 166s; Young to Kinney, April 23, 1864, BYLC, CR 1234 1, box 6, vol. 7, p. 144, image 176s.

96. "The New National Currency," *DUV*, February 3, 1864, 4/1.

97. "Greenbacks *vs* Gold," *DUV*, February 20, 1864, 2/1.

98. Connor to Drum, July 2, 1864, *WOR*, ser. 1, vol. 50, part 2, 889–90.

99. Connor to Drum, July 9, 1864, *WOR*, ser. 1, vol. 50, part 2, 893–94; "The Convention," *SLDTel*, August 10, 1864, 2/3.

100. *GBK*, 204.

101. The *SLDTel* article was also reprinted in the *SFB*, July 14, 1864, 3/2.

102. "Circulating Medium," *DN*, July 6, 1864, 4/1.

103. Connor to Drum, July 9, 1864, *WOR*, ser. 1, vol. 50, part 2, 893–94.

104. Special Order No. 53, July 9, 1864, *DUV*, July 11, 1864, 2/3.

105. Connor to Drum, July 12, 1864, *WOR*, ser. 1, vol. 50, part 2, 899–900.

106. Young to Wells, July 16, 1864, cited in *TSTU*, 238.

107. "A Graphic Description of a Sabbath at the Tabernacle," *DUV*, July 25, 1864, 1/3.

108. Connor to Drum, July 13, 1864, *WOR*, ser. 1, vol. 50, part 2, 901–902.

109. Drum to Connor, July 15, 1864, *WOR*, ser. 1, vol. 50, part 2, 904.

110. McGarry was in San Francisco after escorting the secessionist pirate Ridgley Greathouse to the military authorities. "Arrival," *DUV*, July 26, 1864, 2/3.

111. Drum to Connor, July 16, 1864, *WOR*, ser. 1, vol. 50, part 2, 909–10.

112. Connor to Drum, July 16, 1864, *WOR*, ser. 1, vol. 50, part 2, 910.

113. Drum to Connor, July 19, 1864, *WOR*, ser. 1, vol. 50, part 2, 912–13.

114. Drum to Connor, July 20, 1864, *WOR*, ser. 1, vol. 50, part 2, 914.

115. Connor to Drum, July 24, 1864, *WOR*, ser. 1, vol. 50, part 2, 916–17. Falling on a Sunday, the holiday celebrating the Saints' entry to Utah passed quietly.

116. Ibid.

117. Drum to Connor, July 27, 1864, *WOR*, ser. 1, vol. 50, part 2, 923.

118. "Phase of the New Life," *SLDTel*, July 25, 1864, 2/1.

119. "A Brutal and Bloody Affair," *SLDTel*, August 15, 1864, 2/1; Young to Ellerback, August 18, 1864, BYLC, CR 1234 1, box 6, vol. 7, p. 272, image 305.

120. "Theater at Salt Lake," *DUV*, September 30, 1864, 3/1, reprinted from the *Denver News*.

121. "The Indian Troubles East," *DUV*, July 27, 1864, 2/2.

122. Ware, *Indian War of 1864*, 337, 398–99. Either the 1856 trail killing of Almon W. Babbitt, Utah's secretary of state and ranking Mormon, was forgotten or Cannon knew it was not by Indian hands.

123. "Pocatello Splurging Around," *DUV*, October 24, 1864, 2/2.

124. "Pocatello—the Renowned Shoshoni," *DUV*, October 27, 1864, 2/1; *GHU*, 117.

125. *GHU*, 117–18.

126. Watterson and nine others to Connor, September 17, 1864, *WOR*, ser. 1, vol. 50, part 2, 979–80.

127. Connor, September 22, 1864, *WOR*, ser. 1, vol. 50, part 2, 980. By telegraphing its entire proposed constitution to Congress, Nevada was granted statehood on October 31, before the November election. This resulted in three electoral votes for Lincoln and added to the Republican tally.

128. Drum to Connor, October 3, 1864, *WOR*, ser. 1, vol. 50, part 2, 999.

129. "The California Regiment," *Sacramento Flag*, reprinted in *DUV*, October 25, 1864, 4/1.

130. McDowell to Doty, October 3, 1864, *WOR*, ser. 1, vol. 50, part 2, 1000.

131. Connor to Drum, January 3, 1865, *WOR*, ser. 1, vol. 50, part 2, 1112 (italics added).

132. McDowell to Doty, October 3, 1864, Doty to McDowell, October 21, 1864, and McDowell to Doty, October 22, 1864, cited in MacKinnon, "Utah's Civil War(s)," 306, 306n23.

133. "The Hostilities on the Plains," *Rocky Mountain News*, August 11, reprinted in *SLDTel*, August 23, 1864, 2/3.

134. "Martial Law and Great Times in Colorado," *SLDTel*, August 31, 1864, 2/2. Chivington would become infamous for leading the November 29 massacre at Sand Creek.

135. *TSTU*, 246–47. Communications documenting abrasive relations: Connor to Thomas, October 14, 1864, *WOR*, ser. 1, vol. 50, part 2, 1111; Halleck to Connor, October 16, 1864, *WOR*, ser. 1, vol. 50, part 2, 1013; Connor to Halleck, October 17, 1864, Connor to Drum, October 17, 1864, and Halleck to Connor, October 18, 1864, *WOR*, ser. 1, vol. 50, part 2, 1014–15; Connor to Drum, October 30, 1864, *WOR*, ser. 1, vol. 50, part 2, 1036–37.

136. McDowell to the Adjutant General of the Army, December 17, 1864, *WOR*, ser. 1, vol. 50, part 2, 1100–1101.

137. "Subsistence Stores for the Army," *DUV*, September 14, 1864, 2/2.

138. General Order No. 23, February 24, 1865, *WOR*, ser. 1, vol. 50, part 2, 1147.

139. *CDBY*, 4:2248.

140. *GBK*, 208.

141. Elizabeth Letitia Higginbotham Peery, in Mormon Biographical Sketches Collection [ca. 1900–1975], LDS_CHL, reel 2, box 2, folder 14, item 5, 4–7.

142. MPOT, John D. Murdock Company (1864), Trail Excerpt: Frank M. Gilcrest to Charley, February 9, 1908, in Personal Recollections of F. M. Gilcrest, 2–10.

143. MPOT, William B. Preston Company (1864), Trail Excerpt: Private Journal of Henry Ballard, 1852–1904, 49–60.

144. MPOT, William S. Warren Company (1864), Trail Excerpt: Thomas Waters Cropper, [Autobiography], in *Family History of Thomas Waters Cropper and Hannah Lucretia Rogers* [1957], 22–26.

145. MPOT, William S. Warren Company (1864), Trail Excerpt: Stephen Fairchild Wilson, Reminiscence, 17–23, transcribed from "Pioneer History Collection," Pioneer Memorial Museum [Daughters of Utah Pioneers Museum], Salt Lake City.

146. MPOT, John Smith Company (1864), Trail Excerpt: John Smith, Autobiography, in University of California [Berkeley] Bancroft Library, Utah and the Mormons Collection (n.d.), reel 3, 11–12.

147. MPOT, Isaac A. Canfield Company (1864), Trail Excerpt: Rev. H. N. Hansen, "An Account of a Mormon Family's Conversion to the Religion of the Latter Day Saints and of Their Trip from Denmark to Utah," *Annals of Iowa*, Summer 1971, 722–28, and Fall 1971, 765–67 (italics added).

148. MPOT, William Hyde Company, 1864, Trail Excerpt: William McNiel, Autobiography, in Marjorie Scott Peterson, McNiel family information.

149. MPOT, Warren S. Snow Company, 1864, Trail Excerpt: J. W. Pickett, Autobiography, in Joel Edward Ricks, Cache Valley Historical Material [ca. 1955], reel 4, item 87, 1–2.

150. MPOT, Warren Snow Company, 1864, Trail Excerpt: George William Parratt, *George William Parratt—Personal Journals and Records, 1837–1897 [1999?].*

151. MPOT, William Hyde Company, 1864, Trail Excerpt: Charles Eugene Fletcher, Autobiography, 1911, 145–52.

152. Untitled, *DUV*, October 8, 1864, 3/1.

153. MPOT, William S. Warren Company, 1864, Trail Excerpt: William Adams, Autobiography, January 27–28, 1894.

154. "Outwitting the Danites," *National Tribune*, February 10, 1910, 7/3. George W. McGillen, of Elizabeth, Indiana, was formerly of Company E, Eleventh Ohio Cavalry.

155. "Apprehensive of the Emigration Westward," *SLDTel*, October 7, 1864, 2/1.

156. "How Will You Vote?" *DUV*, October 21, 1864, 2/1; "Bugle Notes of Victory," *DUV*, October 7, 1864, 2/1.

157. "Election for President," *DUV*, October 7, 1864, 2/2.

158. "Bugle Notes of Victory," *DUV*, October 7, 1864, 2/1.

159. Young to Kinney, November 3, 1864, BYLC, CR 1234, 1, box 6, vol. 7, p. 331, image 365s.

160. Stahr, *Seward*, 406.

161. Ibid., 405–406.

162. Seward to Francis Seward, August 17, 1864, cited in Stahr, *Seward*, 407, 635n35.

163. Raymond to Lincoln, Weed to Lincoln, August 23, 1864, cited in Stahr, *Seward*, 405–407; Stahr, *Seward*, 411.

164. "Next Tuesday," *DUV*, November 1, 1864, 2/1.

165. "To-Day's Election," *DUV*, November 8, 1864, 2/1.

166. "Local Matters," *DUV*, November 11, 1864, 3/1.

167. "The Election," *NYT*, November 11, 1864.

168. "From Gen. Grant's Army: Result of the Election," written November 10, published in *NYT*, November 12, 1864.

169. "From Richmond," written November 10, published in *NYT*, November 15, 1864.

170. "How Will You Vote?" *DUV*, October 21, 1864, 2/1.

171. "Eastern Items," *DN*, November 9, 1864, 1/3.

172. "Eastern Items," *DN*, November 16, 1864, 1/3.

173. "From Utah County," *DN*, November 16, 1864, 5/1.

174. "The Victory Is Won—A Nation Is Saved," *DUV*, November 17, 1864, 2/1.

175. "Day of Thanksgiving," *DN*, November 23, 1864, 7/4; "The President's Message," *DN*, December 14, 1864, 10/1; "By Telegraph," *DN*, December 28, 1/2; "Eastern News," *DN*, December 28, 1864, 8/2.

176. Young to Kinney, November 3, 1864, BYLC, CR 1234, 1, box 6, vol. 7, p. 331, image 365s.

177. Salt Lake City's 1860 census lists Charles A. Monk, age 5, born Utah.

178. "A Horrid Assassination." *DUV*, October 31, 1864, 2/1.

179. "Movement of Troops, *DUV*, October 7, 1864, 2/2; "Departure," *DUV*, October 10, 1864, 2/2.

180. "From Salt Lake," *Virginia City Union*, December 6, reprinted in *DUV*, December 30, 1864, 1/5. Black and 'H' Company, with assistant surgeon John King Robinson, were mustered out at Camp Douglas in late October. *SOO*, 109.

181. *JOMO*, 163–64; C. L. Anderson, "Scattered Morrisites," 69.

182. Young to Evelith, November 28, 1864, BYLC, CR 1234 1, box 6, vol. 7, p. 369, image 402s.

183. Young to Wells and Young, Jr., undated, estimated early December 1864, BYLC, CR 1234 1, box 6, vol. 7, p. 378, image 411. William H. Aspinwall was awarded the Panama-to-Oregon mail contract in 1847; the enterprise later became the Pacific Mail Steamship Company, then the Trans-Panama Railroad, connecting across the Isthmus of Panama. Hafen, *Overland Mail*, 40.

184. "Headquarters on the Colorado," *DN*, January 18, 1865, 4/3–5/1.

185. Young to Wells and Young, January 12, 1865, BYLC, CR 1234 1, box 6, vol. 7, p. 433, image 471s.

186. "The Mormons at Cotton Raising," *SFB*, February 20, 1865, 3/7.

187. "Select School," *DUV*, December 1, 1865, 2/4; "Valedictory," *DUV*, December 21, 1864, 2/1.

188. Hibbard, "Fort Douglas," 49.

189. *GGSL*, 155–56, 161.

190. Hempstead married Mary Virginia Whitehill from Pennsylvania; she bore eight children. He died in Salt Lake City at age forty-seven after a debilitating stroke.

191. "Salutatory," *DUV*, December 22, 1864, 2/2.

192. "To the Representatives of the People," *DUV*, December 7, 1864, 2/1.

193. "The Laws of Utah, No. 1," *DUV*, December 7, 1864, 2/1.

194. "An Ordinance, Incorporating the Church of Jesus Christ of Latter-day Saints," in Morgan, "State of Deseret," 223; "The Laws of Utah, No. 2," *DUV*, December 10, 1864, 2/3.

195. "The Laws of Utah, No. 4," *DUV*, December 15, 1864, 2/1.

196. "The Laws of Utah, No. 6," *DUV*, December 22, 1864, 2/4.

197. "The Laws of Utah, No. 10," *DUV*, December 28, 1864, 2/4.

198. "The Laws of Utah, No. 11," *DUV*, December 29, 1864, 2/5.

199. "The Laws of Utah, No. 12," *DUV*, December 30, 1864, 2/3.

200. "The Laws of Utah, No. 13," *DUV*, December 31, 1864, 2/3.

201. "The Laws of Utah, No. 17," *DUV*, January 6, 1865, 3/1.

202. "The Laws of Utah, No. 18," *DUV*, January 7, 1865, 2/4.

203. Young to Wells and Young, Jr., January 12, 1865, BYLC, CR 1234 1, box 6, vol. 7, p. 435, image 473.

7. The Pen, the Sword, Prophecy Unfulfilled, 1865

1. Young in the Tabernacle, January 8, 1865, *CDBY*, 4:2254.

2. *Stockton Independent*, cited in *GHU*, 52, 52n22.

3. The International Order of Good Templars originated in west-central New York and grew rapidly through United States in the peri-war period. "Brethren of Garrison Lodge," *DUV*, January 14, 1865, 1/4; Fahey, *Temperance and Racism*, 1, 151. By 1868 the IOGT claimed more than a half million members in the United States and Canada. Fahey, *Alcohol and Drugs*, 282.

4. Another temperance group, the Dashaway Society, was also active at Camp Douglas. Hibbard, "Fort Douglas," 109n33.

5. "Polygamy," *DUV*, January 3, 1865, 2/1.

6. "The Word of God, as Preached in Great Salt Lake City," *DUV*, January 7, 1865, 2/4 (italics in the original). Joseph A. Gebow, an Indian interpreter, authored three editions of *A Vocabulary of the Snake or Shoshone Dialect*, the first published 1859 at the office of the *Valley Tan* and the second, January 1, 1864, at the *Union Vedette* press. *SOO*, 132.

7. *DUV*, January 10, 1865, 2/1, and January 11, 1865, 2/1 (italics in the original).

8. *DUV*, January 20, 1865, 2/1.

9. *DUV*, January 25, 1865, 2/1.

10. *DUV*, January 28, 1865, 2/1 (italics in the original). Reference is made to Sgt. Ralph Pike, shot and killed in the street in Salt Lake City in 1859.

11. *DUV*, February 1, 1865, 2/3 (italics in the original).

12. *DUV*, February 11, 1865, 2/1; "Gospel in Utah," *DUV*, February 11, 1865, 2/4.

13. *DUV*, February 17, 1865, 2/3 (italics in the original); "Gospel in Utah," *DUV*, February 18, 1865, 2/2.

14. "Welcome," *DUV*, January 18, 1865, 2/1.

15. "Local Matters: Married," *DUV*, March 18, 1865, 3/1.

16. *ATC*, 116.

17. "From the Missouri to the Pacific," signed by "A.D.R." [Albert Deane Richardson], written July 18, published in *Macon Telegraph*, August 2, 1865.

18. A. D. Richardson, *Beyond the Mississippi*, 351.

19. "A Memorable Day," *DUV*, January 23, 1865, 2/1.

20. *RNB*, 92–93, 92n35.

21. *FK*, 272–73; *GGSL*, 164.

22. "An Item for Camp Pedlars," *DUV*, February 6, 1865, 2/4.

23. The *Deseret News* had taken the actions of enlarging sheet size by 50 percent, adding a four-page supplement, purchasing a new Ericsson engine and cylinder press, and copublishing with the *Salt Lake Daily Telegram* at a time when expenses felled the newspaper *Peep o' Day*, suggesting that the *News* was responding to *Vedette* inroads. "Affairs in Utah," *NYT*, written December 12, 1864, published February 26, 1865.

24. Young to Street, January 17, 1865, BYLC, CR 1234 1, box 6, vol. 7, pp. 438–39, image 486s.

25. Young to Creighton, February 15, 1865, BYLC, CR 1234 1, box 6, vol. 7, pp. 464–65, image 504.

26. Young to Rich, February 20, 1865, BYLC, CR 1234 1, box 6, vol. 7, pp. 473–76, image 513s.

27. "State of Deseret: Governor's Message," *DN*, January 25, 1865, 9/2.

28. Doty to Seward, January 28, 1865, Utah Territorial Papers, U.S. Department of State, 617, NACP, RG 59; Morgan, *State of Deseret*, 91. Doty's error of writing "1861" in his letter to Seward is herein corrected.

29. Doty to Seward, January 30, 1865, Utah Territorial Papers, U.S. Department of State, 618, NACP, RG 59.

30. "Brigham as a Comedian," *DUV*, January 26, 1865, 2/1.

31. "The State (?) of Deseret," *Virginia City Territorial Enterprise*, republished in *DUV*, February 15, 1865, 2/3.

32. *CDBY*, 4:2259–61. William A. Hickman claims he twice refused Young's contract to kill Connor, for he perceived Connor as a good and honorable man. Hickman, *Brigham's Destroying Angel*, 166–67.

33. Letter to editor, *DUV*, January 21, 1865, 2/2, 3/1.

34. *New York Herald*, July 13, 1864.

35. Stillé, *Sanitary Commission*, 229.

36. Untitled, *DUV*, February 16, 1865, 2/5. Others tally smaller figures, about 6,700 Jews serving the Union, and 3,000 for the Confederacy.

37. Soldiers' Relief Fund Committee, *Reports*, 49–50.

38. Quinn, "Mormon Hierarchy," 103,105.

39. Young to Daniel Wells and Young, Jr., in Liverpool, February 28, 1865, BYLC, CR 1234 1, box 6, vol. 7, pp. 492–97, image 533.

40. "The Colorado Route," *DN*, March 8, 1865, 8/1.

41. "Affairs in Utah," written March 27, published in *NYT*, April 23, 1865.

42. *ATC*, 100–101.

43. Fonvielle, *Fort Fisher 1865*, 3, 5–6; "Rebel Fears for Wilmington," *Richmond Sentinel*, reprinted in *DUV*, November 22, 1864, 2/2.

44. Butler came under severe criticism for the failed attack; Lincoln relieved him of command.

45. "Again Hurrah!" *DUV*, January 20, 1865, 3/1.

46. *Wikipedia*, s.v. "Alexander Schimmelfennig," last modified January 15, 2015, http://en.wikipedia.org/wiki/Alexander_Schimmelfennig.

47. "The Fate of Charleston," *DUV*, February 22, 1865, 2/1.

48. "The Fall of Charleston," *NYT*, February 22, 1865.

49. "A Sign of the Times," *DUV*, February 23, 1865, 2/1; "Local Matters," *DUV*, February 23, 1865, 3/1.

50. "A Sign of the Times," *DUV*, February 23, 1865, 2/1; "Local Matters, *DUV*, February 24, 1865, 3/1.

51. Young to Wells and Young, Jr., February 28, 1865, BYLC, CR 1234 1, box 6, vol. 7, p. 492, image 533.

52. Burt to Hempstead, March 1, 1865, in "The Great Inaugural and Union Celebration in Salt Lake City, Saturday, March 4, 1865," *DUV*, March 7, 1865, 2/1.

53. "The Great Inaugural and Union Celebration in Salt Lake City, Saturday, March 4, 1865," *DUV*, March 7, 1865, 2/1; Sharp to Hempstead, March 3, 1865, in ibid.

54. "The Celebration," *DUV*, March 3, 1865, 2/1.

55. "The Second Inauguration," *DUV*, March 4, 1865, 2/1.

56. Stahr, *Seward*, 427–28.

57. The full text of Lincoln's address appeared in the *Vedette*, March 8, 1865, 2/2, and in the *Deseret News*, March 15, 1865, 5/2.

58. "The Inaugural Celebration" and "The Re-union at the City Hall," *DUV*, March 6, 1865, 2/1, 2/2.

59. "The Re-union at the City Hall," *DUV*, March 6, 1865, 2/2. John Taylor, Wilford Woodruff, George Q. Cannon, John Sharp, Jeter Clinton, Henry W. Lawrence, and William Jennings attended.

60. "Let us Understand Each Other," *DUV*, March 8, 1865, 2/1.

61. "Affairs at Salt Lake City," written March 20, published in *SFB*, April 1, 1865, 2/3.

62. "Contention and Its Evils—Peace and Its Blessings," *DN*, March 8, 1865, 8/1.

63. Untitled, *DN*, March 8, 1865, 8/4.

64. Young to Wells, March 13, 1865, BYLC, CR 1234 1, box 6, vol. 7, p. 508, image 549s.

65. *GGSL*, 71–75.

66. "Gloria in Excelsis," *DUV*, April 4, 1865, 2/1 (italics in the original).

67. Broadwater, *Ulysses S. Grant*, 137.

68. Josephy, *Civil War*, 385.

69. Though not recorded in *CDBY*, the *Vedette* claimed that Young prophesied in his April 9 conference address that the Civil War would continue another four years. "The Doctors Disagree," *DUV*, April 12, 1865, 2/1.

70. "Gen. R. E. Lee Surrenders His Army to Lt. Gen. U. S. Grant and the Gallant Forces under His Command," *DUV*, April 11, 1865, 2/3, 1/5.

71. A back page held Grant's matter-of-fact, April 9 note to Stanton: "Gen. Lee surrendered the army of Northern Virginia this p.m. upon terms proposed by myself." Untitled, *DN*, April 12, 1865, 9/4.

72. *Wikipedia*, s.v. "Assassination of Abraham Lincoln," last modified February 17, 2015, http://en.wikipedia.org/wiki/Assassination_of_Abraham_Lincoln.

73. "A Deed without a Name," *DUV*, April 17, 1865, 2/1.

74. "Horrible Assassination of President Lincoln, at Ford's Theater, Washington!! Stabbing of Secretary Seward!!" et al., *DUV*, April 17, 1865, 2/1–5, 3/1–4.

75. "Assassination of President Lincoln," *DN*, April 19, 1865, 5/1–4, 9/1–2.

76. "Our Nation Mourning," *DN*, April 19, 1985, 8/1. The double meaning is confirmed in Orson Hyde's letter: "Our prophet and patriarch were killed, and now 'theirs.'" Hyde to Young, April 23, 1865, CR 1234 1, reel 53, box 40, folder 4.

77. Lyman, *Amasa Mason Lyman*, 307, 362; "Funeral Obsequies of President Lincoln," *DUV*, April 21, 1865, 2/2.

78. "To-day," *DN*, April 19, 1865, 8/1.

79. Connor was also away, commanding the District of the Plains.

80. Lyman, *Amasa Mason Lyman*, 363.

81. "The Funeral Ceremonies at the Tabernacle," *DUV*, April 21, 1865, 2/1; "The Funeral Obsequies at the Tabernacle," *DUV*, April 21, 1865, 2/2–3.

82. "Obsequies," *DN*, April 26, 1865, 6/1.

83. Rumfield et al. to Stanton, January 14, 1865, *WOR*, ser. 1, vol. 48, part 1, 522.

84. "Indians on the Overland Route," written January 23, published in *NYT*, January 24, 1865.

85. *SOO*, 148–49.

86. See *SOO*, 157–72; and *GHU*, 121–35.

87. Atwood to Connor, April 26, 1865, *WOR*, ser. 1, vol. 48, part 2, 219–20.

88. "Indorsement," April 26, 1865, *WOR*, ser. 1, vol. 48, part 2, 220.

89. George to Price, May 4, 1865, *WOR*, ser. 1, vol. 48, part 2, 315–16. Thirty-six policemen from each city's twenty wards were to patrol the streets at night.

90. Price to Connor, May 18, 1865, *WOR*, ser. 1, vol. 48, part 2, 500–501. Price repeated this two days later. *WOR*, ser. 1, vol. 48, part 2, 524.

91. Connor to Dodge, July 21, 1865, *WOR*, ser. 1, vol. 48, part 2, 1113.

92. Price to Dodge, August 15, 1865, *WOR*, ser. 1, vol. 48, part 2, 1187–88.

93. Price to Dodge, August 21, 1865, *WOR*, ser. 1, vol. 48, part 2, 1199–1200.

94. General Order No. 20, August 22, 1865, *WOR*, ser. 1, vol. 48, part 2, 1201.

95. Connor to Barnes, April 6, 1865, *WOR*, ser. 1, vol. 50, part 2, 1184–86.

96. Bowles lectured, often to huge audiences, of his group's time with the Mormons; his book on the subject was *Across the Continent*. Colfax and Richardson also published their accounts and gave lectures.

97. *ATC*, 25, 28, 26.

98. *ATC*, 83.

99. "Distinguished Visitors," *DN*, June 14, 1865, 6/3.

100. *ATC*, 407–408 (italics in the original).

101. "Utah," *Boston Herald*, July 19, 1865.

102. "Evening Services, etc.," *DUV*, June 13, 1865, 2/1. Earlier Richardson wrote for the Golden City, Colorado, newspaper. The trip west proved salubrious, for three months later he returned to Utah for five weeks, writing *Beyond the Mississippi*.

103. *ATC*, 84–85.

104. Bowles, *Our New West*, 217.

105. A. D. Richardson, *Beyond the Mississippi*, 349.

106. Young to Wells and Young, Jr., June 20, 1865, BYLC, CR 1234 1, box 6, vol. 7, p. 671, image 717.

107. *ATC*, 113. James Mason of Virginia and John Slidell of Louisiana were Confederate agents intercepted en route to England. They sought aid for the Confederacy.

108. *ATC*, 118–20, 87.

109. "Brigham Young and Speaker Colfax," written June 19, published in *Providence (R.I.) Evening Presss*, July 15, 1865.

110. "Fact or Fiction," *DUV*, June 26, 1865, 2/1.

111. *ATC*, 102. Evidence to the contrary was a February 17, 1865, entry in the *Salt Lake City Directory:* "Scarcely a day passes, but two or three suffering poor people . . . visit Camp Douglas, applying for relief, and even for the chips at the wood pile." G. Owens, *Salt Lake City Directory* (1867), 28.

112. *ATC*, 106–107.

113. Bowles, *Our New West*, 218.

114. *ATC*, 88.

115. "Died," *DUV*, June 15, 1865, 2/1; "Governor Doty's Funeral," *DUV*, June 16, 1865, 3/2; *JDD*, 385.

116. "Arrivals and Departures," *DUV*, July 14, 1865, 2.

117. "Obituary," *DN*, June 21, 1865, 4/3.

118. Young to Wells and Young, Jr., June 20, 1865, BYLC, CR 1234 1, box 6, vol. 7, p. 671, image 717; "Tribute to Our Late Governor," *DUV*, July 31, 1865, 2/3.

119. Young to Wells and Young, Jr., June 20, 1865, BYLC, CR 1234 1, box 6, vol. 7, p. 671, image 717.

120. Reed to J. P. Usher, August 11, 1863, in Appointments, Interior Department, in the National Archives, cited in *JDD*, 438n25.

121. "And Still They Come," *DUV*, June 16, 1865, 3/2.

122. *ATC*, 128. Connor may have told this to Bowles during their long coach ride together.

123. *ATC*, Supplementary Papers, 391. In 1869 Bowles was more emphatic, saying that Mormons "'put their best foot foremost'" but it was "a cloven foot." With Bowles's departure, Mormons began "assailing the government with vituperative language, and persecuting with new zeal the anti-Mormon elements." Bowles, *Our New West*, 208.

124. *ATC*, 391–92. A. D. Richardson's quote is nearly identical and attested by California volunteer James W. Gibson. *New York Herald-Tribune*, November 10, 1865.

125. A. K. Larson and Larson, *Diary of Charles Lowell Walker*, July 28, 1865, 248.

126. *ATC*, 392.

127. *ATC*, 391–92.

128. "The Day We Celebrate," *DUV*, July 4, 1865, 2/1.

129. "The Glorious Celebration," *DUV*, July 6, 1865, 2/1.

130. Ibid.

131. "Oration," *DN*, July 5, 1865, 5/1.

132. Ibid., 5/1, 8/1.

133. "The Meeting at Platt's Hall To-Night—Some Facts Concerning Congressman Ashley," *SFB*, September 18, 1865, 5/5.

134. "Local and Miscellaneous," *DUV*, July 8, 1865, 3/1.

135. "Local and Miscellaneous," *DUV*, July 10, 1865, 3/1.

136. "The Y.M.L.A. Meeting, Last Eve," *DUV*, July 12, 1865, 2/2 (italics in the original).

137. Calder to Young, while Young was traveling in Sanpete County, July 11, 1865, BYLC, CR 1234 1, box 6, vol. 7, p. 692, image 738s (italics added).

138. James Campbell Livingston, Sr., "The Spy," typescript, MS 6881, LDS_CHL.

139. "The Meeting at Platt's Hall To-Night," *SFB*, September 18, 1865, 5/5.

140. "Ashley's Bill," *DN*, February 3, 1869, 8/1. The bill failed as did many others.

141. *JDD*, 366.

142. Mollenhoff, *Madison*, 23.

143. A. E. Smith, "Mephistopheles," 196–98, 239.

144. *JDD*, 341–43; A. E. Smith, "Mephistopheles," 195, 240.

145. Census records list a combined personal worth for him and wife Sarah at two thousand dollars.

146. *JDD*, 344, 366, 383.

147. "The Indians on the Western Route," *DN*, June 11, 1862, 8/3.

148. Indian subsidies improved in 1863. *SF*, 163, 214–15.

149. O. H. Irish, who was delayed in Nebraska awaiting supplies, did not come on-site as superintendent until late August 1864.

150. *JDD*, 42–47; A. E. Smith, "Mephistopheles," 196.

151. Secretary of State Executive Record Book, vol. B, 171, USHS. Inexplicably, Wood was never charged with the attempted murder of Emily.

152. Silas S. Smith to George A. Smith, August 11, 1862, and James Lewis to G. A. Smith, November 8, 1862, George A. Smith Papers, MS 1322, LDS_CHL. Wood was not brought before a local Mormon bishop's court, for Henry Lunt reported to G. A. Smith in February 1863 they had not held such a court for over two years. Lunt to Smith, February 8, 1863, MS 1322, LDS_CHL.

153. See K. N. Owens, *Gold Rush Saints*, 31–56 passim.

154. Sturgeon, "On the Outside Looking In." Sturgeon's emphasis is on the role and treatment of women, particularly widows, in the West in this era.

155. "Iron County Probate Court Minutes, 1852–1896," Family History Library, Salt Lake City, film 0497739, and Utah State Archives, microfilm 3912, reel 1, box 2, folder 5.

156. "Governor James Duane Doty—Utah Territorial Papers," USHS library, film A-703, 2204.

157. Utah State Archives, microfilm 3912, reel 2, box 3, folder 3 (italics added).

158. Utah State Archives, microfilm 3912, reel 1, box 2, folder 11.

159. Elias Smith Journal, MS 1319, reel 1, 63, LDS_CHL.

160. "Governor James Duane Doty—Utah Territorial Papers," USHS library, film A-703, 2248.

161. Many of the signers were not from Iron County and may have never known George Wood. Later, Dalton was killed while evading arrest for polygamy.

162. "Governor James Duane Doty—Utah Territorial Papers," USHS library, film A-703, 2249–56. Sturgeon presents strong circumstantial evidence that this charge was not true.

163. Doty to A. P. Rockwood, [Utah Penitentiary] Warden, Executive Order Book B, 171, USHS. Near this time, Doty granted pardons to several men charged

with larceny or robbery, when the evidence was lacking or extenuating circumstances proved. Doty issued no other pardons for murder.

164. This law was cited by Acting Governor Amos Reed in denying the appeal for clemency for Luce's death sentence in Bunting's murder. "Execution To-day," *DUV*, January 12, 1864, 2/1.

165. "Obituary," *DN*, June 21, 1865, 4/3. Chest pain characteristic of angina, shortness of breath, or other classical symptoms of a cardiac event were not described. No record shows that Doty received a doctor's attention during the seven-day interval.

166. Irish to Dole, June 15, 1865, "Governor James Duane Doty—Utah Territorial Papers," USHS library, film A-703, 2263. Irish explained that legislators George A. Smith and John Taylor attempted to take the role of governor, since territorial law did not address the simultaneous absence of governor and secretary of state.

167. Mollenhoff, *Madison*, 23.

168. It was widely believed among non-Mormons that Judge Leonidas Shaver was poisoned. His 1855 death in Salt Lake City ended questions put to him over the authenticity of George Q. Cannon's citizenship. His funeral was ostentatious, out of proportion with his regard among Mormons. *RNB*, 175–76.

169. Colfax and Bross, together with Justices John Titus and Thomas Drake, Superintendent Irish, and Marshal Isaac Gibbs, were pallbearers. The body of Dr. John King Robinson, murdered in the street, was interred in grave E: 14, near Governor Doty in E: 9.

170. *CDBY*, 4:2276–82; "Obituary," *DN*, June 21, 1865, 4/3.

171. It is not known if any Salt Lake City property passed to Doty's wife. Sarah sold the Loggery to Hugh H. Ernsting on January 31, 1868. Warranty Deed, Winnebago County Register of Deeds Office, doc. 62, 326. This increase in personal wealth would equal $262,000 in 2012 dollars, by CPI (www.measuringworth.com/uscompare/).

172. Neff, *History of Utah*, 396.

173. Thomas A. Marshall was appointed July 23, 1863, but did not serve.

174. Federal efforts to place three subgroups of the Southern Ute bands on a reservation in the San Juan Mountains began in 1863 but failed. Thompson, *Southern Ute Lands*, 4. Extinguishing Indian land claims was not limited to Utah but was part of a national pattern.

175. U.S. House, "Act to Vacate and Sell the Present Indian Reservations."

176. Irish to Dole, September 26, 1864, "Utah Superintendency," No. 60, U.S. Office of Indian Affairs, *Report, 1864*, 169.

177. "Superintendency of Indian Affairs," *DUV*, January 25, 1865, 3/1.

178. U.S. House, "Act to Extinguish the Indian Title to Lands."

179. Irish to Dole, June 29, 1865, "Utah Superintendency," No. 30, U.S. Office of Indian Affairs, *Report, 1865*, 149–50.

180. Peterson, *Black Hawk War*, 139, 144.

181. Hyde to Young, May 29, 1865, CR 1234 1, reel 53, box 40, folder 4.

182. Peterson, *Black Hawk War*, 139, 149. Congress never ratified the 1865 treaty.

183. Ibid., 151, 153. John Wesley Powell later explained the Indian sense of identity being "fixed to the land." Permanently leaving their land caused them to lose this identity, since they became members of the tribe who owned the land to which they moved.

184. Ibid., 156, 119; Floyd O'Neil, pers. comm., March 2014.

185. Records of the Utah Superintendency of Indian Affairs, 1853–70, microfilm M834, roll 1, NAB; "The Indian Treaty," *DN,* June 14, 1865, 6/2.

186. *CDBY*, 4:2275. Indian treaties required the same attention from Congress as those with foreign governments. As legal contracts, they progressed slowly, with delay or denial common. Thompson, "Origins and Implementation," 2.

187. The office of superintendent of Indian Affairs in Utah was abolished in 1870. Thereafter Indian agents reported directly to the U.S. commissioner.

188. Doty to Dole, August 13, 1862, cited in Morgan, *Shoshonean Peoples*, 280–81.

189. Young to Irish, July 22, 1865, BYLC, CR 1234 1, box 6, vol. 7, p. 695, image 741.

190. Connor to Dodge, July 14, 1865, cited in Peterson, *Black Hawk War*, 118n136.

191. "Who Shall Be Governor?" *DUV,* July 22, 1865, 2/1.

192. "The New Governor for Utah," *DUV,* August 12, 1865, 2/1.

193. "The Elective Franchise," *DUV,* July 31, 1865, 2/1.

194. Ibid.

195. *Denver News,* October 16, reprinted in *DUV,* October 21, 1865, 3/2.

196. "Facts about the Powder River Campaign," *DUV,* October 30, 1865, 2/1. Hollister served in the First Colorado Volunteer Cavalry's New Mexico campaign and wrote *The History of the First Regiment of Colorado Volunteers* in 1863, *The Mines of Colorado* in 1867, and an 1886 biography, *The Life of Schuyler Colfax.* In Utah his career as internal revenue collector, part owner of the *Salt Lake Tribune,* and Liberal Party member was distinguished. *GGSL*, 90n11, 159, 230, 301.

197. "An Ovation to General Connor," *DUV,* October 28, 1865, 2/1.

198. Untitled, *DUV,* October 28, 1865, 3/1, and October 30, 1865, 3/2.

199. *GBK,* 208.

200. MPOT, Chronological Company List, accessed May 2013, http://history.lds.org/overlandtravels/companydatelist?lang=eng.

201. "And Still They Come!" *DUV,* October 20, 1865, 2/1.

202. Young to Young, Jr., December 15, 1865, BYLC, CR 1234 1, box 6, vol. 7, p. 865, image 905.

203. Young to Young, Jr., October 18, 1865, BYLC, CR 1234 1, box 6, vol. 7, p. 776, image 816s.

204. "To Our Subscribers," *DUV*, October 30, 1865, 2/1.

205. "Two Hundred Dollars Reward!" *DUV*, November 15, 1865, 2/1.

206. "No Paper Tomorrow," *DUV*, November 22, 1865, 2/1; McMurtrie, *Notes on Early Printing*, 5.

207. "Mormon Toleration," *DUV*, December 5, 1865, 2/1.

208. Hibbard, "Fort Douglas," 49.

209. "A Card," *DUV*, December 19, 1865, 3/2.

210. "Caution," *DUV*, September 9, 1865, 2/1 (italics in the original).

211. Untitled, *DUV*, November 2, 1865, 3/2.

212. "The Mormon Militia Review," *DUV*, November 4, 1865, 3/2.

213. Young to Young, Jr., November 17, 1865, BYLC, CR 1234 1, box 6, vol. 7, p. 828, image 868 (italics added).

214. "Mormon Army," *San Francisco Chronicle*, reprinted in *DUV*, November 27, 1865, 3/2.

215. "Utah," *Daily Leader*, December 18, 1865, 2/2.

216. "Why Is It?" *DUV*, September 29, 1865, 2/1. A search of *CDBY* confirms the brevity of reports published.

217. "The Mormon War," *New York Sunday Times*, November 10, reprinted in *DUV*, December 12, 1865, 2/3.

218. "Affairs in Utah," signed "Delphi," written October 4, published in *NYT*, November 27, 1865.

219. "The Mormon Question, Its Easy and Peaceful Solution," *NYT*, November 28, 1865.

220. "The Late Review," *DUV*, November 7, 1865, 2/1.

221. Ibid.

222. Ibid.

223. Young to Young, Jr., November 17, 1865, BYLC, CR 1234 1, box 6, vol. 7, p. 828, image 868. G. D. Grant was captain of the Overton freight team of the 1865 season, carrying goods for William S. Godbe.

224. Young to Young, Jr., November 17, 1865, BYLC, CR 1234 1, box 6, vol. 7, p. 828, image 868.

225. Young to Hooper, December 5, 1865, BYLC, CR 1234 1, box 6, vol. 7, p. 858, image 898.

226. "The Late Review," *DUV*, November 7, 1865, 2/1.

227. Hibbard, "Fort Douglas," 113, 146n7.

228. "Galvanized" as in "spurred to action."

229. "Local and Miscellaneous," *DUV*, November 25, 1865, 3/2. The Third California Infantry and the First Nevada Cavalry were relieved by the U.S. Eighteenth Infantry in July 1866. Hibbard, "Fort Douglas," 103.

230. "The Review on Saturday," *DUV*, November 27, 1865, 3/1. Michigan veterans were not at peak; many had served three to four years and were angry about not going home. *GGSL*, 87, 87n2.

231. Young to Hooper, December 5, 1865, BYLC, CR 1234 1, box 6, vol. 7, p. 857, image 897.

232. "Mormon Loyalty: Ostensible and Actual," *DUV*, November 29, 1865, 2/3 (italics in the original).

233. "Persecution towards the Soldiers," *DUV*, December 16, 1865, 2/1.

234. Young to Hooper, December 5, 1865, BYLC, CR 1234 1, box 6, vol. 7, p. 857, image 897.

235. "Brigham's Real Intentions," *DUV*, November 30, 1865, 3/1.

236. "Disastrous Fire at Camp," *DUV*, December 20, 1865, 2/1.

237. Ibid.

238. Young to Capt. E. J. Bennett, December 19, 1865, BYLC, CR 1234 1, box 6, vol. 7, p. 870, image 910, and December 20, 1865, BYLC, CR 1234 1, box 6, vol. 7, p. 871, image 911.

239. "Wholesale Market Report," *DUV*, December 20, 1865, 3/3.

240. "Disastrous Fire at Camp," *DUV*, December 20, 1865, 2/1.

241. "Bully for Congress," *DUV*, December 21, 1865, 2/1.

242. *RNB*, 343, 343n6.

Epilogue

1. Buchanan, *Message of the President* (1857), 25.

2. Desertion and illness while en route significantly reduced the number of soldiers.

3. Buchanan, April 6, 1858, cited in Hafen and Hafen, *Utah Expedition*, 332–37.

4. *BOP*, 23–37.

5. Appealing to his Texas friend Sam Houston for help, Mormon Seth M. Blair described the U.S. Army as "traitors, highwaymen, public robbers (who thirst for gold)," and "have [been] raised . . . to murder an innocent and law abiding people." Blair to Houston, cited in MacKinnon, "Into the Fray," 219.

6. Powell and McCulloch both admitted that "a less decisive policy would probably have resulted in a long, bloody, and expensive war." Buchanan, *Message of the President* (1857). McCulloch became a Confederate officer and a leader of the secret Knights of the Golden Circle. He was killed at Pea Ridge, Arkansas, in March 1862. *MR*, 183n3.

7. Guelzo, *Gettysburg*, 3. In his work *At Sword's Point, Part 1*, MacKinnon comments throughout on the Utah Expedition officers' subsequent careers as Civil War officers.

8. Bancroft, *History of Utah*, 451n28; George F. Richards to Edward H. Snow, February 15, 1927, LDS_CHL, CR 100–14, #2, cited in Buerger, "Endowment Ceremony," 104–105, 105n118 (italics added).

9. Young to Rich, April 4, 1861, BYLC, CR 1234 1, box 5, vol. 5, p. 743, image 816s.

10. Young to Walter M. Gibson, July 2, 1861, BYLC, CR 1234 1, box 5, vol. 5, pp. 818–19, image 895s.

11. Young to Bernhisel, Washington, D.C., December 30, 1861, BYLC, CR 1234 1, box 6, vol. 6, p. 78, image 109 (italics added).

12. Goldin and Lewis, " Economic Cost of the American Civil War," 299–326. The valuation in 2012 dollars, by GDP, is per *MeasuringWorth*, accessed May 2015, www.measuring worth.com/uscompare/.

13. August 24, 1861, *CDBY*, 3:1906.

14. George Sims, Salt Lake City, to W. C. Staines in England, February 24, 1862, CR 1234 1, General Correspondence, Outgoing, reel 28, box 19, folder 20, image 59.

15. Aird, Nichols, and Bagley, *Playing with Shadows*, 172–74, 172n8, 173n10, 174n12.

16. McCullough to Smith, August 19, 1861, images 36–37, George A. Smith Papers, Incoming, MS 1322, LDS_CHL.

17. Young to Hooper, Washington, May 30, 1862, BYLC, CR 1234 1, box 6, vol. 6, p. 262, image 299s.

18. Tullidge, *History of Salt Lake City*, appendix, "Journalism," 14.

19. *ATC*, 392.

20. Lindsay Whitehurst, "Dixie May Apologize for Past Confederate, Blackface Imagery," *Salt Lake Tribune*, January 12, 2013; *Wikipedia*, s.v. "Dixie State University," last modified April 6, 2015, http://en.wikipedia.org/wiki/Dixie_State_University.

21. *WOR*, ser. 1, vol. 50, part 2, 374.

22. Ibid., 372–74.

23. Connor to Drum, June 24, 1863, *WOR*, ser. 1, vol. 50, part 2, 492–95.

24. "'Let the Dead Past Bury Its Dead,'" *DUV*, March 21, 1865, 2/1.

25. Alford, *Civil War Saints*, 405. Any person serving for the Union or Confederates, and baptized into the Church of Jesus Christ of Latter-day Saints at any time in his or her lifetime, is classed by Alford as a Civil War Saint. This allows counting some who were not baptized for a quarter to a half century after the war's end and also includes individuals who were excommunicated. The chapter "Mormon Motivation for Enlisting" comes into question, since six of the eleven men discussed were not Mormons when they enlisted.

26. Of 384 total individuals cited, 74 served the Confederates or served the Union only *after* first serving the Confederacy, leaving 310 who were loyal. Of

the 310 who volunteered to serve the Union, 112 became "Saints" on an average of eighteen years *after* the war's end, and as many as sixty-one years later. Of the 198 who were in fact "Saints" while serving the Union, the recruited or conscripted cavalry of Lot Smith consisted of 94 Utah men. (Of these 94, 12 were "presumed" to have been baptized, one was baptized during the war, and one after the war.)

27. Livermore, *Numbers and Losses*, 1–22.

28. Peterson, *Black Hawk War*, 1–2, 361, 361n48.

29. *GGSL*, 157–58; "The Fourth in Utah," *NYT*, July 6, 1871.

30. *JOD*, 17:321, cited in Bigler, *FK*, 342; *JOD* 20:151; *JOD*, 26:156, cited in Underwood, "Millennialism," 50–51.

31. "Our Flag," *Salt Lake Tribune*, July 12, 1885, 5/1.

32. "The Insults of the Year," *Salt Lake Tribune*, July 28, 1886, 2/2.

33. Homer, *Joseph's Temples*, 258, 259n3.

34. Edward Kemble, "The Flag of the Twelve Stars," *SDU*, May 22, 1858, 2/2–3.

35. Quinn, "Flag of the Kingdom," 105–14.

Bibliography

Archival Collections

Anderson, John Alexander, Papers. Anderson Family Papers. Kansas Historical Society, Topeka.

Bleak, James G. *Annals of the Southern Utah Mission.* James G. Bleak Papers, Special Collections. Manuscripts Division, J. Willard Marriott Library, University of Utah.

Dawson, John W., Obituaries for. Manuscript Collections. Utah State Historical Library, Salt Lake City.

Fuller, Frank, Papers. Special Collections. Manuscripts Division, J. Willard Marriott Library, University of Utah.

Harding, Stephen Selwyn, Papers. Harding MSS. Lilly Library, Indiana University, Bloomington.

Historian's Office History of the Church. Church History Library, Church of Jesus Christ of Latter-day Saints, Salt Lake City.

Kansas Historical Collections. Kansas Historical Society, Topeka.

Lincoln, Abraham, Papers. Library of Congress.

Lincoln Financial Foundation Collection. Allen County Public Library, Fort Wayne, Ind.

Mormon Pioneer Overland Travel, 1847–68. Database, https://history.lds.org/overlandtravels/. Church History Library, Church of Jesus Christ of Latter-day Saints, Salt Lake City.

Records of the Utah Superintendency of Indian Affairs, 1853–70. Office of Indian Affairs. Microfilm Publication M0834, Record Group 75.15.13, National Archives and Records housed in Washington, D.C.

Utah Territorial Papers. General Records, U.S. Department of State, Record Group 59.4.3, National Archives and Records housed in College Park, Md.

Young, Brigham, Office Files. Church History Library, Church of Jesus Christ of Latter-day Saints, Salt Lake City.

Young, Joseph A., Journal. Special Collections. Manuscripts Division, J. Willard Marriott Library, University of Utah.

Published Works, Theses, Dissertations, and Presentations

Adler, Jacob, and Robert M. Kamins. *The Fantastic Life of Walter Murray Gibson: Hawaii's Minister of Everything*. Honolulu: University of Hawaii Press, 1986.

————. "The Political Debut of Walter Murray Gibson," *Hawaiian Journal of History* 18 (1984): 96–115.

Aird, Polly. *Mormon Convert, Mormon Defector: A Scottish Immigrant in the American West, 1848–1861*. Norman: University of Oklahoma Press / Arthur H. Clark, 2009.

Aird, Polly, Jeff Nichols, and Will Bagley, eds. *Playing with Shadows: Voices of Dissent in the Mormon West*. Norman: University of Oklahoma Press / Arthur H. Clark, 2011.

Alexander, Robert. *Five Forks: Waterloo of the Confederacy*. East Lansing: Michigan State University Press, 2003.

Alexander, Thomas G., and Leonard J. Arrington. "Camp in the Sagebrush: Camp Floyd, Utah, 1858–1861." *Utah Historical Quarterly* 34 (Winter 1966): 3–21.

Alford, Kenneth L., ed. *Civil War Saints*. Provo, Utah: Religious Studies Center, Brigham Young University, in cooperation with Deseret Book Co., 2012.

————. "Utah and the Civil War Press." *Utah Historical Quarterly* 80 (Winter 2012): 75–92.

Anderson, C. LeRoy. *Joseph Morris and the Saga of the Morrisites (Revisited)*. Logan: Utah State University Press, 2010.

————. "The Scattered Morrisites." *Montana: The Magazine of Western History* 26 (Autumn 1976): 52–69.

Anderson, Lavina Fielding, ed. *Lucy's Book: A Critical Edition of Lucy Mack Smith's Family Memoir*. Salt Lake City: Signature Books, 2001.

————. "The Textual History of Lucy's Book." Signature Books Library, http://signaturebookslibrary.org/?p=9481.

Anonymous. *Minutes of the Apostles of the Church of Jesus Christ of Latter-day Saints, 1835–1893*. 4 vols. Salt Lake City: privately published, 2010.

Appletons' Annual Cyclopaedia and Register of Important Events of the Year 1877. Whole ser., vol. 17. New York: D. Appleton and Co., 1878.

Arrington, Leonard J. "Abundance from the Earth: The Beginnings of Commercial Mining in Utah." *Utah Historical Quarterly* 31 (July 1963): 192–219.

————. *Great Basin Kingdom: An Economic History of the Latter-day Saints, 1830–1900*. Salt Lake City: University of Utah Press and Tanner Trust Fund, 1993.

Bagley, Will. *"A Bright, Rising Star": A Brief Life and a Letter of James Ferguson, Sergeant Major, Mormon Battalion; Adjutant General, Nauvoo Legion.* Collector's Edition Keepsake for vol. 4, Kingdom in the West series. Spokane, Wash.: Arthur H. Clark, 2000.

———. *Blood of the Prophets: Brigham Young and the Massacre at Mountain Meadows.* Norman: University of Oklahoma Press, 2002.

———. *Frontiersman: Abner Blackburn's Narrative.* Salt Lake City: University of Utah Press, 1992.

———. "'One Long Funeral March': A Revisionist's View of the Mormon Handcart Disasters." *Journal of Mormon History* (Winter 2009): 50–116.

———. *Scoundrel's Tale: The Samuel Brannan Papers.* Logan: Utah State University Press, 1999.

———. "A Terror to Evil-Doers: Camp Douglas, Abraham Lincoln, and Utah's Civil War." *Utah Historical Quarterly* 80 (Fall 2012): 314–33.

———. *With Golden Visions Bright before Them: Trails to the Mining West, 1849–1852.* Norman: University of Oklahoma Press, 2013.

Bagley, Will, and Rick Grunder. "I Could Hardly Hold the Pen": Phebe Ann Woolley Davis's Hard Road to Utah and Back, 1864–1865." Unpub. MS in the author's possession.

Bailey, Paul. *Hawaii's Royal Prime Minister: The Life and Times of Walter Murray Gibson.* New York: Hastings House, 1980.

Bancroft, Hubert Howe. *History of Utah, 1540–1886.* San Francisco: History Company Publishers, 1890.

Baskin, Robert Newton. *Reminiscences of Early Utah.* Salt Lake City, 1914; reprint, Salt Lake City: Signature Books, 2006.

———. *Reply to Certain Statements by O. F. Whitney in His History of Utah.* Salt Lake City: Lakeside Printing Co., 1916; reprint, Salt Lake City: Signature Books, 2006.

Beadle, J. H. *Life in Utah; or, the Mysteries and Crimes of Mormonism.* Philadelphia: National Publishing Co., 1870.

Bell, S. B. "Visit to Brigham Young, at Salt Lake City." *Gazlay's Pacific Monthly* 1 (March 1865): 209–12.

Bennett, John Cook. *The History of the Saints; or, an Exposé of Joe Smith and Mormonism.* Boston: Leland and Whiting, 1842.

Bennett, Richard E. "'We Know No North, No South, No East, No West': Mormon Interpretations of the Civil War, 1861–1865." *Mormon Historical Studies* 10 (March 2009): 51–63.

Bierce, Ambrose. *Civil War Stories.* New York: Dover, 1944.

Bigler, David L. "The Aiken Party Executions and the Utah War, 1857–1858." *Western Historical Quarterly* 38 (Winter 2007): 457–76.

———. *Forgotten Kingdom: The Mormon Theocracy in the American West, 1847–1896.* Spokane, Wash.: Arthur H. Clark, 1998.

———, ed. *A Winter with the Mormons: The 1852 Letters of Jotham Goodell.* Salt Lake City: Tanner Trust Fund and J. Willard Marriott Library, University of Utah, 2001.

Bigler, David L., and Will Bagley, eds. *Army of Israel: Mormon Battalion Narratives.* Keepsake ed. Spokane, Wash: Arthur H. Clark, 2000.

———. *The Mormon Rebellion: America's First Civil War, 1857–1858.* Norman: University of Oklahoma Press, 2011.

A Biographical History of Eminent and Self-made Men of the State of Indiana. Vol. 1. Cincinnati, Ohio: Western Biographical, 1880.

Biographical Sketch of the Hon. Lazarus W. Powell, Governor of the State of Kentucky from 1851 to 1855. Frankfort: Kentucky Yeoman's Office, 1868.

Bitton, Davis. *Ritualization of Mormon History, and Other Essays.* Urbana: Board of Trustees of the University of Illinois, 1994.

Bosbyshell, Oliver Christian. *The 48th in the War, Being a Narrative of the Campaigns of the 48th Regiment, Infantry, Pennsylvania Veteran Volunteers, during the War of the Rebellion.* Philadelphia: Avil Printing Co., 1895.

Bowles, Samuel. *Across the Continent: A Summer's Journey to the Rocky Mountains, the Mormons, and the Pacific States, with Speaker Colfax.* New York: Hurd and Houghton, 1866.

———. *Our New West: Records of Travel between the Mississippi River and the Pacific Ocean.* New York: published by subscription only, J. D. Dennison, 1869.

Broadwater, Robert P. *Ulysses S. Grant: A Biography.* Santa Barbara, Calif.: ABC_CLIO / Greenwood, 2012.

Brooks, Juanita, ed. *The Mountain Meadows Massacre.* Board of Trustees of Leland Stanford Junior University, 1950; new ed., Norman: University of Oklahoma Press, 1970.

———. *On the Mormon Frontier: The Diary of Hosea Stout, 1844–1889.* Salt Lake City: University of Utah Press and Utah State Historical Society, 2009.

Browne, John Ross. *Resources of the Pacific Slope: A Statistical and Descriptive Summary.* New York: D. Appleton and Co., 1869.

Buchanan, James. *The Utah Expedition: Message Transmitting Reports from the Secretaries of State, of War, of the Interior, and of the Attorney General, Relative to the Military Expedition Ordered into the Territory of Utah.* 35th Cong., 1st sess., 1857–58, H. Exec. Doc. No. 71. [Washington, D.C., 1858].

———. "Message of the President." Appendix to the *Congressional Globe,* December 8, 1857, 1–7. 35th Cong., 1st sess., 1857–58.

Buchanan, James, and James Bassett Moor, eds. *The Works of James Buchanan.* 12 vols. Philadelphia: J. B. Lippincott, 1908–11.

Buerger, David John. "The Development of the Mormon Temple Endowment Ceremony." *Dialogue: A Journal of Mormon Thought* 34 (Spring–Summer 2001): 75–122.

Bullock, Richard Harvey. "'The Ship *Brooklyn* Story—Volume 2': The Coombs Family." http://shipbrooklyn.com/pdf/coombs.pdf.

Canning, Ray R., and Beverly Beeton, eds. *The Genteel Gentile: Letters of Elizabeth Cumming, 1857–1858.* Salt Lake City: Tanner Trust Fund and University of Utah Library, 1977.

Cannon, Kenneth L., II. "'Mountain Common Law': The Extralegal Punishment of Seducers in Early Utah." *Utah Historical Quarterly* 51 (Fall 1983): 308–27.

———. "Wives and Other Women: Love, Sex, and Marriage in the Lives of John Q. Cannon, Frank J. Cannon, and Abraham H. Cannon." *Dialogue: A Journal of Mormon Thought* 43 (Winter 2010): 71–130.

Carleton, James H. *Special Report of the Mountain Meadows Massacre.* 57th Cong., 1st sess., H. Doc. No. 605. Washington, D.C.: Government Printing Office, 1902.

———. *Mountain Meadows Massacre.* Spokane, Wash.: Arthur H. Clark, 1995.

Carman, Harry James, and Reinhard Henry Luthin. *Lincoln and the Patronage.* New York: Columbia University Press, 1943.

Chandless, William. *A Visit to Salt Lake: Being a Journey across the Plains and a Residence in the Mormon Settlements at Utah.* London: Elder and Co., 1857.

Civil War Sites Advisory Commission. *Report on the Nation's Civil War Battlefields.* Technical vol. 2, *Battle Summaries.* www.nps.gov/abpp/battles/tvii.htm.

Clark, Champ, and Editors of Time-Life Books. *Gettysburg: The Confederate High Tide.* Civil War Series. Alexandria, Va.: Time-Life Books, 1985.

Cleland, Robert Glass, and Juanita Brooks. *A Mormon Chronicle: The Diaries of John D. Lee, 1848–1876.* 2 vol. San Marino, Calif.: Huntington Library, 1955.

Cole, Philip M. *Civil War Artillery at Gettysburg.* New York: Da Capo Press, 2002.

Colton, Ray C. *The Civil War in the Western Territories.* Norman: University of Oklahoma Press, 1959.

Compton, Todd M. *A Frontier Life: Jacob Hamblin, Explorer and Indian Missionary.* Salt Lake City: University of Utah Press, 2014.

Connelley, William E. *A Standard History of Kansas and Kansans.* Chicago: Lewis Publishing Co., 1918. Transcription available at http://www.ksgenweb.com/archives/1918ks/.

Cowley, Matthias F., ed. *Wilford Woodruff: History of His Life and Labors as Recorded in His Daily Journals.* Salt Lake City: Deseret News, 1909.

Cronin, Sean. *The McGarrity Papers.* Tralee, Ireland: Anvil Books, 1972.

Crookston, Douglas O. *Henry Ballard: The Story of a Courageous Pioneer.* Salt Lake City, Deseret Book Co., 1994.

Daughters of the Utah Pioneers. *Pioneer Gunsmiths and Guns.* Salt Lake City: Talon Printing, 2002.

Davis, Rodney O., and Douglas L. Wilson. *The Lincoln-Douglas Debates.* Urbana: University of Illinois Press, 2008.

Dawson, John W. *Charcoal Sketches of Old Times in Fort Wayne.* Edited by Alene Godfrey. Reprinted from the *Old Fort News,* January–March 1959 (articles orig. published in 1872). Fort Wayne, Ind.: Allen County–Fort Wayne Historical Society, n.d.

Detzer, David. *Donnybrook: The Battle of Bull Run, 1861.* New York: Harcourt, 2004.

Deverell, William. "Thoughts from the Farther West: Mormons, California, and the Civil War." *Journal of Mormon History* 34 (Spring 2008): 1–19.

Dick, Everett Newton. *The Story of the Frontier: A Social History of the Northern Plains and Rocky Mountains from the Earliest White Contacts, to the Coming of the Homemaker.* New York: Tudor, 1941.

Dickson, Ephraim D., III. "Protecting the Home Front," and "Appendix B: "Camp Douglas' First Photographer, Private Charles D. Beckwith." In Kenneth L. Alford, ed., *Civil War Saints,* 143–59, 399–403. Provo, Utah: Religious Studies Center, Brigham Young University, in cooperation with Deseret Book Co., 2012.

Douglass, Frederick. *Frederick Douglass: Selected Speeches and Writings.* Edited by Philip S. Foner. Chicago: Chicago Review Press, 2000.

Du Bois, John Van Deusen. *Campaigns in the West, 1856–1861: The Journal and Letters of Col. John Van Deusen Du Bois.* Pencil sketches by Private Joseph Heger; foreword by Durwood Ball. Tucson: Arizona Historical Society, 2003.

Dwyer, Robert Joseph. *The Gentile Comes to Utah: A Study in Religious and Social Conflict, 1862–1890.* Salt Lake City: Western Epics, 1971.

Dyer, Frederick H. *A Compendium of the War of the Rebellion.* Part 1, *Statement of Organizations in the Service.* Des Moines, Iowa: Dyer Publishing Co., 1908.

Eardley, John R. *Gems of Inspiration: A Collection of Sublime Thoughts by Modern Prophets.* San Francisco: Joseph A. Dove, Printer, 1899.

Emmons, David M. *Beyond the American Pale.* Norman: University of Oklahoma Press, 2010.

Evans, Clement A. *Confederate Military History: A Library of Confederate States History.* Atlanta, Ga.: Confederate Publishing Co., 1899.

Fahey, David M. *Temperance and Racism: John Bull, Johnny Reb, and the Good Templars.* Lexington: University Press of Kentucky, 1996.

Fahey, David M., and Jon S. Miller, eds. *Alcohol and Drugs in North America.* 2 vols. Santa Barbara, Calif.: ABC-CLIO, 2013.

Faust, Drew Gilpin. *This Republic of Suffering.* New York: Alfred A. Knopf, 2008.

Fehrenbacher, Don E. *Lincoln: Speeches and Writings, 1859–1865.* New York: Literary Classics of the United States, 1989.

Fielding, Robert Kent. *The Unsolicited Chronicler: An Account of the Gunnison Massacre, Its Causes and Consequences, Utah Territory, 1847–1859.* Brookline, Mass.: Paradigm Publications, 1993.

Firmage, Edwin Brown, and Richard Collin Mangrum. *Zion in the Courts.* Urbana: University of Illinois Press, 1988.

Fisher, Margaret May Merrill, C. N. Lund, and Nephi Jensen, eds. *Utah and the Civil War: Being the Story of the Part Played by the People of Utah in that Great Conflict, with Special Reference to the Lot Smith Expedition and the Robert T. Burton Expedition.* Salt Lake City: Deseret Book Co., 1929.

Fleisher, Kass, *The Bear River Massacre and the Making of History*. Albany: State University of New York Press, 2004.

Fonvielle, Chris E., Jr. *Fort Fisher 1865: The Photographs of T. H. O'Sullivan*. Carolina Beach, N.C.: SlapDash, 2011.

French, Etta Martha Reeves. "A Letter from Stephen S. Harding to William H. Seward." *Indiana Magazine of History* 26 (June 1930): 157–65. Accessed April 4, 2013, http://www.jstor.org/stable/27786440.

———. "Stephen S. Harding: A Hoosier Abolitionist." Master's thesis, University of Arkansas, 1930.

———. "Stephen S. Harding: A Hoosier Abolitionist." *Indiana Magazine of History* 27 (September 1931): 207–29.

Furniss, Norman F. *The Mormon Conflict, 1850–1859*. New Haven, Conn.: Yale University Press, 1960.

Garrett, John. "Harding: The Biography of Stephen S. Harding." Unpub. MS. Available at Abraham Lincoln Presidential Library and Museum, Springfield, Ill.

Gibbs, Josiah. *The Mountain Meadows Massacre*. Salt Lake City: Salt Lake Tribune Publishing Co., 1909.

Gibson, Harry W. "Frontier Arms of the Mormons." *Utah Historical Quarterly* 42 (Winter 1974): 4–26.

Gibson, Walter M. *The Prison of Weltevreden; and a Glance at the East Indian Archipelago*. Boston: C. H. Brainard, 1857.

Godfrey, Donald G., and Rebecca S. Martineau-McCarty, eds. *An Uncommon Pioneer: The Journals of James H. Martineau, 1828–1918*. Provo, Utah: Religious Studies Center, Brigham Young University, 2008.

Gregg, Thomas. *The Prophet of Palmyra: Mormonism Reviewed and Examined in the Life, Character, and Career of Its Founder, from "Cumorah Hill" to Carthage Jail and the Desert, Together with a Complete History of the Mormon Era in Illinois, and an Exhaustive Investigation of the "Spalding* [sic] *Manuscript" Theory of the Origin of the Book of Mormon*. New York: John B. Alden, 1890.

Griswold, Bert Joseph. *The Pictorial History of Fort Wayne, Indiana: A Review of Two Centuries of Occupation of the Region about the Head of the Maumee River*. Vol. 1. Chicago: Robert O. Law, 1917.

Grow, Matthew J. *"Liberty to the Downtrodden": Thomas L. Kane, Romantic Reformer*. New Haven, Conn.: Yale University Press, 2009.

Guelzo, Allen C. *Gettysburg: The Last Invasion*. New York: Alfred A. Knopf, 2013.

———. "Lincoln and Religion." Presented at United States Historical War Era Seminar, Snow College, Ephraim, Utah, August 7, 2013.

Hafen, LeRoy R. *The Overland Mail, 1849–1869*. Norman: University of Oklahoma Press, 2004.

Hafen, LeRoy Reuben, and Ann Woodbury Hafen. *The Utah Expedition, 1857–1858: A Documentary Account of the United States Military Movement under Colonel Albert*

Sydney Johnston, and the Resistance by Brigham Young and the Mormon Nauvoo Legion. Glendale, Calif.: Arthur H. Clark, 1958.

Hance, Irma Watson, and Irene Warr. *Johnston, Connor, and the Mormons: An Outline of Military History in Northern Utah.* Privately printed, 1962.

Hansen, Klaus J. *Quest for Empire: The Political Kingdom of God and the Council of Fifty in Mormon History.* Lincoln: University of Nebraska Press, 1974.

Hardy, B. Carmon. *Doing the Works of Abraham.* Norman, Okla.: Arthur H. Clark, 2007.

Harris, Sarah Hollister. *An Unwritten Chapter of Salt Lake City, 1851–1901.* New York: privately printed, 1901.

Harris, W. R. *The Catholic Church in Utah.* Salt Lake City: Intermountain Catholic Press, 1909.

Hart, Newell. *The Bear River Massacre: Being a complete Source Book and Story Book of the Genocidal Action Against the Shoshones in 1863 and of Gen. P.E. Connor and how he related to and dealt with Indians and Mormons on the Western Frontier.* Preston, Idaho: Cache Valley Newsletter Publishing Co., 1982.

Hartley, William G. "Latter-day Saint Emigration during the Civil War." In Kenneth L. Alford, ed., *Civil War Saints,* 237–65. Provo, Utah: Religious Studies Center, Brigham Young University, in cooperation with Deseret Book Co., 2012.

Heaton, John W. "'No Place to Pitch Their Teepees': Shoshone Adaptation to Mormon Settlers in Cache Valley, 1855–70." *Utah Historical Quarterly* 63 (Spring 1995): 158–71.

Hendricks, W. C., comp. *Governmental Roster, 1889: State and County Governments of California.* Sacramento: State Printing, 1889.

Hewett, Janet B., ed. *The Roster of Confederate Forces, 1861–1865.* Wilmington, N.C.: Broadfoot, 1996.

———, ed. *The Roster of Union Soldiers, 1861–1865.* 31 vols. Wilmington, N.C.: Broadfoot, 2000.

———, ed. *Supplement to the Official Records of the Union and Confederate Armies.* Wilmington, N.C.: Broadfoot, 2001.

Hewett, Janet B., and Joyce Lawrence. *South Carolina Confederate Soldiers, 1861–1865.* Vol. 1. Wilmington, N.C.: Broadfoot, 1998.

Hibbard, Charles Gustin. "Fort Douglas, 1862–1916: Pivotal Link on the Western Frontier." PhD thesis, University of Utah, 1980.

———. *Fort Douglas, Utah: A Frontier Fort, 1862–1991.* Fort Collins, Colo.: Vestige Press, 1999.

Hickman, William Adams. *Brigham's Destroying Angel: Being the Life, Confession, and Startling Disclosures of the Notorious Bill Hickman, the Danite Chief of Utah.* New York: Geo. A. Crofutt, 1872.

Hirshson, Stanley P. *The Lion of the Lord: A Biography of Brigham Young.* New York: Alfred A. Knopf, 1969.

Holley, Val. "Slouching towards Slaterville: Joseph Morris's Wide Swath in Weber County." *Utah Historical Quarterly* 76 (Summer 2009): 247–64.

Holzer, Harold, and Craig L. Symonds. *The New York Times Complete Civil War 1861–1865*. New York: Black Dog and Leventhal, 2010.

Homer, Michael W. "The Federal Bench and Priesthood Authority: The Rise and Fall of John Fitch Kinney's Early Relationship with the Mormons." *Journal of Mormon History* 13 (1986): 89–110.

———. *Joseph's Temples: The Dynamic Relationship between Freemasonry and Mormonism*. Salt Lake City: University of Utah Press, 2014.

———, ed. *On the Way to Somewhere Else: European Sojourners in the Mormon West, 1834–1930*. Spokane, Wash.: Arthur H. Clark, 2006.

Howard, Gordon M. "Men, Motives, and Misunderstandings." *Utah Historical Quarterly* 44 (Spring 1976): 112–32.

Hulbert, Archer Butler, ed. *Letters of an Overland Mail Agent in Utah*. Worcester, Mass: American Antiquarian Society, 1929.

Hundley, Daniel R. *Prison Echoes of the Late Rebellion*. New York: S. W. Green, 1874.

Hyde, John, Jr. *Mormonism: Its Leaders and Designs*. New York: W. P. Fetridge and Co., 1857.

Jenson, Andrew. *Church Chronology: A Record of Important Events Pertaining to the History of the Church of Jesus Christ of Latter-day Saints*. 2nd ed., rev. and enl. Salt Lake City: Deseret News, 1899.

Johnston, William Preston. *The Life of Gen. Albert Sidney Johnston*. New York: D. Appleton and Co., 1878.

Josephy, Alvin M., Jr. *The Civil War in the American West*. New York: Alfred A. Knopf, 1991.

Keehn, David C. *Knights of the Golden Circle: Secret Empire, Southern Secession, Civil War*. Baton Rouge: Louisiana State University Press, 2013.

Kelly, Charles, and Hoffman Birney. *Holy Murder: The Story of Porter Rockwell*. New York: Minton, Balch and Co., 1934.

Kenny, Michael. *The Fenians*. Dublin: National Museum of Ireland, in association with Country House, 1994.

Kirby, William. *Mormonism Exposed and Refuted: or, True and False Religion Contrasted; Forty Years' Experience and Observation among the Mormons*. Nashville, Tenn.: Gospel Advocate, 1893.

Knecht, William L., and Peter L. Crawley. *History of Brigham Young, 1847–1867*. Berkeley, Calif.: MassCal Associates, 1964.

Lamon, Ward H. *The Life of Abraham Lincoln; from His Birth to His Inauguration as President*. Boston: James R. Osgood and Co., 1872.

Langworthy, Franklin. *Scenery of the Plains, Mountains and Mines*. Ogdensburgh, N.Y.: J. C. Sprague, 1855.

Larson, A. Karl, and Katherine Miles Larson, eds. *Diary of Charles Lowell Walker*. 2 vols. Logan: Utah State University Press, 1980.

Larson, Gustive O. "Uintah Dream: The Ute Treaty—Spanish Fork, 1865," *Brigham Young University Studies* 14 (Spring 1974): 361–81.

———. "Utah and the Civil War." *Utah Historical Quarterly* 33 (Winter 1965): 55–77.

Launius, Roger D., and Linda Thatcher. *Differing Visions: Dissenters in Mormon History.* Urbana: University of Illinois Press, 1994.

Lee, Ruth, and Sylvia Wadsworth, eds. *A Century in Meadow Valley, 1864–1964.* Panaca, Nev.: Panaca Centennial Book Committee, 1966.

Lindsay, John S. *The Mormons and the Theatre.* Salt Lake City: Century Printing, 1905.

Lingenfelter, Richard E., and Karen Rix Gash. *The Newspapers of Nevada: A History and Bibliography, 1854–1979.* Reno: University of Nevada Press, 1984.

Linn, William Alexander. *The Story of the Mormons: From the Date of Their Origin to the Year 1901.* New York: Macmillan, 1902.

Livermore, Thomas Leonard. *Numbers and Losses in the Civil War in America, 1861–1865.* Boston: Houghton, Mifflin and Co., 1900.

Long, E. B. *The Saints and the Union: Utah Territory during the Civil War.* Urbana: University of Illinois Press, 1981.

Ludlow, Fitz Hugh. *The Heart of the Continent: A Record of Travel across the Plains and in Oregon, with an Examination of the Mormon Principle.* New York: Hurd and Houghton, 1870.

Lund, William R., ed. *Engineering Geology of the Salt Lake City Metropolitan Area, Utah.* Bull. 126. Salt Lake City: Utah Geological and Mineral Survey, 1990.

Lyman, Edward Leo. *Amasa Mason Lyman, Mormon Apostle and Apostate.* Salt Lake City: University of Utah Press, 2009.

Lythgoe, Dennis L. "Negro Slavery in Utah." *Utah Historical Quarterly* 39 (Winter 1971): 40–54.

MacKinnon, William P., ed. *At Sword's Point, Part 1: A Documentary History of the Utah War to 1858.* Norman: University of Oklahoma Press / Arthur H. Clarke, 2008.

———. "Epilogue to the Utah War: Impact and Legacy." *Journal of Mormon History* 29 (Fall 2003): 186–248.

———. "Hammering Utah, Squeezing Mexico, and Coveting Cuba: James Buchanan's White House Intrigues." *Utah Historical Quarterly* 80 (Spring 2012): 132–51.

———. "Into the Fray: Sam Houston's Utah War." *Journal of Mormon History* 39 (Summer 2013): 198–243.

———. "'I Would See Them in Hell First': Brigham Young, California Troops, and Utah's Civil War(s)." *California Territorial Quarterly* 87 (Fall 2011): 4–17.

———. "'Not as a Stranger': A Presbyterian Afoot in the Mormon Past." *Journal of Mormon History* 80 (Spring 2012): 1–46.

———. "Utah's Civil War(s): Linkages and Connections." *Utah Historical Quarterly* 80 (Fall 2012): 296–313.

Madsen, Brigham D. *The Craft of History.* Salt Lake City: Utah Westerners, 1995.

———. *Glory Hunter: A Biography of Patrick Edward Connor.* Salt Lake City: University of Utah Press, 1990.

———. *The Shoshoni Frontier and the Bear River Massacre.* Salt Lake City: University of Utah Press, 1985.

Martin, George W. "John A. Anderson—A Character Sketch." Kansas Historical Collections 8:15–323.

Mathis, Don Richard. "Camp Floyd in Retrospect." Master's thesis, University of Utah, 1959.

Maxwell, John Gary. *Gettysburg to Great Salt Lake: George R. Maxwell, Civil War Hero and Federal Marshal among the Mormons.* Norman: University of Oklahoma Press / Arthur H. Clark, 2010.

———. *Robert Newton Baskin and the Making of Modern Utah.* Western Frontiersmen Series. Norman: University of Oklahoma Press / Arthur H. Clark, 2013.

Maxwell, William Quentin. *Lincoln's Fifth Wheel: The Political History of the United States Sanitary Commission.* New York: Longmans, Green, and Co., 1956.

May, Dean L. *Three Frontiers: Family, Land, and Society in the American West, 1850–1900.* Cambridge: Cambridge University Press, 1997.

McDonough, Gerald M. *A Short History of the Irish in Utah: The Forgotten Pioneers.* Salt Lake City: Hibernian Society of Utah, 2002.

———. *The Hogles.* Salt Lake City: McMurrin-Henriksen Book, 1988.

McGhie, Frank W. *The Life and Intrigue of Walter Murray Gibson.* Master's thesis, Brigham Young University, 1958.

McMillan, Henry G. *The Inside of Mormonism: A Judicial Examination of the Endowment Oaths Administered in All the Mormon Temples by the United States District Court for the Third Judicial District of Utah.* Salt Lake City: Utah Americans, 1903.

McMullin, Thomas A., and David A. Walker. *Biographical Directory of American Territorial Governors.* Westport, Conn.: Meckler, 1984.

McMurtrie, Douglas C. *The Beginnings of Printing in Utah.* Chicago: John Calhoun Club, 1931.

———. *Notes on Early Printing in Utah outside of Salt Lake City.* Los Angeles: Press of the Frank Wiggins Trade School, 1938.

McPherson, Robert S. *Staff Ride Handbook for the Battle of Bear River—29 January 1863.* Self-published, 2000.

Michener, James Albert, and A. Grove Day. "Gibson, the King's Evil Angel." In *Rascals in Paradise,* 102–32. New York: Random House, 1957.

Missouri General Assembly. *Document Containing the Correspondence, Orders, &c. in Relation to the Disturbances with the Mormons; and the Evidence Given Before the Hon. Austin A. King, Judge of the Fifth Judicial Circuit of the State of Missouri, at the Court-house in Richmond, in a Criminal Court of Inquiry, Begun November 12, 1838, on the Trial of Joseph Smith, Jr., and Others, for High Treason and Other Crimes against the State.* Fayette, Mo.: published by order of the General Assembly of the State of Missouri, 1841.

Moehring, Eugene P. "The Civil War and Town Founding in the Intermountain West." *Western Historical Quarterly* 28 (Autumn 1997): 217–341.

Mollenhoff, David E. *Madison: A History of the Formative Years.* 2nd ed. Madison: University of Wisconsin Press, 2003.

Moorman, Donald R, and Gene A. Sessions. *Camp Floyd and the Mormons: The Utah War.* Salt Lake City: University of Utah Press, 1992.

Morgan, Dale L. *The Great Salt Lake.* Indianapolis: Bobbs-Merrill, 1947.

———. *Shoshonean Peoples and the Overland Trails: Frontiers of the Utah Superintendency of Indian Affairs, 1849–1869.* Edited by Richard L. Saunders; with ethnohistorical essay by Gregory E. Smoak. Logan: Utah State University Press, 2007.

———. *The State of Deseret.* Logan: Utah State University Press, and Utah Historical Society, 1987.

———. "The State of Deseret." *Utah Historical Quarterly* 8 (April, July, and October 1940): 66–251.

Morris, Joseph. *The "Spirit Prevails," Containing the Revelations, Articles and Letters Written by Joseph Morris.* San Francisco: George S. Dove and Co., 1886.

Murphy, Cullen. *God's Jury: The Inquisition and the Making of the Modern World.* New York: Houghton Mifflin Harcourt, 2012.

Musser, Joseph B. "Walter Murray Gibson—Oceanic Adventurer." *United States Naval Institute Proceedings* 52 (September 1926): 1708–32.

Neely, Mark E., Jr. "The Constitution and Civil Liberties under Lincoln." In Eric Froner, ed., *Our Lincoln: New Perspectives on Lincoln and His World,* 37–61. New York: W. W. Norton, 2008.

Neely, Mark E., Jr. "President Lincoln, Polygamy, and the Civil War: The Case of Dawson and Deseret." *Lincoln Lore,* no. 1644 (February 1975): 1–4; no. 1645 (March 1975): 1–4.

Neff, Andrew Love. *History of Utah, 1847 to 1869.* Salt Lake City: Deseret Press, 1940.

O'Brien, Thomas M., and Oliver Diefendorf. *General Orders of the War Department, 1861, 1862 and 1863.* 2 vols. New York: Derby and Miller, 1864.

O'Donovan, Connell. "The Mormon Priesthood Ban and Elder Q. Walker Lewis: 'An Example for His More Whiter Brethren to Follow.'" *John Whitmer Historical Association Journal* 26 (2006): 48–100.

———. "The Orphan Child: Priscilla Mogridge Smith Lowry Williams Staines (1823–1899)." *John Whitmer Historical Association Journal* 32 (Spring–Summer 2012): 79–113.

Orton, Chad M. "'Away Down South in Dixie': A Look at the Secession Movement in Utah." Presented before the Mormon History Association, St. George, Utah, May 1992. MS in the author's possession.

Orton, Brig. Gen. Richard H. *Records of California Men in the War of the Rebellion, 1861 to 1867.* Sacramento, Calif.: State Office, J. D. Young, Supt. State Printing, 1890.

Orwell, George. *Nineteen Eighty-Four.* New York: Harcourt, Brace and Co., 1949.

Owens, G., comp. *Salt Lake City Directory.* [Salt Lake City]: G. Owens, 1867.

Owens, Kenneth N. *Gold Rush Saints: California Mormons and the Great Rush for Riches.* Spokane, Wash: Arthur H. Clark, 2004.

Pedersen, Lyman Clarence, Jr. "*The Daily Union Vedette:* A Military Voice on the Mormon Frontier." *Utah Historical Quarterly* 42 (Winter 1974): 39–48.

———. "History of Fort Douglas, Utah." PhD diss., Brigham Young University, 1967.

Peterson, John Alton. *Utah's Black Hawk War.* Salt Lake City: University of Utah Press, 1998.

Plumb, J. H. *The Death of the Past.* Boston: Houghton Mifflin, 1970.

Potterf, Rex M. "John W. Dawson, Herodotus of Fort Wayne." *Old Fort News* 32 (Summer 1969): 1–14.

Pratt, Orson. "Kingdom of God—Part I." In *Series of Pamphlets,* ser. 1, no. 2. Liverpool, England: R. James, 1851.

Quigley, Dr. H. *The Irish Race in California.* San Francisco: Roman and Co., 1878.

Quinn, D. Michael. "The Culture of Violence in Joseph Smith's Mormonism." *Sunstone* (October 2011):16–28.

———. "The Mormon Hierarchy, 1832–1932: An American Elite." PhD thesis, Yale University, 1976.

———. *The Mormon Hierarchy: Extensions of Power.* Salt Lake City: Signature Books, in association with Smith Research Associates, 1997.

———. "The Flag of the Kingdom of God." *Brigham Young University Studies* 14 (Autumn 1973): 105–14.

Rable, George C. *God's Almost Chosen Peoples, A Religious History of the American Civil War,* Chapel Hill: University of North Carolina Press, 2010.

Rawley, James A. *Turning Points of the Civil War.* Lincoln: University of Nebraska Press, 1966.

Reeve, W. Paul. *Making Space on the Western Frontier: Mormons, Miners, and Southern Paiutes.* Urbana: University of Illinois Press, 2006.

Rémy, Jules. *A Journey to Great-Salt-Lake City.* 2 vols. London: W. Jeffs, 1861.

Rich, Christopher B., Jr. "The True Policy for Utah: Servitude, Slavery, and 'An Act in Relation to Service.'" *Utah Historical Quarterly* 80 (Winter 2013): 50–74.

Richards, Mary Stovall. Review of *God's Almost Chosen Peoples,* by George C. Rable. *Utah Historical Quarterly* 79 (Summer 2011): 283–84.

Richardson, Albert Deane. *Beyond the Mississippi: From the Great River to the Great Ocean.* Hartford, Conn.: American Publishing Co., 1869.

Richardson, James D., ed. *The Messages and Papers of Jefferson Davis and the Confederacy.* New York: Chelsea House–Robert Hector, 1966.

Ricketts, Norma Baldwin. *The Mormon Battalion: U.S. Army of the West, 1846–1848.* Logan: Utah State University Press, 1996.

Roberts, B. H. *Comprehensive History of the Church of Jesus Christ of Latter-day Saints.* Salt Lake City: Deseret News Press, 1930.

Rogers, Fred B. *Soldiers of the Overland: Being Some Account of the Services of General Patrick Edward Connor and His Volunteers in the Old West.* San Francisco: Grabhorn Press, 1938.

Ross, David A. *Critical Companion to William Butler Yeats: A Literary Reference to His Life.* New York: Infobase Publishing / Facts on File, 2009.

Ross, Jeffrey Ian. *Religion and Violence: An Encyclopedia of Faith and Conflict from Antiquity to the Present.* 3 vols. Armonk, N.Y.: M. E. Sharpe, 2011.

Rumfield, Hiram S. "Letters of an Overland Mail Agent in Utah." Edited by Archer Butler Hulbert. *Proceedings of the American Antiquarian Society* 28 (October 1928): 227–302.

Sandburg, Carl. *Storm over the Land: A Profile of the Civil War.* New York: Harcourt, Brace, 1939.

Sanders, Ken, and Will Bagley. "John Varah Long: Forgotten Utah Writer and Pioneer." Unpub. MS, n.d.

Saunders, Richard L., ed. *Dale Morgan on the Mormons: Collected Works; Part I, 1939–1951.* Norman: University of Oklahoma Press / Arthur H. Clark, 2012.

———. *Printing in Deseret: Mormons, Economy, Politics and Utah's Incunabula, 1849–1851.* Salt Lake City: University of Utah Press, 2000.

Schindler, Harold. *Orrin Porter Rockwell: Man of God, Son of Thunder.* Salt Lake City: University of Utah Press, 1966.

Scott, Robert Nicholson, and Henry Martyn Lazelle. *The War of the Rebellion: A Compilation of the Official Records of the Union and Confederate Armies.* Ser. I, 1–53; ser. II, 1–8; ser. III, 1–5; ser. IV, 1–4. Washington, D.C.: Government Printing Office, 1880–1901.

Sears, Stephen W. *Landscape Turned Red: The Battle of Antietam.* New York: Ticknor and Fields, 1983.

Seegmiller, Janet Burton. *"Be Kind to the Poor": The Life Story of Robert Taylor Burton.* N.p.: Robert Taylor Burton Family Organization, 1988.

Shaara, Michael. *The Killer Angels.* New York: Ballantine, 1974.

Smith, Alice Elizabeth. *James Duane Doty: Frontier Promoter.* Madison: State Historical Society of Wisconsin, 1954.

———. "James Duane Doty: Mephistopheles in Wisconsin." *Wisconsin Magazine of History* 34 (Summer 1951): 195–98, 238–40.

Smith, Lucy Mack, Mother of the Prophet. *Biographical Sketches of Joseph Smith, the Prophet, and His Progenitors for Many Generations.* Edited by Orson Pratt. Liverpool and London: S. W. Richards, 1853.

Soldiers' Relief Fund Committee of San Francisco. *Reports of the Treasurer and Secretary of the Soldiers' Relief Fund Committee, of San Francisco, to the California Branch, United States Sanitary Commission, with a Supplement Containing the Receipts by Rev. H. W. Bellows, D.D., during his residence in San Francisco.* San Francisco: S. W. Wade and Co., 1865.

Sprague, John Titcomb. *The Origin, Progress, and Conclusion of the Florida War.* 1848; reprint, Gainesville: University of Florida Press, 1964.

Stack, Peggy Fletcher. "Mormons Warned against Baptizing Holocaust Victims." *USA Today,* March 5, 2012.

Stahr, Walter. *Seward: Lincoln's Indispensable Man.* New York: Simon and Schuster, 2012.

Stanley, Reva. *A Biography of Parley P. Pratt: The Archer of Paradise.* Caldwell, Idaho: Caxton Printers, 1937.

Stashower, Daniel. *The Hour of Peril: The Secret Plot to Murder Lincoln before the Civil War.* New York: Minotaur Books, 2013.

———. "Lincoln Must Die," *Smithsonian* 43 (February 2013): 74–89.

Stenhouse, T. B. H. *The Rocky Mountain Saints: A Full and Complete History of the Mormons.* New York: D. Appleton and Co., 1873.

Stewart, George R. *Pickett's Charge: A Microhistory of the Final Attack at Gettysburg.* Boston: Houghton Mifflin, 1959.

Stillé, Charles Janeway. *History of the United States Sanitary Commission: Being the General Report of Its Work during the War of the Rebellion.* Philadelphia: J. B. Lippincott and Co., 1866.

Taylor, Samuel Wooley. "Walter Murray Gibson, Great Mormon Rascal." *American West: Magazine of the Western History Association* 1 (Spring 1964): 18–27, 77.

Tegeder, Vincent G. "Lincoln and the Territorial Patronage: The Ascendency of the Radicals in the West." *Mississippi Valley Historical Review* 35 (June 1948): 77–90.

Thompson, Gregory Coyne. "The Origins and Implementation of the American Indian Reform Movement: 1867–1912." PhD diss., University of Utah, 1981.

———. *Southern Ute Lands, 1848–1899: The Creation of a Reservation.* Edited by Robert Delaney. Occasional Papers of the Center of Southwest Studies, Paper No. 1. Durango, Colo.: Center of Southwest Studies, 1972.

Thornbrough, Emma Lou. *Indiana in the Civil War Era, 1850–1880.* Indianapolis: Indiana Historical Society, 1989.

Tullidge, Edward William. *History of Salt Lake City.* Salt Lake City: Star Printing, 1886.

Turner, John G. *Brigham Young, Pioneer Prophet.* Cambridge, Mass.: Belknap Press of Harvard University Press, 2012.

Underwood, Grant. "Millennialism, Persecution, and Violence: The Mormons." In Catherine Wessinger, ed., *Millennialism, Persecution, and Violence,* 43–61. Syracuse, N.Y.: Syracuse University Press, 2000.

U.S. Congress. House. "Utah Territory: Message of the President of the United States, May 2, 1860," by James Buchanan. 36th Cong., 1st sess., H. Exec. Doc. No. 78.

U.S. Congress. House. Committee on Foreign Affairs. "Report of Mr. Stanton." 34th Cong., 1st sess., H. Rep. No. 307. *The Executive Documents of the House of Representatives of the United States for the First Session of the Thirty-fourth Congress.* Washington, D.C.: Government Printing Office, 1857.

U.S. Congress. Senate. "Volunteer Troops for Guarding the Overland and Inland Mail and Emigrant Routes." Letter from the Secretary of War, 50th Cong., 2d sess., S. Exec. Doc. No. 70. *The Executive Documents of the Senate of the United States for the Second Session of the Fiftieth Congress.* Washington, D.C.: Government Printing Office, 1890.

———. "Report of the Committee on Territories." 37th Cong., 2d sess., S. Comm. Rep. No. 87. Washington, D.C., 1863.

U.S. Congress. Senate. Committee on Privileges and Elections. *Proceedings before the Committee on Privileges and Elections of the United States Senate in the Matter of the Protests against the Right of Hon. Reed Smoot, a Senator from the State of Utah, to Hold His Seat.* 4 vols. 59th Cong., 1st sess., S. Rep. No. 486. Washington, D.C.: Government Printing Office, 1904–1906.

U.S. Naval War Records Office. *Official Records of the Union and Confederate Navies in the War of the Rebellion.* Guild Press of Indiana, 1999. CD-ROM.

U.S. Office of Indian Affairs. *Report of the Commissioner of Indian Affairs, for the Year 1861.* Washington, D.C.: Government Printing Office, 1861.

———. *Report of the Commissioner of Indian Affairs, for the Year 1863.* Washington, D.C.: Government Printing Office, 1864.

———. *Report of the Commissioner of Indian Affairs, for the Year 1864.* Washington, D.C.: Government Printing Office, 1865.

Unruh, John David, Jr. *The Plains Across: The Overland Emigrants and the Trans-Mississippi West, 1840–60.* Urbana: University of Illinois Press, 1979.

Utley, Robert M. Review of *Indians and Emigrants: Encounters on the Overland Trails,* by Michael L. Tate. *Western Historical Quarterly* 38 (Summer 2007): 228–29.

Van Wagoner, Richard S., ed. *The Complete Discourses of Brigham Young.* 5 vols. Salt Lake City: Smith-Pettit Foundation, 2009.

Vogel, Dan. *Early Mormon Documents.* 5 vols. Salt Lake City: Signature Books, 1995–2003.

Waite, Mrs. C. V. [Catherine Van Valkenburg]. *The Mormon Prophet and His Harem.* Chicago: J. S Goodman and Co., 1868.

Ware, Eugene F. *The Indian War of 1864: Being a Fragment of the Early History of Kansas, Nebraska, Colorado, and Wyoming.* Topeka, Kans.: Crane and Co., 1911.

White, David A. *News of the Plains and Rockies, 1803–1865.* Vol. 4. Spokane, Wash.: Arthur H. Clark, 1998.

White, Jonathan W. *Abraham Lincoln and Treason in the Civil War: The Trials of John Merryman.* Baton Rouge: Louisiana State University Press, 2011.

————. "Lincoln and the Value of Union," "Abraham Lincoln and Civil Liberties," and "The Election That Saved America." Presented at the United States Historical War Era Seminar, Snow College, Ephraim, Utah, August 6–8, 2013.

Whitman, Walt. "A Night Battle, over a Week Since." In "Specimen Days," *Complete Prose Works*. Philadelphia: David McKay, 1892.

Whitney, Horace G. *The Drama in Utah: The Story of the Salt Lake Theatre*. Salt Lake City: Deseret News, 1915.

Whitney, Orson Ferguson. *History of Utah*. 4 vols. Salt Lake City: George Q. Cannon and Sons, 1904.

Woodruff, Wilford. *Wilford Woodruff's Journal*. Edited by Scott G. Kenney. 8 vols. Salt Lake City: Signature Books, 1983.

Wray, Clayton J. "The Story of the Second Murder in Iron County, Utah: Olive Olivia Curtis Coombs." 2002. MS 18990, LDS Church History Library.

Wright, Benjamin Fletcher, ed. *The Federalist, by Alexander Hamilton, James Madison, and John Jay*. New York: Barnes and Noble, 1996.

Young, Brigham, with George D. Watt and Church of Jesus Christ of Latter-day Saints. *Journal of Discourses*. 26 vols. Salt Lake City: Deseret Book Co., 1966.

Young, Richard W. "The Morrisite War." *Contributor* 11 (June 1890): 281–84; 348–50; 369–72; 428–31; 466–471.

Zanjani, Sally. *Devils Will Reign: How Nevada Began*. Reno: University of Nevada Press, 2006.

Newspapers Consulted

Alta California (San Francisco)
Charleston (S.C.) Mercury
Daily Oregonian (Portland)
Daily Union Vedette (Camp Douglas, then Great Salt Lake City, Utah Terr.)
Daily Vedette (Camp Douglas, Utah Terr.)
Deseret News (Salt Lake City)
Fort Wayne (Ind.) Morning Gazette
Holmes County (Ohio) Republican
Indianapolis Sunday Star
London Times
Millennial Star (Manchester and Liverpool, England)
Missouri Republican (St. Louis)
Mobile (Ala.) Register
Mountaineer (Salt Lake City)
New York Daily Tribune
New York Post
New York Times

Ohio State Journal (Worthington)
People's Press (Bluffton, Ind.)
Perrysburg (Ohio) Journal
Richmond (Va.) Daily Dispatch
Rocky Mountain News (Denver, Colo.)
Sacramento Daily Union
St. Louis Democrat
Salt Lake Telegraph
Salt Lake Tribune
San Francisco Bulletin
San Francisco Flag
Santa Fe (N.Mex.) Weekly Gazette
Springfield (Mass.) Republican
Union Vedette (Salt Lake City)
Valley Tan (Salt Lake City)
Weekly Arizonian (Tubac)
Winona (Minn.) Daily Republican
Winona (Minn.) Republican Herald

Index

Brigham Young is abbreviated in subentries as B. Young. Nauvoo Legion is abbreviated in parentheses as N.L.

451

Vedette, 243; accuses Mormon of stealing paper and ink, 333; celebration of Lincoln re-elected, 268; Charles Hempstead, first editor, 226; editors of, 410n203; extensive coverage of Lee's surrender, 303; increase in sheet size, 334; labels Mormon reception of Colfax and visitors as farcical, 311; McLeod's sermon praised, 286; offices moved to city center, 334; personally funded by Connor, 226; published by California Volunteers, 226; publishes lamentations of literary quality, 304; reports disloyal public preaching, 244–45; subscription rates increase, 334; supports former slaves voting, 331–32; touts its financial success, 313; "vedette" defined, 226

Wade, Benjamin Franklin (Ohio sen.): bill fails, 341; as chairman of Committee on Territories, 88; Harding's speech published, 180; introduces bill against polygamy, 341; shown affidavit regarding Dawson, 88
Wade, Jeptha, 59, 61
Waite, Catherine V. (wife): claims Mormons leaders work to entrap Harding, 204; confirms Fuller's affinity with LDS leaders, 112; entrapment of Steptoe, Dawson, 114, 204, 114; on Morrisite homes plundered, 204; writes of Kinney's allegiances to Mormon leaders, 113–14
Waite, Charles B. (judge), 13, 58, 115, 195, 201, 203, 206, 223, 234, 269, 353; as coauthor of Browning bill, 196; documents LDS disloyalty, 58; praised by Connor, 202; resigns judicial post, 204; supports Harding pardon of Morrisites, 153; threatened, 196; on Young's marriage to Amelia Folsom, 202
Walker Brothers, 71, 345
Wandell, Charles Wesley, 411n17; author of mining bill, 236; death, 411n17; dissents on Connor removal, 236; Mountain Meadows visit, 411n17; questions about Meadows massacre

posed by, 411n17; as Reorganized LDS Church missionary, 411n17; as territorial legislator, 236
Ward, Hamilton, Sr. (New York rep.), 341
Ware, Eugene (capt.), 258
Warm Dance, 186
Wasatch Mountain Mining District, 252
Watkins, Anna (Harding's Utah housekeeper), 240
Watkins, Louisa (Harding's housekeeper), 240
wealth, of Brigham Young, 169, 292–93; acquisitions in Hawaii, 293; evidence of, 293; as a joke among local Mormon leaders, 284
Weber Military District, 73
Weed, Thurlow (editor, *Albany Evening Journal*), 267
Wells, Daniel H. (lt. gen., N.L.), 41, 55, 63, 67, 181, 243, 301, 338, 352, 359; and Camp Crittenden, 71; order to Burton to guard Hooper, Kinney, and Chauncey West, 136; order to Lot Smith to form cavalry company, 136–37; order to seize of Utah Expedition supplies, 9; and revival of Nauvoo Legion, 73, 242; war preparations, 9; and weapons/weapon-use, 7, 74–75
West, Chauncey W. (brig. gen., N.L.), 73
Western Union Telegraph, 59
West Mountain Quartz Mining District, 250
Weston, Isaac Mellen: at Robinson's murder, 410n208; *Vedette* editor beaten, threatened, 227–28
Westwood, Phebe, 212–13
Whitehill, Mary Virginia, 419n190
Willard, Ammiel L., 39
Williams, Albina Merrill (first wife of T. S. Williams), 85–86, 87, 355; affidavit alleging misconduct, signed by John T. Caine, 100–101; claims Mormons ordered her husband's killing, 87; unsigned affidavit alleging misconduct, 99–100
Williams, Lydia Phelps (second wife of T. S. Williams), 381n5
Williams, Norma Isabella (daughter of T. S. Williams), 102

8- 14

ML